THE ARTIST AS CREATOR

THE ARTIST AS CREATOR

an essay of human freedom

by MILTON C. NAHM

Baltimore: THE JOHNS HOPKINS PRESS: *1956*

Distributed in Great Britain by Geoffrey Cumberlege
Oxford University Press, London

Printed in U.S.A. by J. H. Furst Company, Baltimore

Library of Congress Catalog Card No. 56-8241

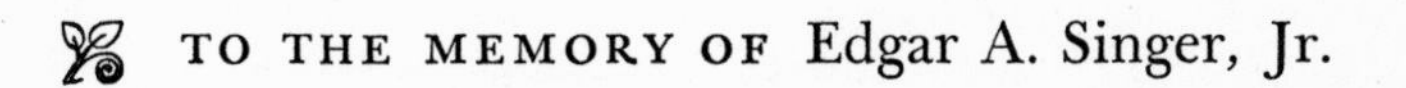

TO THE MEMORY OF Edgar A. Singer, Jr.

AND

Erich Frank

Preface

The Artist as Creator is an essay of human freedom in the arts and in the fine arts. As a systematic examination of originality and intelligibility, it is the obverse side of the coin of aesthetic experience, a fact which has permitted me to refer occasionally to the argument of *Aesthetic Experience and Its Presuppositions*.[1] After the completion of the latter study, it was clear that the tacit assumption of my thinking in aesthetic is human freedom and that its basic problems are encountered in analyses of aesthetic experience, of the judgment and evaluation of art and fine art, and of the activity of the artisan or the fine artist. As will be evident to the reader, I believe that this has been the principal unexamined presupposition of the majority of aesthetic theories and that the specification of the problem since the middle of the eighteenth century has merely made explicit an assumption present to philosophy of art from its beginnings. I believe, also, that human freedom has remained a largely unexamined assumption of aesthetic theory because such problems as the ugly and ugliness have been obscured by a methodology and terminology which are not necessarily unique to philosophy of art or even integrated to this field.

My first effort to specify this problem, "The Theological Background of the Theory of the Artist as Creator," was read before the American Society for Aesthetics, revised for a meeting of the American Philosophical Association, Eastern Division, and published in 1946 in *The Journal of the History of Ideas*. In the intervening years, I have enjoyed the task of elaborating upon the central argument of that paper and testing its validity in more specific ranges of the field of aesthetic.

In writing this essay, I have been interested not only in the

[1] Milton C. Nahm, *Aesthetic Experience and Its Presuppositions* (New York, 1946).

problem of human freedom but in examining the main lines of speculation in the Western tradition concerning the problem. Book I concerns the " great analogy " of the artist to God as creator and maker and indicates, for the historian of ideas, the ways in which a nonaesthetic tradition helped to preserve speculation and support interest in aesthetic values for purposes of its own.

Book II follows upon this clarifying process and I have assumed in it that certain historical solutions to the problems of originality and intelligibility in art have served their historical purposes. In any case, I have suggested in Book II that there is a technique for the production of fine art, and I have done so by indicating the grounds for intelligible criticism of art and fine art.

The critical reader of *The Artist as Creator* may charge, with some justice, that it pays preponderant attention to the idealist tradition in aesthetic and in philosophy of art. I have tried to guard against such prejudice as this would imply. Objectivity is difficult to obtain, however, in a subject which is so inclusive of aesthetic problems, since a systematic account of the issue of human freedom cannot pretend to analyze even all of the greatest thinkers on the subject. I should not be disinclined, however, to assert that, with the obvious and notable exception of Aristotle, the great tradition of speculation in aesthetic has been built by such idealist philosophers as Plato, Plotinus, St. Augustine, Longinus, Kant, Schiller, Hegel, Schopenhauer, and Croce. But even were this not the fact, the problem of the artist as creator as it affects this book could only have originated and been elaborated in a tradition in which the world is assumed to have begun in time and to have been created or made by God. It is not, therefore, by chance that Plato and his followers assume a more important position in the analysis of the " great analogy " than do Aristotle and the Aristotelians.

My indebtedness to philosophers, critics, and artists in speculation upon aesthetic is great. To two philosophers, it is particularly notable. To Erich Frank, who was my colleague at Bryn Mawr College, I owe much, as do all who came in contact with his distinguished thinking. To Edgar A. Singer, Jr., with whom I studied at the University of Pennsylvania, I owe whatever of methodology in terms of empirical idealism may be evident in this essay. The extent of my indebtedness will be even more apparent when I add that the title of this book is a phrase from Singer's "Esthetic and the Rational Ideal," a series of studies published in *On the Contented Life.*[2] To the memory of these two distinguished men, so different in their approaches to philosophy but so alike in their devotion to it, I have dedicated this volume.

The grant of a Fellowship by the Bollingen Foundation made it possible for me, in 1950, to work in libraries in Italy and in England, as well as to experience again many of the works of art mentioned in this book. For that opportunity, I express my gratitude.

Bryn Mawr College
NOVEMBER, 1955

Milton C. Nahm

[2] Edgar A. Singer, Jr., *On the Contented Life* (New York, 1936).

Contents

Contents

I The "Great Analogy"

How exquisitely the individual Mind
(And the progressive powers perhaps no less
Of the whole species) to the external World
Is fitted: – and how exquisitely, too –
Theme this but little heard among men –
The external World is fitted to the Mind;
And the creation (by no lower name
Can it be called) which they with blended might
Accomplish: – this is our high argument. . . .

WORDSWORTH, *The Recluse*

1 Creativity and Freedom

> How in its naked self
> Reason wer powerless showeth when philosophers
> wil treat of Art, the which they are full ready to do,
> having good intuition that their master-key
> may lie therein; but since they must lack vision of Art,
> (for elsewise they had been artists, not philosophers)
> they miss the way; . . .
>
> ROBERT BRIDGES, *The Testament of Beauty*

Into the noble and ennobling theme of human freedom, the tradition of speculation in the West has introduced as a variation the creativity of the artist. The variation, which has tended to celebrate intimations of divine powers resident in the artist and manifest in fine art, has seized upon men's imaginations and has been voiced with conviction and eloquence. In consequence, the creativity of the artist has at times been wholly separated in theory from the theme of freedom; no less frequently, the sustaining theme has been subordinated to the variation. Despite these clearly marked historical tendencies, an essay of the artist as creator is basically a study of freedom. This theme of freedom is exceeded in significance by few in philosophy. It is one which provides the massive background against which much of speculation upon *homo faber* becomes intelligible and to which, in its turn, the creativity of the artist gives its unique interpretation.

It is not necessary to argue that freedom is omnipresent to speculation upon the artist as creator or, indeed, to aesthetic in its entirety as a portion of theory of value, in order to remark its significance and delineate the contours it assumes within the context of art. It is enough to point out at the outset that it is present to the earliest and continues to affect the latest interpretations of the subject. As Plato looks upon the poet as a " shy, wingéd, and holy thing," freed in and by means of divine inspiration from the rules of art, so Croce declares the freedom of art from such activities as morality and technique, the claims of which he believes would deny to this moment of spirit mastery in its own house. Hanslick goes so far as to assert that in music the composer " can remodel nothing," but must " create everything *ab initio*." Valery argues that " the artist's whole business is to make something out of nothing."

Aristotle's writings upon art echo faintly the note of liberating inspiration: "poetry implies either a happy gift of nature or a strain of madness." Their author is well aware, however, of the doubtful privileges, madness or atrabiliousness, which ancient medicine assumed to be concomitants of the divine afflatus. More to the point, however, Aristotle is primarily a naturalist, reluctant to endow the mimetic artist with more than freedom of choice. Whereas, for Plato, the imitative artist is but a facile mirror of the world; for Aristotle he is one who chooses to present men in action as they are, better than they are, or worse than they are. If too literal interpretations of mimesis have obscured the significance of the naturalist effort to sketch the boundaries of a free world of art, metaphorical extensions of the word's implications have been history's compensation for that fact. Aristotle's voice has many modern echoes: it is the nature of poetry, writes one critic, " to be not a part nor yet a copy of the real world . . . but to be a world by itself, independent, complete, autonomous."

To mention Croce and to quote Hanslick, Valery, and Bradley in the context of a tradition which begins with Plato and Aristotle, while omitting mention of the contributions to the theory of the artist as creator made by thinkers in the intervening centuries, overaccentuates the fact that the Western tradition of speculation upon art owes much to the Greek cast of mind, which set the artistic problem in the mold of mimesis. That the problem of the artist's freedom is implicit in the notion that the poet and his fellow makers are mimes is evident in the differing interpretations of the artist which, as we have observed, are offered by Plato and Aristotle. It is also true that the freedom of choice with which classical rationalist philosophy endows the artist plays no small role in forming the conception of creativity. It would not be difficult, in fact, to argue that all aspects and problems of human freedom which have been examined so meticulously within the ethical and metaphysical disciplines have their analogues in classical philosophies of art. It is clear, for example, that the difference between Plato's and Aristotle's interpretations of mimesis implies a basic distinction between determinism and freedom of choice. It could be maintained, also, that the theory of inspiration is potentially the notion of negative freedom, that it is an assertion of freedom from the rules and conditions of art, precisely as Kant occasionally argues that to be free to do what one is obliged to do is to be free *from* natural desires. Equally easily, it may be urged that inspiration presents the analogue to the theory of freedom of the will: the poet so exalted produces an object or event unconditioned by precedent artistic processes. Similarly, the Aristotelian theory of *katharsis* is correlative to the Aristotelian theory of action in ethics and poses the identical problem that freedom in choice of means and determination of end raises in ethical speculation.

Were we concerned to investigate the possibility that speculation on human freedom pervades speculation upon art, these specific issues might well be elaborated. The two millenia of controversy concerning human freedom in creativity present, without doubt, an impressive record in terms of duration alone. It is no less impressive, however, as one in which classical theory is enriched and in which aesthetic problems are given sharper definition. For an essay of the artist as creator, it is singularly important that aesthetic theory has not been too rigidly restricted in its development by the conditions which pertained to its origins. One may suggest this by mention of the fact that the Greeks knew that the problem of art impinged upon that of freedom but had no word for " fine art," whereas for us the term " fine art " means the free or the freeing arts. And if we try succinctly to account for this modern assertion of what was but implicit in ancient theory, while attempting to encompass the general problem of free creativity, we shall not err if we accept for the most part the assumption that modern theory relies upon imagination rather than imitation as the ground for the developed theory of the artist's free powers.[1] Nevertheless, aesthetic history bears out in general the hypothesis that reliance upon imagination makes intelligible the growth and enrichment of the Western tradition of human freedom in the specific context of art. In that context, it is necessary at once to relate art to and to differentiate it and its problems from ethics and metaphysics and the specific issues pertinent to them.

Historically, the assumption that man's creative powers are explicable in terms of this faculty and, therefore, neither conditioned by an instinct to imitate nor limited to a capacity for invention, has established the "science" of aesthetic as a philosophical discipline. As we shall observe, within this discipline and in its relation to other disciplines, the notion of freedom assumes a role no less central, however more obscure it may be, than it plays in ethics.

The chronicle of critical and philosophical speculation which produced theories of imagination sufficiently sound and inclusive to bear the burden of the argument that man is a free creator goes beyond the scope and need of the present essay. Indeed, the material with which we shall deal in this introductory chapter will, of necessity, appear to be drawn from sources all too widely separated and to have been subjected to little or no philosophical analysis. Some justification for the adoption of this mode of presentation rests upon the need to bring before the reader the scattered material of a long tradition; some is implicit in the nature of the case. A sufficient examination of the nature of imagination and the mode of its emergence necessarily involves a consideration of its relation to imitation and

[1] The issue is a doubtful one principally because, as I hold that feelings and imagination are inseparable and since classical theory emphasized the former, it is difficult to accept a hard and fast distinction.

inspiration. The latter terms have been closely associated with imagination in speculation upon artistic activity and provide information concerning both the general and the specific meanings which it has assumed in philosophy of art. Consequently the nature of the problem of the artist as creator can be set before us, and we can follow the issues peculiar to his freedom.

In this connection, we should note at the outset that the revival of learning at first draws principally upon the ancient theory of imitation [2] to free the " liberal " arts from restrictions of technical rules.[3] Scholarship suggests [4] that soon " the artist's invention has subtly shifted from finding what is already there, though hidden, to selecting or creating or fashioning a mental image by human strength alone." The ancient " invention " takes up its abode in the house of the artist: " It is given to poets alone to invent," writes Fracastoro.[5] To the continuing speculation concerning the meaning of " invention," Sir Philip Sidney gives needed point. Of art, Sidney writes that there is none " delivered unto mankind that hath not the works of nature for his principal object." [6] " Only the poet," he adds,

[2] It is well to note that " In the Middle Ages paintings and sculptures were not thought of in relation to a natural object which they seek to imitate but rather in relation to the formative process by which they come into being, namely, the projection of an ' idea ' existing in—though by no means ' created ' by—the artist's mind into a visible and tangible substance . . . and in the exceptional cases in which the procedure of the imitative arts was considered with regard to their relation to a visible model, this model was conceived, not as a natural object but as an ' exemplar ' or ' simile '—that is, as another work of art which served as a pattern." Erwin Panofsky, *Albrecht Dürer* (Princeton University Press, 1943), Vol. I, p. 243.

[3] See, for example, Antonio Palomino's discussion of " liberal " and " mechanical " arts: *El Museo pictórico y escala optica,* Vol. 1, Bk. 2, Ch. I, p. 3. Compare Seneca's remark, " Liberal studies are those which are worthy of being studied by free men." (*Letter* 88)

[4] See Gilbert and Kuhn, *A History of Esthetics* (New York: Macmillan, 1939), p. 186.

[5] Girolamo Fracastoro, *Naugerius, Sive de Poetica Dialogus,* trans. Ruth Kelso, p. 66. See Gilbert and Kuhn, *op. cit.,* on Fracastoro and Dürer, p. 186. It may be noted that Fracastoro makes the comment after remarking, " he is not a poet who employs the common-place."

[6] *The Defense of Poesy,* p. 7.

" disdaining to be tied to any such subjection, lifted up with the vigor of his own invention, doth grow, in effect, into another nature, in making things either better than nature bringeth forth, or quite anew, forms such as never were in nature . . . ." The poet it is who, while he " goeth hand in hand with nature," yet ranges freely " within the zodiac of his own wit."

The most liberal, much less the literal, interpretation of " imitation " scarcely suffices to bear the burden of explaining how poets are sufficiently free of external influences to bring forth " quite anew, forms such as never were in nature." [7] The burden, soon shifted to imagination,[8] is the heavy one of providing a ground for artistic originality, as well as an explanation

[7] *Ibid.*, p. 7.

[8] See Gilbert and Kuhn, *op. cit.*, p. 198: " The rational analysis of the meaning of the term ' imitation ' which the intellectual energy of the literary criticism of the Renaissance precipitated, issued finally in the suggestion that ' imitation ' is imagination or fancy in the modern sense."

The problem is complicated in Renaissance speculation by the effort to extend the range of the theory of creativity beyond poetry—to which the Greeks tended to limit it—to other arts. In his attempt to assert the superiority of painting over poetry, Leonardo da Vinci, for example, writes: " The imagination cannot visualize such beauty as is seen by the eye, because the eye receives the actual semblances or images of objects and transmits them under the sense organ to the understanding where they are judged. But the imagination never gets outside the understanding (sensus communis); it reaches the memory and stops and dies there if the imagined object is not of great beauty; thus poetry is born in the mind or rather in the imagination of the poet who, because he describes the same things as the painter, claims to be the painter's equal! But in truth he is far removed, as has been shown above. Therefore, in regard to imitation, it is true to say that the science of painting stands to painting in the same relation as a body to its cast shadow; but the difference is even greater; because a shadow penetrates through the eye to the understanding while the object of the imagination does not come from without but is born in the darkness of the mind's eye. What a difference between forming a mental image of such light in the darkness of the mind's eye and actually perceiving it outside the darkness! " *Trattato della Pittura*, 15. Quoted from *Paragone*, 18, ed. Irma A. Richter, pp. 49–50.

The issue raised by Leonardo is not only one of imitation and imagination. It concerns his evaluation of rational explanation as superior to all nonnatural explanation. In my opinion, the creative imagination for him is nonrational.

for the emergence of novel works of art.[9] As a critical instrument, imagination is used by writers to rid philosophy of art of vestiges of mimetic theory. Its function in the tradition of aesthetic and artistic speculation is not limited, however, to displacing imitation as the core of theory. It is entrusted with autonomous creative powers of its own.

An acute remark by Sir Francis Bacon suggests the essence of the powers which speculation attributed to this faculty.[10] Poetry is "a kind of learning . . . truly belonging to imagination"

[9] By way of illustration, Leonardo da Vinci argues that there is a difference basic to a differentiation among the arts: "In imitable sciences," he writes, "the student can attain equality with the master and can produce similar fruit. These sciences are useful to the imitator, but they are not of such excellence as those which cannot be passed on in heritage like other goods. Among inimitable sciences painting comes first. It cannot be taught to those not endowed by nature like mathematics, where the pupil takes in as much as the master gives. It cannot be copied like letters where the copy has the same value as the original. It cannot be moulded as in sculpture where the cast is equal in merit to the original; it cannot be reproduced indefinitely as is done in the printing of books. It remains peerless in its nobility; alone it does honour to its author, remaining unique and precious; it never engenders offspring equal to it; and this singleness makes it finer than the sciences which are published everywhere . . . ." *Trattato della Pittura*, 8; *Paragone*, 8, ed. Irma A. Richter, pp. 28–29.

Leonardo is to be compared and contrasted in this regard to Albrecht Dürer, another of the great initiators of the modern conception of originality and novelty in art. E. Panofsky argues (*Albrecht Dürer*, Vol. 1, p. 281) that whereas "the divine nature of the painter's science transforms the painter's mind into an image of the mind divine," Leonardo da Vinci "deliberately avoids" the expression "created" and used the word "generate." For Dürer on the other hand the painter is able "to call into being something that never was." Panofsky (*op. cit.*, p. 280) quotes the following from Dürer: "The mind of artists is full of images which they might be able to produce; therefore, if a man properly using this art and naturally disposed (*genaturt*) therefor, were allowed to live many hundred years he would be capable—thanks to the power given to man by God—of pouring forth and producing every day new shapes of men and other creatures the like of which was never seen before nor thought of by any other man" (Animus artificum simulacris est refertus, quae omnia incognita prius [!] cum in humanis tum aliarum rerum effictionibus in dies prolaturus sit, si cui forte multorum seculorum vita et ingenium [!] ac studium artis huius ususque divinitus contigerit)."

[10] "On the dignity and advancement of learning," *The Physical and Metaphysical Works of Lord Bacon*, II, xiii, 96 ff.

which is justly to be esteemed " of a Divine nature " precisely because " it raises the mind, by accomodating the images of things to our desires, and not, like history and reason, subjecting the mind to things." By the eighteenth century, Addison does not hesitate to assert that the more specific employment of affecting the imagination " has something in it like Creation." [11] The more general estimate of the freedom attributed to the faculty takes forms not too dissimilar from that made by Lord Kames: ". . . man is endued with a sort of creative power: he can fabricate images of things that have no existence . . ." [12] For Lord Kames, in fact, imagination is " this singular power of fabricating images without any foundation in reality . . . ."

The attribution of autonomy and originality to the imagination is noteworthy. No less so is the concern expressed by critics that a sole dependence upon the new instrument will justify the artist's denial that technique is still essential or that he is subject to the conditions implicit in art. Bacon, it is true, does mention the " measure of words " to which poetry as a kind of learning is confined. He remarks, nevertheless, that poetry is " extremely licentious," an obvious inference if only because this art belongs to imagination " which being unrestrained by laws, may make what unnatural mixtures and separations it pleases." An older tradition saves imagination from too derogatory criticism in Bacon's writing; but neither Dr. Samuel Johnson nor Lord Kames is constrained to abate the attack by consideration of the " Divine nature " with which inspiration is presumed to endow imaginative art. Consequently, it is precisely what Lord Kames [13] takes to be the significant facts concerning imagination—its " acting without controul " and its ability to " fabricate ideas of fine visible objects, of more noble and heroic actions, of greater wickedness, of more surprising events, than ever in fact existed "—that provide the rationalist with the ground for his attack.

[11] *The Spectator*, No. 421.
[12] Henry Home, *Elements of Criticism* (5th ed., 1774), pp. 518–19, 524.
[13] Henry Home, *Elements of Criticism*, p. 524.

Of imagination in general, Dr. Johnson observed that it is " a licentious and vagrant faculty, unsusceptible of limitations, and impatient of restraint," a faculty which " has always endeavoured to baffle the logician, to perplex the confines of distinction, and burst the enclosures of regularity." [14] Whatever of the rationalist predilection for classical severity and the learned doctor's own tendency to formulate doctrinaire rules Johnson's remark exhibits, it does nevertheless suggest the more specific problem in philosophy of art which supporters of the theory of imagination had shortly to face. To display fancy constantly or to indulge it without control, writes Alexander Gerard, " leads poets to describe improbable events and unnatural characters, and to search for unseasonable wit and ill-timed splendour." [15] Gerard suggests that judgment might well have been employed and have directed the poets " to imitate nature with exactness, and study simplicity of expression." What Mark Akenside, in *The Pleasure of Imagination*,[16] calls " high capricious powers " which " lie folded up in man," had been used to purchase freedom in the coin of novelty at the expense of art's intelligibility.

Imagination may well be the clue offered by the history of aesthetic to the solution of two problems proposed by Plato in *Ion*, the first posed by the suggestion that the poet borrows his subject matter from other arts, such as those of the charioteer and the law-giver, the second that " he who has no knowledge of a particular art will have no right judgment of the sayings and doings of that art." Nonetheless, the emancipation of the painter, the sculptor, or the poet from the need to *know* the techniques of the craftsmen who supply the content of arts by an insistence only that he *imagine* is a long and painful process.

The plea for the artist that he be valued as one who, by use

[14] *Rambler*, No. 125, p. 287.

[15] *An Essay on Genius* (1774), pp. 76–77.

[16] Akenside (1744), pt. 1, p. 23, lines 222 sq. I quote from the edition of 1818.

of imagination, creates another nature out of the material that actual nature gives has an enduring history. Kant repeats it,[17] but his systematization of aesthetic speculation in the *Kritik of Judgment* provides a context which transforms while it transmits the plea. The third critique not only analyses the judgment of taste and its objects. In it, Kant tries to formulate a theory of imagination so comprehensive as to meet the requirements of both artistic originality and art's intelligibility. Into it, the riches of eighteenth-century criticism flowed, and upon it the authors of the great aesthetic theories of the nineteenth and twentieth centuries drew for their own philosophies of artistic freedom.

The first requisite for the creative artist, Kant argues, is "originality." The free artist is, however, the genius compact not alone of imagination but of understanding as well. He possesses no mere "capacity to produce original nonsense"; in him "Imagination . . . submits to the constraint of the Understanding," and he submits the rich material furnished by originality to the "talent cultivated in the schools" for its execution and its form.[18]

To form imagination into a philosophical instrument adequate for the requirements laid down by sound theory for freedom in terms of both originality and intelligibility is, of course, not Kant's single-handed accomplishment. Rather, it is the result of centuries of speculation. To it contributed poets, critics, and philosophers so varied in point of view as Muratori, Gracían, Huarte, Bacon, Hobbes, Addison, Shaftesbury, Duff, Young, Kant, Coleridge, Wordsworth, Hegel, and Croce.[19] In

[17] Kant's *Kritik of Judgment*, trans. Bernard, sec. 49, p. 198. See *infra*, Ch. IV-V, for a fuller treatment of Kant's notion of the genius.

[18] Kant's *Kritik of Judgment*, sec. 47, p. 193 and sec. 49, p. 201.

[19] See *infra*, Ch. IV-VI. George Puttenham in *The Arte of English Poesie*, p. 19 interestingly enough regards "our maker or Poet" as one "holpen by a cleare and bright phantasie and imagination," yet one also of "sounde iuegement and discourse," who by means of these well affected parts "as by a glasse or mirrour, are represented vnto the soule all maner of bewtifull visions, whereby the inuentiue parte of the mynde is so much holpen, as without it no man could deuise any new or rare thing."

the course of that speculation, as we have implied, the doctrine of mimesis assumed a subordinate role, victim finally of the controversy between the ancients and the moderns. More significantly for the problem of human freedom, however, while philosophers, poets, and critics abandoned the long-lived and authoritative notion that art is imitation, they clung to the tradition of inspiration.

There are, of course, variations in theory concerning the relations of artistic imagination and artistic inspiration. Whereas some writers use imagination and inspiration as if they were alternative terms, it is clear that once the issue is faced, a difficult problem is presented. We have already mentioned the shift from the notion of discovery to selection, to "creating or fashioning a mental image by human strength alone."[20] The instance suggests the difficulty faced by theorists who move from the mimetic to the imaginative theory, while yet retaining the belief that inspiration still exercises an influence. Girolamo Fracastoro's *Naugerius, Sive de Poetica Dialogus* shows, in the first step from imitation to invention, the substitution of one natural explanation for another. The author is explicit in his recognition of the skills required by the poet;[21] but no less evident is the difficulty he encounters in proceeding from the nonnatural ground, inspiration, to a natural ground for invention. Despite the bow he makes to the "gods" who "have condescended to speak oracles" in him, Fracastoro believes that poets "alone invented that divine speech" which they use. Nonetheless, however diminished his dependence upon external sources for the product of his craft may be, the maker is believed to be inspired.[22]

[20] See above, p. 7.

[21] Fracastoro, *op. cit.*, p. 65: the poet "first began to modulate sounds, to select the musical, and reject the unmusical . . . to give attention to sonority and smoothness, and in short to all the other beauties of language."

[22] *Ibid.*, p. 65: "As soon as he had joined all the beauties of language and subject and had spoken them, he felt a certain wonderful and almost divine harmony steal into him, to which no other was equal. And then he observed that he was, as it were, carried out of himself."

Not only do doubts assail those writers who ask whether the sources of inspiration are external or internal to the artist; the most profound skepticism likewise attaches to the notion that *furor poeticus* does in fact explain the artist's creative powers.[23] Yet, in spite of such skepticism and uncertainty concerning the more specific interpretations of the theory, the central tenets of the doctrine that the ground for freedom from rules of art and for artistic originality is inspiration are not basically affected. Two facts of significance emerge in this connection. The first is the tenacity with which writers of the most diverse theories of imagination cling to the ancient doctrine of inspiration. The second is the ostensibly monolithic character of the tradition of inspiration itself.

As an instance of the tenacity with which one aspect of the theory of inspiration has been held, it will suffice to mention and later return to the words of a modern realist who has developed a theory of imagination. Precisely as Fracastoro describes the poet as feeling "a wonderful and almost divine harmony steal over him," so Samuel Alexander writes that "every artist is in his degree like Shakespeare, who was a reed through which every wind from nature or human affairs blew music."[24]

The notion of the artist as a passive recipient of the message of the Muses has become a commonplace in artistic criticism. It is unnecessary to determine whether Fracastoro influenced Alexander or even whether they drew upon a common source.[25]

[23] See, for example, Castelvetro, *Poetica d'Aristotle*, Ch. IV, 65, 11, cited by Gilbert and Kuhn, *A History of Esthetics*, p. 173. Castelvetro doubts that Plato seriously advocated the doctrine.

[24] *Beauty and Other Forms of Value*, p. 74: "Great artists know or believe that they are inspired from something outside themselves . . . . The artist's creativeness conceals from us his real passivity . . . ."

[25] See *infra*, Ch. V, p. 175. The two principal sources are Plato's *Ion* and Longinus' *de Sublimitate*. Plato remarks that there is no invention in the poet "until he is inspired and out of his senses." Longinus' writing exerted enormous influence upon modern theory. He maintains that "the effect of genius is not to persuade the audience but rather to transport them out of themselves . . . . What inspires wonder casts a spell upon us . . . ."

It is difficult, however, wholly to explain in terms of coincidence or historical influence the identity of assumptions that the artist is inspired as the ground common to the accounts we shall now instance, accounts which illustrate divergent metaphysical, psychological, and physiological presuppositions for philosophy of art. These we discover in Huarte's theory of humours, Duff's theory of association of ideas, and Kant's theory of productive imagination.

Huarte, to whom criticism owes much in the formation of the tradition of the genius in art, bases his theory of imagination upon the assumption that "all the governing Faculties in Man . . . require each their particular Temperament to perform their Functions as they ought." [26] In his naturalist interpretation, based on the theory of qualities, Huarte maintains that heat is the "Instrument with which the Imagination acts; in as much as this quality raises the Figures in making them boyl as it were." He interprets Plato to mean by inspiration that the wit, "by means of which, some have without Art or Study spoke such subtle and surprizing things, and yet true, that were never before seen, heard, or writ, no nor even so much as thought of," is mixed with madness. Imagination for Huarte absorbs the function of inspiration and "produceth prodigious Conceptions, and such as astonished *Plato*."

In contrast to Huarte and his theory of humours, William Duff writes of original genius against a background of association of ideas.[27] He urges that enthusiasm is the "glowing ardor of Imagination" which, "finding no objects in the visible creation sufficiently marvellous and new, or which can give full scope to the exercise of its powers, naturally bursts into the ideal world, . . . depending in its excursion wholly on its own strength, its success in this province of FICTION will be proportionable to the plastic power of which it is possessed."

Kant, denying the applicability of the theory of association of

[26] *Examen de Ingenios* or *The Tryal of Wits*, trans. Bellamy (1698), pp. 17–20.

[27] *An Essay on Original Genius* (1767), pp. 178–79. See Walter Kaufman, "Heralds of Original Genius," p. 204.

ideas to aesthetic judgment and to creativity, maintains that "genius is the exemplary originality of the natural gifts of a subject in the *free* employment of his cognitive faculties." [28] It is characterized by the "unsought undesigned subjective purposiveness in the free accordance of the Imagination with the legality of the Understanding . . ." The author of a work of genius "does not know how he came by his Ideas." [29] his skill cannot be communicated,[30] and the creative aspect of his operations is "ineffable."

We see, therefore, that the explanation of imagination may vary as widely as do "temperament" or "humours," "association of ideas," and "faculty-theory" of mind, while the theory of its originality remains tied to the ancient notion of *furor poeticus.* But not only is there evidenced a reluctance to abandon the theory of inspiration in accounting for originality in imagination, there is, at least ostensibly, evidence that the theorists present the tradition of inspiration as if it were monolithic in character. Two millenia of speculation upon the artist appear to have altered it little, as is evident from the following illustrations, selected from the wealth of material the literature of enthusiasm affords: Shelley writes of "hierophants of an unapprehended inspiration," and so echoes the words of Socrates in the *Apology*: "I went to the poets . . . I took them some of the most elaborate passages in their own writings, and asked what was the meaning of them . . . . I must say that there is hardly a person present who would not have talked better about their poetry than they did themselves. Then I knew that not by wisdom do poets write poetry, but by a sort of genius and inspiration; they are like diviners and soothsayers who also say many fine things, but do not understand the meaning of them." Robert Bridges, in *The Testament of Beauty,* asserts that reason, "in its naked self," is powerless, for philosophers "must lack vision of Art." Plato's *Symposium*

[28] *K. d. U.,* trans. Bernard, secs. 49, 50, p. 203.
[29] *Ibid.,* sec. 46, p. 189.
[30] *Ibid.,* sec. 47, p. 191.

provides the *locus classicus* for " vision " or " communion " attained by " having got beyond ' science ' into direct contact with ' beauty.' "[31] More specifically with reference to what we should now call the " fine artist "—Plato's " light, wingéd, and holy thing "—it is " not by art " that the poet sings but " by power divine." In *Laws,* we learn that of judgment, the correlative to art, " the poet . . . when he sits down on the tripod of his muse, is not in his right mind; like a fountain, he allows to flow out freely whatever comes in, and his art being imitative, he is often compelled to represent men of opposite dispositions, and thus to contradict himself; neither can he tell whether there is more truth in one thing that he has said than in another."[32] Similarly, for Croce, " the true artist, in fact, finds himself big with his theme, he knows not how; he feels the moment of birth drawing near, but he cannot will it or not will it."[33]

The fact that philosophers, critics and poets have clung to the notion of inspiration, and the additional evidence afforded by the monolithic nature of what they so evidently believe to be the answer to the problem of the artist's creativity, would be less striking and suggestive were we not to consider two additional and, as we shall see, related details. The first is the profundity of theories of imagination formulated by thinkers such as Descartes, Spinoza, Kant, and Bergson principally, for metaphysical and epistemological disciplines. The second is the fact that such general theories have been used to clarify significant issues concerning freedom other than that of artistic creativity. A classical instance is Spinoza's analysis of *conatus* in the *Ethic.* But it is more important for our present task to point out that significant consequences have resulted within the aesthetic universe of discourse from the application of sound theories of imagination. Aesthetic experience and aesthetic judgment have

[31] A. E. Taylor, *Plato,* pp. 230-31. See M. C. Nahm, *Aesthetic Experience and Its Presuppositions,* Ch. II, p. 36.

[32] *Op. cit.,* 719 c-d.

[33] *Aesthetic,* p. 51.

been liberated by this means from intrusive moral, economic, scientific, and religious claims concerning the value or disvalue of works of art. Works of art and works of fine art have been brought within the scope and under the rules of this faculty. The problem of the judgment of taste has been generalized, in consequence, in order to differentiate the fine from the technical arts and to permit evaluation, interrelation, and classification of the fine arts themselves.

In contrast, obscurity characterizes the general theme of freedom as it verges on the artist, an obscurity the more perplexing because the basic problems of the artist as creator have been stated clearly at various times in aesthetic speculation. By way of illustration, Plato and the eighteenth-century critics could scarcely have presented the artistic problem less ambiguously than they did in terms of originality and intelligibility. If we now recall the fact that the theory of inspiration has so constantly impinged upon speculation concerning the artist as creator, while it has been less pervasive in analysis of other aspects of aesthetic, we may at least assume that the obscurity derives from relating the artist to inspiration.

However premature this suggestion may be, the facts to which it will be applied are evident. Sober philosophical speculation has been frequently abandoned and replaced by either expressions of revulsion or fascination as philosophers and critics have approached the subject of the artist, a subject which one might presume to be the core of the problem of freedom in art and the presupposition of the free judgments and experiences which have been analyzed in sober terms. If the revulsion has led to neglect of the problem, fascination has led to worse. Robert Frost is eminently correct in suggesting that "the best way out is always through," but it has evidently required a courage stouter than that possessed by the critical to face, much less journey through this "stricken field." Those interpreters of the artist as creator who have yielded to their fascination in the problem appear to have followed one of two courses. The first has been to place the artist in strange company—the magician, the soothsayer, the prophet, and the madman—and thereafter to abandon him, surrounded by the maenad rout, the seers, and the practitioners of magic. The alternative has been only ostensibly less extravagant. In otherwise sober philosophical analyses, the artist and his powers have been described uncritically in absolute and categorical terms. Thus, Croce, who regards art as expression and expression as "free inspiration,"[34] holds that the artistic fact is "*altogether completed* in the expressive elaboration of impressions,"[35] while another expressionist, Bernard Bosanquet, is in no less categorical mood as he makes contrary assertions: artistic freedom is the "*complete self-determination*" of one whose imagination "lives in the powers of his medium."[36]

It is a matter of no small moment, as we shall see, to discover the ground for such conviction as both Croce and Bosanquet express. At present, however, we are more interested to indicate that the absolutism of treatment, as well as the tone of conviction with which it is expressed, not only accompanies such auxiliary and peripheral questions as that concerning the way the imagination operates but also, and with no diminution whatsoever, is directed to the problem of the artist's creativity itself. Indeed, so categorical are the assertions concerning the artist's freedom or his lack of it, and so antithetical the conclusions drawn, that the reader might infer that the writers in question believe either that no problem is presented or that, if there is a problem, no alternative to their inferences is possible. From the superabundant evidence of this attitude, it will suffice for our purposes to touch briefly upon the writings of a psychologist, a philosopher, and an archaeologist. Each, as we shall see, tends to put the problem beyond possible solution.

The psychologist in question, C. J. Jung, insists that any reaction to stimuli is susceptible to causal explanation. For

[34] *Ibid.*, p. 51. The italics in this and in the following quotation are mine.
[35] *Ibid.*, p. 50.
[36] "Croce's *Aesthetic*," p. 273 and *Three Lectures on Aesthetic*, p. 62.

him, however, the " creative act " is the absolute antithesis to mere reaction and one which " will forever elude the human consciousness." [37]

The philosopher makes his assertion on more general grounds. Erich Frank denies [38] that creation is possible in nature and presents his argument in metaphysical terms.[39] His conclusion is that " even the finest accomplishment of the human spirit is not real creation, for all human creation presupposes as its matter the world which man has not created himself."

Let us turn to the archaeologist. " The artist's confidence in his own unlimited power to create," writes Rhys Carpenter, is unfounded; but if he loses the illusion that he possesses this unlimited power " he can no longer act." [40]

The accord among metaphysician, psychologist, and archaeologist that the problem of the artist as creator may be disposed of in such categorical terms is interesting enough in itself. Even more interesting, however, is the fact that, whether the hypothesis adopted by the absolutists be that the artist is creative but that his creativity is beyond analysis or that he is unfree but must work under the illusion of freedom, the writers in question seem never to have inferred that their own central theme precludes the possibility that a meaningful essay of the artist as creator may be developed. On the contrary, they continue to speculate concerning the nature of art and the conditions for artistic creativity or aesthetic experience. It is quite possible to assume that their speculation seems less extravagant than that which began on the assumption of the poet's divine frenzy only because they have substituted a contemporary for an archaic terminology.

[37] *Modern Man in Search of a Soul,* p. 177. " Any reaction to stimulus may be causally explained." Jung's statement sharpens a distinction between freedom and " blind mechanism " implicit in Croce's aesthetic.

[38] *Philosophical Understanding and Religious Truth,* p. 57: " Creation in the true sense of the word is utterly impossible in nature . . . ."

[39] *Ibid.*, p. 57: ". . . an ultimate origination, an absolute coming into existence which is not dependent upon any cause of a similar order of being is unthinkable . . . ."

[40] " The Basis of Artistic Creation in the Fine Arts," pp. 30–31.

The evidence for the latter point is that what follows from the premises of the absolutists is no less startling than are the premises of the ancient argument that the poet produces great poetry because a god has breathed spirit into him. An instance is provided by Jung who, as we have seen, concludes that the creative action " will forever elude the human consciousness." The psychologist does grant that the scientist is able to describe both creativeness and freedom of will as " processes." [41] However, " the creative aspect of life which finds its clearest expression in art baffles all attempts at rational explanation." One may well wonder that Jung does not hesitate to resolve " the secret of artistic creation." And that he does attempt its resolution—and indeed includes as well the " effectiveness of art " in the solution—by identifying the creativity of the artist with " the state of *participation mystique* " can mean only that the problem does not " baffle all attempts at rational explanation." Rational explanation includes defining and identifying. Confusion is merely worse confounded as Jung's argument proceeds. It is remarked that the problem of *homo faber* may in fact be divided into " two separate and distinct tasks " for the psychologist: that of explaining " the formation of a work of art "; and that of revealing " the factors which make a person artistically creative." [42]

Let us postpone for the moment an evaluation of the metaphysician's denial to the artist of creative powers and, turning to Carpenter's restriction of the latter to mere illusion of freedom, attempt to discover in the archaeologist's conclusions whatever may bear upon the distinction made by Jung between

[41] *Modern Man in Search of a Soul,* p. 177. Cf. *ibid.,* pp. 198–99.

[42] Jung's insistence that reason is incapable of coping with the problem of artistic creativity repeats certain of Croce's aesthetic conclusions, more particularly that expression is " free creation " and that artistic genius " is always conscious; otherwise it would be blind mechanism." Jung's inference concerning the analyzability of the object of art made, in contrast to the creativity of the artist, is also asserted by Croce and, in both instances, makes the process of art and the creativity of artists dissimilar and separable. See Croce's *Aesthetic,* pp. 15, 50, 51, 116.

the process of forming the work of art and the process in which the artist is artistically creative. Carpenter maintains that the attribution to the artist of an " unlimited power to create " is wholly incompatible with the fact that " to the trained beholder every painting proclaims not merely its maker, but also its date and environment." [43] For him, the artist's creations show " a manner appropriate to a school or group, which in turn takes its ordered place within a phase or style pointing back to its predecessors and forward toward its successors."

It is at this point that the heartening forthrightness of the pragmatist's denial to the artist of creativity and his attribution to him of only the " illusion of freedom " suggests that all absolutism employs Procrustean methods. Carpenter knows the central problem and asks his own question concerning it in the clearest terms: " If the artist were wholly free to create, why should not each of his creations be completely unique . . . ? " The emphasis in the question is no doubt on the word " wholly " in the previous and " completely " in the last question. But the uniqueness of the product of the fine artist is precisely what the metaphysician asserts in terms no less categorical than those in which the pragmatist expresses his denial. Croce, for example, does not hesitate to maintain that the intuition is a unique individual. It may be granted at once that the point upon which Carpenter insists lends added strength to his absolutism. He maintains that creativity implies uniqueness, and uniqueness precludes classification. The inference is that intelligibility within a class or genus would be the obvious sacrifice required to assure the artist freedom to create.

We may be prone to accept this positivist method, even though it must be admitted that to leave the ground for the artist's " illusion " of freedom without examination commends itself no more than does Croce's assertion that the artist does not will to create but creates [44] or Frank's generalization that " creation is a miracle the idea of which human reason alone

[43] " The Basis of Artistic Creation in the Fine Arts," pp. 30–31.

[44] *Aesthetic,* p. 51.

cannot grasp."[45] But we are less likely to accept the positivist view once we realize that we are here presented with not only one absolutism, pragmatist though it may be, in conflict with its psychological and metaphysical correlates, but also that by implication a view like Carpenter's runs counter to the tradition in Western speculation which has led to the distinction between fine and technical arts. Neither " a manner appropriate to a school or group " nor " a style " relating a work of art to predecessors or successors suffices to provide for a distinction between a work of art and a work of fine art, precisely because neither characterization touches upon the validity or invalidity of the assumption that by the work of fine art men have meant " unique " in the sense of a work of " free " or a product of " freeing " art.[46]

As we have observed, the principal historical function of imagination has been that of marking off an aesthetic universe of discourse. It is, likewise, precisely the possibility of such demarcation which has permitted aestheticians to proceed upon the hypothesis that there are unique works of fine art. It may be argued, certainly, that to declare that the work of art or the work of fine art is free does not of necessity imply that the artist is likewise free. It may be argued, in fact, that the classical statement that art is a " state of capacity to make," serves precisely the function of freeing the work of art in space and time from the maker,[47] an argument reminiscent of Jung's effort to distinguish the task of explaining " the formation of a work of art " from that of revealing " the facts which make a person artistically creative." It is none the less impossible to maintain without argument that a work of art so freed is identical with a natural object or event occupying a spatial-temporal locus dif-

[45] *Philosophical Understanding and Religious Truth*, p. 61.

[46] Carpenter uses the words, " fine arts," in the title of his lecture, but the " work of art " is employed in his argument. He remarks (*op. cit.*, p. 33) that " The individual artist attains his own status by submission to the contemporary trend."

[47] See *infra*, Ch. I, p. 30.

ferent from the perceiver—precisely because the maker, in some sense as a free agent, intends to produce a free work of art.

There remains, therefore, the possibility that the artist possesses more than the "illusion of freedom," if it be true that we mean by fine art either a work of art separated by means of technique from its maker or "freeing" art, i. e., art which satisfies by process the condition for freeing the judgment and experience of the aesthetic perceiver from preoccupations wholly nonaesthetic. The latter possibility would permit use of "unique" in a general aesthetic sense, i. e., as a term intended to show that a work of fine art has an unique aesthetic value within an unique universe of discourse. It is owing to its author's failure to elaborate upon these implications of "free" that the categorical and absolutist tone of Carpenter's conclusion is exaggerated.

It may well be that the foregoing statements by psychologist, philosopher, and archaeologist, however categorical, provide a pattern for speculation superior to that which uses the terms "fine art" and "fine artist." Whatever difficulties are raised by assertions that there is absolute freedom in artistic creation beyond demonstrable relation to the making of art, that there is no freedom in artistic making and, by implication, that all art is intelligible because it is technical or that the word "creation" should be restricted to reference to God's acts and making —it is evident that to introduce the terms "fine art" and "fine artist" does open floodgates of speculation no less difficult to close.

Are works of fine art products of artists who, as Plato and many another believed, work "not by wisdom" but by a "sort of genius and inspiration"? Is the motive for such production an effort, as Lascelles Abercrombie suggests, to "escape from the privacy" of the artist's own mind in order to "become the property of the whole world"?[48] Is their "birth in beauty" owing to a "reasoned state of capacity to make" or to an imaginative power which goes beyond explanation in terms of

[48] *The Theory of Poetry*, p. 80.

such rational capacity? Are the objects or events we call " fine art " merely private expression, or must public art become private intuition and private expression become public communication in order to merit aesthetic evaluation?

That these and a host of similar and no less difficult questions are implicit in the hypotheses of fine art and fine artists must be admitted. It should be noted, however, that there is nothing contradictory in the suggestion that a free art may produce an object or event unique in consequence of freedom and that it may produce an object or event intelligible in consequence of the fact that it is an art. It is possible, likewise, that the words " creative " and " free " may be so ambiguous in aesthetic usage as to mean productive of both the unique or the intelligible. In any case, it is clearly impossible to answer on *a priori* grounds the question whether the " creations " of fine art do or do not take their place " within a phase or style pointing back to its predecessors and forward toward its successors." The basic assumption of the present essay of human freedom in art is that a means-end relation may be specified between fine art and the work of fine art. Our preliminary investigation will be devoted to the historical context of the absolutist position. At the moment, it is necessary only to point out that Jung's assertions concerning creativity differ little from those which abound in the eighteenth century, of which a notable instance is Edward Young's " genius," one capable of " accomplishing great things without the means generally reputed necessary " to the end of producing " an original." [49]

The assumption that an essay of the artist as creator may specify the means-end relation holding between fine art and the work of fine art implies that criticism and judgment may likewise be soundly grounded, in so far as the latter are conditioned by an analyzable artistic process, operating within an unique universe of discourse. These are hypotheses contrary to the basic assertion that creativity is beyond reach of " all attempts at rational explanation." Whether, however, valid

[49] *Conjectures on Original Composition,* p. 49.

inferences may be drawn from the object of art, either to the nature of the process by which it is produced or to the artist who produces it, presents no small portion of the general problem.

It has seemed to many writers that inferences from the work of art to the creator or limited to the former avoid many of the problems raised by the artist as creator simply because they rest on more objective grounds than do analyses of the feelings and mental processes of the artist. It has been of value to present a preliminary account of a controversy concerning two processes, creativity and art, and to record certain conclusions to which speculation has arrived. Nonetheless, the presentation of the account or of the conclusions has provided little more information concerning what is separated from the artist by the process of art or concerning artistic freedom than has been derived concerning the processes themselves.

It would seem rash, therefore, to maintain not only that there are works of fine art but also that such objects and events as the following objects of art are also products of free art: the Greek temple at Segesta; the cathedral, campanile, and baptistery at Pisa; the cathedral at Chartres; della Robbia's " Visitation " in Pistoia; the descending cadences of Mozart's *Concerto No. 21 in C; Antigone; King Lear;*

> . . . a shelfy coast
> Long infamous for ships and sailors lost,
> And white with bones;

El Greco's " Ecstasy in the Garden "; Vermeer's " Woman Weighing Gold "; Van Dyck's " Portrait of a Gentleman "; Turner's " Steam, Speed, and Rain "; Monet's " Rouen Cathedral "; Kolbe's *Adagio*; Verrocchio's " Colleoni Monument "; the Medici Chapel; the Sistine Chapel; and Leonardo da Vinci's anatomical drawings.

To enumerate works of fine art before we know what a work of art is, much less what a work of fine art is, requires some preliminary justification. Yet, one may designate objects and events which appear to merit the term "fine art" without assuming, as some writers have done, that simple enumeration suffices for the solution to the problem or that a multiplication of instances satisfies its conditions.[50] The separation of such objects and events from their makers provides a merely negative argument for the freedom of either the artist or the work of fine art. The obvious objection to the negative argument is encountered at once, moreover, in the need to distinguish artistic from natural objects and events, both of which occupy loci separate from the perceiver. It may be pointed out simply that one's credulity is subjected to a lesser strain by assuming that such objects and events as merit consideration in terms of aesthetic judgment and evaluation are products of a means-end relation yet to be specified than that they have occurred either by chance or by the accidental correlating of the separate processes of creativity and art. The probability is such that, taking it into account, we may proceed immediately to ask what condition, in terms of this simple assumption, must be satisfied in order to answer the two questions which are raised at once, namely, what is a work of art? and what is a work of fine art? The answer is certainly that if art be taken at the outset to mean what the classical literature of philosophy has asserted, i. e., the technical and forming processes by which an object or event is produced, we evidently need to know what structure produced by that forming or making process is common to the various objects which are called fine art and belong to the various arts.

The chronicle of art is rich in insights which craftsmen have provided in their efforts to describe the structure of the work of art. One instance, a description of a recital of Bach's *Suite in B Minor, for flute and strings,* will serve our immediate purposes. This bit of acrid humor occurs in Aldous Huxley's *Point Counter Point.* What strikes the reader at once is the variety of things a complex work of art may be imagined to be.

[50] By way of illustration, Maurice Bedel's "The Rights of the Creative Artist" (UNESCO) may be cited.

At Tantamount House, Huxley writes, "a dozen anonymous fiddlers and cellists scraped" at the conductor's bidding. "And the great Pongileoni glueily kissed his flute. He blew across the mouth hole and a cylindrical air column vibrated . . . . In the opening *largo* John Sebastian had, with the help of Pongileoni's snout and the air column, made a statement: there are grand things in the world, noble things; there are men born kingly; there are real conquerors, intrinsic lords of the earth . . . ." Then, "exquisitely and simply melodious," the Rondeau provokes in the poet the Sarabande, "a slow and lovely meditation on the beauty . . . of the world . . . a beauty, a goodness, a unity . . . ." [51]

Mr. Huxley ponders the strange antitheses his own imagination has presented: between "Pongileoni's snout and the cylindrical air column" and the "slow and lovely meditation of the poet upon beauty"; between Bach's "statement," "there are grand things in the world," and the vehicle for that statement, the fiddlers as they draw "their rosined horsehair across the stretched intestines of lambs." The immediate result of his pondering the contrast between the Caliban's cave of the instruments of art—the snout, the air column, and the sheep intestine —and the haunt of Ariel—the "long Sarabande," the "algebra" cutting "capers," and the poet slowly meditating his "lovely and convincing certitude"—is that here is "a beauty, a goodness, a unity that no intellectual research can discover, that analysis dispels, but of whose reality the spirit is from time to time suddenly and overwhelmingly convinced."

That this reality is beyond attainment by intellectual research or that it is one which analysis dispels, as Mr. Huxley would appear to believe, are issues concerning the philosophic question of the real which will soon engage our attention.[52] The point of our present interest may more profitably be the fact that, while Mr. Huxley believes beauty to be ineffable, judgment to be unanalyzable, and aesthetic experience to be

[51] *Point Counter Point*, pp. 26 ff.

[52] See *infra*, pp. 29 ff.

inexplicable on rational grounds, he does present for his and our imagination three great traditional bases for the explanation and judgment of the structure of art. That Mr. Huxley's outlook is sufficiently mystical to dismiss them or that it may be argued that these suggestions appear in the context of a work of art and should not be regarded, therefore, as the novelist's own opinion is, likewise, not our present concern. Rather, we are interested in the brief presentation of various structures suggested for works of art which criticism has examined in contexts more technical than that of *Point Counter Point.*

What are the three great traditional theories of the structure of the work of art to which Mr. Huxley's description may be correlated and by examination of which we may hope to determine whether analysis of any one or of the three in their interrelation will cast light on the nature and sources of creativity? [53] Mr. Huxley's interest in the tools and materials of art—the snout and the rosined horsehair—suggests the theory of art as making; his mention of the "grand things in the world" implies the theory of art as symbolization; and the Rondeau which provokes in the poet "a slow meditation upon beauty" is the theory of art as creative imagination, called expression.[54]

Each of these analytically distinct philosophies of art, that of making, of symbolization, and of expression, assumes that the "real," i. e., the product of the artist's art and the object of aesthetic judgment, is the structure of the work of art, respectively as object made, as sign symbolized, and as image expressed. What are the grounds for the claim made for each theory that it provides an answer to the question, what is a work of art? Secondly, are the various theories compatible with each other?

[53] There are four theories of art implicit in Mr. Huxley's description but the fourth, the formal theory, has been dealt with at considerable length in my *Aesthetic Experience and Its Presuppositions,* Ch. II-V. For our present purposes, we may draw the necessary inferences concerning formal theories from an examination of the "unity" implied in the hypothesis of expressionism.

[54] Compare, for example, R. Collingwood's description of aesthetic experience as an autonomous activity which "arises from within . . . [and] is not a specific reaction to a stimulus proceeding from a specific type of external object," *The Principles of Art,* p. 40.

The ground for the claim that making provides a sound basis for judgment in art is that this process may be differentiated from acting and that the structure produced by tools and techniques and ordinarily called an artefact is an object or event separated from the maker.[55] The ground for the claim that symbolization provides a sound basis for judgment in art is that the science of signs—iconology—may mark out classes of " intrinsic meanings " which " refer in reality to aspects of one phenomenon, namely, the work of art as a whole." [56] The ground for the claim that expression provides the clue to the meaning of art is that only imagination or intuition forms impressions into unique and individual images or works of art.[57]

Such, in brief, are the grounds for the argument that there is the work of art. Are the theories compatible to the degree that we can, from them, determine what the structure of the work of art is? If we turn to a work of fine art written about the cathedral at Chartres, one of the objects or events we have judged to be a work of fine art, we may both illustrate the theories in question and suggest, as well, a problem which the critic overlooks but which is crucial for the philosopher who attempts to answer the question. Henry Adams, in *Mont St. Michel and Chartres,* describes the cathedral in ways which accord with the great traditional theories: He quotes [58] Viollet-le-Duc, and the cathedral is understood in terms of " making ": " Toward the beginning of the thirteenth century, the architect of the Cathedral of Chartres sought out entirely new window combinations to light the nave from above . . . . For the first

[55] See the classic statement of the problem in Aristotle's *Nicomachean Ethics,* 1140 a 1 seq. Compare *ibid.,* 1105 a 27: ". . . the products of the arts have their goodness in themselves . . .".

[56] E. Panofsky, *Studies in Iconology,* pp. 16–17.

[57] B. Croce, *Aesthetic as Science of Expression.* To call an " intuition " or " image " or " expression " a " structure," even in the loose sense in which we have thus far used that term, may appear to run counter to the expressionist's contention that the work of art need not be made. Still, " expression " is the forming process, i. e., it is the objectification of " impressions " and, in these senses, therefore, a " structure."

[58] *Op. cit.,* p. 114.

time one sees at Chartres the builder deal frankly with the clerestory, or upper fenestration, occupying the whole width of the arches, and taking the arch of the vault as the arch of the window. Simplicity of construction, beauty in form, strong workmanship, structure true and solid, judicious choice of material, all the characteristics of good work, unite in this magnificent specimen of architecture . . . ." But it is not only a work of art as made; the Cathedral is "a symbol of unity; an assertion of God and Man in a bolder, stronger, closer union than ever was expressed by any other art . . . ." [59] And, finally, ". . . Chartres expressed, besides whatever else it meant, an emotion, the deepest man ever felt,—the struggle of his own littleness to grasp the infinite." [60]

Each object or event which we earlier called a work of fine art could be described in the identical structural terms, i. e., as products of making, of symbolizing, and of expressing, which Adams uses in describing Chartres. [61] Few critics of literature or art would seriously question their relevance; fewer still would recognize any incompatibility among them. As for the philosopher of art, it is doubtful that he would offer too strenuous objection either to the identification or the assertion of the complementary character of two of the traditional theories, making and symbolization.[62] It is evident, in support of the argument that the theories are at least complementary, that

[59] *Ibid.*, p. 45.

[60] *Ibid.*, p. 106.

[61] This is in contrast to the tendency of classical writers to consider poetry as unique among the arts. Artists and critics of the Renaissance maintained that painting and sculpture were not mechanical or servile but liberal or divine. See Leonardo da Vinci's suggestion that the lesser praise given to the painter than to the poet is owing to the fact that "as painters did not know how to plead for their own art she was left without advocates for a long time. For painting does not talk; but reveals herself as she is, ending in reality; and Poetry ends in words in which she eloquently sings her own praises." *Paragone* 20, *Trat.* 46, ed. I. Richter, p. 52. Schopenhauer's treatment of music is the modern analogue to the classical selection of poetry as unique.

[62] To such a conclusion, various analysts of music would object. Cf. Hanslick, *The Beautiful in Music,* pp. 151–52: "Nature does not supply us with the art-elements of a complete and ready prepared system of sound, but only with

the theory of making assumes that, by means of technique, a form has been imposed upon material, that the material embodies this form, and that what the maker conceives to be the end of his art, the perceiver knows as an intelligible form. Inasmuch as this embodied form is separated from the maker by the act of making[63] and is yet presumably intelligible in terms of the artist's intention,[64] historians of aesthetic have rarely hesitated to conclude that this is a ground for judgment of the work of art, not merely as an imitation or a copy, but, indeed, as a symbol.

Controversy concerning theories of the structure of the work of art arises once we ask not whether expression is compatible with making and with symbolizing—inasmuch as it is—but rather whether a theory of art as technique or symbolization is compatible with that of expression.[65] In the most radical statement of the latter theory, that of Benedetto Croce, and in its most illuminating elaboration, in the writings of R. G. Collingwood, it is clear that the answer is in the negative. The expressionist insists that "the aesthetic fact is altogether completed in the expressive elaboration of impressions." [66] "If the symbol be conceived as separable," Croce argues, art is "aping science." Not only is the theory of symbols declared to be incompatible with that of art as expression; the theory of making or technique is likewise declared alien to it.[67] And these in-

the crude matter which we utilize for our music. Not the voices of animals, but their gut is of importance to us; and the animal to which music is most indebted is not the nightingale, but the sheep."

[63] See *supra*, p. 30.

[64] See Aristotle's remark, *E.N.* 1140 b 23, that in art "he who errs willingly is preferable . . ." and *Poetics* 25. 1460 b 20, where Aristotle argues that "if the poet meant to describe the thing correctly, and failed through lack of power of expression, his art itself is at fault." See *ibid.* 1460 a 27: "If, however, the poetic end might have been as well or better attained without sacrifice of technical correctness . . . the impossibility is not to be justified, since the description should be, if it can, entirely free from error." Trans. by I. Bywater.

[65] See *infra*, Ch. VII et seq. See also my *Aesthetic Experience and Its Presuppositions*, Ch. X–XIX.

[66] Croce, *Aesthetic*, p. 50.

[67] *Ibid.*, Ch. XV. Cf. R. G. Collingwood, *The Principles of Art*, p. 111: "The

compatibilities, it is asserted, derive from the fundamental thesis that art is free: " if by art be understood the externalization of art, then utility . . . [has] . . . a perfect right to enter into it; that is to say, the right to be master in one's own house." [68]

We thus observe that, if our sources of information concerning art and fine art, the work of art and the work of fine art, and the artist and the fine artist depend upon a description of the structure of the work of art in which traditional theories are compatible, we face difficulties which appear to belie the sound and objective grounds so frequently assumed to render the object produced by art more readily available for analysis than are the feelings of the artist or the processes he uses. It is noticeable, however, that the expressionist tends to hold that the ground for the incompatibility of the theories of structure lies not so much in the structure of the image as in the intuition or imagination of the artist, i. e., in that first moment which is held to be autonomous, essential to but independent of other moments of spirit. This is significant, principally because it suggests that it is difficult to change the locus of the problem from the process of creativity to the structure of the work of art.

In a sense, therefore, we have arrived by the alternative route of the work of art and its structure at the repetition of the tentative conclusion to which the problem of the creativity of the artist appeared to lead. The expressionist's insistence upon the process of creativity is accompanied by assertions that not even the artist can know the nature or will the creation of the images which are identified with art. This would appear to reiterate within a philosophical context Bridges' conviction that reason lacks the " vision " necessary for an understanding of art, Jung's assertion that the creative processes " will forever elude the understanding," and Huxley's notion that we search for what " no intellectual research can discover."

means-and-end, or technique, terminology . . . is inapplicable . . . . Expression is an activity of which there can be no technique."

[68] Croce, *Aesthetic*, p. 116.

The fact is, however, that even a brief analysis of the relation or nonrelation of structural theories of art yields more than mere repetition of statements concerning the artist as creator. In the first place, the grounds for the assertion that the image is incompatible with symbol or object are now more explicit. Secondly, some suggestion of the difficulty of relating artist to process and object of art has been presented. Finally, and most significantly, we discover that however tempting it may be to seize upon the presumed objectivity of the work of art or of fine art as a ground for inferences concerning the artist as creator, it is impossible to avoid by this means the need to discriminate those aspects of freedom which have been asserted to be unique to creativity. The fact is brought home by what appears in the writings of the expressionists: namely, that the theory is a statement which its authors believe to be an integral part of the theory of inspiration, which, as we have seen, has accompanied the theory of imagination in the aesthetic usage. Croce holds, in fact, that "expression is free inspiration." [69]

The identification of expression as a theory both of the structure of art and of artistic and critical freedom with the recurrent and monolithic theory of the inspired artist leads us then to ask what precisely specifies the freedom of inspiration and what, according to ancient and modern theories, differentiates it from other accounts of the artist's freedom? A preliminary answer is made available by comparing and contrasting its classical formulation in Plato's writings with Aristotle's theory of making and the Atomists' conception of human willing and cosmic creating. And with this tentative answer we may also arrive at some clue to the factor or factors in the tradition of the inspired artist which will account for the recurrence of this monolithic theory, as well as the source of the evident compulsion it has exercised upon speculation in philosophy of art and aesthetic.

[69] *Aesthetic,* p. 51. Cf. Collingwood, *The Principles of Art,* pp. 126 ff. Cf. Huxley, *supra,* p. 28.

Some writers have been led by the homogeneity of the tradition of inspiration in speculation upon art to identify freedom and inspiration. Were the terms in fact analytically related, the comparison and contrast we propose to undertake would be meaningless. In any case, it is clear that Croce's use of the two terms " free " and " inspiration " argues that for him no such analytical relation holds,[70] precisely as it is clear that to be " inspired " has had in history a more limited application than has to be " free." We may assume that the relation between " free " and " inspired " is a synthetic one.

The most evident differentiation to which the three classical theories of freedom which touch upon the problems of making and creating are susceptible is that between natural and nonnatural explanations of the processes under consideration. To the former classification belong Aristotle's theory of free choice and the Atomists' description of freedom in cosmic making and in human acting; to the latter, the Platonic theory of the inspired artist. It will suffice, at the moment, to indicate the background of the theory of inspiration, in its nonnatural context, as a philosophy in which " the whole sphere of nature, the empirical world . . . remains absolutely separated from the real existence of the transcendent ideas." [71] Aristotle rejects the transcendence,[72] as do the Atomists. But whereas for Aristotle the theory of free choice in art is formulated within a teleologically definable philosophy of nature, the Atomists present their theories of freedom in terms of strict ateleological defining.

Let us examine, first, the two natural theories of freedom

[70] It will suffice here to point out that Croce obviously intends to avoid, if possible, two aspects of the traditional theory of inspiration in putting forward his own argument for the artist's creativity: the first is " some controlling force outside the artist "; (see Collingwood, *The Principles of Art,* p. 126) ; and, secondly, the curious combination of freedom and bondage which such " controlling force outside the artist " has led speculation to assume concerning the artist.

[71] E. Frank, " The Fundamental Opposition of Plato and Aristotle," p. 171.

[72] *Ibid.,* p. 34: " Aristotle rejects the transcendence, the *chorismos,* of the ideas . . . ." Cf. *ibid.,* p. 183: " Aristotle is the most imposing representative

and their differences and then turn to the nonnatural notion of inspiration. For Aristotle making, as is acting, is a state of rational capacity, to be analyzed in a philosophy in which freedom of choice is assumed to be a natural endowment.[73] The reasoned state of capacity to make " is concerned with coming into being, i. e., with contriving and considering how something may come into being which is capable of either being or not being." [74] The capacity for making is actualized in the realm of the " variable," and, although art is a " state . . . involving a true course of reasoning," Aristotle holds that, owing to the variability, we are concerned with " what may occur otherwise." The origin of what " may come into being which is capable of either being or not being " is in the maker, not in the thing made. The scope and meaning of what may be called " voluntary making " is indicated by the Aristotelian suggestion that " in art he who errs willingly is preferable." [75]

In the specific fields of art of which Aristotle has written, mainly in *Poetics* and in the latter portion of *Politics,* we are informed of the meaning of the suggestion that the moving principle is in the agent, " he being aware of the particular circumstances." In *Poetics,* the phrases, the poet " has chosen " and may make a " wrong choice " are reiterated. Probable impossibilities and errors are not only permitted but are to be preferred " if the end of art be thereby attained." [76] In *Politics,* Aristotle not only classifies the kinds of music but also generalizes the problem to include the various choices we may make in pursuing the art. In general, the artist chooses and by means of technical skill makes actual the potentialities of the material

of that attitude of purely theoretical objectivity and faithful phenomenological observation which are the chief characteristics of the descriptive sciences of nature and of philologico-historical research."

[73] *E. N.* 1114 b 1 ff.

[74] *Ibid.,* 1140 a 10 ff.

[75] *Ibid.,* 1140 a 23 ff.

[76] *Poetics,* trans. Butcher, 1460 b 25. Aristotle writes (*ibid.,* 1460 b 8) that the poet, " being an imitator, like a painter or any other artist, must of necessity imitate one of three objects—things as they were or are, things as they are said or thought to be, and things as they ought to be."

of the arts. What the poet, for example, " should aim at " is indicated in terms of the word " nature " or " natural." [77]

Aristotle begins with imitation as the genus of arts, proceeds to differentiate the arts in terms of manner, media, and objects and concludes that, in terms of free choice, the artist actualizes the potentialities to produce an object analogous to " a living organism or any whole composed of parts " which " must not only have an orderly arrangement of parts, but must also be of a certain magnitude." [78]

To a consideration of the merits and limitations of Aristotle's theory of freedom of the artist as maker and to the theory of art he proposes, we shall return.[79] In general, Aristotelianism emphasizes the intelligibility and rationality of the artistic process.[80] As we shall see, this leads to the suggestion that the poet should " preserve the type," while yet ennobling it. In general, the theory's conclusions are in contrast to those of the Atomists and to the inferences drawn from the theory of inspiration. So intent, indeed, is Aristotle upon establishing a natural theory of freedom for the artist that it has been held doubtful that his philosophy, which emphasizes freedom of choice of means, will permit interpretation in terms of the choice of ends as well.[81] Art and acting are specifically differentiated in the theory in that " the products of the arts have their goodness in themselves, so that it is enough that they should have a certain character, but if the acts that are in accordance with the virtues themselves have a certain character it does not follow that they are done justly or temperately." [82] Finally, Aristotle's conception of de-

[77] For example, *Poetics*, 1449 a 15: " Having passed through many changes, [tragedy] found its natural form, and there it stopped."

[78] *Poetics*, VII, trans. Butcher.

[79] See *infra*, Ch. VII, pp. 221 ff.

[80] *Poetics*, XV.

[81] Cf., W. D. Ross, *Aristotle*, pp. 200–201.

[82] *E.N.* 1105 a 27–30. Cf. H. H. Joachim, *The Nicomachean Ethics*, p. 13: ". . . the important thing is the product: not his state of mind, will, or purpose in the making, but the character of what is made. The products of the crafts (techniques, productive arts) are relatively free, independent of the personality of the maker. They have their goodness or badness in themselves. An artist

liberation and choice is ambiguous to the degree that it is a matter of controversy whether or not the agent is free.[83]

It is notable that the seeming clarity of Aristotle's statement concerning freedom of choice is paralleled in the description of phenomena and of their becoming, as well as in human willing, in the philosophy of the ancient Atomists. The Atomists' writings, whether one consider the fragments of the philosophies of Leucippus, Democritus, Epicurus, or the *De Rerum Natura* of Lucretius, impinge upon cosmological problems of making and creating and center attention upon the problem of human freedom in willing and in acting. But in these speculative fields, classical Atomism examines creating and freedom methodologically using identical principles for both. Within a tradition of speculation which has served as model and pattern for physical explanation, economical and inclusive in its scope, the principal phenomenon of cosmology and human freedom to be explained comes to be the emergence of the novel, i. e., of " new beginnings," [84] both in the world of nature and in human willing. No less significantly, it should be emphasised that ancient Atomism examined this, among other philosophical problems, without recourse either to psychological teleology [85] or to a divine creator.[86]

or craftsman is ' good ' if his works are good: and his works stand on their own merits . . . . in action the all-important thing is the state of mind of the agent—his will, purpose, motives: for his end is acting in a certain way, ' living well,' and not anything beyond the acting—in production the maker's will, motives, method of operation and actual making are of importance only so far as they affect the character of the product."

[83] Cf. Joachim, *op. cit.*, p. 110, where the issue is raised in terms of the alternative, that the purpose, which is " nothing mysterious or miraculous," is the " expression of man's nature " or that " our good and bad actions express a ' deliberate decision ' which appears to emerge without intelligible development, and without intelligible connexion with the rest of man's nature and the environment in which he lives." Joachim holds that both interpretations may be substantiated from passages in Aristotle's works.

[84] See, for example, Lucretius' *De Rerum Natura.* The most significant passages are II. 215–24, 251–73.

[85] See Aristotle's *de Gen. Animal.*, E 8. 789 b 2.

[86] See Plutarch's *Strom.* 7 (D 581): " Democritus the Abderite supposed the universe to be infinite because it had not been fashioned by any Maker."

The suggestions implicit in classical Atomism concerning novelty, creativity, and freedom important for our problem are best examined against the background of Leucippus' proposition that "nothing occurs at random, but everything for a reason and by necessity."[87] What Leucippus intends is indicated in the mention by Epicurus of laws of nature (*foedera natura*), the basis of his philosophy, the first principle of which is that "nothing is created out of nothing." As Bailey points out, "the laws of atomic being require that the atoms should fall eternally without meeting."[88] But Epicurus maintained[89] that there is a "certain freedom in the motion of atoms . . . namely an inherent declination as is proved by the phenomena."[90]

The issue of the "swerve" or "declination" is elaborated in Lucretius' *De Rerum Natura*.[91] It is remarked in this poem that "bodies must swerve a little; and yet not more than the least possible." Doxographers and commentators have pondered the crux they believe to be presented at this juncture: whether the swerve or declination of atoms from the movement to which they are necessitated by natural law is introduced by the post-Democritean Atomists either to provide an explanation of the fact that atoms do overtake each other—as is evident in phenomena—or to provide a ground for human freedom. It is evident, however, that no dilemma is presented, inasmuch as the philosophical problem to be resolved is identical in either instance.[92] The swerve of atoms is employed methodologically to produce compounds of atoms, i. e., to

[87] Fr. 2. See my *Selections from Early Greek Philosophy*, p. 160.

[88] *The Greek Atomists and Epicurus*, pp. 317–18.

[89] See my *Selections from Early Greek Philosophy*, 174, fr. 50. Cf. *ibid.*, frs. 47, 51.

[90] See Bailey, *op. cit.*, p. 317. Bailey refers to Cicero's *de Nat. Deor.* i. 25. 70, in which it is noted "hoc dicere turpius est quam illud quod volt non posse defendere."

[91] *Op. cit.*, Bk. II, lines 196–253.

[92] See Bailey, *op. cit.*, pp. 320–21. See also his discussion on pp. 318–20, especially the quotation from Diogenes of Oenoanda: "if destiny be believed in, then all advice and rebuke is annihilated."

explain Heraclitean process in a theory which attempts to take account of Parmenidean *Being* by resorting to indivisible bodies —varying infinitely in geometrical properties. It is thus intended to account for what is novel, namely, the phenomenal change in a qualitatively perceptible universe. No such novelty is explicable in terms of the necessitated motions of atoms.[93] But, similarly, the swerve or declination of the atoms is used to explain what must be explained if we are to speak meaningfully concerning free human action, i. e., what is novel and not necessitated. For, as Lucretius maintains, a man's "own will" must be permitted to make "for each a beginning" and thus avoid the enthrallment which follows "if all motion is ever linked together and a new motion ever springs from another in fixed order and first-beginnings do not by swerving make some commencement of motion to break through the decrees of fate, that cause follow not cause from everlasting." [94]

For Lucretius, the making of a cosmos in which phenomenal change is possible is the making of a world in which atoms may be compounded and separated. The origin of phenomena and the origination of free acts presents the identical problem of change to be accounted for in specifically different ranges of phenomena.[95] "For each," i. e., for phenomenal process and for willing, there must be a "beginning." In the case of compounded atoms, i. e., phenomena, "the begetting bodies of matter do beget different things." Thus, the theory of Anaxagoras that "all things though latent are mixed up in things" is held to be incorrect.[96] Novelty emerges in the formation of

[93] Lucretius, *On the Nature of Things*, trans. Munro, pp. 48–49. "If they were not used to swerve, they would all fall down . . . through the deep void, and no clashing would have been begotten nor blow produced among the first beginnings: thus nature never would have produced aught." Bailey (*op. cit.*, p. 83) cites Simplicius to the effect that "the atoms move in the void and catching each other up jostle together" but remarks that "Epicurus certainly conceived of a theoretic condition in which before a single collision had occured the atoms were all moving in the same direction without catching each other up."

[94] *De Rerum Natura*, II, 251 ff.

[95] *Ibid.*, II, 253–311.

[96] *Ibid.*, I, 895. Cf. Bailey, *De Rerum Natura*, II, Appendix I, pp. 537–56:

phenomena by means of a process which may be regarded as " creative "; and free acts of will are actions novel in the sense that they are not wholly explicable in mechanical terms.

It is noteworthy that writers within the tradition of the Atomist philosophy established by Leucippus and Democritus judge the issue of freedom to be crucial to the degree that they are prepared to limit, in order to account for novelty, the mechanist world view in which laws of necessity apply. The emergence of " new beginnings " is explicitly stated to be the problem for which the declination or swerve of the atoms is provided as the solution and its introduction destroys the universality of the proposition, " nothing occurs at random, but everything for a reason and by necessity."

The Aristotelian theory of free choice in making emphasizes the intelligibility and the typicality of the product of the maker's art. The Atomists' theory of freedom emphasizes originality and novelty in the fields of cosmology and of human action. In Plato's theory of inspiration, the problem of artistic freedom is related to the poet and rhapsode in a context which presents for Plato the problem that Aristotle later resolved in terms of voluntary making. Plato's theory combines natural and nonnatural principles of explanation. To it we shall now turn, examining it in some detail and making explicit the inferences needed to understand the conception of the artist as creator in the tradition in which Plato's writings are a most significant influence. We shall then return to the presumed identification of freedom and inspiration in Croce's theory and, by comparing and contrasting Aristotelian, Atomist, and Platonic hypotheses, attempt to answer the main question: Why has the notion of inspiration recurrently tended in monolithic restatements to preëmpt speculation concerning the artist as creator?

" If . . . you hold that the elements combine without changing their nature, nothing can be created from them, whether animate or inanimate." See Lucretius, *op. cit.*, II, 62–65, ". . . I will explain by what motion the begetting bodies of matter do beget different things and after they are begotten again break them up . . . ."

Plato's use of inspiration is largely limited, as regards the problem of art, to the poet. Later speculation extended its application to other arts.[97] As we shall see, the Western tradition of the artist as creator was influenced, as regards inspiration, by the Hebraic-Christian Revelations.[98] For our purposes, we should note that Plato evidently used the term " inspiration " in the context of philosophy of art, to emphasize a cleavage within the conception of artistic productivity itself. For him, the line of that cleavage runs between the aspect of freedom which may be called artistic creativity and that best denominated mimetic and technical craft. The point is the more remarkable because the author of the *Republic* has decreed that the poet should be " anointed with myrrh," that there should be set upon his head " a garland of wool," but that he should also be sent " away to another city." But even this exile of the artist from the ideal commonwealth by the lawgiver and the severe censorship to which such fine art is to be subjected are but the marks of external servitude to which the poet, the painter, and the sculptor are condemned. Its internal analogue derives from the nexus of the art itself, from the art to which the poet is bound, and it is this which evokes the Spartan denial to that " light and wingéd and holy thing " of the doubtful privileges of living in the commonwealth. Plato argues that the poet displays a " shallow versatility " which permits him to make everything.[99] Indeed, Plato adds—and, in so doing brings technique as well as function and subject matter well within the scope of his attack—he does so by " a rapid method " which admits of many variations; and all of these methods are of such kind as to be put most rapidly into action, as if one would " take a mirror, and turn it round in every direction."

[97] Cf. *supra*, p. 31.

[98] Cf. *infra*, Ch. v, pp. 170 ff.

[99] See A. S. Ferguson, " Plato and the Poet's ΕΙΔΩΛΑ," p. 138. *Republic*, trans. Davies, 596 C 25 ff.: The poet belongs to the class of " extraordinarily ingenious persons " who can not only " construct all manufactured articles . . ." but also " produces everything that grows out of the ground, and creates all living things, himself among others; and, in addition to this, heaven and earth and the gods and all the heavenly bodies, and all beings of the nether world."

It is true that Plato is at this point contrasting the production of useful objects to the copying of them. Systematically, however, his inquiry concerns the function (ἔργον) by which these images may be defined. The principal implication of the inquiry is this, that the artist is receptive rather than productive, an unfree mime rather than a free creator, one who merely appears to produce novelty. In this, Plato does contrast the imitative artist to the man inspired.[100] The principal issue is the clearer, once we recall the criteria for the standards of art to which Plato, in *Laws,* believed the Egyptians adhered and for which he commends them. The Egyptians, he writes, " fixed and exhibited . . . patterns . . . in their temples and no painter or artist is allowed to innovate upon them, or to leave the traditional forms and invent new ones." [101] The inference to be drawn is evident. Craft or making does not produce novelty; nor should its practitioner attempt to make it do so.

The bondage imposed upon the artist by the laws and censorship of the state and the at least ostensible subservience of the artist to the strictures of mimetic art clearly enough poses the problem which Aristotle attempted to solve by his theory of freedom of choice in making. Nor are the possibilities for freedom wholly foresworn by Plato himself.[102] If, however, we remain within the context of Plato's writings of the middle period, the bondage so imposed makes Plato's *Ion* the more extraordinary as an enunciation of the implications of artistic inspiration. For while it is in itself Plato's poetic expression that the poet is " taken possession of " by God, who " sways the souls of men in any direction he pleases," it is Plato's philosophical inference that the artist in being inspired is freed from the " rules of art "; from the specific limitation imposed in the injunction that a craftsman must proceed rightly and from the general requirement that the practitioner acquire " a knowledge of a whole art."

[100] Cf. Bosanquet, *A Companion to Plato's Republic,* pp. 380–81, and Ferguson, *op. cit.,* pp. 139 ff.

[101] *Op. cit.,* trans. B. Jowett, 656.

[102] See *infra,* Ch. II, pp. 68 ff.

The consequences of Plato's speculation are significant. In the first place, it is evident, as we have observed, that he entertains serious doubts that the craftsman or technician is enabled by Τέχνη to produce genuine novelty. In so far as novelty poses the problem of the artist, it is implied that inspiration does provide an answer and that the inspired artist may produce it.[103] Secondly, Plato makes no effort to relate the rational process, art, to the nonnatural (i. e., super-rational), inspiration. In this, Plato's method, as relates to freedom in making, is in sharp contrast to that of the Atomists. It is true that the latter introduce the swerve of the atom in a world in which necessity is the primary law, but their speculation concerning freedom is still related to the movements of bodies in the void. In contrast, Plato's argument does not relate art and inspiration within the universe of discourse of art. Thirdly, the specific freedom accorded the artist is negative, i. e., he is freed from the requirement that he make " right judgments of the sayings and doings of that art," and, therefore, from judgments, his own and those of others, of correctness or error.[104] Finally, it is significant that Plato presents this theory of the artist's freedom from the rules of art and of the divine compulsion which " awakens lyrical and other numbers "[105] as well as the presumption of inventiveness in him while under the sway of inspiration, at the divergent levels of theology and craft. This he does in *Ion* by recourse to an extraordinary analogy between

[103] This would appear to be a portion of what is implied in *Ion* 534 C: " Had he learned by rules of art, he would have known how to speak not of one theme only, but of all." Tynnichus, it is added, " wrote nothing that anyone would care to remember, but the famous paean . . . one of the finest poems ever written, simply an invention of the Muses . . . ." Trans. B. Jowett.

[104] Compare *Laws* 719, trans. B. Jowett: ". . . the poet, according to the tradition which has ever prevailed among us, and is accepted of all men, when he sits down on the tripod of the muse, is not in his right mind; like a fountain, he allows to flow out freely whatever comes in, and his art being imitative, he is often compelled to represent men of opposite dispositions, and thus to contradict himself; neither can he tell whether there is more truth in one thing that he has said than in another."

[105] *Phaedrus,* 245.

the "iron rings," attracted by the stone of Heraclea, and the poets who, in their turn, "take inspiration from them."[106] Under the sway of God, Plato argues, the soul is inspired. And so manifestly is poetry the handmaiden to theology that Plato is led to urge of the poet that "there is no invention in him until he is inspired and is out of his senses, and the mind is no longer in him: when he has not attained to this state, he is powerless and is unable to utter his oracles."[107]

It is significant that Plato emphasizes the differentiation between inspiration and art, which receives its fuller elaboration in *Phaedrus*.[108] It is more significant that the freedom achieved by the artist from the rules of art is purchased by what would appear to be a greater bondage of entering upon a "state of unconsciousness" and of being a mere instrument for a divine will.[109] And, finally, there are suggestions of even wider impli-

[106] See my *Aesthetic Experience and Its Presuppositions*, Ch. x, xi.

[107] *Ion*, 534. Plato offers some elaboration of the theory: "God takes away the minds of poets, and uses them as his ministers, as he also uses diviners and holy prophets . . . . For in this way the God would seem to indicate to us and not allow us to doubt that these beautiful poems are not human, or the work of man, but divine and the work of God; and that the poets are only the interpreters of the Gods by whom they are severally possessed."

[108] *Op. cit.*, 245: "he who having no touch of the Muses' madness in his soul, comes to the door and thinks that he will get into the temple by the help of art—he, I say, and his poetry are not admitted."

[109] The curious combination of freedom and servitude noted by Plato (cf. *Ion*) and accepted by the Platonists of Alexandria, as well as by some Patristic philosophers, is not an aspect of classical speculation alone. Jung writes, for example (*op. cit.*, pp. 194–95) that "every creative person is a duality or a synthesis of contradictory aptitudes. On the one side he is a human being with a personal life, while on the other side he is an impersonal, creative process. Since as a human being he may be sound or morbid, we must look at his psychic make-up to find the determinants of his personality. . . . Art is a kind of innate drive that seizes a human being and makes him its instrument. The artist is not a person endowed with free will who seeks his own ends, but one who allows art to realize its purposes through him. As a human being he may have moods and a will and personal aims, but as an artist he is man in a higher sense—he is 'collective man'—one who carries and shapes the unconscious, psychic life of mankind. To perform this difficult office it is sometimes necessary for him to sacrifice happiness and everything that makes life worth living for the ordinary human being."

cations in this relating of theology and of the freedom of the artist. In certain remarkable passages in *Symposium*,[110] Plato tells us that the wisdom which understands that " through Love all the intercourse and converse of god with man, whether awake or asleep, is carried on " is " spiritual," whereas " all other wisdom, such as that of arts and handicrafts, is mean and vulgar." The context in which this dichotomy between inspiration and art is expressed is important. Plato speaks of the creative Eros, " a great spirit, (δαίμων) and like all spirits he is intermediate between the divine and the mortal," whose " power " is that of interpreting " between gods and men, conveying and taking across to the gods the prayers and sacrifices of men, and to men the commands and replies of the gods."

Eros is the " mediator who spans the chasm which divides them," and through him " the arts of the prophet and the priest . . . find their way." The object of love, Plato tells us, is " birth in beauty." The systematic problem is clearly presented: [111] " All creation or passage of non-being into being is poetry or making, and the processes of all art are creative; and the masters of arts are all poets or makers." Thus, in a theory of artistic inspiration, we are brought to the problem of " creation or passage of non-being into being." The explanation is on natural grounds. It is an explanation of poetic making in terms of a process analogous to the natural one of sexual reproduction. The problem it proposes to solve by reference to the natural process is, however, one complicated by the nonnatural status of the transcendent ideas.[112]

That Plato may be putting forward the theory of poetic inspiration in a satire mainly aimed at rhapsodes such as Ion may be true. The fact should not obscure the central inference which affected the tradition of the artist as free creator. Plato holds that the condition for inventiveness is that the poet has been " inspired and is out of his senses, and his mind is no

[110] *Op. cit.*, 202–203, trans. Jowett.

[111] *Symposium*, 205.

[112] See *supra*, p. 35.

longer in him." [113] And we may well profit by what the tradition of creativity in art made of this inference. The more extravagant implications of the notion have lent themselves to such suggestions as that of Edward Young, who, in his *Conjectures on Original Composition,* writes of the " genius " that he " differs from a good understanding as a magician from a good architect . . . ." [114] There is, however, another side to Young's thought which, while influenced by the fantastic notions associated with inspiration and little less by the astounding assertions made in the eighteenth century concerning the genius, is yet sober and brings the problem into the context of philosophy. For, to continue the quotation, the distinction between " genius " and " good understanding " is like that between magician and good architect in that the man inspired " raises his structure by means invisible," the man of good understanding " by the skilful use of common tools."

The point upon which Young insists is that the inspired genius is one who possesses the " power of accomplishing great things without the means reputed necessary to that end." We are met in this elaboration of Plato's statement of the ancient notion of inspiration by a contrast between the great artist and the craftsman who proceeds by means of technical processes, the rules for which were laid down for art by the Aristotelians. But the eighteenth century retains, also, the Platonic notion of the inspired artist as one freed from subjection to rules. And it is prepared to free him, as Maurice Morgann frees him, from nature as well as art: " True Poesy is *magic,* not *nature;* an effect from causes hidden or unknown." [115]

[113] The relation of this theory to Aristotle's conception of *katharsis* and to that of therapy for bacchic women is obvious.

[114] *Op. cit.,* ed. Steinke, pp. 45–46, 49.

[115] *Essay on the Dramatic Character of Falstaff,* pp. 71 ff., Morgann continues: " To the Magician I prescribed no laws; his law and his power are one; his power is his law. Him, who neither imitates, nor is within the reach of imitation, no precedent can or ought to bind, no limits to contain . . . . Means, whether apparent or hidden, are justified in Poesy by success; but then most perfect and most admirable when most concealed."

The influence of the Platonic theory is not limited to the genius, to means-and-ends, and to nature. The Platonic-Longinean [116] notion of the inspired artist who thought " little of minute correctness " and the men who were " far removed from flawlessness " finds its way into the philosophical structure of Kant's *Kritik of Judgment* in the distinction between art and beautiful art. For Kant, " every art presupposes rules by means of which in the first instance a product, if it is to be called artistic, is represented as possible." [117] But beautiful art cannot devise the rule by which its product is brought about. Beautiful art " does not permit the judgment upon the beauty of a product to be derived from any rule, which has a *concept* as its determining ground, and therefore has at its basis a concept of the way in which the product is possible."

We observe in Kant's writing upon the creative artist an effort to bring a poetical and mystical will-o-the-wisp into a philosophical structure, for which the framework of reference is teleological defining. We shall shortly consider whether the continuity of thought in the Western tradition of the artist as creator can be accounted for solely on philosophical grounds.

However philosophical Kant's approach to the aesthetic problem, his terminology, as we have seen, still includes inspiration, genius, and ineffability. Their retention by so sober a thinker as the author of the *Kritik of Judgment* again suggests the monolithic character of the tradition of the inspired artist and the firm hold this speculation has exerted upon the imaginations of poets, critics, philosophers of art, and aestheticians. But not only has the theory of inspiration tended to preëmpt speculation concerning the artist as creator. It has also presented the issue concerning the structure of the work of art which we do well to recall. For the tradition of inspiration is of primary interest to us in so far as it casts light upon the reasons for the

[116] Longinus, *de Sublimitate*, particularly Ch. xxxvi.

[117] *Op. cit.*, p. 189. See also secs. 46, 47. Kant remarks that " artistic skill cannot be communicated; it is imparted to every artist immediately by the hand of nature." (Bernard's translation, p. 191.)

incompatibility of the theory of expression with the structural theories of symbolization and making. Let us proceed, therefore, to a consideration of the theory of inspiration in comparison and contrast to the theories of freedom offered by the Aristotelian and the Atomists' theories of making and creating.

We have observed that the Atomists' theory of freedom implies that there is genuine originality and novelty. But the world-image constructed by ancient Atomism is the model of scientific objectivity and so has lent itself to the great formulations of natural philosophy in the seventeenth and eighteenth centuries. We have observed that the later classical Atomists destroyed their own scientific hypothesis as one available for classical physics and mechanics by the introduction of the swerve of the atom to account for originality, freedom, and novelty. It should now be noted that the ancient theory is made available the more easily for the modern scientific world-image for precisely the reasons that make it less readily available for speculation concerning artistic creativity: its theory of freedom is not formulated in terms of either maker or creator and it does not introduce among its explanatory principles teleological hypotheses. Atomism offers no analogue as a cosmogony or cosmology to the human creator or maker in art: "To escape from the old notion of the divine guidance of the world," writes Cyril Bailey, "the Atomists had set up a materialist philosophy directed solely by uniform laws of cause and effect." [118]

The importance of this point for an explanation of the recurrence of the figure of the artist as a creator and for the monolithic character of the theory of inspiration is emphasized as we

[118] *The Ancient Atomists and Epicurus,* pp. 320–21. It is interesting to note that Bailey maintains that "The 'swerve' of the atom is, no doubt, as the critics have always pointed out, a breach of the fundamental laws of cause and effect, for it is an assertion of a force for which no cause can be given and no explanation offered. For if it be said that the atom swerves because it is its nature to do so, that is merely to put 'nature' as a *deus ex machina* on a level with 'necessity' as it was conceived by some of the early physicists . . . . Epicurus . . . tried to escape from the *impasse* without abandoning a materialist position . . . ."

return to a consideration of the Aristotelian theory of art. The theory rivals in continuity and influence the Platonic hypothesis of the artist as creator and that of inspiration but it does so as a theory of art and of its rules. As we have observed, Aristotle's theory presents the notion of an intelligible art and of a natural theory of freedom. That Aristotle's artist is a maker rather than a creator is important. It is more important to notice, however, that in the history of the conception of the artist as creator, more particularly in eighteenth-century speculation, the Aristotelian principle that making is in the agent rather than in the object made is emphasized at the expense of the rules of art precisely as a result of increased interest in the theory of inspiration and creativity.[119] For the most part, the original pattern is clear and persistent. And this would appear to be due to the fact that Aristotle "has no theory . . . of divine creation," that he does not think of God as the creator of the world,[120] and that it is "but rarely that he ascribes purposive action to God." [121] These are facts reflected in the ostensible emphasis which makes the work of art, rather than the agent, the center of interest.[122]

Our suggestion, then, is that the theory of the artist as an inspired creator persists and recurs because interest in it is

[119] See *infra*, Ch. IV, pp. 137 ff. Once perfectibility of technique is introduced as a possible end for artistic technique, the influence of the artist as creator exerts an almost magnetic influence upon the Aristotelian theory.

[120] W. D. Ross, *Aristotle*, p. 184. See *infra*, Ch. IV, p. 137, n. 1, for a modification of this view.

[121] *Ibid.*, p. 79.

[122] Ostensible, if we take literally what is maintained in *Poetics*, namely, that "in art he who errs willingly is preferable." Cf. *E.N.* 1105 a 27. It would appear to me that the statement is to be understood in terms of the fact that his theory of virtue as a mean state between excess and defect takes actions, feelings, and pleasures and pains to be the matter for the form imposed by the agent himself in producing the actualization of the appetitive soul's potentialities. In the theory of making the matter is what is imitated, the form the imitation, and the choice—"he who errs willingly is preferable"—may produce a work of art which imitates better than, worse than, or the same as what is imitated. A man who prefers a state other than that of virtue is not to be preferred. He is judged, rather, to be vicious.

derived and sustained by the figure of a world creator and that in periods of speculation in which this interest is dominant, the theory of technique and craft reflects the influence of the notion of creativity.[123] And, at least tentatively, it may be suggested that one of the main reasons for the central argument of Plato's philosophy of artistic inspiration and of creation is that this philosophy includes the image of a cosmic demiurge, as well as the notion of God " beyond this world which he [Plato] considers, therefore, to be merely created." [124]

The suggestion must, however, be tentative. Philosophers of art like Bosanquet and Croce do not merely repeat the content of a tradition in which the image of a cosmic maker appears. And to explain the problem of artistic creativity a genetic theory alone will not suffice. Moreover, in considering the meaning of Croce's statement that expression is free inspiration, we must remember that the Italian thinker's philosophy, as is that of Bosanquet, is firmly rooted in the philosophy of German idealism and that the latter is asserted in its interpretation of art as a theory of freedom. Much, then, derives from philosophical sources and, more specifically, from Kant's proposition that " the taste in the beautiful is disinterested and free " and from Hegel's assertion that the work of art may be a work of fine art because of our capacity to regard the latter as it presents itself to " sensuous apprehension," liberated from " the apparatus of its merely material nature " through " the productive fancy of the *artist* ".[125]

If we assume that Croce's aesthetic of creativity most ade-

[123] Note, for example, Shaftesbury's comparison of the poet to a " divine Prometheus under Jove," and the even more extraordinary fact that Aristotle himself was held in such esteem that his presumed infallibility and divinity provided proponents of his theory with a conception sufficiently like that of deity to compensate for what the original Aristotelian theory of art may have appeared to them to lack.

[124] E. Frank, " The Fundamental Opposition of Plato and Aristotle," pp. 171–72. Frank maintains that in this Plato " transgresses . . . the boundary of the peculiarly Greek notion to which the world, nature itself, is God . . . ."

[125] *The Introduction to the Philosophy of Fine Art*, trans. Bosanquet, pp. 103, 108, 112.

quately illustrates the point that the freedom of the artist is philosophically grounded, it might be argued that we do discover in it not only the influence of Kant and Hegel but also the daring of a mind stimulated by Vico, by the tradition of metaphysical conflict between freedom of will and free choice, and by the great ethical statements concerning human freedom which have appeared in the writings of Plato, Aristotle, St. Augustine, Kant, and Hegel. But what we observe at once is that, granted this hypothesis, the general metaphysical and ethical theories of freedom have not, in their transition to aesthetic, escaped the influence of the image of the cosmic creator and maker, theological and poetical implications, and both the theories of inspiration and of genius. Schiller's theory that art is play is adopted from Kant's analysis of the judgment of taste and argues that the artist is freed from strictures of both sense and intellect. [126]

But, as we have already noted, the ancient theory of play, which also affects Schiller, is not entirely free of the influence of the theory of *katharsis*, and the latter has its roots in part in that of inspiration. Hegel's rationalism in aesthetic makes its bow to both the notion of the genius and of inspiration.[127] The tradition does have its realist and natural ground in the notions of freedom as emancipation from the passions and in the examination of sensuous media and ideas. But it uses no less, as is evident in the writings of Schopenhauer and Nietzsche, the nonnatural approach of inspiration until, for the latter philosopher, aesthetic is " truly a prodigy."

But even were we to urge that the problem of the artist as creator has its source in what Frank calls the fundamental opposition between Plato and Aristotle,[128] we should face difficulties were we to try to state that problem in philosophical terms alone. Even were it granted that the divergences within the tradition itself are extreme instances of the initial philo-

[126] See my *Aesthetic Experience and Its Presuppositions,* Ch. VII.
[127] See *infra,* Ch. V, pp. 165 ff.
[128] See *supra,* p. 35.

sophical opposition,[129] we come to a straightforward statement to the contrary by Croce. He maintains that Hegel's aesthetic—a philosophy of art which takes cognisance of meanings, symbols, media and techniques, as well as of feelings—fails precisely because it is a philosophy of art: " there is nothing philosophically contradictory," remarks Croce with specific reference to the Hegelian dialectic of symbolic, classical and romantic stages of art, " because the philosophic problem has not yet emerged " in art.[130]

It is evident that Croce intends to deny that artistic creativity or aesthetic experience is subject to judgment in terms of truth or falsity. Equally evident is the fact that he denies to aesthetic any ontological reference. More closely related to the problem of the present essay, however, is his denial that aesthetic expression is comprehended in terms of freedom of will. To will is to choose, he remarks, and aesthetic expression is prior either to choice or to will. It would appear, therefore, that if " expression is free inspiration " is the basic proposition of Croce's aesthetic, the meaning of the word " free " as it refers to artistic processes is not identical to its philosophical connotation.

Yet, curiously enough, the alternative to the influence of the post-Kantian tradition of speculation upon freedom, namely, that Croce's notion of artistic creativity is part and parcel of the tradition of inspiration, appears upon closer inspection to be untenable as well. Croce's artist as creator whose freedom is unconditioned does wear the garb of the ancient and inspired poet: he does not plan what he expresses. He is unconscious in expressing the image he does express.[131] But if this aesthetic of creativity insists upon one fact to the exclusion of all others concerning artistic freedom it is that artistic and aesthetic expression are autonomous. In epistemological terms, expression

[129] Instances of such opposition are: that for Nietzsche, aesthetic evaluation is a " prodigy "; for Hegel, a rational process; for Schiller, art is play; for Croce this is denied.

[130] *What is Living and What is Dead in the Philosophy of Hegel,* p. 122, trans., D. Ainslie.

[131] See *supra,* p. 17.

is essential for all other stages of spirit but stands in need of none. But to assert the freedom of the artist in this sense is to insist, also, upon an essential differentiation between the theory of imagination-expression and that of inspiration. The classical theory of inspiration is based upon the hypothesis that there is a " controlling force outside the artist." [132] It is this that has made Shelley's phrase " hierophants of an unapprehended inspiration " so apt a description of the artist who is at once free and in bondage to an external agent, whether God or the Muses.

It is now clear that the qualifying adjective " free " in Croce's " expression is free inspiration " is intended to deny the assumption by ancient theorists that the poet is made subservient to or that he is taken possession of by the God who, as Plato wrote, " sways the souls of men in any direction he pleases," and who is in fact the source of freedom and invention. If, however, this is what does distinguish expression from the ancient notion of inspiration, we do well to examine more carefully our assumption that the tradition of inspiration is in fact the monolithic one we have judged it to be.

There is no doubt that inspiration recurs constantly as an explanatory principle. There is, equally, no doubt a nominal uniformity in its use throughout the centuries. It will be recalled that the term was retained as the theory of imagination was elaborated, in contrast to the gradual disappearance of the notion of imitation. This is in part explicable because the name " inspiration " is used monolithically, while it is applied in two senses, the one implying an external agency, the other the autonomous inventive powers of the artist. The former sense, the notion that the artist is under the control of an external force, is as foreign to the theory of art as imagination as is the notion of mimesis.

Neither interpretation explains the tenacity with which inspiration is retained in speculation or why it, in contrast to

[132] The phrase is R. G. Collingwood's. See *The Principles of Art,* p. 126. Cf. B. Bosanquet's remark on Croce's *Aesthetic*: " Beauty . . . lives in the creative imagination, and there alone . . . ." " Croce's Aesthetic," p. 261.

mimesis, is molded to the uses of imagination. The solution to these problems is, however, clear. The internalization and naturalization of the problem of freedom and originality by means of imagination, i. e., the change in locus of the originating power or faculty from the Muses or Gods to man is of great significance. But for the theory of the inspiration the inventive and originating powers of the inspired artist are in fact not his own but those of the divinity that possesses him. In the theory of imagination those same powers are attributed to the creative artist as if he were God.[133] Eros and the demiurge are the grounds for invention and the means by which the product of inspiration escapes the rules of art and the artist the need for judgment upon a whole art. What is monolithic about the tradition of inspiration is not the locus of the agency which inspires the artist but the figure of divinity which adheres to the word. The theory of expression-imagination as a theory of autonomous freedom, while it has doffed the theological habiliments, retains the sub-religious flavor. Whereas the theory of inspiration for the most part insists upon an external agency as the ground for artistic freedom, the theory of expression-imagination makes of the artist the analogue to God. The association of the theory of inspiration with speculation upon the artist as creator has been facilitated simply because it makes explicit the figure of divinity which is implicit in the notion of artistic creativity in theories of imagination.

The character of our heritage of two millenia of tradition concerning artistic freedom thus begins to take form and the reasons for the absolutism and conviction of statement concerning the artistic become clearer. The dominant feature of that tradition, sustained in part by " inspiration," has been the great analogy of the artist to God, the cosmic creator and maker. More specifically, the analogy has tended to interpret artistic freedom in terms of two external relations by which God's freedom is gauged. Those relations are to ideas and to matter.

[133] See *infra*, Ch. v, pp. 173 ff.: Shaftesbury's comment on inspiration, applicable both to the ancient and the modern theory.

The clearest discernment of the problem is found in George Puttenham's comparison of the poet, " as we may say of God: who without any travell of his diuine imagination, made all the world of nought, nor also by any paterne or mould . . . ." [134]

In contrast to the nominal uniformity of inspiration, the tradition of the analogy by means of which the freedom of the artist has been explained presents an explicit conflict concerning the relations we have mentioned. Thus, whereas Keats writes superbly:

> . . . Poesy alone can tell her dreams,
> With the fine spell of words alone can save
> Imagination from the sable chain
> And dull enchantment,[135]

Wordsworth holds:

> . . . many are the Poets that are sown
> By Nature; men endowed with highest gifts,
> The vision and the faculty divine,
> Yet wanting the accomplishment of verse.[136]

Similarly, for one critic, Sir Walter Raleigh, " the elementary passions, pity and love, wrath and terror, are not in themselves poetical; they must be wrought upon by the word to become poetry." [137] For another, Lascelles Abercrombie, on the contrary, the moment of imaginative experience " possessed the poet's mind the instant the poem began . . . , was *conceived*, as an inspiration." [138] For Abercrombie, " it existed before the verbal art of the poem was commenced, just as it exists in us after the verbal art was finished. For though it could not have come to us except in these very words, and, in this consideration, may be identified with the verbal art, since we can only have what the language can give us; yet, once it has come into

[134] *The Arte of English Poesie,* ed. Arber, pp. 19–20.

[135] " The Fall of Hyperion," 1, 7–15.

[136] " The Excursion," I, 76–80.

[137] *Style,* p. 115.

[138] *The Theory of Poetry,* p. 58.

complete and vivid existence, it can be attended to and remembered apart from the words."

The issue, the conflict, and the conviction are all sharpened once the opposition in terms of the artist's freedom is expressed at the philosophical level. As we have observed, the point at which Croce asserts that " the externalization of art " proffers utility and morality the right to be master in art's own house is precisely the point at which Bosanquet asserts the " complete self-determination " of the artist in terms of the medium.[139] It is significant that this is not a consequence of conflict between art as expression and as realism but rather one between two theories of expression which draw upon a common philosophical source.[140] Once the issue is joined, the specific points of the conflict become evident. Bosanquet assumes that technique is " our medium of intercourse through the body and through natural objects " in the field of art. That such a relation holds between the artist and a medium, Croce specifically denies: [141] " The search for the *end of art* is ridiculous, when it is understood of art as art " and " Expression does not possess *means,* because it has not an end." [141]

Collingwood, whose aesthetic is an elaboration of Croce's, acutely observes that his own notion of creativity is open to the " too probable objection " concerning the term.[142] What he asserts is that " to create something means to make it non-

[139] *Three Lectures on Aesthetic,* p. 62: " Every craftsman . . . feels the peculiar delight and enjoys the peculiar capacity of his own medium. This delight and sense of capacity are of course not confined to the moments when he is actually manipulating his work. His fascinated imagination lives in the powers of his medium; he thinks and feels in terms of it; and it is the peculiar body of which *his* aesthetic imagination and no other is the peculiar soul." Cf. Croce, *Aesthetic,* pp. 20, 70, particularly the remark that " division annihilates the work."

[140] See Hegel's *The Philosophy of Fine Art.* Hegel holds that freedom requires the expression and representation of spiritual interests in plastic shapes. The alternative, he maintains, is to regard art as fully determined " in the wilderness of unfettered fancy," where the " form would be at the mercy of mere chance."

[141] *Aesthetic,* pp. 51, 112.

[142] *The Principles of Art,* pp. 128–29.

technically" but "voluntarily" and "consciously." But the person who makes need not be "acting in order to achieve any ulterior end; he need not be following a preconceived plan; and he is certainly not transforming anything that can properly be called a raw material."

Samuel Alexander is no less certain that the antithetical theory of creation is sound. Creative imagination in art does create a new reality, but this is done by "moulding the material of the art to express a purpose." And "art of all kinds, including fine art, constructs the work of art out of physical materials, wood or stone or pigments or words, or, as in music, tones, or, as it may be, bodily movements as in the dance . . . ." This, then, is a theory of good craftsmanship, in which the maker "takes faithfully the steps necessary" to the end of constructing his product "*as perfectly as he can.*"[143]

It is clear that Croce and Collingwood imply that the artist as creator is free in a superhuman sense and, more specifically, that his powers differ radically from those ordinarily attributed to *homo faber*. The point is clearer once we consider the significance which philosophy has attributed to man's freedom to make. To deny that man has free will is to raise a metaphysical question which, whether it pertain to the relation of mind and body or to that of cause and effect, remains for all practical purposes highly abstract. But to assert that man is free beyond his powers to make a work of fine or free art, to appreciate it, or to judge it, is ultimately to denigrate the power which, many philosophers believe, distinguishes man as man, i. e., his power to make or shape with tools an object or event. Making is the aspect of man's control of nature which, for imagination, is far less a function of abstract rational powers than of rational powers in process of making or constructing something. One may go so far, indeed, as to assert that it is possible to conceive a world in which men are not free to act. It is impossible to conceive a world in which men do not make

[143] *Beauty and Other Forms of Value*, pp. 14, 17, 53. (Italics mine)

and in which they do not extend their powers and the scope of their powers through art and technique.

Making is in fact a function of the power Bergson believes distinguishes " the two main lines of evolution of animal life . . . the Arthropods and the Vertebrates." [144] For while instinct and intelligence " have each as their essential object the utilisation of implements," the implements of instinct are " organs supplied by nature and hence immutable," whereas those of intelligence are " invented tools, and therefore varied and unforeseen." Instruments and tools as means to the control of nature appear to be unlimited in variety and infinite in power. If we think, then, of the artist, whose production of fine art or of images is presupposed by technical skill in the one instance and is unconditioned in the other, we appear to have come upon the supreme artificer, endowed with unconditioned freedom.

To describe the artist in terms of such creativity is to urge that he possesses divine powers. To maintain, as Bosanquet does, that he possesses the freedom of complete self-determination is likewise to predicate of man superhuman freedom. But even to suggest, as Alexander does, that the artist is a good craftsman who performs " as perfectly as he can " has a no less clear analogue in theology. It is, indeed, as we shall see, the conflict of theologies which is the source of the incompatibility of theories of the artist as creator and of the structures of art. Coleridge believed that poetry is " a dim analogue to creation." Robert Browning expresses in two divergent and conflicting accounts of creating what the analogue implies.[145] Of Abt Vogler's extemporization upon music, Browning writes

. . . For think, had I painted the whole,
Why, there it had stood, to see, nor the process so wonder-
worth:
Had I written the same, made verse—still, effect proceeds
from cause,

[144] Henri Bergson, *The Two Sources of Morality and Religion*, p. 19.
[145] *Op. cit.*, vi–vii.

Yet know why the forms are fair, ye hear how the tale is told:
It is all triumphant art, but art in obedience to laws,
Painter and poet are proud in the artist-list enrolled:—
But here is the finger of God, a flash of the will that can,
Existent behind all laws, that made them and, lo, they are!
And I know not if, save in this, such gift be allowed to man,
That out of three sounds he frame, not a fourth sound, but
a star.
Consider it well: each tone of our scale in itself is nought;
It is everywhere in the world—loud, soft, and all is said:
Give it to me to use! I mix it with two in my thought;
And there! Ye have heard and seen: consider and bow the
head!

In suggesting that "here is the finger of God," that the musician has powers identical with the "Existent behind all laws, that made them . . .", the poet discerns two significant facts, namely, that to the artist as creator are attributed miraculous powers and that his divine freedom in creating consists precisely in his capacity to transcend "art in obedience to laws."

But if the musician, as creator, displays miraculous powers in Browning's poem, the painter and poet remain within the rolls of art, of "art in obedience to laws," in the realm in which "effect proceeds from cause." And it is this conception of the fine artist, conceived on analogy to God, the Maker, which finds its full poetic expression in Browning's *The Ring and the Book*: [146]

I find first
Writ down for very A B C of fact,
"In the beginning God made heaven and earth;"
From which, no matter with what lisp, I spell
And speak you out a consequence—that man,
Man,—as befits the made, the inferior thing,—
Purposed, since made, to grow, not make in turn,
Yet forced to try and make, else fail to grow,—
Formed to rise, reach at, if not grasp and gain
The good beyond him,—which attempt is growth,—
Repeats God's process in man's due degree,
Attaining man's proportionate result,—

[146] *Op cit.*, I, 707–33.

Creates, no, but resuscitates, perhaps.
Inalienable, the arch-prerogative
Which turns thought, act—conceives, expresses too!
No less man, bounded, yearning to be free,
May so project his surplusage of soul
In search of body, so add self to self
By owning what lay ownerless before,—
So find, so fill full, so appropriate forms—
That, although nothing which had never life
Shall get life from him, be, not having been,
Yet something dead may get to live again,
Something with too much life or not enough,
Which, either way imperfect, ended once:
An end whereat man's impulse intervenes,
Makes new beginning, starts the dead live,
Completes the incomplete and saves the thing.

In suggesting that man " Repeats God's process in man's due degree, / Attaining man's proportionate result," Browning discerns what the " great analogy " between the fine artist and God, the maker, has implied, that man is " bounded, yearning to be free," that his powers are human, not superhuman, and that his freedom consists precisely in appropriating forms, in completing the incomplete, not in creating, but perhaps in " resuscitating " within the limitations of human powers.

Aesthetic theory is heir to one of the great theological and metaphysical controversies of history. The Western tradition of speculation upon the artist as creator is radically affected by a dual analogy, that between the artist and God the creator, in the Hebraic-Christian tradition, and that between the artist and the cosmic maker in Plato's philosophy. The widespread influence of these analogies upon our notions of creativity, novelty, originality, and intelligibility will be clear as we proceed. That this influence has been thorough will be no less evident as we examine the problem of ugliness, the formation of the theory of genius, and the legacy of other perplexing issues with which speculation has endowed modern aesthetic.

Our eventual problem remains to ascertain the meaning of the statement that the artist is one who brings about the " passage from non-being into being." This we can approach best by examining first the results of the tendency in speculation to elevate power and knowledge to omnipotence and omniscience. And, in this connection, we do well to remember that theology, which has frequently provided religion with the numerous arguments with which the latter has attempted to restrain the artist, is in its turn curiously enough, if not the ultimate, at least the conserving source for the Western world's dual theory of the unconditioned freedom of the artist as creator, as it has been for the alternative notion of the artist as an analogue to God the maker with limited powers.[147] We shall see, as we examine the grounds for aesthetic value, precisely how significant the theory of the artist as creator has been in the history of concepts and ideas.[148]

Our immediate task, however, is to examine the conflict of cosmologies which provides the context for the conflict of aesthetic theories in which are present the opposing views of artistic freedom. To this, we turn in the next chapter.

[147] Cf. Werner Jaeger, *The Theology of Early Greek Thinkers*, p. 2: "If the continuity of the ancient Greek tradition was never entirely broken in Europe, it is due to the fact that Greek philosophy kept it alive. But this would not have been possible had not the same philosophy, as *theologia naturalis*, served as the basis for the *theologia supernaturalis* of Christianity."

[148] See *infra*, Bk. II, particularly Ch. VI.

2 The "Great Analogy"

. . . a dim analogue to creation.

COLERIDGE

David Hume mentions the "intangling brambles" raised to cover and protect the weaknesses which a considerable part of metaphysics derives from "the craft of popular superstitions." In the preceding chapter, we sought to indicate the tenacity with which the bramble, "inspiration," has clung to the notion of the artist as creator and what it has obscured. It would appear that we are now similarly about to entangle our essay of the artist's freedom in what is no less a product of the craft that Hume mentions. That possibility is implicit in the statements that the monolithic theory of artistic inspiration has sustained, while yet obscuring, the conviction that man as creator is free in some sense as God is free and that tradition has interpreted divine freedom equally as creativity and making.

The course of this essay is not determined in this regard by a dearth of alternative and possible analogies. For Plato, the artist is like a mirror; for John Galsworthy, he is like a fisherman of odds and ends; [1] and for E. M. Forster, he is like a bucket lowered for "something which is normally beyond . . . reach." [2] Moreover, these modern writers recognize a bifurcation in the artist, parallel to that which has led the principal thinkers in the Western tradition to weigh his powers in terms of a God who originates and constructs. Galsworthy believes that the artist is a "welder" of what is "fished up"; Forster believes that what, as a bucket, he brings up from the uncon-

[1] *The Creation of Character in Literature* (The Romanes Lecture), pp. 3–5.

[2] "The Raison d'Etre of Criticism in the Arts," *Two Cheers for Democracy*, p. 123.

scious is also subjected to " technical ingenuity and worldly knowledge."

Interesting as these and the no doubt innumerable other analogies available to philosophical speculation may be, the pattern of the analogy of the artist to God is unique. It would appear to be the ground for other analogies; it deals with the core of the problem basic to speculation upon the artist as creator; and it states that problem of freedom in terms of the central notions of knowledge and power. Even should it prove to be wholly " the product of popular superstitions," we should do well to avail ourselves of the information its analysis offers for the history of ideas. As we shall show, however, its value is not simply historical. A tradition so persistent as this has proved to be is one which owes its interest not only to alien and intrusive elements but to aspects integral to the aesthetic problem as well.

As we have observed, the analogy turns in general terms upon the relation of the artist and of God to ends and to matter, in explanation of the individual product of the creative process. We shall present the problem, at the cost of some repetition, successively at the levels of the aesthetic, the cosmological, and the microcosmic conflicts.

The Aesthetic Conflict

Croce's statement that " expression is free inspiration " means that the artist is a free creator, Bosanquet's that " imagination is the mind working under great reservations which set it free," that the artist is a free maker. The statements are antithetical, although integral to the theory that art is expression. The implications of the philosophers' statements are applicable to the structure of art as well as to the artist and will serve as illustrations of an entire tradition.

Each philosopher states the problem of the artist as creator in terms proper to the aesthetic context. For Croce, the aesthetic moment of spirit is expression or intuition. The artist forms or expresses. He does not create in terms of ends—the search for which Croce maintains is " ridiculous." [3] Nor is his expressing or creating properly describable in terms of the forming of matter. He forms impressions, it is true but, to guard against " a . . . kind of invasion and confusion," it is pointed out specifically that " the hither side of the lower limit is sensation, formless matter, which the spirit can never apprehend in itself as simple matter." [4] What is formed or expressed is the " individual expressive fact," distinguished as intuition, image, or individual from what intellectual knowledge relates.

For Bosanquet, art is expression, and the artist forms or expresses. The product of his expression is " a new individual expression." But, although Bosanquet describes the craftsman as " feeling the peculiar delight " and enjoying " the peculiar capacity of his own medium," the imagination is itself described as the mind " working *under great reservations* which *set it free*." It is true that these reservations are not held to be consequent to a subordination of imagination to the " total structure of real fact and truth." Rather, Bosanquet maintains that imagination constitutes an alternative world which has a structure of its own. This structure is, in its turn, describable in terms of ends, of which, as we have seen, Croce rids his own aesthetic.[5] Whereas for Croce expression and technique are distinct, as are aesthetic and practice, for Bosanquet there is aesthetically meaningful method or technique, applicable to that second Crocean " limitation," matter.[6]

For Bosanquet, as for Hegel, freedom is " true originality " which is " true objectivity." For Croce, objectivity as a problem of freedom is relevant not to aesthetic expression but to free-

[3] *Aesthetic*, p. 17. Aesthetic is " free from concepts." Cf. *infra*, Ch. III.

[4] *Ibid.*, p. 5.

[5] For Bosanquet, the world of imagination is one with a " method and purpose of its own, and having for its goal a different type of satisfaction from that of ascertained fact." See *Three Lectures on Aesthetic*, pp. 28–29.

[6] *Ibid.*, p. 34. Bosanquet holds that imagination must " acknowledge . . . certain limitations," among which is that " imaginative expression creates the feeling in creating its embodiment."

dom of choice or freedom of will in the realm of practice. As an aesthetic problem, freedom of choice is ruled out because the artist is not related to ends.[7] Similarly, expression is distinguished from freedom of will,[8] i. e., from the "*practical* spirit."

Systematically, Croce constructs a theory of artistic creativity which undercuts both free will and free choice.[9] The logical priority of intuition, asserted by identifying art, intuition, imagination, and expression, differentiates the free creativity of the artist from the freedom manifested in technique, action, or intellection. In contrast, for Bosanquet such procedure threatens the relation of the mind to the external world.[10]

[7] *Aesthetic,* p. 51. "To choose is to will: to will this and not to will that and this and that must be before us, expressed. Practice follows, it does not precede theory . . . ."

[8] *Ibid.,* pp. 47–48: ". . . will independent of knowing is unthinkable."

[9] Croce's statements concerning the unconditioned freedom of art and the artist appear to be unambiguous. What he intends, however, is complicated by several facts which will be evident in our later considerations of the problems of creativity. The complication which it is well to indicate at this point is systematically grounded. Croce asserts that "freedom is the very essence of every spiritual form, and with the denial of the freedom of that form is denied the form itself." (E. T., *Philosophy of the Practical,* p. 183) Generically, therefore, freedom is descriptive of all spirit and to ascertain its specific form for art as expression presents a difficulty. What that difficulty is will be evident as we proceed with Croce's analysis of art. Croce's identification of art as "free inspiration" should be contrasted to his notion that "The Spirit is freedom, and in order to be so, not in the abstract, but in the concrete, it must also be necessity." (*Ibid.,* p. 180) There is ample evidence that, should we concentrate upon one line of his speculation, Croce may be interpreted to mean that the "necessity" of art is provided by nonaesthetic factors, e. g., "no poet creates his poem outside definite conditions of space and time . . . [and] the historical situation is given to him." Another illustration is the statement, "He is a true poet who feels himself at once bound to his predecessors and free," which appears on the same page. In the light of Croce's denial of an "end" to art, it is of interest that he maintains (*ibid.,* p. 48) that "The end, then, in universal, is the concept itself of will." But there is no doubt that in placing intuition in a status prior to will, Croce undercuts the problem of artistic feeling as correlative to either choice or will in the historical sense of those terms by interpreting it in terms of unconditioned creativity. (See Raffaello Piccoli, *Benedetto Croce,* pp. 123 ff. and pp. 198 ff.)

[10] "Croce's Aesthetic," *Proceedings of the British Academy,* Vol 9, p. 271:

Despite this divergence between Croce's and Bosanquet's interpretations of the theory of expression-imagination, traceable to the disparate nature of the tradition of creating and making, the English philosopher's theory of freedom is not unaffected by the notion of creativity. Both philosophers have inherited the spirit of a tradition, while doffing its trappings. The poet-philosopher, Coleridge, in suggesting that poetry is " a dim analogue to creation," is wholly within that tradition. Inasmuch as it is only within that tradition that we may discern plainly the full implications of the key word " creation," we shall indicate its principal implications before turning to the cosmological conflict which is the prototype for the aesthetic conflict. Coleridge, in fact, echoes the account of God's creation of the world in Genesis, as reinforced by such classical philosophical progenitors as Philo,[11] St. Augustine,[12] and, notably, Athanasius, in the denial to man of such freedom. Athanasius states the problem as follows: " For God creates, and to create (το κτίζειν) is also ascribed to men; . . . Yet does God create as men do? . . . Perish the thought; we understand the terms in one sense of God, and in another of men. For God creates, in that He calls what is not into being, needing nothing thereunto; but men work some existing material (ὑποκειμένη ὕλη) ." [13]

" We see how this philosophy reinforces Croce's devotedness to the undivided expression. But the contention seems on the way to become ridiculous. It has destroyed our meeting point with ourselves . . . , and now it offers to destroy our medium of intercourse through the body and through natural objects . . . . Externality is a character of the world and a sign and vehicle of spiritual achievement, and there can be no doubt that the creative imagination yearns towards externality, and externality in some special medium."

[11] See H. Wolfson, *Philo,* Vol. 1, p. 172: " God's unity in the sense of uniqueness thus makes it impossible for anything else to be regarded as uncreated and as creative. On the basis of this conception of the unity of God, it would be therefore impossible for Philo to accept Plato's ideas as being uncreated and as also being creative by their own power." Compare *ibid.,* p. 201 and, more specifically, p. 221: " 'To act . . . is the property of God, and this we may ascribe to any created being; the property of the created is to suffer.' "

[12] *De Libero Arbitrio,* l. 2. See also *De div. quaest.,* LXXXIII and cf. *ibid.,* LXXXIII, *quaest.* XLVI, 2.

[13] " De Decretis, or Defence of the Nicene Definition," *A Select Library of*

The Western tradition of creation reflects the spirit of this denial to man of God's miraculous powers. It is significant, however, that once the theological terminology has fallen into disuse, the use of the word " analogous " has sufficed to endow the artist with freedom commensurate with that attributed to the Deity, at least as regards omnipotence and omniscience.[14] This has sufficed for consideration of the fine artist as one with power to produce by his art or imagination unique individuals and to transcend natural laws.[15] To account for the artist's presumed capacity to produce unique individuals, a specification of the general theory of the emergence of novelty in essences and immortal souls has been employed. The presumption that the artist is capable of transcending natural law is but a specification of the theory that God has power to perform miracles. The two general issues are among the principal points of differentiation between the Hebraic-Christian theory of God's creativity and the classical view of " making " put forward by Plato. To an examination of these opposed views we shall now turn.

The Cosmological Conflict

The aesthetic issue is analogous, so far as the freedom of the artist is concerned, to that presented in the bifurcated heritage of cosmic creating and making, the philosophical implications of which may be drawn from the well-known historical conflict of cosmologies evident in the comparison and contrast of Plato's *Timaeus* and the account of the world's creation in Genesis.

Nicene and Post-Nicene Fathers of the Christian Church, IV, 77, Cf. *ibid.*, 19 and " de Orat.," II, 22. See also, Note 1 above, but compare Wolfson, *op. cit.*, pp. 300–01.

[14] The capacity for continuous creation is not stressed. For the general problem of God's attributes see I. Husik, *A History of Mediaeval Jewish Philosophy*, pp. xxii-iii and G. B. Burch, *Early Mediaeval Philosophy*, pp. 76–77.

[15] It should be noted, however, that Browning's musician does not create *ex nihilo*. Compare Croce, *op. cit.*, pp. 5–6, on the " passivity " of matter, and the " notion of it as a mere limit."

The classical theory of cosmic making in *Timaeus* introduces into philosophy " for the first time the image of a creator god." [16] Plato is well aware of the difficulties of the problem.[17] But of the two models after which a builder might frame the world, Plato holds that the world-maker "looked to the eternal " rather than " to that which has come to be." The ground for this is a theory of causation.[18]

Shorey remarks of this cosmic process, that " a demiurgos or supreme artisan does not precisely create the universe out of nothing but reduces a vaguely visioned pre-existent chaos to a cosmos." [19] This demiurgos, which Cornford identifies with the world soul,[20] imposes upon uncreated matter the eternally existing forms, to make after their model or pattern the structure of the universe.

The theory put forward in *Timaeus* is one of τέχνη or making, not of creation. The demiurge works upon already existing material. The model for the structure made is, as we have observed, the eternal world of ideas. The contrast between making and creating is well set forth by Erich Frank, with specific reference to " the new conception of the world and God " as compared to the Greek conception of the world, or nature, or God: ". . . the Platonic God did not really create the world. He only transformed the chaos into a cosmos. Thus, God was not a true creator; he was merely an artificer, an architect who shaped the world out of eternal material which he had not created, but which was given to him; and he built

[16] F. M. Cornford, *Plato's Cosmology*, p. 34.

[17] *Timaeus* 28 c (*Plato's Cosmology*, trans. Cornford) : " the maker and father of this universe it is a hard task to find, and having found him it would be impossible to declare him to all mankind."

[18] *Ibid.*, 28 a-b: ". . . all that becomes must needs become by the agency of some cause; for without a cause nothing can come to be. Now whenever the maker of anything looks to that which is always unchanging and uses a model of that description in fashioning the form and quality of his work, all that he thus accomplishes must be good. If he looks to something that has come to be and uses a generated model, it will not be good."

[19] *What Plato Said*, p. 332.

[20] *Plato's Cosmology*, pp. 176–77.

it in conformity with the Idea which again was eternal and independent of him." [21]

More specifically, and with reference to St. Augustine, Frank draws the significant inference that ". . . the world was created by God out of nothing and this creation was due to God's absolute free will, not to any logical or other necessity, or to any Idea outside of himself." [22] In this statement, Frank has laid emphasis upon the meaning of " creation " as the bringing into being of something *ex nihilo,* not only with reference to matter [23] but also to forms or ideas.[24]

[21] *Saint Augustine and Greek Thought* (The Augustinean Society, 1942), p. 5. A. E. Taylor denies, by implication, the validity of this type of interpretation of Plato. See, for example, *Plato: The Man and His Work,* pp. 443–44: " It seems plain that the *Timaeus* knows of no external limitations imposed on God's will by conditions independent of God himself." Taylor's view is that Plato's demiurge is a true " creator."

[22] *Op. cit.,* p. 5.

[23] See *infra,* Ch. III, pp. 110 ff., for St. Augustine's treatment of matter.

[24] Whereas the problem of matter has been of primary importance in the history of philosophy of art, that of forms or ideas has been of greater importance for aesthetic. See my *Aesthetic Experience and Its Presuppositions,* especially Ch. II-IV. The issue involved in the analogy of the artist to God in His relation of ideas has received less attention than that of His relation to matter. E. Frank, *Philosophical Understanding and Religious Truth,* p. 75, n. 8, quotes A. E. Taylor's *Varia Socratica,* p. 178 ff.: " The guiding principle of Greek thinking is the Nous, the intellection of that which exists. That which the Nous perceives as being present actually exists and at the same time must needs be as it is; it is an *eidos,* an ' idea,' something that can be seen." Frank also quotes, *ibid.,* p. 75, n. 10, *De Somniis,* 14, 76: " God, when He gave birth to all things, not only brought them into sight but also made things which before were not, not just handling material as a *demiurge, an artificer,* but being Himself its *creator.*"

The passage subjected in the Middle Ages to most dispute was St. Augustine's concerning the status of ideas in relation to God, in *De Diversis Quaestionibus* LXXXIII, ed. Migne, Vol. 6, pp. 11 ff. The following quotation is a portion of Q. 46, *de ideis* (30): " Quis autem religiosus et vera religione imbutus, quamvis nondum possit haec vera religione imbutus, quamvis nondum possit haec intueri, negare tamen audeat, imo non etiam profiteatur, omnia quae sunt, id est, quaecumque in suo genere propria quadam natura continentur, ut sint, Deo auctore esse procreata, eoque auctore omnia quae vivunt vivere, atque universalem rerum incolumitatem, ordinemque ipsum quo ea quae mutantur, suos temporales cursus certo moderamine celebrant, summi Dei legibus contineri

It is this conception that Puttenham echoed concerning the poet who resembles God " who without any trauell to his diuine imagination, made all the world of nought, nor also by any paterne or mould as the Platonicks with their Ideas do

et gubernari? Quo constituto atque concesso, quis audeat dicere Deum irrationabiliter omnia condidisse? Quod si recte dici vel credi non potest, restat ut omnia ratione sint condita. Nec eadem ratione homo, propriis sunt creata rationibus. Has autem rationes ubi arbitrandum est esse, nisi in ipsa mente Creatoris? Non enim extra se quidquam positum intuebatur, ut secundum id constitutueret quod constituebat: nam hoc opinari sacrilegum est. Quod si hae rerum omnium creandarum creatarumve rationes in divina mente continentur, neque in divina mente quidquam nisi aeternum atque incommutabile potest esse; atque has rerum rationes principales appellat ideas Plato: non solum sunt ideae, sed ipsae verae sunt, quia aeternae sunt, et ejusmodi atque incommutabiles manet; quarum participatione fit ut sit quidquid est, quoquomodo est . . . ."

The issue had been argued by St. Irenaeus as follows: ". . . if this set of things was made after the likeness of that, in what other likeness shall the latter in its turn be made? For if the Framer of the world did not make these of himself, but like a workman of no consequence, and as a boy learning his first lesson, transferred them from patterns not his own, whence had he whom they [the Gnostics] call The Deep the forms of that order which first emanated from him? " (*Five Books of St. Irenaeus Against Heresies*, trans. John Keble, bk. 2, Ch. 7, pp. 110–11) Another notable example is St. Anselm's remark (*Monologium*, trans. S. N. Deane, Chap. IX, pp. 55 ff.) in distinguishing " in what sense those things which were created may be said to have been nothing before their creation." He holds that nothing can conceivably be created by anyone " unless there is, in the mind of the creative agent, some example, as it were, or (as is more fittingly supposed) some model, or likeness, or rule. It is evident, then, that before the world was created, it was in the thought of the supreme Nature, what, and of what sort, and how, it should be." There was nothing, " so far as the creator's thought is concerned, through which, and according to which," beings were created. In chapter X, Anselm draws the analogy between the process and that " when an artisan is about to make something after the manner of his craft, he first expresses it to himself through a concept." He takes care, however, to point out in chapter XI, that the " analogy is very incomplete . . . . For the supreme Substance took absolutely nothing from any other source, whence it might either frame a model in itself, or make its creatures what they are; while the artisan is wholly unable to conceive in his imagination any bodily thing, except what he has in some way learned from external objects . . . nor can he perform the work mentally conceived, if there is a lack of material, or of anything without which a work premeditated cannot be performed." The notion of freedom and necessity is raised at once: ". . . these inner expressions of the works they are to create phantastically suppose." [25] But what is presupposed by the notion of creativity in contrast to artisanship is of greatest significance for us, once it is translated in terms of freedom. Brehier notes that for Plotinus " L'Un est avant tout la ' puissance de toutes choses '; mais il n'est aucune de ces choses." [26] Foster infers that " the doctrine of Creation attributes to God an autonomous activity of will." [27] It awaited a brilliant paper by Wolfson on the philosophy of Philo to make evident the fundamental difference between Plato's and the Alexandrian's evaluation of God's power over the laws of nature, to indicate the fundamental grounds for the divergences, and to make the basic inferences concerning the divergent interpretations of man's freedom.[28] Wolfson remarks that both Plato and Philo believe

differ in the creative substance and in the artisan: that the former expression, without being taken or aided from any external source, but as first and sole cause, could suffice the Artificer for the performance of his work, while the latter is neither first, nor sole, nor sufficient cause for the inception of the artisan's work . . . ." The view is presented cogently and simply in the words (*ibid.*, Ch. XII), " it is equally certain that whatever the supreme Substance created, it created through nothing other than itself . . . ."

[25] *The Arte of English Poesie*, p. 3.

[26] *La Philosophie de Plotin*, p. 42.

[27] " The Christian Doctrine of Creation and the Rise of Modern Natural Science," *Mind*, N. S., 43, pp. 460–65. The issue concerning God's relation to ideas is clearly put by M. de Wulf, *History of Mediaeval Philosophy*, Vol. 1, p. 117: ". . . since things have been created in conformity with the divine types or ideas, these ideas are the ultimate source of all contingent reality and the supreme foundation of the intelligibility of essences . . . . Exemplarism radically transforms one Platonist theory: the Ideas which for Plato co-exist with God, become God himself considered in the infinite perfection of his knowledge. Already Philo had effected a similar fusion of doctrines, but it was in its Augustinean form that exemplarism was known to the Middle Ages . . . ." Compare E. Gilson, " La Matière et les Formes," *Introduction à l'Étude de Saint Augustin*, ed. 1949, pp. 260–61. See St. Augustine's question (*The City of God*, Book XII, Chap. 26, in *A Select Library*, p. 243) : " And if God, as Plato continually maintains, embraced in His eternal intelligence the ideas both of the universe and of all the animals, how, then, should He not with His own hand make them all? Could He be unwilling to be the constructor of works, the idea and plan of which called for His ineffable and ineffably to be praised intelligence? "

[28] Harry Austryn Wolfson, " Philo on Free Will," *Harvard Theological Review*, XXXV (1942), No. 2, pp. 138–40.

that the laws of nature " were implanted by God in the universe as an act of good will." [29] Plato held, however, that once implanted, they could " never be upset," while Philo believed that " God may change the order of natural events when it serves some good purpose."

The reason for this historical divergence is of crucial importance for our consideration of creation, cosmological or artistic, and relates to the opposition between Athens and Alexandria in the weighing of God's power to change " the order of natural events." F. M. Cornford argues that inasmuch as " Reason must be content to sacrifice the less important advantage and achieve the best result attainable, ' Plato's Demiurge ' is not strictly omnipotent.[30] In arranging the world he could not group physical qualities in such a way as to secure all the ends he desired." [31] But Philo's God, on the contrary, " may change the order of natural events when it serves some good purpose." As Wolfson points out, " there is no room for miracles in the philosophy of Plato." [32] Philo's God " is philosophically the Demiurge of Plato." There is room, however, in the Alexandrian philosopher's system of thought for miracles, inasmuch as Philo's God retains " the essential characteristics of the

[29] *Ibid.*, pp. 138–39.

[30] *Plato's Cosmology*, p. 176; cf. *ibid.*, 209 ff.

[31] Cf. A. O. Lovejoy, *The Great Chain of Being*, p. 54: " This expansiveness or fecundity of the Good . . . , as Plato clearly implies, is not the consequence of any free and arbitrary act of choice of the personal Creator in the myth; it is a dialectical necessity. The Idea of the Good is a necessary reality; it cannot be other than what its essence implies; and it therefore must, by virtue of its own nature, necessarily engender finite existents . . . . It follows that every sensible thing . . . cannot but be, and be precisely what it is . . . . The goodness of God–in the language of religion–is a constraining goodness; he is not, in Milton's phrase, " free to create or not," nor free to choose some possible kinds of beings as the recipients of the privilege of existence, while denying it to others. And since the characteristics that each of these has are also, upon Platonistic principles, inherent in the eternal Idea of it–in just that distinctive possibility of being of which it is the realization–neither God nor the creatures could conceivably have been or done aught other than what they are or do."

[32] *Ibid.*, pp. 139–40. But cf. Frank, *op. cit.*, p. 75, n. 10 (quoted *supra*, n. 24).

miracle-working Jehovah of the Hebrew Scriptures . . . . Philo held that God may change the order of natural events . . . ."

This moment in Alexandrian speculation is crucial for the unfolding theory of creation throughout the centuries of later tradition. It was then that the aura of the miraculous emanated. Eventually, in the theory of art and the history of aesthetic, it first re-formed and later supplanted in some forms of expressionism the classical theory of making.

The Microcosmic Conflict

From the conflict of the cosmic theory of making and that of creation, the Western tradition derives divergent interpretations of freedom. Its thinkers try, however, to reconcile them. The conjunction of the miracle of creation and the notion of freedom without condition or restraint, on the one hand, and of rational making and conditioned freedom, on the other, leads speculation eventually to search for the grounds of human freedom in both nonrational creative and rational sources. It is owing to the relating in philosophy of macrocosm and the analogous speculation in theology concerning the significance of man's creation in God's image which provides one means of transition from the notion of cosmic to that of human freedom for the artist.[33] From the ancient conception of man as a microcosm are drawn inferences concerning what man makes freely in consequence of possessing a rational soul, inferences which parallel those drawn concerning the nature of God's freedom and the world He fashions or creates. The theory of demiurgic making includes an interpretation of man, whose microcosmic soul is analogous to the macrocosmic world soul. The theory of God's miraculous powers to create supplants the demiurgic and microcosmic analogy with the dogma of man created in God's image. But the inferences concerning freedom without conditioning factors which has been attributed to the fine artist are

[33] Cf. *infra*, Ch. v, pp. 168 ff.

already implicit within the interpretation of the microcosmic soul, made explicit for human freedom by Philo's effort to reconcile Greek philosophy and Hebraic theology.

Both Plato and Philo regard man as a microcosm of the macrocosm. Plato maintains, however, that man makes under the laws of nature and by necessity. Philo, whose God "has reserved for himself the power of freedom to upset the laws of nature which He established in the world at the time of its creation," has "endowed man with a similar power of freedom to upset the laws of nature to which he is subject.[34] Acts of the will are "absolutely of man's own free choice," determined neither by God nor "by any of the natural causes" by means of which His purpose is effected in the universe.[35] In the Hebraic-Christian tradition, the belief that God created man in His image suffices to guarantee for humanity freedom adequate to ground responsibility, and this it attempts despite the dogmas of God's foreknowledge and man's fall from grace through Adam's sin.

We tend to reflect upon this opposition of theory concerning the nature of man's soul principally in its religious and moral connotations. We tend to take less seriously the words of the poet and the critic, in part because we assume that they are committed by their arts to metaphorical and allusive expression. The result is that we are not prone to interpret literally words such as Sir Philip Sidney's concerning the poet: "lifted up with the vigor of his own invention . . . hand in hand with nature, not enclosed within the narrow warrant of her gifts, but freely ranging within the zodiac of his own wit." [36] We are dulled by the interpretation of inspiration as an end, rather than as either a poetic allusion to freedom or as significant of the "great analogy." We, therefore, fail to read aright, within the great tradition of the analogy of the artist to God, the explanation of that maker who bestows "a Cyrus upon the world to make

[34] Wolfson, "Philo on Free will," *Harvard Theological Review*, xxxv, p. 163.
[35] *Ibid.*, p. 138.
[36] *The Defense of Poesy*, ed. Cook, pp. 7–8.

many Cyruses " because the " Heavenly Maker of that maker, who, having made man in His own likeness, set him beyond and over all the works of that second nature." Sidney insists that this superiority " in nothing he showeth so much as in poetry . . . with no small argument to the incredulous of that first accursed fall of Adam,—since our erected wit maketh us know what perfection is, and yet our infected will keepeth us from reaching it." [37]

We are, certainly, no less likely to accept literally the words of those who, rejecting the principle of creation, develop the notion of the artist like unto a maker divine. Yet, for the rational Shaftesbury, " a poet is indeed a second *Maker*; a just Prometheus under Jove." [38] In his " Letter concerning Enthusiasm," Shaftesbury maintains that " No poet . . . can do anything great in his own way without the imagination or supposition of a divine presence," whether the latter be spectral or real.[39]

That we judge this to be metaphor is understandable and the judgment is, no doubt, in part correct. It should be made plain, however, that these are but the more palpable evidences of the influence of the " great analogy " upon the conception of the fine artist and his art. The pattern for these and the more subtle attributions to the fine artist of divinity are fixed for the Western tradition of philosophy of art once the macrocosmic-microcosmic analogy is given its anthropomorphic presentation in *Timaeus* and once St. Augustine, that " exemplar of Middle Ages " whose earlier writings upon art fall within the scope of the Neoplatonic tradition, destroys *de Apto et Pulchro* and refers with contempt to poetic utterances as " mere wind and smoke." [40]

As regards the Platonic notion of the relation of microcosm

[37] *Ibid.*, pp. 8–9.

[38] Anthony, Earl of Shaftesbury, *Characteristics of Men, Manners, Opinions, Times, etc.*, Vol. I, p. 36.

[39] *Ibid.*, pp. 8–9.

[40] *Confessions*, bk. 1, Ch. XVII.

and macrocosm, it suffices for our present purposes to point out that in *Timaeus,* not only has the earlier notion of Eros as the begetter given way to *nous; nous* has been replaced by the notion of the *demiurgos.*[41] The problem of the *Sophist,*[42] expressed in the question, " Can we imagine that being is devoid of life and mind, and exists in awful unmeaningness an everlasting fixture? " has received a partial answer in the hypostatization of the efficient cosmic cause. The answer is significant not only for cosmic making but for the making of the beautiful as well. Neither chance nor an irrational power governs all things.[43] Mind orders all things, in both men and in the cosmos.

Cornford suggests that " the kernel of Plato's ethics is the doctrine that man's reason is divine and that his business is to become like the divine by reproducing in his own nature the beauty and harmony revealed in the cosmos, which is itself a god, a living creature with soul in body and reason in soul . . . ." [44] But man's ethical life depends for its proper functioning upon the mixture of the " limited " and the " unlimited." The pleasures he is permitted are those unmixed with pain,[45] induced by the experience of objects " turned off from lathes, from rulers and patterns of angles," including, among others, " beauties of pure colors, beauties of form, the straight line and circle and the plane and solid figures." Similarly, the demiurge makes the world in the form of a sphere, the most uniform of all solid figures, a universe constructed on the plan " to make it most nearly like the every way perfect and fairest of intelli-

[41] Cf. F. M. Cornford, *Plato's Cosmology,* p. 25: ". . . in the Philebus (26E) we hear that all things that become must have some cause (αἰτία), and this is immediately identified with ' the maker ' (τὸ ποιοῦν) ; ' what becomes ' and ' what is made ' are two names for one thing. As in the *Timaeus,* the Craftsman (τὸ δημιουργοῦν) is substituted as the equivalent of ' the maker ' and of ' the cause '; and later (28D) this cause is said to be Intelligence, the King of Heaven and Earth."

[42] *Op. cit.,* trans. Jowett, 249.

[43] *Philebus,* 28.

[44] *Plato's Cosmology,* p. 34.

[45] See my *Aesthetic Experience and Its Presuppositions,* Ch. III, pp. 112 ff.

gible things." And in making the human body, the gods copied the round figure of the universe and "bound the two divine revolutions in a spherical body, and we now call our head, our divinest member and sovereign of all the rest." [46]

Both the cosmos made by the demiurge and the beautiful forms made by man are objects of rational speculation and explanation. They are the products of free choice, conditioned because the demiurge is not in full control either of matter or of ideas.[47] By means of the "image of a creator god," Plato has fixed in the philosophy of art the notion of artistic freedom in terms of intelligibility.

To advocates of the contrasting belief in creativity, neither the divine process nor the analogous one employed by the artist is wholly, if at all intelligible. What God as creator does transcends rational explanation and is explicable in terms of no technique.[48] The basic issue has been succinctly stated in another context by Whitehead: "Creativity is the principle of *novelty*." [49] Plato's account of demiurgic making, it has long been asserted, is intelligible precisely because it explains the production only of the typical, the class, and what may be categorized.[50] From this explanation in rational terms, it is main-

[46] *Timaeus*, trans, A. E. Taylor, 44 D.

[47] F. M. Cornford, *Plato's Cosmology*, p. 37: ". . . Plato's Demiurge, like the human craftsman in whose image he is conceived, operates upon materials which he does not create, and whose inherent nature sets a limit to his desire for perfection in his work. He has been pictured as confronted with 'all that is visible' in a chaos of disorderly motion. For this disorder he is not responsible, but only for those features of order and intelligible design which he proceeds to introduce, 'so far as he can.' . . . the Demiurge is not the sole cause of Becoming . . . . Nor does the Demiurge create that Receptacle of Becoming in which the images of the Forms are mirrored. This is not mentioned among the works of Reason; it is as independent of the Demiurge as the world of Forms. The Forms, again, he does not create; they are not made or generated, but eternally contribute an element of order to Becoming, because an ordered world will be more 'like himself', that is to say, better, than a disorderly one."

[48] Cf. Erich Frank, *Philosophical Understanding and Religious Truth*, p. 57; quoted *supra* Ch. I, p. 20.

[49] *Process and Reality*, p. 31.

[50] In this connection, it is interesting to note that Whitehead makes creativity the ultimate category in metaphysics.

tained that creativity, expressed in terms of the poet's inspiration from Plato to Croce and intended to account for the unique individual, is lacking.

The contrasting statements concerning the artistic means by which the individual is produced are aesthetic expressions of a conflict which appears in the main tradition of God as creator. In speculation in the medieval period, the interest of philosophers and theologians centered upon the nature of the soul and its immortality, discussed at times in terms of the return of the soul to the world soul or the persistence of its individuality.[51]

That the problem is central to aesthetic and to the theory of the artist as creator is evident in the history of such statements as Aristotle's that " the poet . . . should preserve the type and yet ennoble it. In this way Achilles is portrayed by Agathon and Homer," [52] and such contrasting statements as Croce's, " Don Quixote is a type; but of what is he a type, save of all Don Quixotes? A type, so to speak, of himself." [53]

The principal philosophical attempts to resolve the problem of individuation reappear aptly in their aesthetic contexts. For Croce, " intuition," the form of knowledge contrasted with the " logical " and identified with the aesthetic stage of spirit, is precisely knowledge of the *individual.* And Croce denies not only matter but specifically the validity of the assertion that " space and time . . . are the forms of intuition." [54] Intuition

[51] This speculation is explicit in the terminology of modern aesthetic. " The feeling for the medium," writes Bosanquet, " the sense of what can rightly be done in it only or better than in anything else, and the charm and fascination of doing it so—these, I take it, are the real clue to the fundamental question of aesthetics, which is ' how feeling and its body are created adequate to one another.' It is parallel to the question in general philosophy, ' Why has the soul a body.' " (*Three Lectures on Aesthetic,* pp. 60–61.)

[52] *Poetics,* xv.

[53] *Aesthetic,* p. 34.

[54] *Aesthetic,* p. 4. He does so on the ground that " we have intuitions without space and without time: the colour of a sky, the colour of a feeling, a cry of pain . . . ; these are intuitions which we possess, and with their making space and time have nothing to do." Cf. *ibid.,* p. 5.

reveals in a work of art " not space and time, but *character, individual physiognomy*." But the *principio individuationis* of the demiurgic theory is either a function of matter or of spatial-temporal coordinates. Thus, for Constantin Ritter, Plato's argument in *Timaeus* means that the individual is " whatever appears as extended in space (the various positions in space are all different) and as such an object appears only once, as something individual." [55] Ritter maintains that Platonic theory means, at this point, that " Each Idea indicates the essence of the individual appearances in so far as it is knowable." [56] Some Platonists have interpreted this to mean that the additional inference may be made that Plato in this way provided for the emergence in the receptacle of the individual and the novel.[57]

It may scarcely be denied, however, that for Plato essences are archetypal. In the field of art, his search for the canon of beauty,[58] his praise of the conservatism of Egyptian art,[59] and his evident dislike and mistrust of novelty in sculpture and poetry,[60] are aesthetic consequences of a doctrine which, as it takes on its Aristotelian form, led the realists of the Middle Ages to urge that universals " are *the more Real in proportion as they are the more universal*." [61] It is by means of the theory of inspiration, as we have observed, that Plato proposes to account for what goes beyond rational explanation in the passage from nonbeing to being. The Stoic, Hebraic, and Christian interest in the personality and individuality of man not only suggests the difficulties which the Western tradition has found to be inherent in the view which subordinates the value of the

[55] *The Essence of Plato's Philosophy*, p. 210.

[56] *Ibid.*, p. 210.

[57] Cf. A. E. Taylor, *Plato: The Man and His Work*, pp. 443–44: " The Demiurge really is thought of as a true ' Creator ' and everything sensible has ' emerged ' as the result of a process . . . the world is always in ' evolution ', even if the evolution never began and will never come to an end."

[58] See M. C. Nahm, *Aesthetic Experience and Its Presuppositions*, Ch. IV.

[59] *Ibid.*

[60] *Laws*, 657, 660.

[61] See W. Windelband, *A History of Philosophy*, trans. J. H. Tufts, p. 290. Compare *ibid.*, pp. 232–33, 252–55, and 287 ff.

individual to that of the form or type, or which interprets the significance of the individual substance in terms only of its capacity to manifest the type; it also provides the background for the assertion, within the theory of the artist as creator, of the unconditioned uniqueness of the work of fine art and the unlimited freedom of the fine artist.

The alternative which the tradition of creativity in the philosophy of art has accepted is an interpretation to be understood in terms of one of theology's miracles, i. e., in terms of the existence of unique and individual souls, free and endowed with personality.[62] In aesthetic, the interpretation has centered upon a theory of the production of unique and individual works of art,[63] created by an artist liberated from the rules of technique. The general theory is clearly stated by Croce, for whom " the impossibility of choice of content completes the theory of the *independence* of art." [64] But the close relation of the theory of the soul and of the image is not neglected: " since every work of art expresses a state of the soul, and the state of the soul is always individual and always new, the intuition implies infinite intuitions . . . all are original, each one incapable of being translated into the other." [65]

We have presented, in general outline, the principal phases of the " great analogy " which has dominated speculation in the Western tradition of the philosophy of art and from which has emerged the notion of the fine artist endowed with freedoms analogous to those attributed to God the creator and maker. How influential that analogy has been is evident in one quotation. We have seen that, in contrast to Croce, Bosanquet's interpretation of Hegelian aesthetic is a deepening and specification of the demiurgic theory of making, rational and intel-

[62] Cf. Bosanquet, *Three Lectures on Aesthetic,* p. 62: " His [every craftman's] fascinated imagination lives in the powers of his medium; he thinks and feels in terms of it; it is the peculiar body of which *his* aesthetic imagination and no other is the peculiar soul."

[63] Cf. *supra,* Ch. II, pp. 65 ff.

[64] *Aesthetic,* p. 51.

[65] *The Essence of Aesthetic,* pp. 56–57.

ligible throughout. Yet even Bosanquet writes that "it is very dangerous to say that beauty is the aim of art . . . if it means to us that we know beforehand what sort or type of thing our beauty is to be. For beauty is above all a creation, a new individual expression in which a new feeling comes to exist. And if we understand it so, there is not much meaning in saying that it is the aim of art, for we do not know beforehand what it is to be."[66]

Our central problem in an essay of the artist as creator is the establishment of a theory of fine art adequate to account for the emergence of the novel and unique yet intelligible work of fine art. Bosanquet's words would appear no less to deny this possibility than do those of Collingwood, who so clearly attempts to guard art as expression against "theophobia." Collingwood asserts that art is creation in the sense that a man can make "non-technically, but yet consciously and voluntarily."[67] This means that "the person who makes these things is acting voluntarily; he is acting responsibly; but he need not be acting in order to achieve an ulterior end; he need not be following a preconceived plan; and he is certainly not transforming anything that can properly be called a raw material."

If a technique of fine art poses the main problem of the artist as a creator of a unique and intelligible individual, why not proceed immediately to an analysis of that problem? The answer is, in part, historical. In a sense, the aesthetic and the theological problems of creativity are so closely united that they must first be disengaged. An instance will demonstrate this: St. Augustine's notion that the saint is free because he is unable to sin, while other men are free in the sense that they are able not to sin, is clearly not an aesthetic statement nor was it intended as such. Yet it does much to clarify the early theory of ugliness and the eighteenth century's notion of the genius as a free maker. There remains, however, a more fundamental problem which suggests the course this essay now takes. Before

[66] *Three Lectures on Aesthetic,* p. 109.
[67] *The Principles of Art,* pp. 128–29.

the history of art emerged as a discipline for the analysis of art as a craft and before the philosophy of art in its more technical statement developed in modern times, speculation concerning the artist as creator received its principal study in biography and in inferences drawn from the study of such abstractions as the " beautiful," the " ugly," the " sublime," and the " tragic." The latter speculation had its own value but it also contributed to the continuity of European speculation upon art and its making.

The problem of freedom as it derives from the relation of the agent to ideas becomes an aesthetic issue in the consideration of types such as the beautiful and the sublime.[68] Its significance for our understanding of freedom in art turns upon the fact that the tradition of the artist as creator sustained in this aspect of speculation what was implicit in the type as aesthetic value. Freedom, as a problem of the agent's relation to matter, is ultimately naturalized to aesthetic speculation concerning technique and media.[69] But before either the problem of aesthetic value or of technique in relation to media emerged, the " great analogy " had effected its influence. The controversy concerning freedom as omniscience or knowledge centered upon the problem of the genius; that concerning freedom as omnipotence or power was directed to a search for a solution to the problem of the ugly.

The development of the theory of genius is a largely modern phenomenon.[70] The problem of the ugly was formulated in terms of the " great analogy " in the earlier period in which controversy began to affect the tradition of the artist as creator or maker. To the latter issue, that of the ugly and of ugliness, we shall now turn.

[68] See *infra,* Ch. x.
[69] See *infra,* Ch. VIII.
[70] See *infra,* Ch. IV, pp. 127 ff.

3 The Ugly

. . . Deus bonus est, unde malum?
. . . the trackless labyrinth of verbalism . . .

The later Platonic theory of ideas tends to convert the idea of the good into the conception of power. It is asserted that being is inconceivable without motion, life, soul, and mind. We have already mentioned the development of *nous* and cause into the demiurge in *Timaeus*.[1] It is not necessary, at this juncture, to elaborate a principal theme of Neoplatonic and Augustinean interpretations of Plato's theory of ideas, that of the location of ideas in *nous* in the former and of the *rationes seminales* in the latter philosophy.[2] The conception of the genius in art is formulated, principally in the seventeenth and eighteenth centuries, in terms of this problem of knowledge. It is certainly true that the problems of epistemology and power in their relation to freedom may not be wholly separated.[3] Nonetheless, it is power in relation to matter which raises the problem of evil and it is principally the problem of evil which conditions speculation upon the ugly and ugliness. Once omnipotence is

[1] *Vide supra,* Ch. II, p. 77 ff. See Plotinus, *Enneads,* 5.4.1, on the "power" of the "First, the perfect."

[2] See E. Gilson, *Introduction à l'Étude de Saint Augustin,* Ch. 2, pp. 259–60. See *supra,* Ch. II, p. 70, n. 24.

[3] This is not in any sense to deny that the notion of the genius as the "great man" is foreign to ancient theory of art. See Plato's *Ion* 532 and Longinus' *de Sublimitate,* particularly the suggestions concerning what William Smith translated as "a lofty and tow'ring genius" (*Dionysius on the Sublime,* 4th ed. [London, 1770], pp. 23–24, 62–63). The method here employed is principally dictated by the fact that it was Longinus' writing on inspiration and sublimity which influenced the great development of the theory of genius. It should be emphasized, as it will be later, that the notion of omnipotence did affect the notion of omniscience. As will be observed, Aristotle saw clearly that the problem of ugliness is one of defect and error, i.e., is not beyond judgment. See *infra,* this chapter, pp. 118 ff.

asserted to be a divine perfection and the issue is joined concerning the eternality or creation in time of matter, the ugly becomes the aesthetic analogue to evil.

As the analogy is elaborated, the theory designed to explain the ugly and ugliness becomes no less a budget of paradoxes than is that of evil. That it should parallel and equal in paradox the speculation summed up in the query, " si Deus bonus est, unde malum? " is surprising, on at least one count. If one consider the human situation and man's precarious state, the constancy with which theologians and moral philosophers encounter difficulties in tracing evil to its source and in accounting for its presence is scarcely to be wondered at. And that the complexities of the situation should drive speculation to investigate the metaphysical and theological grounds for evil is the less startling, inasmuch as the major tradition in ethical thought has not asserted its autonomy so definitively as has the aesthetic. Specifically, since the eighteenth century and, more particularly, under the influence of Kantian theory of judgment, the conception of free imagination has tended, as we have noted, to exclude judgments concerning being or the religious or moral value or disvalue of works of fine art.[4] It is precisely in the consideration of the ugly and of ugliness that the moral, theological, and ontological implications which the establishment of a unique aesthetic universe of discourse has tended to exclude from aesthetic speculation again arise.

Here, again, Croce and Bosanquet well illustrate the point. No more determined efforts have been made to free aesthetic from the strictures of theology and morality than those of the two expressionist philosophers. Yet, their writings exemplify the fact that the specific analogy of evil and the ugly and the more general analogy of the fine artist as creator to God would appear to have obscured for both the fact that the sought-for autonomy of art has disappeared. Thus, in writing upon the ugly, Croce does not hesitate to assert that " in so far as the

[4] See *supra*, Ch. I, pp. 9 ff.

theoretic activity is also practical activity . . . the polarization of good and evil, which in that case are called beautiful and ugly, true and false, takes place . . . ."[5] Not only are distinctions thus broken down in practical activity; the ontological problem is likewise raised.[6] The point is even clearer in Bosanquet's remark that the "root of ugliness" is discovered in "the pretension to pure expression."[7] The connotation of "pretension" can only be one related to the moral vice of pride.

It may be supposed that Croce's and Bosanquet's difficulties derive from their systematic accounts of the universe. The paradoxical character of the theory of the ugly remains, however, as is evident at a point at which metaphysical systems do not intrude. It is one of the anomalies of contemporary theories of expression, for example, that, once Lessing had differentiated the arts into the spatial and the temporal[8] and then had proceeded further to distinguish beauty into the formal and the expressive,[9] on the grounds of this distinction, the ugly, which historically has been judged to be contrary to beauty and therefore incompatible with it, has not only entered the aesthetic fold but has actually come to be judged beautiful. This is not a merely theoretical conclusion.[10] It has been employed as a

[5] *Philosophy of the Practical,* p. 205. He insists that the "pure theoretic activity, considered in itself cannot be polarized."

[6] *Ibid.,* p. 202. "The judgements that we give when we judge an action to be foolish or wicked, a statement false, a work of art ugly, are all metaphysical. In delivering them we do not mean to say that there is an *existence* called error, ugliness, foolishness, but only that there is a given existence and that another is wanting."

[7] *Three Lectures on Aesthetic,* p. 106. Cf. *The Value and Destiny of the Individual,* p. 215: ". . . the essence of the evil attitude is the self-maintenance of some factor in a self both as good and also as against the good system."

[8] *Laocoon,* trans. Ellen Frothingham.

[9] *Ibid.,* p. 11: ". . . it follows necessarily that whatever else these [i. e., the imitative] arts aim at must give way completely if incompatible with beauty." Cf. p. 153: ". . . painting as a fine art will not express it [i. e., ugliness]" and p. 156: "I must call attention to the fact that painting and poetry do not stand upon the same footing in this respect. In poetry . . . ugliness of form loses its disagreeable effect almost entirely by the successive enumeration of its coexistent parts."

[10] Cf., B. Bosanquet, *A History of Aesthetic,* p. 433, as an example.

rule for technique in sculpture,[11] the art which served Lessing as the basis for the original distinction.

It would be difficult in any circumstance to accept the ugly without some reservation as an aesthetic category or problem, were we forced also to accept the implications of the statement, " the uglier a being is in nature, the more beautiful it becomes in art." It is certainly true that Rodin's " La Vielle Heaulmière," various of Rembrandt's anatomy lessons, Tennessee Williams' *A Streetcar Named Desire*, Edgar Allan Poe's " The Facts in the Case of M. Valdemar," and Milton's

> A cry of Hell Hounds never ceasing bark'd
> With wide *Cerberean* mouths full loud, and run
> A hideous Peal . . .[12]

do suggest the validity of what Aristotle and Kant contended, namely, that natural ugliness is transformed into artistic value once it has been made mimetic or symbolical by means of art. On the other hand, if there are aesthetic categories, it is necessary to assume that some limitations must be accepted and it is difficult to believe that there can be, as would appear to be implied in this statement, an identity of aesthetic contraries.[13]

One may be tempted, certainly, to discuss the problem of the ugly as meaningless and relegate it to that "trackless labyrinth of verbalism " within which Croce includes it. We should do so, however, at a loss to our understanding of human freedom and to the comprehension of the manner in which the conception of artistic creativity was formed in the Western tradition

[11] E. g., Rodin's " La Vielle Heaulmiere." See Rodin's *Art*, p. 45: ". . . it often happens that the uglier a being is in nature, the more beautiful it becomes in art." Rodin insists, *ibid.*, pp. 44–45, that what " is considered ugly in nature often presents more *character* than that which is termed beautiful, because in the contractions of a sickly countenance, in the lines of a vicious face, in all deformity, in all decay, the inner truth shines forth more clearly than in features that are regular and healthy . . . it is solely the power of *character* which makes for beauty in art . . . ." (Trans. R. Fedder)

[12] *Paradise Lost*, II, 654 ff.

[13] The fundamental difficulty is, as we shall see, that a structural problem has been confused with an evaluational one. See *infra*, Ch. IX–X.

of speculation. This is true despite the ample suggestion which history makes that the ugly and ugliness are problems over which has been cast the spell of miracles. This is suggested not only by the notion that the beautiful and ugly as expressed are, in fact, identical; but also in the long-lived tradition that, whereas perfection of technique produces beauty, the ugly is owing to defect. Furthermore, it is immediately evident that absolutism, the mark of theory affected by the analogy of the artist to God, is, if possible, magnified in the speculation concerning grotesque, the distorted, and the ugly.

This absolutist attitude, which is part and parcel of the tradition of the artist as creator, is directed toward the problem of the ugly and of ugliness in Bosanquet's suggestion that the determination of the self is got by " discipline under the spirit that is the outer world," and in Croce's that " Activity is the deliverer, just because it drives away passivity," and that in expressing impressions man frees himself from them.

The issue is, then, precisely that of power. As Bosanquet clearly sees, it is power and freedom directed to the " medium of intercourse through the body and through natural objects " which occasions the problem of the ugly.[14] As Plato's demiurgos works in " world-stuff " he has not created, so Bosanquet's artist frees himself in external media. As St. Augustine's God creates *ex nihilo,* so Croce's artist expresses what may be called impressions but which merely are passivity or negativity in contrast to activity.

The ugly itself is described by both theorists in similarly absolute terms. For Bosanquet, there remains a possibility that there is " true ugliness " which " must mean, if it means anything, invincible ugliness, such as no sane imagination can see as beauty." [15] For Croce ugliness cannot be " *complete,*" i. e., no ugly event is " without any element of beauty." [16]

[14] " Croce's Aesthetic," *Proceedings of the British Academy,* Vol. 9, pp. 267–271.

[15] *Three Lectures on Aesthetic,* p. 97.

[16] *Aesthetic,* p. 78. Compare Collingwood, who denies that the artist works with " raw materials." See *supra,* Ch. I, p. 57.

It is important to recognize that Bosanquet's theory of the ugly not only follows directly from the philosophical view that "externality is a common character of the world and a sign and vehicle of spiritual achievement," [17] but that, paradoxically enough, its moral connotations are no less explicit. "Insuperable ugliness" is found in the "region of insincere and affected art," its root being "the pretension to pure expression, which alone can have a clearer and positive failure." [18]

Of Croce's theory of the ugly, Bosanquet makes the succinct remark that that which has "no expressive form by which it embodies anything . . . for aesthetic purposes . . . is nothing," [19] and that the theory itself means, if properly interpreted, that "the ugly is the purely inexpressive." [20] In a formal and limited sense, this is an accurate description. But "unsuccessful expression," for Croce, is to be understood in terms of the larger distinction between value and disvalue. In the latter context, the ugly is to be contrasted to "activity that unfolds itself freely." Like Bosanquet's notion of the ugly, Croce's is, again paradoxically enough, not free from moral implications. The ugly would appear to be a function of matter, which is "mechanism, passivity; it is what the spirit of man suffers, but does not produce." [21] What matter does produce is, in fact, "animality, whatever is brutal and impulsive in man, not the spiritual dominion, which is humanity."

[17] *Three Lectures on Aesthetic*, p. 106. Compare *A History of Aesthetic*, p. 435: ". . . what we have to dread as ugliness insuperable either by healthy perception or by the 'characteristic' of art, is not the narrow, the rude, the terrible, the grotesque, or even the vicious when frankly and forcibly revealed for what it is; as plainly represented in their apparent ugliness, these elements become modifications of the beautiful. We must look for insuperable ugliness in its highest degree in the falsely beautiful produced by the confusion of aims and feelings in conscious representation, *i. e.* in art. We shall find it in the sentimental presented as touching, in the effeminate as tender, in the feeble taken to be delicate, the tawdry taken to be brilliant, and the monstrous taken to be strong . . . ."

[18] *Three Lectures on Aesthetic*, p. 106.

[19] *Ibid.*, p. 97.

[20] *Ibid.*, p. 103; cf. pp. 104–105.

[21] *Aesthetic*, pp. 5–6.

The moral is not, however, the immediately significant implication. The ugly is to be contrasted to " free inspiration," which in turn is grounded in a theory of autonomous freedom.[22] Its ground would appear to be the Aristotelian privative conception of matter, interpreted by Croce to mean " the lower limit " which " spirit can never apprehend in itself as simple matter. This it can only possess with form and in form, but postulates the notion of it as a mere limit." [23] The ugly itself and as such. however, cannot exist,[24] although there can be " degrees of ugliness." [25]

If we inquire, not concerning the grounds for asserting the nonexistence of the ugly, namely, the nominal existence but actual nonexistence of matter, but concerning what would appear to be the basic reason for the denial to the ugly of existence, we come to the core of the theory of freedom and to hints of its derivation from the analogy of the artist to God. Croce remarks, in elaborating his inference that the completely ugly is impossible, that if there were no element of beauty, the ugly would " for that very reason cease to be ugly, because it would be without the contradiction in which is the reason for its existence." [26] At what point would such contradiction appear? At the point at which " disvalue would become nonvalue; activity would give place to passivity." The problem is thus placed within the larger context of value-theory.[27] It is significant, however, that value and disvalue are terms for a process

[22] *Ibid.*, p. 6. Matter and form ". . . are not *two acts of ours*, opposed to one another; but the one is outside us, and assaults and sweeps us off our feet, while the other inside us tends to absorb and identify itself with that which is outside." (Italics mine)

[23] *Ibid.*, p. 5.

[24] *Aesthetic*, p. 79: " If the ugly were *complete*, that is to say, without any element of beauty, it would for that very reason cease to be ugly . . . ."

[25] *Ibid.*, p. 79. There are " degrees of ugliness," " from the rather ugly (or almost beautiful) to the extremely ugly," a condition which Croce contrasts with that of the beautiful which " does not possess degrees."

[26] *Aesthetic*, p. 79.

[27] *Ibid.*, pp. 77–78.

of conflict and struggling.[28] The presupposition of this process is clearly "no trackless labyrinth" but a cosmic struggle. "Whether they [the contraries] are to be thought of dualistically, as two beings or two orders of beings, like Ormuzd and Ahriman, angels and devils, enemies to one another; or as a unity, which is also contrariety," Croce does not pretend to decide. But that the first is Gnostic, with a firm philosophical foundation in Plato's dualism of demiurgic making and something external and uncreated by the maker, and the second Neoplatonic, sufficiently suggests the direction in which the statement moves. If we recall that the God of Genesis creates *ex nihilo,* that matter, for Croce, is nonexistent, and the ugly as such does not exist, we locate the general problem even more specifically. And we should also better comprehend the meaning of Bosanquet's assertion that "if it [the ugly] is not plastic, i. e., has no expressive form by which it embodies anything, then, for aesthetic purposes it is nothing." [29]

The issue is still confused because the factors which have affected it are complex to a degree. In the development of speculation upon the ugly, there has entered not only the theological analogy of God's creation or making of the world, but a second analogy, that of evil to the ugly. An additional complication is offered by the nontheological, Aristotelian interpretation of the ugly, which places emphasis upon the transformation undergone by natural objects or events as they become imitations and symbols in the work of art. We have had some inkling of the complexities of the ugly as a problem by the intrusion of ontological, religious, and moral implications in its consideration within the aesthetic universe of discourse. Some additional forewarning is got from Croce's twofold theory of the ugly as nonexistent, "the distinctive consciousness of

[28] *Ibid.,* pp. 77–78. "Absence of value is not sufficient to cause disvalue, but activity and passivity must be struggling between themselves with the one getting the better of the other; hence the contradiction and disvalue of the activity that is embarrassed, impeded, or interrupted."

[29] *Three Lectures on Aesthetic,* p. 97.

the beautiful and the ugly, . . . based on the conflicts and contradictions in which aesthetic activity is developed." [30]

The clarification of these issues is at least partially possible once we examine the theological and moral conflict in which the aesthetic problem has its origin. The prototype of the notions that the fine artist enjoys unconditioned freedom and that his freedom is imagination operating in a medium, working out its capacities and limitations is the "great analogy." More specifically, it is the analogy in that aspect in which God's powers are judged in terms of matter. With the enormous history of the subject our argument need not be involved.[31] Its principal structure was formed in the philosophies of Plato and Aristotle and sufficiently developed by Plotinus and St. Augustine for this essay, by reference to these classical sources, to determine its aesthetic and nonaesthetic implications. Plato's tendency to interpret the good in terms of power provides a ground for a theory of evil of sufficient scope to include the problem of the ugly. Plotinus argues the analogy of evil and moral evil to the ugly and artistic ugliness in terms of matter. Augustine accepts the parallelism of evil and ugliness developed by Neoplatonism and argues the issue of freedom, both for God and for man, in terms of the nonexistence of matter. The notion of miraculous and creative powers operating in the artistic as well as in the moral and religious fields is thus established.

The general paradox which presents itself to the theologian, the moralist, and by analogy to the philosopher of art is clearly put by the Stoic, Lactantius:

If [God] neither wills nor is able, [to abolish evils], He is

---

[30] *Aesthetic*, p. 79.

[31] The problem is implicit in the theory of becoming from Thales through Aristotle. Concerning ugliness, the most interesting early speculation is that of Heraclitus. See, for example, M. C. Nahm, *Selections from Early Greek Philosophy*, p. 91, fr. 46, "Opposition unites. From what draws apart results the most beautiful harmony. All things take place by strife." See *ibid.*, p. 94, fr. 99: ". . . the most beautiful of apes is ugly in comparison with beings of another kind, and the most beautiful of earthen pots is ugly in comparison with maidenkind."

> both malicious and feeble; and so is not God. If He wills and is able, whence then are evils, or why does He not abolish them? [32]

In Plato's philosophy, the basic difficulty is clearly stated, as is the inference drawn from it: " Evils . . . can never pass away," he writes, " for there must always remain something which is antagonistic to good." [33] In providing a ground for that " immortal conflict going on among us," [34] however, the ambiguity with which the factor opposed to the good is examined has served to enhance its value for later speculation. Plato's own description of the making of the world by the demiurge is one in which what comes to be is " sensible " and " generable," in contrast to the " eternal " model.[35] A more elaborate account,[36] calling attention to a third term in addition to the " model " and its " transient visible copy," brings in the " receptacle," " a natural matrix for all things," capable of receiving all kinds in itself but " bare of all forms."

What, precisely, the nature of this third term " which never perishes " is in *Timaeus* presents a problem with which scholarship has wrestled for centuries.[37] The Aristotelians interpret it

[32] *De Ira* 13. Quoted by Paul Elmer More, *The Religion of Plato,* pp. 236–237.

[33] *Theatetus,* trans. Jowett, 176.

[34] *Laws* 908.

[35] *Timaeus* 28–29.

[36] *Ibid.,* 48 e–49 a, 50 c–d, trans. A. E. Taylor. Cf. *ibid.,* 52: ". . . the form is one thing, self-same, never born, never perishing, never receiving anything else into itself from without nor entering anywhere into anything else, invisible and imperceptible to any sense; it is that, in fact, which it is the function of thinking to contemplate. A second thing is that which bears the same name and is like the first, but is perceptible to sense, is born, is continually in motion, comes to be in a place and again vanishes out of it, is apprehended by opinion based on sense. Our third term, once more, is in every case, *space* which never perishes but provides an emplacement for all that is born . . . ."

[37] See Zeller, *Plato and the Older Academy,* p. 312, where it is described as " the mere form of Materiality." Compare also, Zeller, *ibid.,* p. 296, n. 9, with reference to *Timaeus* 69 a, for a discussion of the Platonic use of ὕλη and its relation to the later philosophical application of the term to " signify the abstract concept of material substratum." Compare also, A. E. Taylor's *A*

to mean the unformed material substratum got by logical privation; [38] a modern commentator, A. E. Taylor, maintains, on the contrary, that " the cosmology of Timaeus is a cosmology without ' matter,' " [39] and that Plato, in the significant passage, is writing only of space or extension.[40]

Zeller, after examining the evidence, practically dismisses the possibility of ascertaining Plato's meaning.[41] The preponderance of evidence suggests that the third term is space, place, or extension and this interpretation has exerted wide influence upon speculation concerning individuals and particulars. Yet, whatever may have been Plato's intention and however probable it is that the spatial interpretation is correct, there is little doubt that the Neoplatonists believed that Plato meant matter.[42] It may be true that the popular platonists of the early Roman Empire " were in error when they taught that Plato held ' matter ' to be the source of evil." [43] It was nonetheless within the limits of this interpretation that the Western tradition of speculation upon evil and the ugly formed and was developed.[44]

In the Neoplatonic interpretation, the source of evil is matter. For Plato it is precisely the problems of freedom and necessity, within the limitations imposed upon the maker, by what Neo-

Commentary on Plato's Timaeus, p. 493; notes to *Timaeus* 69 a 6; and Baeumker, *Problem der Materie*, pp. 126–188.

[38] See note 2, above.

[39] *A Commentary on Plato's Timaeus*, p. 178.

[40] See *supra*, Ch II, p. 80. This view is in agreement with that of Constantin Ritter, while F. M. Cornford denies that " the body of the universe " has been reduced by Plato to " mere extension."

[41] *Op. cit.*, pp. 295–341.

[42] Taylor, *op. cit.*, p. 78.

[43] *Ibid.*, p. 78. Taylor holds that, as Plato maintains in the *Laws*, " ' souls ' are the real causes of all evil as well as of all good." Cornford, *op. cit.*, pp. 176 ff., argues that motions and active powers other than the demiurge " are perpetually producing undesirable effects."

[44] It is significant that the formation of the tradition of philosophy of art within the " great analogy " brings the interpretation of the receptacle in terms of matter and space into relation with the problem of individuation, while the notion that the maker of the world is " soul " is related to the problem of the indivividual artist.

platonism interpreted to be matter, which give rise to the problem of evil.[45] The demiurge no more creates the receptacle than he creates the forms.[46] It is desire for perfection which is the ground for the making of the world, for " he was good, and none that is good is ever subject to any motion of grudging." [47] Inasmuch as God desired that all things should become as similar as possible to himself, his desire was not for anything bad. Some light upon the argument in *Timaeus* is provided by an earlier judgment in the *Republic*: " God and the things of God are in every way perfect." [48] The ground for this statement is clear: God, being truly good, is the cause of well-being.[49] Moreover, " the good is not the cause of all things, but of the good only."

If then God is not the author of the evils in the world and has but partial control in his ordering of the processes in this world, the causes of evils " are to be sought elsewhere, and not in him." Evil is thus real; God's powers are limited; but, although those powers are not coextensive with the things of the world, it is held that God exercises complete power over what he does make; his " creations are indissoluble." [50]

[45] *Timaeus* 48 e: ". . . the generation of this our world came about from a combination of necessity with understanding, but understanding overruled necessity by persuading her to conduct the most part of the effects to the best issue." (Trans. A. E. Taylor)

[46] See Cornford, *Plato's Cosmology*, p. 37: ". . . like the human craftsman in whose image he is conceived," God " operates upon materials which he does not create, and whose inherent nature sets a limit to his desire for perfection in his work."

[47] *Timaeus* 29 e, trans. A. E. Taylor.

[48] *Op. cit.*, 381 a–b, trans. Jowett.

[49] *Ibid.*, 379.

[50] See Taylor, *A Commentary on Plato's Timaeus*, p. 72: " Evil is real," arising either in consequence of matter or of agents who may be " real agents " and who may be " not perfectly wise and therefore not perfectly good." Concerning the indissolubility of God's creations, it is remarked that " all that is bound may be undone . . . only an evil being would wish to undo that which is harmonious and happy." Compare Wolfson, *supra*, Ch. II, p. 72, on Plato's and Philo's conceptions of freedom. See also, Plato's mythological presentation in *Politicus* 272 ff., in which he speaks of " cycles " and explains the occurrences after " the earth-born race had all perished." It is of interest that the pilot of

What, then, are the principal inferences to be drawn with reference to the problem of evil and the derived problems of ugliness from Plato's account of the demiurge and the construction of the world? It would appear that Plato's God is an artist and the world a work of art,[51] rather than that his God is intended to be an object of worship [52] or that the world is to be judged to be equal in value to its maker; [53] that evil is real; [54] and that God is not omnipotent.[55] It is the first and the latter two points which most nearly concern the theory of evil and ugliness.

Plato's God is not an object of worship; neither is he responsible for the existence of cosmic evil. Plato presents a rationalist interpretation of freedom in terms of responsibility. Cornford contrasts Plato's interpretation to that of Galen: " We say that certain things are impossible by nature and these God does not even attempt; he only chooses the best among the things that come about." [56] Galen is no less aware of the contrasting conception of God, implicit in the revelation of the

the universe " let the helm go," that the " universal creature " ruled, following the instructions of God, " as far as he remembered them," and that " from God, the constructor, the world received all that is good in him, but from a previous state came elements of evil and unrighteousness." (Trans. Jowett)

[51] F. M. Cornford, *Plato's Cosmology*, pp. 27, 37.

[52] *Ibid.*, p. 35. Compare More, *The Religion of Plato*.

[53] See A. E. Taylor, *A Commentary on Plato's Timaeus*, p. 78: ". . . the world *is* not God, but something derived from and dependent on God," and, consequently, " it cannot be as good as God Himself." Cf. E. Frank, *Philosophical Understanding and Religious Truth*, pp. 56–57.

[54] This inference would hold whether its source be regarded as matter or as souls, i. e., " real agents " which " are not perfectly wise and therefore not perfectly good " or whether, as Cornford suggests, " Plato recognises in the working of the universe, a factor which confronts the divine Reason and is neither ordained nor completely controlled by it." The latter would mean that " irrational and merely necessary motions and changes, with casual and undesigned results, actually occur in Nature at all times, as well as those which are subservient to rational ends." (*Plato's Cosmology*, p. 209)

[55] See Cornford, *ibid.*, p. 209: The demiurge is not represented as " an omnipotent creator who had designed the whole contents of the universe " but " as a craftsman who ' takes over ' materials in disorderly motion and does the best he can with them."

[56] Galen *U. P.* xi, 14. Quoted by Cornford, *op. cit.*, p. 36. For Plato, there

Old and New Testament: " For Moses, God has only to will to bring matter into order, and matter is ordered immediately."

In *Timaeus,* God makes the cosmos because " he was good, and none that is good is ever subject to any motion of grudging." With the Platonic assumptions, Plotinus [57] and St. Augustine [58] are in general agreement. In both philosophies, God's power in producing or creating the world is examined in terms of matter, which, in contrast to Plato's treatment, is specified and by reference to which emerges the problem of the ugly. For Plotinus, there is a formal identification of evil and ugliness, which one method, it is assumed, will suffice to explain.[59] For Augustine, evil and ugliness are to be understood in terms of deficiency, but, whereas evil is deficiency of being, ugliness

is an " errant cause," which may be matter, and there are errant motions. In the universe, there are movements and alterations not related to design or to good. It would appear that Plato is attempting to work out a theory of responsible freedom and making, the basis for which is a teleology which likewise implies mechanism. In this sense, Plato is offering in *Timaeus* a picture of the world in which reason rules necessity, as Cornford remarks (*op. cit.,* p. 209), " only for the most part." The demiurge's designs would operate upon a universe analogous to an organism, definable in terms of unity and good. But the parts of the universe may be described in mechanical terms.

[57] Plotinus, *Enneads* 1.4.1, asks " How then could the most perfect remain self-set—the First Good, . . . how could it grudge or be powerless to give of itself, and how at that would it still be the Source? " (Stephen MacKenna's translation, which is used throughout)

[58] St. Augustine's Platonism in these respects is less evident. God, for him, is both transcendent and describable in terms of predicates. He writes that " God is the supreme good, above all good, and for that reason He is unchanging." (Quoted by M. C. D'Arcy, " The Philosophy of St. Augustine," *A Monument to St. Augustine,* p. 185) More specifically, he offers (*The City of God,* Book xi, Ch. 23) as the " good and simple " reason for the world's creation that " a good God made it good; and that the things created, being different from God, were inferior to Him, and yet were good, being created by none other than He." (*A Select Library of the Nicene and Post-Nicene Fathers of the Christian Church,* Vol. II, p. 217)

[59] *Enneads,* 1.6.6: " We may say even that Beauty *is* Authentic-Existents and Ugliness is the Principle contrary to Existence; and the Ugly is also the primal evil; therefore its contrary is at once good and beautiful, or is Good and Beauty: and hence the one method will discover to us the Beauty-Good and the Ugliness-Evil."

is deficiency of form or of beauty.[60] Fundamentally, for both philosophers, the issue turns on God's freedom and responsibility and, in a derivative and analogous sense, upon the freedom of the artist.

For Plotinus, freedom, responsibility, and ugliness are issues to be resolved in terms of a dynamic pantheism in which the "One is perfect," "seeking nothing, possessing nothing, lacking nothing." Metaphorically, it "has overflowed, and its exuberance has produced the new."[61] For Augustine, freedom, responsibility, and ugliness are issues to be resolved in terms of a creative God.

For Plotinus, "all that is fully achieved engenders"; "the offspring is always minor";[62] matter, the final offspring, the mother and nurse of generation, the matrix of primitive matter in space, void of form, is not created. It is "prefigured," but not in time; it is neither space nor place, which is posterior to matter and to body.[63] It is, rather, the indeterminate, in contrast to the One.[64] It is nonbeing.[65]

[60] *Contra Epist. Manich.* xx, xliii, 49: ". . . let us abhor this heresy which has been led by faith in its fancies to represent the divine substance as extended and diffused through space, even through infinite space, and to cut short one side so as to make room for evil, not being able to perceive that evil is not nature, but against nature; and to beautify this very evil with such visible appearance, and forms, and consistency of parts prevailing in its several natures, not being able to conceive of any nature without those good things, that the evils found fault within it are buried under a countless abundance of good things." (*A Select Library of Nicene and Post-Nicene Fathers of the Christian Church*, Vol. iv, p. 150) Compare *De Natura Boni*, iv, P. L. 42, 553: "Proinde cum quaeritur unde sit malum, prius quaerendum est quid sit malum: quod nihil aliud est quam corruptio, vel modi, vel speciei, vel ordinis naturalis." In *L'Esthétique de Saint Augustin et ses Sources*, p. 141, K. Svoboda interprets Augustine to mean that "La beauté existe donc tant que la nature des choses dure. Le contraire véritable des qualités en est la privation, par example le contraire de la voix, c'est le silence . . . ."

[61] *Enneads*, 5.2.1.

[62] *Ibid.*, 5.1.6.

[63] *Ibid.*, 2.4.11–12.

[64] *Ibid.*, 2.4.5. Matter is "indetermination needing The First to its determination."

[65] *Ibid.*, 3.6.7: "It lives on the farther side of all these categories and so has

In contrast, for Augustine, matter is created by God.[66] The world is made of a formless matter, " which matter, out of nothing." In this act of creation, a miracle as it was for Philo, is discovered St. Augustine's affirmation of God's freedom and independence: " Quia voluit, fecit." [67] This act of *will*—in contrast to the prefigured existence of Plotinus' matter,—is a free act.[68]

We come, at once, in these statements concerning the One, God, freedom, and matter, to the interrelated problems of responsibility, evil and ugliness. More significantly, as we shall indicate, in the Plotinean and Augustinean philosophies of art, the analogy of the artist to God serves to provide ideally the ground for each significant statement made by Croce and Bosanquet concerning the ugly and ugliness. Let us begin with the dynamic pantheism of Plotinean philosophy.

" As necessarily as there is Something after the First," writes Plotinus, " so necessarily there is a Last: this Last is Matter, the thing which has no residue of good in it: here is the necessity of Evil." [69] Being and those beyond being are good and among neither can evil have a place. Plotinus suggests that evil may be an image of being or perhaps something still further removed than an image.[70] He envisages the possibility that it may be " absolute formlessness," below " all patterns, forms, shapes, measurements, and limits."

What, then, of the relation of formless matter, " the necessity of Evil," to the One, whose perfection does not permit grudging

no title to the name of Being. It will be more plausibly called a non-being, and this in the sense . . . of veritable Not-Being . . . a bare aspiration towards substantial existence . . . a phantasm unabiding and yet unable to withdraw—not even strong enough to withdraw, . . . so absolute its lack of All Being."

[66] *Confessions,* XII, Ch. 8. Compare *Ad Orosium,* 1.2 and *De Div. Quaest.,* 83. See Gilson, *Introduction à L'Étude de St. Augustin,* pp. 253 ff.

[67] *Ad Orosium,* 1.2.

[68] *De Diversis Quaestionibus,* 83, q. 22: " Ubi nulla indigentia nulla necessitas, ubi nullus defectus, nullus indigentia. Nullus autum defectus in Deo: nullo ergo necessitas."

[69] *Enneads,* 1.8.7.

[70] *Ibid.,* 1.8.3. Cf. Wolfson's *Philo,* I, 301.

and whose nature requires generation, even though "the offspring is always minor"? [71] To ask this question is to inquire concerning the One's responsibility for both evil and ugliness.[72] Plotinus' reply is implicit in his statement of the fundamental philosophical question: "From such a unity as we have declared The One to be, how does anything at all come into substantial existence, any multiplicity, dyad, or number?" [73] There is offered first the famous answer that what we are "to conceive as rising in the neighborhood of that immobility" must be "a circumradiation—produced from the Supreme but from the Supreme unaltering—and may be compared to the brilliant light encircling the sun and ceaselessly generated from that unchanging substance." [74] There is, indeed, ugliness in this world; but this cosmos may not be condemned as less than beautiful.[75]

The reason immediately offered for this lack of ground for condemnation and the assertion that the cosmos "stands as a stately whole, complete within itself," is of significance for aesthetic. The basic issue is, however, God's freedom. Divergent answers have been given to the question, to what extent is the One free? [76] No small part of the difficulty in evaluating

[71] *Ibid.*, 5.1.6.

[72] It should be noted that, in contrast to St. Augustine's views, Plotinus holds that the universe exists eternally, insisting upon "the utter absence of a beginning to it." (*Enneads*, 3.2.1.) The cosmos is subsequent to "the providence ruling in the Universe as a universal consonance"; but it is "subsequent not in time but in fact of derivation." (*ibid.*) It should also be noted that, as Plato's demiurge forms the world, so for Plotinus "the Divine Intelligence, preceding it in Kind, is its cause as being the Archetype and Model which it merely images, the primal by which, from all eternity, it has existence and subsistence."

[73] *Enneads*, 5.1.6.

[74] *Ibid.*, 5.1.6.

[75] *Enneads*, 3.2.3. Cf., "No charge can be laid against its source . . . if a considered plan brought it into being it would still be no disgrace to its maker."

[76] See Whittaker, *The Neo-Platonists*, p. 77, E. Bréhier, *La Philosophie de Plotin*, pp. 40, 177 ff., P. Henry, "La Problème de la liberté chez Plotin," *Rev. Néoscolastique*, XXXIII (1931) and "Néoplatonisme Grec.," *Rev. de Met. et de morale* XXVI (1919).

Plotinus' answer derives from the ambiguity, persistent in Alexandrian philosophy, that God is transcendent, while philosophers yet affirm predicates of him. [77] This Philonic heritage is, in turn, complicated by the influence of Stoicism, more particularly by the Stoic assumption that purposiveness and mechanism are not incompatible. Plotinus does maintain that there is necessity in the operation of natural law for the cosmic process —and here we do well to recall Plato's insistence that the laws of nature could not be upset by God.[78] Thus, the " Kosmos of Parts " comes into being by " sheer necessity." Plotinus adds that this universe is not intelligence and reason but ". . . the meeting ground of Necessity and Divine Reason." [79] He formulates the problem clearly enough,[80] maintaining that neither automatic activity nor chance will account for the existence and coherent structure of this universe. Rather, we are told, " since we hold the eternal existence of the Universe, the utter absence of a beginning to it, we are forced, in sound and sequent reasoning, to explain the providence ruling in the Universe as a universal consonance with the divine Intelligence . . . .[81] As we have noted, Plotinus holds that the cosmos is subsequent not in time but in fact of derivation.[82] In this sense, the divine Intelligence is the cause of the cosmos as its archetype and model. This model it merely " images."

[77] See *Enneads*, 2.9.1: " When we speak of The One and when we speak of the Good we must recognize an Identical Nature; we must affirm that they are the same—not, it is true, as venturing any predication with regard to that (unknowable) Hypostasis but simply as indicating it to ourselves in the best terms we find."

[78] See above, Ch. II, pp. 72 ff. Compare *Enneads*, 3.1.10: " To sum up the results of our argument:—All things and events are fore-shown and brought into being by causes; but the causation is of two Kinds; there are results originating from the Soul and results due to other causes, those of environment."

[79] The problem is, as we have seen, how the One makes the universe existent. The explanation offered is in terms of emanations, i. e., by the overflow from the One and by the introduction of intermediate entities. *Nous* it is that actually brings the cosmos into being.

[80] *Enneads*, 3.2.1.

[81] *Ibid.*, 3.2.1.

[82] See above, Ch. III, p. 98.

Within this framework, Plotinus, in the first treatise on Providence, formulates the alternative possibilities: " the denial of any controlling power " or " the belief that the Kosmos is the work of an evil creator." [83] The first possibility is ruled out on grounds inherited from the necessity and rationality explicit in the Platonic theory of demiurgic making. The argument against the alternative is made in terms of a direct attack upon the Gnostics, on the ground that the latter have introduced a plurality of intellectual essences.[84] Gnosticism would make " the world one of the Primals, and with it the Matter from which it emerges." [85] To accept the Gnostic notion would mean, according to Plotinus, that evil would antedate the world and we should be obliged to admit evil in the One.

Having ruled out the possibility that either such a plurality of intellectual essences or that chance opposes the creative process, while yet granting that evil and ugliness are present in the cosmos, Plotinus accounts for their existence in the world in terms of what impedes the overflowing goodness of the One in producing the world. He does this, both for cosmic and artistic making, in terms of that " prefigured Matter," upon which the productive forms in both cosmos and art operate.

Matter, as we have observed, is neither space nor place. Rather, it is the indeterminate; [86] it is nonbeing; [87] and it is correctly called evil.[88] Inasmuch as evil and ugliness are identical and may be examined by the same method,[89] matter is also

[83] *Enneads,* 3.2.1.

[84] *Ibid.,* 2.9.5; compare 2.9.12 and 2.9.13.

[85] *Ibid.,* 2.9.12.

[86] Matter is " indetermination needing The First to its determination." *Enneads,* 2.4.5.

[87] *Ibid.,* 3.6.7: " It lives on the farther side of all these categories and so has no title to the name of Being. It will be more plausibly called a non-being, and this in the sense . . . of veritable Not-Being . . . a bare aspiration towards substantial existence . . . a phantasm unabiding and yet unable to withdraw—not even strong enough to withdraw, . . . so absolute its lack of Being."

[88] *Ibid.,* 3.6.12.

[89] *Enneads,* 1.6.6. Cf. *ibid.,* 3.6.11. Compare Baeumker, *Das Problem der Materie,* p. 415.

correctly called ugly. In calling it evil, "we are right only if we mean that it is not amenable to modification by The Good; but that means simply that it is subject to no modification whatever." [90]

The differing characterizations of matter as nonbeing, as indetermination, and as evil which Plotinus employs, lay his philosophy open to charges of terminological inconsistency. Yet, the ostensible inconsistency is actually the outgrowth of the fact that the problem of matter and ugliness is approached metaphysically. Had matter been an issue to be considered in terms of the One beyond predication and of the "prefiguration" of that which is beyond determination, the use of the term "nonbeing" would have sufficed. The changing world is, however, both a fact and a problem, the latter to be resolved cosmologically in terms of intervenient emanations, aesthetically in terms of the microcosmic artist, his art, and the product of his art in processes analogous to the cosmic ones.

Our principal interest is the analogy between *nous*, the second hypostasis of the Plotinean system and the locus of the Platonic ideas, and the artist who practises his art. We may dismiss the relation of the One and matter, i. e., the relation which gives rise to the notions that matter is nonbeing and that ugliness, like evil, is simply defectiveness. These notions are merely correlative to those in the theory of absolute creativity and freedom which assert that there are absolutely beautiful objects and events. Such absolute power is incompatible with ugliness or its existence. It is consistent with the notion that there is a form of knowing, namely, inspiration, which transcends rationality and it rightly asserts that there is a return and procession to the source of all things, the One.

As the problem is considered in the cosmological and in the artistic realms, Plotinus asks, "But why does the existence of the Principle of Good necessarily comport the existence of a Principle of Evil?" [91] The question is answered in the sugges-

[90] *Enneads*, 3.6.11.
[91] *Enneads*, 1.8.7.

tion that " the All " is made up of contraries and " could not exist if Matter did not." The nature of the cosmos is " a blend "; what comes into it from God is good; from underlying matter, " not yet brought to order by the Ideal-Form " comes evil and ugliness. In cosmological terms, the ugly is the consequence of a conflict of contraries.[92] It is to be understood in terms of the dual facts that *nous* makes the world and that in *nous* are the Platonic ideas. Neither in Platonic nor Neoplatonic theory can evil or ugliness be accounted for by reference to ideas which are evil or ugly: neither " the repulsive " nor " the products of putridity " have their idea.[93] Moreover, compounds are not included under ideas and Plotinus' aesthetic theory is a study of compounded objects, i. e., objects compounded of form and matter.

The analogy between *nous* and the artist is clear. It is " in virtue of the form or idea introduced by art " [94] that the block of marble becomes beauty and this form or idea " is in the designer before ever it enters the stone." [95] It must be emphasized that the artist achieves in Plotinus' philosophy an incomparably greater freedom than does the technical artist in Plato's speculation. In part, this is owing to the context of the philosophy in which the subject is treated. For Plotinus, " the One . . . has overflowed, and its exuberance has produced the new." [96] More specifically, the arts do not give a bare reproduction of the thing seen.[97] They go back to " the Ideas from

[92] Compare Chrysippus' theory of evil, as given by Aulus Gellius (quoted by P. E. More, *The Religion of Plato*, p. 235) : " Nothing is more utterly blind and stupid than those who think that goods could exist if there were not also evils in the world. For as goods are the contrary of evils, it is necessary that both should exist together, each supporting the other by a kind of mutual resistance."

[93] *Enneads*, 5.9.14; compare Plato, *Parmenides*, 130.

[94] *Enneads*, 5.8.1.

[95] *Ibid.*, See Whittaker, *Neo-Platonism*, p. 92: " The arts themselves—which as creative ideas are in the soul of the artist—have a beauty surpassing that of the works that proceed from them."

[96] *Ibid.*, 5.2.1.

[97] *Ibid.*, 5.8.1.

which Nature itself derives." Moreover, Plotinus argues the autonomy of the arts and power to improve upon nature.[98] The freedom of the artist is rationality in technique.[99]

The measure of the artist's freedom for Plotinus is evident, as we contrast this analysis of rational technique with that of Plato's speculation. For Plato, as we have seen, the artist is free only to produce a specious novelty; his technique produces imitations twice removed from reality; his freedom is got only by inspiration which transcends art.[100] But if Plotinus' conception of an artist, whose free creative powers operate as ideas by means of technique, indicates an increase in artistic freedom, it is nonetheless true that the artist's freedom is not omnipotence. And it is precisely within the limitations of the autonomy of the art's creative power that Plotinus offers his theory of an ugliness, which, *ex hypothesi,* is ineradicable.

The measure of Plotinus' contribution to the notion of the artist as creator is in part got by examining the way in which the cosmic and artistic analogy is developed in the study of ugliness, in part by the awareness of an autonomous freedom implicit in his knowledge of the work of art. It is creative freedom gained through knowledge of the necessity imposed by matter which provides in each instance the ground for the Plotinean answer to the problem of ugliness. The principle is stated in the tractate on Providence: "Evil by definition is a falling short in good, and good cannot be at full strength in this Sphere where it is lodged in the alien: the good here is in something else, in something distinct from the Good, and this something else constitutes the falling short for it is not good." [101]

It is in consequence of this interpretation that Plotinus maintains that evil is ineradicable. He offers two reasons for the fact: the first, that "thing will always stand less than thing";

[98] *Ibid.* "They are holders of beauty and add where nature is lacking."

[99] *Ibid.* "Pheidias wrought the Zeus upon no model among things of sense but by apprehending what form Zeus must take if he chose to become manifest to sight."

[100] See above, Ch. I, p. 42.

[101] *Enneads,* 3.2.5.

secondly, that "all things come into being through it [the Good], and are what they are by standing away from it." [102] In terms of the cosmos, this means for Plotinus that it is not sound to condemn the cosmos "as less than beautiful, as less than the noblest possible in the corporeal," [103] nor may one justly condemn the source of the cosmos for the latter's lack of beauty. In support of this, Plotinus abandons the ateleological hypothesis which explains the metaphysical relation of the One and matter. In explaining the cosmos, a pseudo-teleology is employed, reminiscent of Plato's theory, in a system which replaces explicit demiurgic making by dynamic emanations.[104]

In the world, "to linger about the parts is to condemn not the Kosmos but some isolated appendage of it" and "in the entire living Being" to "fasten our eyes on a hair or a toe [to neglect] the marvellous spectacle of the complete Man." So, too, by analogy of the artist to *nous*, the creative artisan converts the necessity of working upon material into a positive value. Plotinus argues that not everything is as good as anything can be. Reason wills things as they are and "in its reasonable act" produces "even what we know as evil." Sovereign reason cannot desire all that is good. Precisely as Plato urged that the sculptor need not make all the parts of the statue beautiful in order to produce a beautiful statue,[105] so "an artist would not make an animal all eyes." [106] Should we ask that the world be otherwise,

---

[102] *Ibid.*, 3.2.5.

[103] *Ibid.*, 3.2.3.

[104] *Ibid.* "The world . . . if a considered plan brought it into being . . . would still be no disgrace to its maker." That world is "a stately whole, complete within itself, serving at once its own purpose and that of all its parts which, leading and lesser alike, are of such a nature as to further the interests of the total." The passage continues in a vein reminiscent of Plato: "It is therefore impossible to condemn the whole on the merits of the parts which, besides, must be judged only as they enter harmoniously or not into the whole, the main consideration, quite overpassing the members which thus cease to have importance."

[105] *Republic*, IV. 420.

[106] *Enneads*, 3.2.11.

> we are like people ignorant of painting, who complain that the colours are not beautiful everywhere in the picture: but the Artist has laid on the appropriate tint to every spot. Or we are censuring a drama because the persons are not all heroes but include a servant and a rustic and some scurrilous clown; yet take way the low characters and the power of the drama is gone; these are part and parcel of it.[107]

Within the pattern of Plotinus' philosophy, the hypothesis of power and of goodness, potential in the One and exercised without grudging, includes the theory of the artist as a creator in relation to matter. With reference to the teleology of the cosmos and of art, ugliness is necessary for the beautiful. The contrast of contraries contributes to the work of art. The echo of this recurs both in Croce's and Bosanquet's aesthetic. For Plotinus, by analogy, the " ordinance of art " must, like that " ordinance of the Kosmos," be in keeping with the intellectual principle as " expression of its essential being." The reason-principle which emanates from the One " sets up a conflict of part against part " and " at war with itself in the parts which it now exhibits, it has the unity, or harmony of a drama torn with struggle." [108] The comparison is to a harmony emerging directly " from the conflicting elements themselves." It is this conflict which again echoes in Croce's theory, converted into a conflict of values. For Plotinus, the issue is made specific by reference to music, in which tones, high and low, are the product of the rational principles which meet in the " unit of Harmony." In the universe at large we similarly find " contraries "; but while its members everywhere clash, the total being is the manifestation of the rational principle.

As Croce discovers in matter the ground for passivity and brutality, so Plotinus similarly finds in it the ground for evil. So too, for Bosanquet, ugliness becomes a form of pretense and a lack of integrity. In Plotinus' thought, the ground is prepared for this intrusion of the moral into the artistic realm, with the

[107] *Ibid.*, 3.2.14.
[108] *Ibid.*, 3.2.16.

consequence that in interpreting ugliness he employs a double analogy, that between the artist and God and that between evil and ugliness. Plotinus specifies the problem of power in relation to matter in terms of good by urging that the evil in the "single Soul will stand a good thing in the universal system; what in the unit offends nature will serve nature in the total event." [109] Freedom, both of the creator and the man of action, is postulated as a requirement:

> If man were all of one piece—I mean, if he were nothing more than a made thing, acting and acted upon according to a fixed nature—he could be no more subject to reproach and punishment than the mere animals. But as the scheme holds, man is singled out for condemnation when he does evil; and this with justice. For he is no mere thing made to rigid plan; his nature contains a Principle apart and free.[110]

St. Augustine's philosophy of art is primarily Neoplatonic. What does it contribute to the notion of the artist as creator in the "great analogy," in its specific reference to freedom and ugliness? That ugliness is interpretable, as has been observed above, as the appearance of evil is a proposition difficult to evaluate in the context in which Augustine offers it. It would appear to be a natural development of the converse of Plato's theory that of all ideas that of beauty is the most evident in the realm of sight and hearing.[111] Again, perhaps the best known suggestion made by Augustine concerning ugliness follows from the assumption that, had no one sinned, "the world would have been filled and beautified with natures good without exception."[112] Augustine maintains that although the sinful will violated the order of its own nature, it did not on that account escape the laws of God. But

> . . . as the beauty of a picture is increased by well-managed shadows, so, to the eye that has skill to discern it, the universe

[109] *Enneads,* 3.2.17.
[110] *Ibid.,* 3.3.4.
[111] See *Phaedrus,* 250.
[112] *The City of God,* XI, 23.

is beautified even by sinners, though, considered by themselves, their deformity is a sad blemish.

Yet this is, as regards the need for shadows in the perfection of a picture, an echo of Plotinus' words in the *Enneads*.[113]

Indeed, to suggest that St. Augustine did contribute to the theory of ugliness in any other sense than to transmit Neoplatonic theory of art would appear to ignore his conviction that the Platonists were the greatest of philosophers, that he destroyed his writing called *de Apto et Pulchro*, and that his writings on the subject belong to that earlier period of his speculation, in which the influence of Neoplatonism was dominant. Yet it is precisely by taking cognizance of these facts that his novel contribution does become clear. It is the historical consequences of the Augustinean conception of individuality and personality, both of which initially affected the philosophy of history and ethics rather than aesthetics or philosophy of art, which eventually contribute to the notion of the artist as free creator and of his responsibility or lack of it for ugliness and the ugly. As Erich Frank has argued " the conception of personality is a necessary correlate to the conception of free will." [114]

We may ascertain the reasons for our difficulties in obtaining a precise differentiation of St. Augustine's own writings from those of Neoplatonism concerning freedom and ugliness and, at the same time, some notion of the grounds for the historical development of freedom implicit in personality and individu-

[113] *Enneads*, 3.2.11: " We are like people ignorant of painting who complain that the colours are not beautiful everywhere in the picture . . . ."

[114] " St. Augustine and Greek Thought," p. 9. Frank argues, (*ibid.* pp. 8–9), that Greek philosophy held that " the soul had been torn away from its original union with God," that " this separation, the *principium individualitatis*, was considered as the original sin," and that " to atone for it, the soul became incarcerated in the body as a prison again and again. Man's morality consisted in the attempt to shake off his corporeal individuality by fighting against the body and its senses in order to transsubstantiate himself into pure and divine Reason." Frank argues that Augustine claimed that the human body and the sensible world in general " cannot be evil, since they were created by God " and that man's sin, for Augustine, " no longer consisted in his being a definite

ality, by referring principally to two points, to his conception of man and matter.[115] Plotinus holds that " the embodied lives by virtue of a Form or Idea: individual or partial things exist by virtue of Universals." [116] Man is a microcosm of the world which is rational in consequence of its making by *nous*. For St. Augustine, man is created by God in the image of God.[117] Augustine hints that man's efforts are creative.[118] And the hint is the stronger in the light of the analogy of evil and ugliness, inasmuch as man does have free will.

The significant point is, however, that St. Augustine believes that God created the world by an act of will [119] and that He creates matter.[120] The world is made of " a formless matter, which matter, out of nothing." Evil is deficiency [121] and the corruption of beauty is ugliness." Augustine's view is not wholly consistent; [122] but he is consistent in maintaining that, while

individual or in his body, but rather in the rebellion of his personal will against the will of God . . . in his being attached to the objects of creation instead of being attached to the Creator."

[115] See *supra*, Ch. II, pp. 74 ff.

[116] *Enneads*, 3.2.4.

[117] *De Trinitate*, XIV, Ch. xii, 16: " There is, then, a nature not made, which made all other natures . . . and is without doubt more excellent than those which it has made, than . . . the mind of man, made after the image of Him who made it." (*Select Library* . . . , Vol. III)

[118] ". . . Thou hadst subjected to me what Thou createdst beneath me. And this was the true temperature and middle region of my safety, to continue in Thine image . . . ." (*Confessions*, VII, Ch. vii, 11). Emanuel Chapman, *St. Augustine's Philosophy of Beauty*, p. 77, interprets the passage to mean that " the artist continues the image [of God] in a special way, and in a certain manner art may be said to be the highest natural likeness of the activity of God . . . through the illumination of art man can engender works in his own image which resemble God."

[119] " Quia voluit, fecit," *Ad Orosium*, 1.2.

[120] *Confessions*, XII, Ch. viii; compare *Ad Orosium*, 1.2 and *De Div. Quaest.*, 83. See Gilson, *Introduction à L'Étude de St. Augustin*, pp. 253 ff.

[121] *Contra Epistolam Manichaei*, Ch. 35–40 (arranged): " The whole of that which is called evil is . . . corruption; . . . Whatever is corrupted is deprived of some good; . . . Corruption does harm only as displacing the natural condition; . . . whatever tends to decrease tends to non-existence; . . . what is non-existent is nothing . . . in any corporeal thing, the corruption of beauty is ugliness."

[122] Matter is the principle of change and the receptacle of forms (*De Genesis*

God creates *ex nihilo* and so creates matter, the artist does not create but forms matter already created.[123] The distinction obviously turns on the conception of God's will, held to be a free act.[124] Some indeed deny that God is omnipotent. Augustine writes of those who " affirm that there is a nature which God Almighty did not create, but of which at the same time He fashioned this world." [125] The controversy arises because there are those who deny that God is almighty reason " from their carnal familiarity with the sight of craftsmen and house-builders, and artisans of all descriptions, who have no power to make good the effect of their own art unless they get the help of materials already prepared." In drawing the distinction from this between the " formed " and the " formable," he emphasizes the assertion that " God made all things from nothing." [126]

In the inferences drawn from the distinction between God and the artist, St. Augustine's philosophy appears to repeat the Neoplatonic theory of the ugly as defect in a metaphysical sense. In both philosophies, there would appear to be, for art, an ineradicable element of matter and, therefore, of ugliness, precisely as this notion persists in Bosanquet's phrase, " invincible ugliness." Only in so far as the artist may employ the ugly to produce the beautiful whole, does he seem powerful enough to overcome the bondage of his craft to matter.[127]

contra Manich., I.7, 11; *De Gen. ad Litt.*, 1, 14, 28). It is also nonexistent (*De dive sis quaest.* 83, q. 54). Matter does not exist prior to things in time but it precedes forms in terms of causality. Also, matter is nonexistent as regards God's responsibility for evil, it is existent " non omnino nihil " in terms of its relations to forms and the informing process.

[123] *Confessions*, XI, 5. " For it was not as a human worker fashioning body from body . . . he assigns to it already existing, and as it were having a being, a form, as clay, or stone, or wood, or gold, or such like."

[124] *De Diversis quaest.*, 83, q. 22: " Ubi nulla indigentia, nulla necessitas; ubi nullus defectus, nulla indigentia. Nullus autem defectus in Deo: nulla ergo necessitas."

[125] *De Fide et Symbolo*, II, 2. (*Select Library* . . .) Compare J. Maritain, *Art and Scholasticism*, pp. 63–64.

[126] Augustine, *ibid.*, II, 2. God " made out of nothing the things which he did make."

[127] The problem in Augustine's theory of beauty is complicated by the theory

With the largely Neoplatonic conclusion concerning the ugly, St. Augustine apparently was content. His principal interest in freedom is brought forth by the problems of free will and predestination. The main content of the analogy between God and man lay, not between God and the artist, but between God and the saint, whose freedom is described as the inability to sin. Yet, the pages of modern aesthetic theory develop the Augustinean interpretations of the implications of Platonism for man's freedom and for the problem of ugliness,[128] as well as the " great analogy " of which these problems are a part. We learn that God is not good; [129] that God is good but not omnipotent; [130] that God is good but that evil is not what it seems to be; that God is good but that evil is a necessary condition for the good of the whole and for our knowledge of the good.

There can be little question that the Platonic treatment of the question of the ugly and of ugliness was sustained and transmitted within the tradition of creativity and making in the speculation, partly theological, partly moral, which elaborated Neoplatonism in Italy.[131] Augustine and Dionysius the Areopagite are the " most famous exponents " of the mystic tradi-

of " natural illumination." See Chapman, *op. cit.*, p. 77, where it is remarked that " all art depends on the natural illumination of art," which is explained in the following terms (p. 61): " The mind which is variable is submitted to the immutable and necessary regulative ideas. The immediate intuition of these forms is called illumination." In the light of the divine illumination, the mind makes its judgment, which " has the character of oughtness and necessity." Chapman argues that " error is in the judgment when it is of a part only and not of the whole object," and " Measure, form, and order are said to be bad when they are inferior to that which they should be, or when they are applied to objects where they do not agree, or when applied inharmoniously." The reference is to *De Vera Relig.*, XXXVI, 66.

[128] The reader's attention is drawn, not only to Croce and Bosanquet, but to Dessoir, Volkelt, Schlegel, Hegel, Lipps, and Dessoir. See B. Bosanquet, *A History of Aesthetic*, especially pp. 301 and 338. See also Listowel's *A Critical History of Modern Aesthetics*, pp. 270–72.

[129] Schopenhauer and von Hartman.

[130] Kant.

[131] Nesca A. Robb, *Neoplatonism of the Italian Renaissance*, p. 17 ff. on the relations of Italian speculation to that of Alexandria, as well as the influence of Cassiodorus and St. Isidore of Seville.

tion in Alexandrian philosophy which affected the artists and writers of the Renaissance.[132] In Dionysius' *On the Divine Names,* the good is celebrated " as beautiful and as Beauty." [133] " The absolutely Evil is neither existing nor good, nor generative, nor productive of things being and good." [134] The analogy between evil and ugliness is accepted and developed.[135]

It would be erroneous to conclude that the scholars of the Renaissance did not alter the theory of the ugly which had its origin in Platonic and Alexandrian philosophies. Other influences, notably that of the Aristotelian theory of art,[136] affected them, as did the naturalist tradition [137] of Alexandrian interpretation. Aside from such external influences, however, their own speculative ventures led to altered interpretations. To cite but one illustration, Leone Ebreo, in the *Dialogues of Love,* one

[132] *Ibid.,* pp. 17–18.

[133] *Op. cit.,* trans. John Parker, sec. VII, p. 39.

[134] *Ibid.,* sec. XX, p. 55. Cf. sec. XXI, pp. 59–60.

[135] Sec. XXVII, p. 65: ". . . neither is the Evil in bodies. For deformity and disease are a defect of form, and a deprivation of order. And this is not altogether an evil, but a less good; for if the dissolution of beauty and form and order become complete, the body itself will be gone."

[136] See *infra,* the present chapter, pp. 115 ff.

[137] Robb, *op. cit.,* pp. 17–18, on the influence of Avicenna. The curious mixture of Biblical and philosophical sources is perhaps sufficiently illustrated by Pico della Mirandola's statement in " On the Dignity of Man " (trans. by Elizabeth Livermoore Forbes, *Renaissance Philosophy of Man,* p. 224) : " God the Father, the supreme Architect, had already built this cosmic home we behold, the most sacred temple of His godhead, by the laws of His mysterious wisdom. The region above the heavens He had adorned with Intelligences, the heavenly spheres He had quickened with eternal souls, and the excrementary and filthy parts of the lower world He had filled with a multitude of animals of every kind. But, when the work was finished, the Craftsman kept wishing that there were someone to ponder the plan of so great a work, to love its beauty, and to wonder at its vastness. Therefore, when everything was done (as Moses and Timaeus bear witness) , He finally took thought concerning the creation of man. But there was not among His archetypes that from which He could fashion a new offspring, nor was there in His treasurehouses anything which He might bestow on His new son as an inheritance . . . . At last the best of artisans ordained that the creature to whom He had been able to give nothing proper to himself should have joint possession of whatever had been peculiar to each of the different kinds of being . . . ."

of the most influential of Neoplatonic writings, remarks of matter that " Chaos . . . must have existed without form before the creation of the world: for the presence of form in the world proves that it was created in time and made anew, while the formlessness or stuff of which it is made proves, not a temporal beginning, but age-old eternity." [138] He holds that the good is being, the bad privation, but adds that, although there is a mean between the beautiful and the ugly, there is none between absolute good and evil, having already declared that the beautiful and the good are not identical and that not everything that is not beautiful is ugly.[139]

Speculation like Leone Ebreo's concerning the beautiful and the ugly is both valuable and interesting. It forms part of the tradition of the " great analogy." Yet, it is clear that what novelty it displays derives solely from its intricacy as metaphysical speculation. Historically, it is of interest because one may so clearly discern in it and in its variants the metaphysical materials which come to be for Croce the basis of aesthetic theory, namely, that there is no ugly but only degrees of ugliness. This assertion of the artist's freedom by Croce is a declaration of complete artistic freedom, to which not even matter is opposed. Historically, it is the correlative to the theory of absolute beauty, integral to the theory of art as expression. Both are the consequences of a theory of power, divine or mortal.

The puzzle in the theory of the ugly and of ugliness in its context of freedom is not presented by Croce's denial that there is absolute ugliness. The explanation of this aesthetic inference is discovered in the fact that there is a clear prototype of the issue involved in the history of speculation concerning the relation of God the creator to matter. On the other hand, there remains a genuine puzzle in speculation concerning absolute

[138] *Op cit.*, p. 284. Cf., p. 283. (I have used Friedeberg-Seeley and Barnes' translation of the *Dialoghi di Amore, The Philosophy of Love.* For Leone Ebreo and his relation to the Neoplatonic movement, see Karl Gebhardt's edition.)

[139] *Ibid.*, p. 256. See also, pp. 429–30.

ugliness which derives from the conception of the demiurge in relation to matter. This is amply illustrated in Bosanquet's philosophy of art. It is evident, so long as matter is judged to be beyond analysis or remains unanalyzed in terms of medium, structure, technique, or symbols, it will be dealt with as if its sole interest were in the locus of a something or a nothing related to God or the artist as an abstract problem. The issue can then be one of negation or privation or deficiency; but no very interesting possibilities for analysis in terms of ugliness will present themselves.

In this sense, Bosanquet is certainly correct in his conclusion that what has "no expressive form by which it embodies anything is 'nothing.'" It is interesting, however, that while he does maintain systematically that "externality . . . is a sign and vehicle of spiritual achievement" and that, in aesthetic terms, there is "invincible ugliness,"—both points being implicit in the theory of making—he proceeds no farther. As a historian of aesthetic, he is well aware of the analyses of media or plasticity, of signs and symbols, and of feeling which a tradition less closely allied to the analogy of the artist to God had substituted for the monolithic tradition which associated the ugly with matter as such. Bosanquet urges that modern speculation upon aesthetic begins when Lessing deduces the distinction between poetry and painting "from the nature of their respective media." [140] He sees clearly the significance of Aristotle's remark in *Poetics* that delight in imitation may extend to objects which are "painful to see" [141] and that we "delight to view

[140] *A History of Aesthetic,* p. 223.

[141] *Ibid.,* pp. 57–59. It should further be remarked, in the elucidation of the conception of the ugly, that Aristotle is arguing the problem in terms of the aesthetic pleasure of learning and that an ugly thing is transformed from a mere object or event by means of technique into a sign or symbol in the material of art. It should further be remarked that the process of symbolization results from the artist's practice of technique and that by means of technique the idea in the craftsman's mind is transferred to other objects or media, in which it is recognizable as what the artist intended the object or event to signify, i. e., his interpretation of it. This is to suggest again the notion of freedom of choice in the Aristotelian system. It should be noted that Aristotle

the most realistic representations of them in art, the forms for example of the lowest animals and of dead bodies." Bosanquet urges that "the fascination of ugliness in representative art was a newly observed phenomenon . . . . Not the content of the likeness, but something, whatever it might be, involved in the fact of its being a likeness at all, was thus suggested to be the secret of its attraction." It should be pointed out, also, that Bosanquet recognizes the value of Kant's similar suggestion that the "ugly is capable of being beautifully portrayed in art"[142] and, in writing of Kant's theory of the sublime, further remarks that "it was the true forerunner of all aesthetic theory which brings apparent ugliness within the frontier of beauty."[143]

As is suggested in these remarks upon Aristotle's and Kant's theories of the ugly, Bosanquet does begin by their means to analyze out of that monolithic matter the factors essential to a clear statement of the problem of the ugly in terms of technique,[144] media, and symbols. He does not, however, sufficiently emphasize the significant statement Kant makes concerning the impossibility of representing the ugliness associated with what excites disgust.[145] Yet, that he is well aware that feeling as well as media and symbols must be taken into account in a theory of ugliness is sufficiently indicated by his analysis of Lessing's *Laocöon*. He not only judges Lessing's distinction between poetry and painting "from the nature of their respective media" to constitute the beginning of modern speculation upon aesthetic but urges that "all beauty . . . is ultimately

rejects the demiurgic theory of making, although *Physics* 8, 199 a 8 is reminiscent of this process. And, finally, it seems likely that Aristotle avoids the difficulties inherent in the notion of the ugly as deficiency or privation simply because for him unformed matter is a privative notion, i. e., logically possible but ontologically impossible.

[142] *A History of Aesthetic*, p. 275.

[143] *Ibid.*, p. 275.

[144] See Kant's remark that it is the "representation" which makes the difference, *K.d.U.*, sec. 48, trans. Bernard, pp. 194–95, and, *ibid.*, p. 193: "A natural beauty is a *beautiful thing*; artificial beauty is a beautiful representation of a thing."

[145] *K.d.U.*, p. 195. Cf. *infra*, Ch. XI, pp. 294 ff.

expressiveness, and its substance and foundation falls away if the artist is not mastered by some burden or import for which he desires to find utterance." [146]

Bosanquet has suggested, in these historical analyses, the possibility of discovering the ground for ugliness by analysis of technique, expression of feeling, or significance and symbolization. Each may present a possible problem to be solved by the artist. Moreover, taken together as the whole work of art, another problem is presented. That Bosanquet should urge that there is " invincible ugliness " is consistent with this atomization of matter into its various artistic functions; that he should at the same time insist upon the complete freedom of the artist derives from the notion of the genius, rather than from that of the artist's omnipotence, as we shall see in the next chapter.

Croce's assertions that the ugly is nonexistent and that there are " degrees of ugliness " derive from considering the ugly as a function of matter, first in terms of passivity and defect, and secondly, in terms of the presumed analogy between evil and ugliness, which in its turn is derivative from the treatment of matter as the source of man's passivity and brutality. As we have observed, the assertions that the ugly is nonexistent and that there are absolutely beautiful objects or events created by artists endowed with unlimited freedom to produce original works of art are correlative. It would follow, in this interpretation of ugly, that no work of art could be ugly, should this proposition preclude the possibility that the object of art be made, expressed, signified, or formed.[147]

There is, however, another and quite different sense in which " the ugly " and " ugliness " are used with connotations of defectiveness and nonexistence. It is evident, for example, that the Augustinean theory of evil and ugliness is grounded in theory which must assert that value is both primitive and per-

[146] *A History of Aesthetic*, pp. 223, 227.

[147] That the absolute ugly has a meaning as a regulative principle will be argued later, Ch. XI, pp. 306 ff.

vasive. In consequence, the explanation of nonvaluable objects or events, whether they be evil or ugly, will necessarily be expressed in terms of defectiveness, i. e., as " turning away from the good," with the obvious implication that if value is ultimate as an existential hypothesis, defect may mean nonexistence or partial existence. It should be noted that this is precisely the ground for Croce's argument, in the aesthetic context, for the nonexistence of the ugly. Aesthetic is expression, the first moment of spirit. In contrast to passivity, which is grounded in matter, this first stage of spirit is activity and valuing.[148] In this sense, expression is temporally prior and opposed to what does not exist.

There is, however, another meaning of expression or intuition, which suggests a quite different interpretation for what, from the aesthetic point of view, is nonexistent. Croce maintains that there are not only primitive intuitions; we can also intuit, in terms of " the whole . . . which determines the quality of the parts." [149] A work of art " may be full of philosophical concepts," wherein " the total effect of the work of art is an intuition." It is in the latter sense, in which the emphasis is laid upon the temporal rather than upon the logical priority of intuition, that Croce argues, in the *Philosophy of the Practical,* that " the judgments that we give when we judge an action to be foolish or wicked, a statement false, a work of art ugly, are all metaphorical. In delivering them we do not mean to say that there is an *existence* called error, ugliness, foolishness, but only that there is a given existence and that another is wanting . . . but what is meant by the negative form of those judgments is that such an act is this and not another, that it is utilitarian and not moral, a commercial and not a literary or scientific fact, and so on." [150]

Now this situation resembles that which theorists of art as technique have examined, although Croce denies that art is

[148] See, however, the *Philosophy of the Practical,* pp. 195–205.
[149] *Aesthetic,* pp. 2–3.
[150] *Op. cit.,* pp. 202–03.

technique and, on the contrary, insists that it is imagination. Kant, who suggests that "beautiful art is the art of genius," [151] holds that it is superior to natural beauty precisely because "it describes as beautiful things which may be in nature ugly or displeasing," [152] a suggestion which brings within the context of genius the meaning of Aristotle's remark, concerning objects which are "painful to see." [153] But what Kant and Aristotle mean is not, however, what Croce maintains. For the former, the natural, the naturally ugly, or, indeed, the aesthetically neutral, may be made aesthetically valuable by means of technique. Aristotle, by way of illustration, compares the work of art to an organism, presumably meaning that an artist who employs the rational state of capacity to make produces an organic whole. For Croce, on the contrary, technical processes do not enter into the aesthetic evaluation of complex philosophical concepts in expression, so as to differentiate it from the evaluation of the expression of "primitive" impressions.[154] He denies the validity of such a contrast precisely on the grounds that what the artist does is not explicable in terms of the means-end relation. The artist's act of expression is, as we have seen, antecedent to such choosing as is implicit in the relating of means to ends.[155]

The differences here emphasized are fundamental to a differentiation of the theories of artistic creativity and making as they impinge upon the ugly. What Kantian and Aristotelian technical theory of art implies is perhaps best illustrated by analogy to the ethical distinction between motive and intention. The first term refers to the desired or desirable results of action, the second to all the foreseen results, including those not desired by the agent. A similar distinction may be made available to the philosophy of art. We may abstract from the context

[151] *Kritik of Judgment,* sec. 47, trans. Bernard, p. 192.

[152] *Ibid., sec.* 48, trans. Bernard, pp. 194–95.

[153] *Poetics,* 4.1448 b 10. Cf. *Rhetoric,* 11, 137 b. See above, n. 141.

[154] There is a quantitative distinction among expressions.

[155] See *Philosophy of the Practical,* pp. 195–205.

of the work of art that aspect upon which, we may assume, the artist proposed to concentrate his attention. Such would appear to be symbolism and technical expression in Michelangelo's "Last Judgment," expression without too great attention to technical perfection in Cezanne's "The Bathers," or technique in Cellini's "Perseus." We may assume, on the other hand, that the artist is in fact a creative genius and, therefore, omnipotent. The latter assumption may suggest that what he creates is instantaneously created or that he may employ with equal power all factors which enter into the structure of the work of art. Unless we proceed on one assumption or the other, we shall be forced to judge as defective precisely those aspects of the work of art which the artist has not intended to emphasize or which he could not perfect with the technical skill he displays in that aspect of the work of art which corresponds to the product of his motive, i. e., what he desires to produce in contrast to all of the foreseen consequences of his making. To argue, for example, that because Dali sacrifices intelligible or pleasing symbols to his enormous powers of draftsmanship and design, such paintings as "Soft Construction with Boiled Beans" or "The Persistence of Memory" are ugly may be simply to misunderstand the difference between what is lacking by intention or underemphasis and what is in fact ugly. It is meaningful to maintain that El Greco in producing "The Burial of the Count Orgaz" produced what he desired, i. e., the effect of otherworldliness, by intentional distortion. To argue that the distortion is ugly is an elliptical mode of expression. The basic point is that the artist produces a symbol, an expression, and a constructed medium in consequence of the conditions of his art. Defect is not a particularly significant clue to ugliness. It may be a clue to the artist's end of making. The alternative is a theory of "instantaneous creation," which, in fact, is suggested by the theory of the artist as creator, more particularly in those aspects of it dictated by the tradition of inspiration.

We come now to the analogy within the "great analogy,"

that between evil and ugly, of particular evils and ugliness. The shortest way with dissenters is to assert the need to judge an aesthetic object or event on aesthetic grounds and to substantiate the argument by making valid a distinction between making and acting. In the historical context, this has meant that evil implies "reference to the *will*," and is "properly referred to actions," [156] whereas making is an art, properly referred to objects and events. It has been argued, however, that there is, by implication, a moral requirement laid upon the artist to employ technique with integrity.[157] If the argument is valid, its validity is certainly established in the aesthetic integrity of the work of art, with such consequences as we have observed in Bosanquet's assumption that ugliness may derive in part from pretense and display itself in the work of art. [158] Disregarding the question whether in fact the artist's making is or is not action, we get to the root of the problem if we recall that actions may be represented or symbolized in sculpture, painting, and drama, as well as described in music and poetry. If we ask whether ugliness derives from the representation of evil actions, motives, intentions, and results, the answer is not unequivocal. It is evident, for example, that the figures of Lucifer, of Judas, of Satan, and of the Serpent in the morality plays were hideous and that they were both intended and expected to be. It is no less evident that there are many instances of ugliness which do not represent or symbolize evil. If Rodin's "La Vielle Heaulmiere" represents the appearance of "mala," his sculptured Balzac does not. Yet, if the former is ugly, certainly the latter is no less so. Quintin Metsys' "Portrait of Margarita of the Tyrol" represents an ugly woman, judged by some, indeed, to be the ugliest princess ever portrayed. The truth or falsity of this statement is, however, independent of whether or not Margarita is moral or immoral, a saint or a sinner. A like

[156] See for example, Abbott's *Kant's Theory of Ethics*, p. 151.

[157] J. Maritain, *Art and Scholasticism*, pp. 8, 11, *et passim*.

[158] "The root of ugliness," it will be recalled, lies in "the pretension to pure expression."

inference may be drawn concerning Velasquez' portrayals of court dwarfs.

These instances serve not only to underline the distinction between making and acting but also to emphasize the function of technique in representing. They serve to introduce, as well, the more general problem. Evil presents a moral or a theological issue. Such issues are, for aesthetic, specific instances of nonaesthetic signs. The general question posed is not whether evil is ugly. Rather, it is the problem, how nonaesthetic signs are made integral to works of art which in some instances are also works of fine art. It is this general problem which Aristotle and Kant offer to solve in terms of technique. Each, the first implicitly, the second explicitly, suggests that by means of craft the ugly or displeasing in nature may become pleasing or beautiful and, more specifically, that the evil, the painful, and the ugly in nature may be converted into objects or events of aesthetic value. This may result either from art serving as the technical means by which the artist brings the natural fact or event into the unity or whole of the work of art or from the acceptance of art as the precondition necessary for the proper use of the predicate, aesthetic.

It should be observed, in the first place, that in this respect evil occupies no unique status in aesthetic and, secondly, that it presents no unique problem. To answer the question how evil becomes beautiful or ugly in a work of art is in fact to ask what must be asked in each instance of the transformation of a nonaesthetic sign, object, or event into an aesthetic symbol. The problem is identical, whether the object, event, or sign derives from the philosophical, moral, logical, or religious fields.[159] The artist appears to recognize no *a priori* limitation on such signs, as is evidenced by Dante's selection of Ugolino, Picasso's of Guernica, or Joyce's of Mrs. Bloom.

If, then, the ugly and ugliness are explicable neither in terms of privation, defect, nor appearance of evil, the obvious possi-

[159] See M. C. Nahm, *Aesthetic Experience and Its Presuppositions*, Ch. v and x.

bility remains to be examined, namely, that they may be required, as Plotinus maintained, to provide artistic contrast and needed conflict. To adopt this explanation is, in fact, to recognize that the artist's freedom is conditioned by a plan or purpose or idea. It implies that within the limitations of the conditions laid upon his powers, the artist frees himself, converting what may be an actual impediment into a value. It recognizes the fact that the hideous and the evil may present a problem of greater degree of difficulty than do other nonaesthetic signs and objects or events.

In this context, too, we see more clearly the relevance of the analogue to motive and intention to which we have drawn attention. The artist must turn to his uses not only those aspects of media which he desires to use for results he intends. He is forced to employ those aspects of technique or signs which are presented by the task before him as brute fact and to employ them in terms of all the foreseen consequences of his making.

A no less significant inference to be drawn from the theory so well presented in ancient philosophy in terms of the contrast of light and shade, and one which philosophy of art came to interpret in terms of variety in unity, relates primarily to the theory of art as expression. Too great concentration upon a single natural referrent for the aesthetic object, a referrent which may be either aesthetically neutral or displeasing in its nonartistic state, may produce sufficient uneasiness to hinder or even destroy aesthetic experience. It is probable that this explains Kant's remark that disgust is a feeling impossible to represent. It may be that techniques employed to isolate signs which induce this feeling—and perhaps those of fear and rage—are significant less for indicating the difficulties presented for aesthetic depiction of the ugly than for demonstrating that signs for such feelings must be presented in company with other signs, techniques, or feelings. If so, one may infer that a precondition for aesthetic value is variety in unity.

This does not mean that the theory of variety in unity provides a definitive answer to the problems of the ugly and of ugliness.[160] The work of art as a whole is no less the object of judgment of fact than is the work of art as a more limited structure. Only if we are prepared to examine more fully the ugly, the sublime, the tragic, the comic, and the beautiful,[161] can we ascertain the place of the work of art as a whole in aesthetic evaluation.

At the beginning of this chapter, we suggested that the historical tradition of the ugly and of ugliness is rooted in the Platonic conception of a freedom for the maker conditioned by something, which history took to be matter, external to him. We have indicated, also, the Philonic-Augustinean tendency to interpret man's freedom by analogy to God's and to interpret it in terms of the denial of the existence of matter. We have observed the difficulties inherent in the notion that ugliness is defect, negation, or privation. The alternative, as we have suggested, is the historical assertion that ugliness is necessary for the conflict of contraries which produces the aesthetic object.

This, in its turn, raises the other important issue with which the " great analogy " of the artist's freedom has been concerned: the explanation of the fine artist as one who employs means to ends. This is a specification of the general problem of God's freedom as omniscience, implicit in Plato's philosophy in the relation of the demiurge to ideas which are external and eternal. The problem of the ugly and of ugliness leads directly, therefore, to that of the genius, the analogue to the divine creator and maker.

[160] For further discussion of the problem, see *infra,* Ch. VIII.
[161] See *infra,* Ch. IX and X.

4 The Genius

. . . it is, as it were, a fragment of Divinity.

SCHELLING

Kant maintains that genius is the talent for beautiful art.[1] He intends to emphasize the superiority of artificial beauty over natural beauty, and this he does by maintaining that the art of genius is superior precisely because it is able to describe as beautiful things which may be " in nature ugly or displeasing." [2]

For the historian of aesthetic, the collocation of concepts and problems explicit and implicit in these remarks is of extraordinary interest. In the first place, their context is a systematic account of judgment which, as Kant believed, " makes possible the transition from the realm of the natural concept to that of the concept of freedom," specifically applied to art.[3] Secondly, it is precisely in the art of genius that Kant locates the capacity to make the ugly identical with its contrary. The power attributed here to genius is one which, as was observed in the previous chapter, has added no little to the force of a tradition in which the artist's power and knowledge are implicitly or explicitly analogous to God's. Finally, as will be evident as we proceed, Kant's suggestion implies that the distinction between freedom to know and freedom to make, which arises in historical considerations of God's relation to ideas and matter, begins to blur once the conception of genius is elaborated and the problems of art are subjected to systematic and technical analysis.

Despite this convergence of ideas and problems, it is erroneous to interpret the genius solely or even principally by reference to the ugly, which speculation tended to consider the test

[1] *K.d.U.*, sec. 48, trans. Bernard, p. 193.
[2] *Ibid.*, pp. 194–95.
[3] *Ibid.*, Introduction, IX, p. 40.

of his most striking powers. For one school of philosophy of art, the genius is the maker of beautiful objects; for another, the producer of the sublime which transports men out of themselves. It is well to point out that these are not only classificatory but also value terms. Our present argument, however, is simply that such extensions of the meaning of the genius for an essay of the artist as creator are significant as they derive from the interpretation of the artist's freedom by analogy to God's in relation to ideas.

We have observed at length the interest of critics and philosophers in the presumed capacity of the poet and his fellow artists, once inspired, to go beyond the rules of art.[4] As we shall see, speculation in the eighteenth century, in which the notion of the genius was most interestingly investigated, came to concentrate upon the implication in the theory of inspiration that the poet could know without being trained or taught.[5] It converted the problem into a philosophical one when, having asked how the genius could execute works of beautiful art, it replied in the words of one of its poets that the genius has "the power of accomplishing great things without the means generally reputed necessary to that end." [6]

It is apparent that such a statement clarifies only to a limited extent terminology used by classical writers to account for originality got by divine inspiration. We do well, however, to make much of even such limited gains in clarity, as we shall discover upon being made aware of the facts which led one historian of aesthetic to pronounce upon the "cult of genius" with "attendant superstitions." [7] Such clarifications lead to or accompany a sharper delineation of basic problems. The ugly, for example, comes in this process to lose its theological cast and is judged correctly to be a problem of aesthetic types and

[4] See *supra*, Ch. I.
[5] Compare Plato in *Meno* and *Phaedo* and Longinus, *de Sublimitate*, II, 1.
[6] Edward Young, *Conjectures on Original Composition*, p. 49.
[7] See Croce, *Aesthetic*, p. 15.

values.[8] As the speculation concerning genius and its presumed powers continued, the abstract analogy of the fine artist to God underwent continued humanization and naturalization. Accompanying that process and owing to the persistent attention paid to the problems of originality and intelligibility, aesthetic proceeds directly from the notion of art as types to working hypotheses concerning techniques, generic and archetypal symbols, theories of feeling and imagination, as well as more detailed studies of forms, styles, and patterns.

While in these many and varied aspects of speculation, the abstract analogy of the fine artist to God was naturalized to art in the eighteenth century, two aspects of this process are especially significant for our present essay.[9] If objects and events such as the Greek temple at Segesta or Mozart's *Concerto No. 21* manifest in their uniqueness and display in their aesthetic value the fact of artistic originality and so of the artist's freedom, the suggestion that they are original has often implied that their makers are men whose stature does not permit them to be fitted comfortably into the categories which human beings make use of to classify and so to understand their fellows. One experiencing " birth in beauty " is easily led to accept the genius as unique. He may as readily accept as unique the event or object made, for reasons clearly implicit in the lines from Alexander Pope's *An Essay on Criticism*:

> In Poets as true genius is but rare,
> True Taste as seldom is the Critics share;
> Both must alike from Heav'n derive their light,
> These born to judge, as well as those to write.[10]

If the work of fine art escapes analysis in terms of the means-end relation because it is the product of genius, so, likewise, it is argued, does the judgment of that work of fine art. If the

[8] This is but one illustration of the contribution which the conception of genius has made to aesthetic speculation. As we shall see, it is closely related to the difficulty of classifying the fine arts, which in its turn pertains to problems of art's originality, intelligibility, and novelty.

[9] See above, Ch. I, pp. 15 ff.

[10] *Op. cit.*, lines 11 ff.

analogy of the fine artist to God centers the artist's freedom upon the relation of the creator to ideas as ends of making, we discover that omniscience is the central issue, regardless of whether the fine artist is freed from rules of technique or the critic from rules of criticism.

The background for these two central problems of genius in the eighteenth century may be sketched rapidly and amplified as need arises. As we shall observe, in the century itself, we discover at once a reaction against a misunderstood Aristotelianism in art and criticism, as well as the beginnings of a less dogmatic and traditional interpretation of Aristotle's own writings. We find, as well, a considerable body of literary and artistic criticism, principally of interest for this essay because it provided Kant with empirical data for his systematic account of aesthetic experience, of the judgment of taste, and of the artist as genius. And, finally, there is increasingly evident a naturalist approach to the problems of freedom in art.

The historical development of the conception of genius in modern times,[11] as it affected the period of our interest, may likewise be presented rapidly. Zilsel holds that the use of the word "genio" came about 1550 in the hands of the painter-engineers, Leonardo, Vasari, and Telesio, to carry both the connotations "creative" and "newly creative."[12] Panofsky remarks, however, that "Leonardo, the 'scientist,' would have been much surprised, and possibly somewhat offended, had anybody called him a 'genius'" and adds that "it was not until the middle of the sixteenth century that a great sculptor and painter, named Michelangelo, could be called 'divino,' and some more decades had to pass before the philosophers of Mannerism, such as Giovanni Paolo Lomazzo, could transform Ficino's theory of beauty, celestial influences and 'creative' ideas into a metaphysics of art."[13]

[11] Cf. *supra*, Ch. I, for account of the inspired poet.

[12] *Die Entstehung des Geniesbegriffes.*

[13] E. Panofsky, *Albrecht Dürer*, Vol. I, p. 282. Panofsky maintains, *ibid.*, pp.

By 1700, according to Lange-Eichbaum, the word " genius " had come to mean not only " the incomprehensible and mysterious creative force animating certain human beings," but also its principal earlier connotation came to be applied to " the individuals manifesting this force." [14] What has been called the " new theory of creative freedom in the arts," [15] incorporated in the conception of original genius, which may be traced through its common European inheritance in the history of the words " ingenious," " ingenio," " furor poeticus," and the notions of " wit " and " humours," is grounded on the religious notion of the inspiration, of the seer, and the prophet. But if, as is suggested, the notion of genius " never loses its religious sub-flavour," [16] this is principally owing to the hypostatization of creative and demiurgic freedom.[17]

We come upon the " religious sub-flavour " in the writings of men of all ages concerning the genius.[18] The primary difficulty is to determine the degree to which writers simply affect the

281–82, that it " was for Dürer—encouraged, perhaps, by Agrippa of Nettesheim, who . . . was the most important intermediary between Ficino and Germany, and who had already dared to include architects, painters and other ' craftsmen ' among those who may become inspired by the Saturnian ' furor melancholicus ' —to claim for artists what the Florentine Neo-Platonists had reserved for ' seers ' (' vates ') : the quality of genius." Compare Lange-Eichbaum, *The Problem of Genius*, pp. 6 ff., who follows Zilsel and maintains that " about 1650, in the baroque period, the notion of the genius assumed its modern stamp . . . ."

[14] W. Lange-Eichbaum, *The Problem of Genius*, pp. 6 ff.

[15] See Paul Kaufman's " Heralds of Original Genius " in *Essays in Memory of Barrett Wendell.* Kaufman holds that William Sharpe's *Dissertation on Genius*, published in 1755, is the first formulation of the conception of genius in its literary application.

[16] Lange-Eichbaum, *op. cit.*, p. 6.

[17] Cf. *supra*, Ch. I and *infra*, Ch. V and Ch. VI.

[18] The great instances are Plato, whose poet writes " not by wisdom alone " but by " genius and inspiration " and in whom there is no invention until he is " inspired " by God and " out of his senses "; Longinus, who writes that " other qualities prove their possessors men, sublimity lifts them near the mighty mind of God "; Edward Young, who holds that " Heaven will not admit of a partner in the accomplishment of some favorite spirits; but rejecting all human means, assumes the whole glory to itself . . . . Hence genius has ever been supposed to partake of something Divine "; and Shaftesbury, whose poet is " a second *Maker*; a just Prometheus under Jove."

terminology of religion. Whether, by way of illustration, Joseph Trapp expresses discontent with the conception of the inspired poet or with the terminology employed when he decries the "fables" and statements concerning that "Fire or more than human Impulse," with which the age appeared to distinguish the true poet from prosaic writers,[19] is a question less significant than is the fact that he writes at the time at which men were making the important methodological shift to analysis in terms of imagination.[20]

A later significant consequence of this shift is the lifting of the poet from the class of *vates* to that of man endowed with primitive epistemological powers.[21] The more immediate consequence, and indeed the core of the theory of genius, is the fact that while writers like Addison still speak of "creation," the "heralds of original genius" approach this analogue to the ancient controversy concerning God's relation to external ideas in terms of the artist's relation or nonrelation to means and ends. It is natural, in the context of the century's thinking, that Young should contrast the original, which "rises spontaneously from the vital roots of genius," [22] with imitations. And it should be noted that the latter are "often a sort of manufacture wrought up by those mechanics, art and labor, out of preexistent materials not their own." The central problem of genius is clear, however, once Young uses "spontaneously" to mean "accomplishing great things without the means generally reputed necessary to that end." [23]

[19] *Lectures on Poetry*, p. 32.

[20] See *supra*, Ch. I, pp. 7 ff.

[21] Cf. *infra*, Ch. V.

[22] *Conjectures on Original Composition*, pp. 45–46.

[23] Young's treatment of originality and means-end relation in conjunction is no isolated phenomenon in the eighteenth century. In 1748, William Jackson asks *Whether Genius be born, or acquired?* After describing genius as "a property of the soul," he proceeds to maintain not only that it is beyond the power of human art to give musicians invention but also that "no means which the knowledge and practice of the art can furnish, ever succeeded to give ear and genius, where nature denied them." (*Op. cit.*, pp. 186, 194) It should be noted that Jackson believes that genius must also have talents. Compare John

Croce, as we have noticed, denigrates the "cult of genius" and its attendant "superstitions." It is evident, however, that his assertion that expression "does not possess *means*, because it has not an end," [24] is a commonplace of speculation in the eighteenth century in which men were consciously or unconsciously expressing their own attitudes toward the great analogy of the artist to God. Nor were they all convinced that genius is, as their great precursor, Longinus, had maintained, "born, and does not come of teaching." [25] As the author of *de Sublimitate* had added that "some effects of natural genius alone can only be art," so writers like Alexander Gerard argue that it is judgment which reviews the plan formed by fancy. Gerard's remark that "every work of genius is a whole . . . so organized as to become altogether subservient to a common end," [26] differs from its modern demiurgic analogue in that Bosanquet, for example, does not believe it possible to argue that beauty is the end or aim of art.[27] Yet Gerard's fancy, which forms the plan, is not unlike the imagination, of which Bosanquet remarks that although you cannot lay down beforehand where the end or aim of art will take you, nevertheless "all the material and physical process which the artist uses . . . has been elaborated and refined, and, so to speak, consecrated by ages of adaptation and application in which it has been fused and blended with feeling . . . and that is how . . . feelings get their embodiment, and embodiments get their feeling."

The parallelism between the eighteenth-century theory of genius and contemporary theories of the fine artist is evident.

Pinkerton, *Letters on Literature*, No. 30, p. 207, who remarks that "Poetry knows no rules. The code of laws which Genius prescribes to his subjects, will ever rest in their own bosoms."

[24] *Aesthetic*, p. 112.

[25] *de Sublimitate*, II, 1–3.

[26] *An Essay on Genius*, p. 84. Gerard writes that "fancy could not have forced the regular plan of an epic poem . . . if judgement had not, from the consideration of this end, and the repeated comparison of it with the means which imagination proposed for accomplishing it, discovered, in what situation every incident would produce the very greatest effect."

[27] *Three Lectures on Aesthetic*, p. 1. Cf. pp. 108 ff.

There are essential differences, too, the historical reasons for which sufficiently explain the general evolution of the term "genius." The eighteenth century employed the term in part as an instrument for freeing speculation concerning art and criticism from the bondage of Aristotelianism. Its constructive contribution to the theory culminated in a systematic and affirmative statement concerning the meaning of artistic freedom by Kant; and few philosophers of art in the nineteenth and twentieth centuries have been unaffected by the theory of genius formulated in the *Kritik of Judgment.*

Let us examine in greater detail these historical aspects of the conception of the genius and the relation of that historical development for the problem of human freedom. We may illustrate easily the opposed attitudes of writers in both the seventeenth and the eighteenth centuries toward the traditional Aristotelianism. Robert Wolseley has asked "Shall we lay aside the Prescriptions of *Aristotle* contrary to the experience of near *2000* years, and practise hereafter by his new Dispensatory?" [28] while Rymer had characterized the greatest English poets as "unhappy . . . through their ignorance or negligence of these fundamental Rules and Laws of *Aristotle.*" [29] Yet, by the time Alexander Pope wrote that

> Music resembles Poetry, in each
> Are nameless graces which no methods teach,
> And which a master-hand can reach.
> If, where the rules not far enough extend
> (Since rules were made but to promote their end)
> Some lucky License answer to the full
> Th' intent propos'd, that License is a rule,[30]

the controversy concerning what we should now call fine art turned precisely upon the value of those "rules . . . made but to promote their end," which the Aristotelians had nurtured

[28] Preface to *Valentinian, A Tragedy.* Quoted in Spingarn, *Critical Essays of the Seventeenth Century.*

[29] Preface to the Translation of Rapin's *Reflections on Aristotle's Treatise of Poesie.* (Arranged) See Spingarn, *op. cit.*

[30] *An Essay on Criticism,* lines 141 ff.

to the detriment of an understanding of Aristotle's theory of free choice and the meaning of his use of "inspiration." [31]

More specifically than Pope, Edward Young urged that there are in poetry "mysteries not to be explained but admired," holding that "a genius differs from a good understanding, as a magician from a good architect; that raises his structure by means invisible, this by the skilful use of common tools." [32] The controversy centered, as we have observed,[33] upon the uses of the word "invention," which now comes almost wholly within the compass of speculation upon genius. Of the latter, Alexander Gerard clearly held that it is the faculty required to account for the new and the original.[34] To the former term, "invention," the connotations of omnipotence still adhere.[35] But we observe the tendency of the period to move from speculation upon power to speculation concerning knowledge and from mystical to natural explanation in such writings as William Duff's. *An Essay on Original Genius* makes originality and invention functions of the "plastic imagination." [36]

[31] It will be recalled (see *supra*, Ch. I, pp. 36 ff.) that Aristotle's analyses of voluntary and involuntary action, deliberation and free choice in the *Nicomachean Ethics*, Book III, suggest for art that the conditions for freedom are that the forming principle is in the agent and that there be knowledge of particular circumstances. Aristotle argues that we may choose among means but that the end is fixed. This theory of art as wholly comprehensible in terms of means and ends dominates criticism until the emergence of theories of imagination and wit. One reaction to Aristotle's theory which is of interest in the context of the present chapter is Addison's: "We no longer pay a blind veneration to that barbarous Peripatetic jingle, those obscure scholastic terms of art, once held as oracles; but consult the dictates of our own senses, and by late invented engines force nature herself to discover plainly her most hidden recesses." Joseph Addison, "An Oration, In Defence of the New Philosophy," *The Works of Joseph Addison*, Richard Rawlinson ed., (6 vols. London, 1893), VI, 609.

[32] *Conjectures on Original Composition*, ed. Steinke, p. 49.

[33] See above, Ch. I, pp. 36 ff.

[34] *An Essay on Genius*, p. 8.

[35] See, for example, William Jackson's remark in *Whether Genius be born, or acquired?*, pp. 194–95, to the effect that "invention" is "a creation of something not before existing."

[36] *Op. cit.*, p. 89. Duff specifies the nature of genius as follows: ". . . above

The poets, critics, and philosophers were striving to account for the original or novel in terms of invention, and those who embraced the theory of inspiration denied that the problems could be solved wholly or in part by explanation of art in terms of rational technique. They had clear vision concerning the nature of the problem, as well as knowledge and insight which led them to the fountainhead of speculation on the subject of freedom and genius. Not only had Plato written of the poet as inspired genius but, after distinguishing him from the mimetic artist, presented the propositions that the inspired artist so freed need have " no knowledge of a whole art " nor need he " make right judgments of the sayings and doings of that art." [37] Plato is the ultimate source of the eighteenth century's notions concerning genius,[38] but Longinus, in that great critical writing, *de Sublimitate,* fixes for that age the image of the great man and of great art. And, indeed, Longinus stresses a crucial implication of the question which was ultimately to concern art and fine art, namely that there are profoundly moving works of art whose makers evidently think " little of minute correctness." [39]

all, it is distinguished by an inventive and plastic Imagination, by which it sketches out a creation of its own, discloses truths that were formerly unknown, and exhibits a succession of scenes and events which were never before contemplated or conceived." The measure of the advance made with reference to imagination is well illustrated by comparing Duff's remarks to those of George Puttenham, in *The Arte of English Poesie,* p. 18, in his comments upon critics: ". . . whatsoever deuise be of rare inuention they terme it phantasticall, construing it to the worst side . . . ." He holds, however, that " For as the euill and vicious disposition of the braine hinders the sounde iudgement and discourse of man with busie & disordered phantasies, . . . so is that part being well affected, not onely nothing disorderly or confused with any monstrous imaginations or conceits, but very formall, . . . that by it as by a glass or mirrour, are represented vnto soule all maner of bewtifull visions, whereby the inuentive parte of the mynde is so much holpen, as without it no man could deuise any new or rare thing." Duff writes, *op. cit.,* p. 86, that ". . . by the word ORIGINAL, when applied to Genius, we mean that NATIVE and RADICAL power which the mind possesses, of discovering something NEW and UNCOMMON in every subject on which it employs its faculties."

[37] *Ion,* 538. Compare *Laws* 719.

[38] But see *infra,* Ch. v, p. 171 on possible native sources of theory of inspiration.

[39] *de Sublimitate,* xxxvi, 1, 3.

The suggestion clearly allies technique and judgment to crafts, but denies their relevance to products of free genius.

Of the eighteenth-century writers affected in one way or another by the theory of genius, many, like Pope, Addison, Shaftesbury, Burke, Hutcheson, and Home are of stature sufficient to warrant serious consideration by later speculation for their intrinsic merits. Some, like Young, Duff, Gerard, and Jackson are important principally because their writings were influential. But the writings of both the greater and the lesser men entered the tradition of the artist as free creator which flowed into Kant's *Kritik of Judgment*.[40] It is this great work in philosophy which has as core for its aesthetic part the proposition that " taste in the Beautiful is alone disinterested and free satisfaction." [41] Indeed, it is this which leads Bosanquet to write that in the third critique Kant gave aesthetic consciousness its " final negative definition " [42] in terms of freedom.

We have noticed that criticism in the eighteenth century tends to emphasize a denial of Aristotle's authority, while nineteenth- and twentieth-century speculation concerning genius rarely escapes Kant's influence. Our examination of the later history of the theory of freedom as it was expressed in terms of genius depends, therefore, upon a knowledge of the tradition of genius which flowed into the third critique; with the native climate of Kant's thought in which the tradition grew; and with the fruits of that growth in the speculation concerning freedom as a conception integral to that of the fine artist.

It is important to observe, at the outset, that Kant's assumption that the judgment of taste is " purposive without purpose " is elaborated on grounds which readily serve to bring his later notion of genius into the tradition of both the demiurgic and the creative analogy. Kant holds that the " purposiveness with-

[40] For Kant's indebtedness to the English writers, see Schlapp, *Anfänge von Kant's ' Kritik des Geschmacks '* and *Kant's Lehre vom Genie und die Entstehung d. Kritik d. Urtheilskraft.*

[41] *K.d.U.*, sec. 6, p. 54, trans. Bernard.

[42] *A History of Aesthetic*, p. 265.

out purpose " characteristic of this form of judgment is possible " so far as we do not place the causes of the form in a Will, but yet can only make the explanation of its possibility intelligible to ourselves by deriving it from a Will." [43] No less important is the fact that his theory of genius is the more easily affected by the English critical and philosophical writings on the subject because his own earlier theory of judgment emphasizes native endowment.[44]

These aspects of Kant's earlier speculation are most significantly brought in the *Kritik of Judgment* within a framework of freedom clearly stated in the *Kritik of Pure Reason*: " Freedom (independence) from the laws of nature is no doubt a liberation from compulsion, but also from the guidance of all rules " [45] is the general statement which Kant gives in the transcendental dialectic. It is no less forcibly specified for the aesthetic of genius: " *Art* . . . is called free . . . . But it is not inexpedient to recall that in all free arts there is yet requisite something compulsory." [46] And, in elaborating upon this specification, Kant holds that spirit insures originality, while mechanism is that " without which the *spirit*, which must be free in art and which alone inspires the work, would have no body and would evaporate altogether . . . ." [47]

Kant's systematic effort to reconcile the creative and demiurgic notions of freedom for the artist, both in its contribution to aesthetic and in its deficiencies, is not merely a recounting of material provided by English essayists on genius. It is much clarified, however, by a knowledge of their problem, of the quarrel between the ancients and the moderns, and of the speci-

[43] *K.d.U.*, sec. 10, p. 68, trans. Bernard.

[44] *K.d.R.V.* A 133, p. 177, trans. Kemp Smith. In contrast to the understanding, which Kant believes can be instructed and " equipped with rules," judgment " is a peculiar talent which can be practised only, and cannot be taught. It is a specific quality of so-called mother-wit; and its lack no school can make good." It is, thus, a natural talent or gift.

[45] *Ibid.*, A 447, pp. 410–11, trans. Kemp Smith.

[46] *K.d.U.*, sec. 43, p. 184, trans. Bernard.

[47] *Ibid.*, sec. 43, pp. 184–85.

fication which they gave to the ancient problem inherited from Plato and Longinus. And, as we shall see, not the least interesting of their writings were efforts to reconcile the two traditions of freedom.

The reconciliations were certainly the more difficult in view of the continuing and obdurate acceptance by able men of the notion that Aristotle's rules of art provided the *sine qua non* for the practising artist.[48] Yet, although Aristotle had denied validity to the theory of the cosmic demiurge, there are passages in his writings which suggest vestiges of the theory and recall its applicability to art.[49] In the eighteenth century, the heirs to the Aristotelian tradition in art, with the exception of those who were committed to its rules as if the latter were the pronouncements of a divinity, are forced by the vigor of the writings of proponents of novelty and originality to reformulate their own philosophies of the artist. In this sense, the true heir to the Aristotelian theory in the century of speculation concerning the genius is Shaftesbury, precisely as he is the thinker before Kant who most interestingly attempts to reconcile the demiurgic hypothesis of intelligible freedom with the ancient theory of inspiration.

It was not until 1782 that the most extreme claim was made for genius, invention, and novelty by Pinkerton in his *Letters of Literature*: " Invention " is then, as " the parent of novelty, the superlative qualification of poetry "; poetry " knows no rules "; and " the code of laws Genius prescribes to his subjects, will ever rest in their own bosoms." [50] Genius, Pinkerton believes, is the " supreme arbiter and lord of Nature's whole domain; her superior, her king, her God." But late as this

[48] See above, this chapter, p. 132.

[49] See, for example, *Physics* II, 8, 199 a 12: " Now surely as in intelligent action, so in nature . . . . Now intelligent action is for the sake of an end; therefore the nature of things also is so. Thus if a house, e. g., had been a thing made by nature, it would have been made in the same way as it is now by art; and if things made by nature were made also by art, they would come to be in the same way as by nature." (Trans. R. P. Hardie and R. K. Gage)

[50] *Op. cit.*, Letter IX, p. 57, and Letter XXX, p. 207.

paean of free creativity was, its anticipations were, as we have seen, little less extreme. Shaftesbury opposed the notion of unconditioned originality but he also attempted to formulate in intelligible terms the demiurgic theory of freedom in art into which some infusion of the notion of free creativity had seeped.

It is not so much with extremists like Pinkerton that we are now concerned for an understanding of Shaftesbury and Kant and for some illumination concerning the growth of naturalism in the whole approach to the problem of genius, as with what may be called mixed theories of genius, i. e., theories in which the conceptions of originality and intelligibility are loosely conjoined. Such instances are to hand in the writings of Alexander Gerard, Henry Home, and Joseph Addison.

Gerard in *An Essay on Genius* concentrates upon invention, making this, as we have observed, the faculty of genius.[51] It is fancy[52] which collects the materials which are at once the ground for this inventive power and the object of the author's choice. On this view, imagination sets in every possible light the images or sentiments, thus putting them in the poet's power to judge whether they " ought to be rejected or retained." [53]

We are thus introduced by Gerard to a theory of genius which, thus far, reinterprets the Aristotelian theory of free choice in terms of imagination. And, no less rational than its ancient predecessor, Gerard's theory of fancy or imagination is subject in its power " to the same limitation as our power over the natural world." [54] Thus, it can " produce an endless variety of complex notions " from a stock of simple ideas. But precisely as we can create no new substance, " so neither can we, except in perhaps a few very peculiar instances, imagine the idea of a single quality which we have never had access to observe." [55] This is likewise true of the " boldest fiction " of the poets, those which least resemble anything in nature but which are composed of parts which exist in nature.

[51] *Op. cit.*, p. 8.
[52] *Ibid.*, p. 44.
[53] *Ibid.*, p. 58.
[54] *Ibid.*, p. 101.
[55] *Ibid.*, p. 101.

The reasons for Gerard's limitations upon the powers of genius to create are significantly related to intelligibility and, finally, to judgment.[56] Gerard's is, indeed, a clear statement concerning the requirement that the work of art be intelligible.[57] But his writing shows as well the strains to which that requirement was being subjected in the eighteenth century. By way of example, in discussing judgment, it is evident that Gerard believes genius to be in some peril from this commodity.[58]

Gerard's fears that his own theory of genius is inadequate to account for invention and for the new and this fear presents no less a conflict than his insistence that genius for the arts implies not only the power of invention but also that of execution for the presentation of what he imagines to other men.[59] To do this the "real genius" must execute its inventions by instruments and in manners well known and long in use.[60] The tone of Gerard's writing thus contrasts with Shaftesbury's conviction that the problems raised by genius' originality and the emergence of novelty in art may be resolved in Aristotelian terms. That conviction is no less clearly in contrast to the

[56] See *infra*, Ch. VI, pp. 184-85.

[57] Cf. *ibid.*, pp. 104–06: "If we lose sight altogether of the beaten path of memory, we shall be in danger of missing our way in the winding paths of imagination . . . even in cases where the greatest latitude is allowed to invention, care must be taken that the off-spring of genius bear some relation to the portrait of nature, which memory retains." Trains of ideas, he adds, lead genius often to invention and these it must remember for just judgment.

[58] *Ibid.*, pp. 388–89. Acute judgment "will discover even the smallest blemish in what fancy produces" and its scrupulous canvass and its requirements of "greater excellence than the imagination can attain" will not only extinguish the "ardor" of the faculty of imagination but will "enervate its inventions, deprive them of force and spirit, and substitute an insipid correctness in its place." So well aware is Gerard of the dangers present to genius in too finely balanced and acute a judgment that he argues that "it is almost better to give fancy an uncontrouled range, than to break its vigour by the continual restraint of an overscrupulous judgment." Indeed, "an uncommon acuteness" of judgment will "absolutely destroy genius, unless the imagination be as uncommonly comprehensive . . . ."

[59] *Ibid.*, pp. 416–17.

[60] *Ibid.*, p. 423. ". . . a much greater degree of genius was displayed," he remarks, "by those artists who first brought these instruments to use." Cf. *ibid.*, pp. 419–20.

assumption made by another eighteenth-century writer, Henry Home, Lord Kames, that the demiurgic theory of the artist is inadequate. In Home's writing, the conflict within the theory is the more striking because the author of *Elements of Criticism* writes of the genius in terms of creative imagination, described as "a sort of creative power,"[61] while yet the analysis of the work of art is orthodox in its Aristotelianism.[62] In accord with the tradition of τέχνη, he urges that "it may be justly laid down for a rule, That in works of art, order and regularity ought to be governing principles."[63] The conflict is present, yet it takes an interesting course in the history of aesthetic speculation. "Regularity, proportion, order, and colour," essential to beauty are not so essential to "grandeur."[64]

Hutcheson takes the decisive step, implicit in Home's last mentioned statement: "Grandeur and *Novelty* are two Ideas different from *Beauty*, which often recommend Objects to us."[65] Such a distinction, decisive as its results prove to be,[66]

[61] See *supra*, Ch. I, p. 10.

[62] *Ibid.*, p. 23: "Every work of art that is conformable to the natural course of our ideas, is so far agreeable; and every work of art that reverses that course, is so far disagreeable. Hence it is required in every such work, that, like an organic system, its parts be orderly arranged and mutually connected, bearing each of them a relation to the whole, some more intensely, some less, according to their distinction: when due regard is had of these particulars, we have a sense of just composition, and so far are pleased with the performance." Compare Hutcheson's remark, *An Inquiry into the Original of our Ideas of Beauty and Virtue*, Preface xii-xiii: "*. . . we find ourselves pleas'd with a* regular Form, *a Piece of* Architecture *or* Painting . . . ." In those Ideas which have "what we commonly call sensible Perception in them, *the Pleasure arises from some* Uniformity, Order, Arrangement, Imitation . . . ."

[63] *Elements of Criticism*, pp. 216–17.

[64] *Ibid.*, p. 216. The echo of *de Sublimitate* is heard: "The spectator is conscious of an enthusiasm, which cannot bear confinement, nor the strictness of regularity and order: he loves to range at large; and is so enchanted with magnificent objects as to overlook slight beauties or deformities."

[65] *An Inquiry into the Original of our Ideas of Beauty and Virtue*, 5th ed., sec. 6, xiii, p. 84. Hutcheson adds that "The Reason of this is foreign to the present subject." We need but recall Young's remark in *Conjectures on Original Composition* (ed. Steinke, p. 50) to supply at least one reason: "There is something in poetry beyond prose reason; there are mysteries in it not to be explained, but admired, which render mere prose-men infidels to their divinity."

[66] See *infra*, Ch. VI, pp. 204 ff.

derives from the inadequate reconciliations by men such as Gerard in *An Essay on Taste* and Addison in the *Spectator*, as well as from Shaftesbury's stand against the nonnatural explanation of genius.

Gerard's discussion of genius is, again, a mixed theory. On the one hand, the mystery of invention and creation is like that of the magnet, "inexplicable."[67] Yet, genius, by association of ideas, "designs a regular and well proportioned whole." Similarly, "fine imagination" alone can produce genius, yet the latter must be able to express its designs in "apt materials." Both materials and taste are essential to it.[68]

Gerard discovers that invention on the one hand and materials and taste on the other are irreconcilable. The result is a dualism. Addison's similar dualist tendencies lead him to write of two kinds of genius. There are "Prodigies of Mankind" who need neither the arts nor learning, but there are also those "of a different kind" who "have formed themselves by Rules, and submitted the Greatness of their natural Talents to the Corrections and Restraints of Art." Addison suggests that the distinction rests less upon originality or lack of it than upon the different manner in which originality manifests itself.[69] He is no less aware of the dangers facing the genius who submits to rules than of those facing the "Prodigies of Mankind." The former may "cramp their Abilities too much by Imitation," the latter may throw their gifts away upon "trifles" and "nonsense." But while the latter dangers to

[67] *An Essay on Taste*, pp. 168–69.

[68] *Ibid.*, p. 172. Genius, Gerard writes, is the "grand architect which not only chooses the materials, but disposes them into a regular structure. But it is not able to finish it by itself. It needs the assistance of taste, to guide and moderate its exertions." Genius is "never found where taste is altogether wanting."

[69] *The Spectator*, No. 160, pp. 234–35. "In the first it is like a rich soil in a happy Climate, that produces a whole Wilderness of noble Plants rising in a thousand beautiful Landskips, without any certain Order or Regularity. In the other it is the same rich Soil under the happy Climate, that has been laid out in Walks and Parterres and cut into Shape and Beauty by the Skill of the Gardener." (Ed. Henry Morley)

which novelty leads the genius are vividly illustrated by the instance of the man who diverted himself by tossing eggs in the air, there is no doubt that for Addison the final test of the conception is originality.[70]

Whereas Hutcheson's distinction between beauty and novelty is an assertion for which no argument is offered and Gerard's and Addison's efforts to reconcile the differing aspects of art through genius remain inconclusive, Shaftesbury's monolithic naturalism is strongly argued and its conclusions are illuminating. His sympathies fall, it is true, wholly on one side, on that of the demiurgic conception of freedom, descended to genius.

Shaftesbury's famous remark that "a poet is indeed a second *Maker*; a just Prometheus under Jove," is so frequently quoted that its context is too frequently ignored. The context—the "Soliloquy or Advice to an Author"—indicates clearly its author's allegiance to the technical and rational interpretation of the poet, his identification of the demiurgic theory of making with the notion of the genius, and his distaste for the "insipid race of mortals" whom the moderns are "contented to call poets."[71] Shaftesbury's poet gains his title neither for "having attained the chiming faculty of a language" nor for "an injudicious random use of wit and fancy." Where Young deplores the notion that the poet employs the mechanic arts, Shaftesbury asserts that he is "a real master, or architect in the kind," who employs means to ends.[72]

What Shaftesbury in fact does contribute to the theory of the

[70] *Ibid.*, ". . . very few Writers make an extraordinary Figure in the World, who have not something in their own Way of thinking or expressing themselves that is peculiar to them, and entirely their own."

[71] *Op. cit., Characteristics of Men, Manners, Opinions, Times,* Vol. I, p. 135 ff. (Ed. John M. Robertson, London, 1900)

[72] *Ibid.*, p. 136: "Like that sovereign artist or universal plastic nature, he forms a whole, coherent and proportioned in itself, with due subjection and subordinacy of constituent parts. He notes the boundaries of the passions, and knows their exact tones and measures; by which he justly represents them, marks the sublime of sentiments and action, and distinguishes the beautiful from the deformed, the amiable from the odious."

artist as creative genius is likely to be obscured by two facts, the first, that his aesthetic theory appears in a context of moral speculation,[73] the second, that his opinions are more significant outside the context of the contemporary controversy concerning the sublime than a casual judgment would suggest.[74] As for the first point, the moral context, it need be urged only that Shaftesbury does have an autonomous theory of art, despite his interest in moral sense; for the second, it is necessary here only to indicate that the problem of the sublime is raised in this century principally to account for the freedom of the artist to produce novelty.[75] Thus, Shaftesbury writes that "Astonishment is of all other passions the easiest raised in raw and inexperienced mankind," [76] but he also sees that "As for the Sublime, though it be often the subject of criticism, it can never be the manner or afford the means." [77] The point of the criticism is clear. What Shaftesbury wants [78] is that "our authors had considered of a model or plan, and attained the knowledge of a whole and parts . . . ."

[73] See, for example, *ibid.*, p. 136, his remark that "The moral artist who can thus imitate the Creator, and is thus knowing in the inward form and structure of his fellow-creature, will hardly, I presume, be found unknowing in himself, or at a loss in those numbers which make the harmony of a mind. For knavery is mere dissonance and disproportion."

[74] The point is that Shaftesbury abhors the notion that criticism may transcend the mere ascription of error and explanation in terms of means and ends as technique or craft. He likewise stands out against the contemporary theory of inspiration. He remarks (*ibid.*, Vol. I, p. 157) that "'Tis easy to imagine that, amidst the several styles and manners of discourse or writing, the easiest attained and earliest practised was the miraculous, the pompous, or what we generally call the sublime," since "Astonishment is of all other passions the easiest raised in raw and inexperienced mankind." The quotation appears, relating his criticism to the sublime, in "Advice to an Author," *Characteristics of Men, Manners, Opinions, Times,* p. 169.

[75] See *infra*, Ch. VI.

[76] "Advice to an Author," *Characteristics of Men, Manners, Opinions, Times,* p. 157.

[77] *Ibid.*, p. 169. See also "Miscellaneous Reflections," *Characteristics of Men,* Vol. I, pp. 316–17. "An English author would be all genius. He would reap the fruits of art, but without study, pains, or application. He thinks it necessary, indeed . . . to show the world that he errs knowingly against the rules of art"

[78] *Ibid.*, p. 317.

This is a plea for method and technique, in contrast to the denial that the inspired genius works with means-ends, a plea moreover directed precisely to a consideration of the freedom of the artist, a freedom which Shaftesbury interprets in terms of self-mastery and self-determination, after the model of God's freedom in the rational, Platonic tradition. It is usual, he holds, " with mankind to act absolutely by will and pleasure." [79] One must, on the contrary, get freedom by control of " inclination and will " and by recognition of the fact that " things are stubborn and will not be as we fancy them, or as the fashion varies, but as they stand in nature." [80]

In his elaboration of this essential restatement of the analogy of the artist to the demiurgic maker in *Timaeus* who is an artisan or architect fashioning the world but one incompletely in control of materials, Shaftesbury does state the problem in terms of the " copyist after nature." This survival of the theory of imitation does not, however, much affect the principle, which is a general one: " Nature will not be mocked." Conflict is essential in the imposition of natural rules, rules which Shaftesbury regards as means for getting control of nature whose " decrees and instincts are powerful," as " her sentiments " are " inbred." As for the poet, " he should set afoot the powerfullest faculties of his mind, and assemble the best forces of his wit and judgment, in order to make a formal descent on the territories of the heart; resolving to decline no combat, nor hearken to any terms, till he had pierced into its utmost provinces and reached the seat of empire." [81]

The contemporary association of genius with the ancient theory of enthusiasm and revelation, Shaftesbury puts aside as metaphorical and unbelievable.[82] The ancient notion of the

[79] " Advice to an Author," *Characteristics of Men*, pp. 137–38. Cf. p. 142.

[80] *Ibid.*, p. 228.

[81] *Ibid.*, pp. 228–29.

[82] " A Letter Concerning Enthusiasm," *Characteristics of Men*, pp. 6–7. Of the ancients, he admits, " it was never surely the business of poets in those days to call *revelation* in question, when it made evidently so well for their art." But, he remarks (*ibid.*, p. 6), while it " must . . . have appeared in any,

tutelary genius appeals to him.[83] Nonetheless, it raises a serious problem. Although the notion of the genius suggests primarily a bifurcation of the self, practice within this bifurcated self presents difficulties: " One would think," Shaftesbury writes, " there was nothing easier for us than to know our own minds, and understand what our main scope was." [84] Yet we are faced by the " obscure implicit language " of our minds. And the inference is clear: " No more can a genius alone make a poet, or good parts a writer of any considerable kind," than can the horse alone make the horseman, nor limbs the wrestler or the dancer.[85]

The freedom of the genius has, in fact, but one condition: " 'Tis on themselves that all depends." For this philosophy of the art of the genius is presupposed by notions of freedom as self-knowledge and self-determination. To assert freedom of a wholly creative kind is to assert that a man " has undoubtedly

but especially a poet of those times " natural " to address himself in raptures of devotion to those acknowledged patronesses of wit and science," it is impossible that the modern " who is known never to have worshipped Apollo, or owned any such deity as the muses, should persuade us to enter into his pretended devotion and move us by his feigned zeal in a religion out of date."

[83] He notes, in " Advice to an Author," p. 112, the antique opinion " That we have each of us a daemon, genius, angel, or guardian spirit, to whom we are strictly joined and committed from our earliest dawn of reason, or moment of our birth." But he conceives that " the very utmost the wise ancients ever meant by this daemon companion " was " no more than enigmatically to declare, that we had each of us a patient in ourself; that we were properly our own subjects of practice; and that we then became due practitioners, when by virtue of an intimate recess we could discover a certain duplicity of soul, and divide ourselves into two parts." Shaftesbury is led to another and far more significant speculation. See *infra*, Ch. v, pp. 173 ff.

[84] *Ibid.*, p. 113. See also, *ibid.*, p. 151: " 'Tis at present the boast of almost every enterpriser in the Muses' art, ' That by his genius alone, and a natural rapidity of style and thought, he is able to carry all before him; that he plays with his business, doing things in passing, at a venture, and in the quickest period of time.' " Rather, men require (*ibid.*, pp. 180–81) " that main preliminary of self-study and inward converse . . . the wisdom of the heart to the task and exercise of the brain, in order to bring proportion and beauty into their works . . . . That their composition and vein of writing may be natural and free." (*Ibid.*, p. 180)

[85] *Ibid.*, p. 127.

surpassed himself" and this for Shaftesbury means "that they [men] have in some manner differed from themselves, and are somewhat worse or better than their common rate."[86] This is a miracle and irrational: ". . . there is that, which being wholly metamorphosed and converted, we are in reality transformed and lost."[87] Far better, indeed is the compliment given to great men and princes, "That they have acted like themselves, and suitably to their own geniuses and character." Only thus are our actions and makings comprehensible.[88]

How, on this hypothesis of rational and demiurgic genius, may one account for originality and novelty? If "every just work" is produced by means which are natural, i. e., "natural rules of proportion and truth" and if "the creature of their brain must be like one of Nature's formation,"[89] how may we distinguish the merely technical from the beautiful work of art? The answer accords with the analogy of the work of art to an organism, a notion as old as the discussions in the Academy and the Lyceum. Shaftesbury extols the justness of the whole, in which the particulars "yield to the general design."[90] The variety of nature affords the genius his opportunity, but it is an opportunity which also presents pitfalls for those with neither invention nor design. Shaftesbury believes nature to be so varied that whatever she forms is distinguished "by a peculiar original character, which, if strictly observed, will make the subject appear unlike to anything extant in the world besides."[91] It is this effect that the good poet and painter seek to

[86] *Ibid.*, p. 182.

[87] "A Letter Concerning Enthusiasm," *Characteristics of Men*, p. 184. Note also, that ". . . 'tis the known principle of philosophy to teach us ourselves, keep us the self-same persons, and so regulate our governing fancies, passions, and humours, as to make us comprehensible to ourselves . . . . For, let but the search go freely on, and the right measure of everything will soon be found."

[88] See *infra*, Ch. XI.

[89] "An Essay on the Freedom of Wit and Humor," *Characteristics of Men*, Vol. I, p. 96.

[90] *Ibid.*, p. 94; cf. pp. 28–29, 96. Shaftesbury adds that "Thus the best artists are said to have been indefatigable in studying the best statues: as esteeming them a better rule than the perfectest human bodies could afford."

[91] *Ibid.*, pp. 95–96.

prevent. They " hate minuteness, and are afraid of singularity," the images or characters of which would appear " capricious " and " fantastical." As Aristotle tends to value the type, so, too does Shaftesbury exhort the genius—the men of invention and design—to go to " the many objects of nature," and not to form the idea of their work from the " particular one."

It is art, the rule, and comprehensibility which Shaftesbury extols. A painter with any genius " understands the truth and unity of design; and he knows he is even then unnatural when he follows Nature too close, and strictly copies Life . . . . However, his piece, if it be beautiful, and carries truth, must be a whole, by itself, complete, independent, and withal as great and comprehensible as he can make it . . . ." [92]

The grounds for the controversy concerning genius are such as present themselves early in the theological speculation concerning the relation of God to external ideas. No half-hearted reconciliation, such as Addison's, will suffice to bring together views so diametrically opposed as those of Shaftesbury, with his " second *Maker* " or his " real master, or architect in the kind," and Edward Young's " magician," who employs " means invisible."

It is this great and bifurcated analogy, unreconciled by the controversy of the eighteenth century, which affects what for Kant is essentially the issue of freedom. His method in attacking the problem is to offer a systematic statement concerning creativity, which he interprets in terms of spirit, and making, which he examines in terms of mechanism. Once the problems of the genius as a free artist are systematized, the relevance of novelty, technique and intelligibility is slowly brought to the fore as a problem for post-Kantian speculation upon genius in the arts and the fine arts.

Kant's own attack upon his inherited problem of genius is, as we have remarked, a reconsideration of the problem of freedom in aesthetic terms.[93] The general line of his approach is

[92] *Ibid.*, p. 94; cf. pp. 28–29.

[93] See *supra*, Ch. IV, pp. 135 ff.

clear enough, inasmuch as it is evident that for him the problem of freedom implies originality and law-abidingness.[94] How the inspired artist and the technically equipped artist may be a single individual fine artist presents in fact the issue: whether what is original and ineffable is compatible with what is mechanical and technical. It will suffice for our present purposes merely to present some suggestions which Kant makes. In the first place, Kant holds that the originality of the genius "can only furnish rich *material* for products of beautiful art," while both execution and form require talent "cultivated in schools."[95] Kant tends to associate the originality of genius, which furnishes the materials of beautiful art, with the "play" of the artist's powers, but the freedom thus assured is never judged to be caprice.[96] Perhaps Kant's most important suggestion concerning genius appears in the context of his efforts to conjoin the ineffable and the mechanical at the level of the relations of the arts, not only in terms of the faculties of imagination and understanding but also in terms of the ideas of reason.[97] In this way, Kant proposes to undercut the notion

[94] One difficulty which arises is that Kant asserts that spirit expresses "the ineffable elements," although the "ineffable" applies to the *productive* powers of making and not of judgment. The traditional notion of genius appears in Kant's denial that industry or science can teach the relation of imagination and understanding. (*K.d.U.*, sec. 49, p. 202)

[95] *K.d.U.*, sec. 48, p. 193. Kant amplifies the point in his suggestion (*ibid.*, p. 196), that "by taste the artist estimates his work after he has exercised and corrected it by manifold examples from art or nature; and after many, often toilsome, attempts to content himself he finds that form which satisfies him. Hence this form is not, as it were, a thing of inspiration or the result of a free swing of the mental powers, but of a slow and even painful process of improvement, by which he seeks to render it adequate to his thought, without detriment to the freedom of the play of his powers."

[96] *Ibid.*, sec. 49, pp. 201–02: "Imagination . . . submits to the constraint of the Understanding" and is subject to "the limitation of being conformable to the concept of the latter." It is interesting that Hegel allies this "freedom" of the productive powers in Kant's aesthetic with the notion of "purposiveness without purpose" and concludes that for Kant the means-end relation holding for fine art was "subconscious and undiscovered."

[97] Kant urges (*ibid.*, sec. 49, p. 198) that when experience becomes too commonplace we remold it in accord with the imagination, "in accordance with

which had developed in the eighteenth century in such writings as Duff's and Gerard's that originality may be accounted for in terms of the association of ideas. More significantly, however, his evident aim is to provide, by an examination of imagination, a ground for the creation of another nature " out of the material that actual nature " gives to that faculty.[98] For Kant, a nature such as art provides is neither got by aping nor is it imitation. The " happy relation " of the faculties can be taught by no science, nor can it be acquired by industry.[99]

Kant grasps firmly the systematic problem. He asserts that expression provides the means by which the subjective state of mind brought about by the ideas of reason " as an accompaniment of the concept " may be communicated to others, i. e., how the " ineffable element in the state of mind implied by a certain representation " may be made " universally communicable." [100] In general, he suggests that the solution to the problem, whether the expression be in speech, painting, or sculpture, " requires a faculty of seizing the quickly passing play of Imagination and of unifying it in a concept (which is even on that account original and discloses a new rule that could not have been inferred from any preceding principles or examples), that can be communicated without any constraint [of rules]." [101]

The suggestion is fruitful, but difficulties present themselves in its application to the beautiful arts. Kant sees clearly enough that a beautiful art is neither to be valued in mercenary terms nor wholly explained in terms of nonaesthetic purposes. On the side of the mental powers, he urges that the imagination is set at liberty, that the mind rises aesthetically to ideas, that

analogical laws, but yet also in accordance with principles which occupy a higher place in Reason."

[98] *Ibid.*, sec. 49, p. 198. See also the remark (*ibid.*, p. 198) that the " material supplied to us by nature in accordance with this law of Reason can be worked up into something different which surpasses nature." See *infra*, Ch. VI on the ideas of reason as " limiting conceptions."

[99] *Ibid.*, sec. 49, p. 202.

[100] *Ibid.*, p. 202.

[101] *Ibid.*, sec. 49, p. 202.

there is play of the mental faculties, and that the mind is strenghtened by its feeling of freedom, spontaneity, and independence of natural determination.[102]

The most significant consequence of the theory of genius as comprised both of originality and talent is, as has been suggested, the inference that there are beautiful arts, that they may be classified, and that the judgments upon which such classifications are grounded may be correct or incorrect—this in the face of the definition [103] of a genius as one with "a *talent* for producing that for which no definite rule can be given . . . *originality* must be its first property." [104]

The general ground for Kant's classification of the beautiful or fine arts is that of space and time.[105] A search for the metaphysical ground for the classification of the fine arts is a tantalizing task, principally of value because it does show the well-delineated vestiges of the analogy of the artist to the creator: ". . . we ought only to describe as Art," Kant maintains, "production through freedom, *i. e.*, through a will that places Reason at the basis of its actions." [106] And this statement, in turn, appears to rest upon the supposition that the determining ground of the judgment of taste lies in "the concept of that which may be regarded as the supersensible substrate of humanity." [107]

[102] *Ibid.*, sec. 53.

[103] *Ibid.*, sec. 46, p. 189.

[104] In this connection, it should be remembered that Kant remarks of the products of genius (*ibid.*, sec. 46, pp. 189–90) that they "ought not to spring from imitation, but must serve as a standard or rule of judgment for others," and that genius itself "cannot describe or indicate scientifically how it brings about its products . . . . Hence the author of a product for which he is indebted to his genius does not know himself how he has come by his Ideas; and he has not the power to devise the like at pleasure or in accordance with a plan, and to communicate it to others in precepts that will enable them to produce similar products."

[105] He judges them to be arts of speech, shaping arts, and the arts of beautiful play of sensation. Rhetoric, poetry, sculpture, architecture, painting, music, and arts of color are thus brought within the scope of the arts of genius.

[106] *K.d.U.*, sec. 43, p. 183.

[107] *Ibid.*, sec. 57, p. 233.

If, however, the relation in theory of originality and mechanism raises tantalizing possibilities for metaphysics, their reconciliation in practice, i. e., the interrelating of spirit to actual mechanisms, does so no less for aesthetic: " In poetry," Kant writes, " there must be an accuracy and wealth of language, and also prosody and measure." [108] From this, the seed, grow such elaborations of mechanism as the study of media, symbols, and feelings which characterize philosophies of art in the nineteenth century.

Of these elaborations, Hegel's classifications of the fine arts in *The Philosophy of Fine Art* is one of the most complex and elaborate, precisely as it is one of the most famous. But even Hegel's double classification of the arts in terms of media and of phases of spirit remains, for the most part, an investigation of the interrelations of mechanisms. In any case, it so little touches upon the central problem, i. e., upon that correlate of the means-end relation, the aesthetic relation of the arts and their classification, that we may ignore its complexities. We may content ourselves with what, in the light of the problem of this essay, Hegel does to reveal the core of the Kantian theory of genius. This we may easily do if, after recalling Hegel's tribute to Kant's writings as those of a man with an artistic sense of a profound and philosophic mind, we also recall that Kant writes in the aesthetic context of " purposiveness without purpose." As Edward Young had written of the " means invisible " which the original poet employs, Hegel comments that Kant holds that the beautiful has the " form of teleology," [109] meaning that the teleological character is perceived in the object without the idea of an end. Hegel adds the comment that " the beautiful . . . exists as teleological in itself, without means and end revealing themselves in it as distinct aspects." For Hegel, with his comprehensive grasp of the aesthetic problem, this suggests that " in contemplating beauty, we are not conscious of the conception and of the subsumption under it." [110]

[108] *Ibid.*, sec. 43, p. 185.
[109] *Introduction to Hegel's Philosophy of Fine Art*, trans. Bosanquet, p. 149.
[110] *Ibid.*, p. 148.

It is in their recognition of this dual problem that we best measure the contribution of the post-Kantian writers upon genius to the theory of freedom and fine art. Their expression of the issue is not without its own obscurity. Hegel's remark that, in Kant's interpretation " the teleological correspondence of the inner and outer is the immanent nature of the beautiful object," is sufficient indication of the metaphysical and terminological difficulties, but these alone do not obscure the problem. The " immanent teleology " of the metaphysician is no less affected by the great analogy of the fine artist to God than is Croce's freely inspired artist, " big with his theme, he knows not how " or Shelley's " hierophants of an unapprehended inspiration " who " even whilst they deny and abjure . . . are yet compelled to serve . . . ." For what Hegel discerns in Kant's aesthetic is a more sophisticated and more naturalist interpretation of the ancient specification of the genius as in some sense either mad or prophetic.[111]

Conceptually, it is in terms of the genius as madman and as one granted the prophetic gift that the hoary superstition of the genius begins to emerge from the great analogy of the fine artist to God the creator and maker and to present, in the form of epistemological primitivism, the implications of the means-end relation.

Let us turn, therefore, to the historic ways in which men have argued that the genius, as original, may be thought to succeed in the making of a work of fine art, even though he ignore rules or, indeed, would appear never to have subjected himself to the disciplines ordinarily needed to acquire them. By relating the notion of the free genius to theories of madness and primitivism and, finally, to the notion of the prophet, we may come to understand at once the psychological grounds for the recurrences of the notion of the genius and the significant knowledge he is presumed to have.

[111] *Ibid.*, p. 149.

5 The Genius and the Prophet

And the Sibyl with raving mouth, uttering words solemn, unadorned, and unsweetened, reaches with her voice a thousand years because of the god in her.

HERACLITUS

The Genius as Irrational

Plato's deliverance of the poet from bondage to imitation and technique is couched in terminology which, through the connotations of the word " inspiration," suggests that the poet's frenzy is identical with madness. Indeed, invention is a condition for poetry and for this the poet must be ". . . out of his senses and the mind no longer in him." The historical notion of poetic inspiration is closely associated with Plato's statement. Elaborations of the assertions that poets do not speak by any rules of art and that " God takes away [their] minds, and uses them as his ministers, as he also uses diviners and holy prophets, in order that we who hear them may know them to be speaking not of themselves who utter these priceless words in a state of unconsciousness, but that God himself is the speaker," [1] have appeared to be poetic metaphor. It is startling, consequently, to note that so rationalist a philosopher as Aristotle not only offers " a strain of madness " as the alternative explanation of poetry to " a happy gift of nature " (in which case a man is " lifted out of his proper self "), [2] but that in *Problems*, the Stagarite speculates upon the close relation between insanity and genius.[3]

It is necessary here neither to suggest the close relation of

[1] *Ion* 534, trans. B. Jowett.

[2] *Poetics* XVII.

[3] *Op. cit.*, XXX.I. " Why . . ." he asks, " are all men who are outstanding in philosophy, poetry or the arts, melancholic? " Most of those who have handled poetry, he asserts, have suffered from " black bile."

the Platonic quotation to the passage in the *Laws* concerning the corybantic frenzy nor to examine the relation of the question presented by Aristotle to his own theory of *katharsis* in *Poetics and Politics*.[4] Nor is it necessary for our present purposes to trace the long association in speculation between the genius and the madman. What is notable is a concentration of attention in speculation on genius upon precisely that problem to resolve which Plato and Aristotle both introduced the theory of divine madness into their writings upon art.

That the artist's powers are necessarily and sufficiently conditioned by irrationality is an argument rarely, if ever, maintained in all seriousness. Still, Lange-Eichbaum, in his *Genie-Irrsin und Ruhm* suggests not only the more limited Aristotelian inference but the possibility that insanity may resolve the problem of the genius.[5] The grounds for this possibility have been presented clearly by Schopenhauer who after examining some parallels [6] concludes that the genius and the madman are in contact at the point where connections and relations are mistaken.[7] The evident point of this suggestion is precisely the ancient one, namely the possibility that madness provides a possible mode of escape from restrictions of rationality and permits a consequent achievement in terms of novelty, originality, and uniqueness. Lange-Eichbaum remarks, for example,

[4] See M. C. Nahm, *Aesthetic Experience and Its Presuppositions*, p. 284. Compare *Politics* 1341 a 12.

[5] This is reflected in the same author's *The Problem of Genius*. See, for example, the statement on p. 140: " Almost everywhere, and especially in the subjective fields of imaginative writing, religion, and music, gifted ' insanity ' gains the victory over simple, healthy talent . . . . This does not signify that genius is itself ' insane,' but that the mentally disordered person is more likely than the sane person to become famous . . . ."

[6] *The World as Will and Idea*, trans. R. B. Haldane and J. Kemp, Vol. I, pp. 250–51.

[7] *Ibid.*, pp. 250–55. " The madman has a true knowledge of what is actually present, and also of certain particulars of the past, but . . . he mistakes the connection, the relations, and therefore falls into error and talks nonsense," while the genius " also leaves out of sight the knowledge of the connection of things, since he neglects that knowledge of relations which conforms to the principle of sufficient reason."

that the experience of the psychopath is "enlarged" by the very condition that all psychopathic experience is "a response to especially light stimuli."[8] Exceptional mobility of the ideational life, hunger for stimuli, craving for novelty—these are conditions which permit the psychopath to "get glimpses into numerous domains," and to have experiences "altogether exceptional." The inference is obvious: "What makes one individual more effectively creative than another is an exceptional capacity for bringing his dream stratum into play simultaneously with his reason, or in rapid alternation therewith."[9]

It is not difficult to overemphasize the importance of this speculation and it has been overemphasized more often than not. To imply that "the tint . . . of the entirely new" makes its way into the work, a tint which "lies outside the bounds of sane and reasonable talent as displayed in art," does suggest that the association of genius and madness is owing precisely to the fact that the latter provides a "life which follows laws peculiar to itself." This would appear to be conterminous with Kant's "other nature," which imagination constructs from the nature presented to us and so to provide the condition for the evasion of such technical requirements as art ordinarily stipulates.

To resolve the problem of fine art by identifying genius and madness is illogically to convert the arational or the nonrational into the irrational. Indeed, the difficulties of such identification have long been evident to psychologists. Thus Freud grants that "the artist has also an introverted disposition and has not far to go to become a neurotic," but he adds that "a true artist knows how to elaborate his day-dreams so that they lose that personal note which grates upon strange ears and become enjoyable to others; he knows too how to modify them sufficiently

[8] *The Problem of Genius*, pp. 127–29. The emphasis upon novelty and lack of restraint is interesting: "Thus in very various ways does the tint of the peculiar, of the different, of the entirely new, make its way into the work," a factor which "lies outside the bounds of sane and reasonable talent as displayed in art." Cf. *ibid.*, p. 131.

[9] *Ibid.*, p. 129.

so that their origin in prohibited sources is not easily detected." [10]

The identification of the fine artist as genius and the madman is fruitful for speculation concerned only with instances in which the mad genius controls the material and techniques of art. It is, in theory, precisely the transcendence of this condition which is presumed to provide for the emergence of novelty. Thus the burden of proof of the identification must necessarily rest upon those who assert it. If, however, we seek neither proof nor disproof for the theory but, rather, keep in mind the problem, i. e., the imagined means by which men produce original works of art while yet escaping servitude to techniques of science and art, we may at least explain the recurrence of the notion. It is well to recall, in this respect, the recurrence of words associated with the prophetic powers attributed to the raving sibyl. One modern instance will suffice:

> To straightforward talent there must be added, to make genius, this 'daemon,' and it seems that the daemon, the inner voice, is founded on the psychopathic element. For the daemonical, which is the essence of genius, embraces the inexplicable, the spiritually creative and original, and the whole gamut of strange passions and uncommon ideas.[11]

In this instance, the emphasis is upon the "certain loosening"

[10] *Introductory Lectures on Psychoanalysis,* p. 314. Compare, for the significance of the latter portion of the quotation, Freud's *Wit and the Unconscious.* Compare Jung's *Modern Man in Search of a Soul,* p. 177. Cf. also, Julius Portnoy's *A Psychology of Art Creation,* pp. 12–14, for a statement concerning the limitations of psychoanalytical explanation of the phenomena of artistic creativity. An example is the following: "A poet can be ecstatic and not mad in a pathological sense. Euplastos implies malleability, the artistic capacity to feel itself into the nature of the thing is to create. The actor fits into the character he portrays, he becomes someone other than himself temporarily. In a deranged mind primitive animism dominates the scene. The trees whisper, the birds mock, the psychotic is not himself; he claims to be a legendary prophet. His hallucinations and delusions are no longer malleable for practical purposes, since he is incapable of communicating his feelings through an accepted art form." (*Op. cit.,* p. 12)

[11] E. Kretschmer, *The Psychology of Men of Genius,* p. 17.

in a great proportion of geniuses " of . . . relations to custom and tradition " upon a " disintegration of instinctive life and established ways of thinking," a process which " at some favorable point, can lead on to new and astonishing rearrangements of ideas."

It is true that the demonical is here identified with " the psychopathic structures in the personality." But the word itself has interesting connotations which we shall examine, while the notion of the loosening of the genius's relations " to custom and tradition " fits clearly into a generic form of primitivism which has proved to be no less influential a conception than has madness in forming the common notion of the genius and his powers and which, likewise, will be seen to have its roots in the notion of the genius as prophet.

Primitivism and Genius

Writers who use the conception of primitivism in their account of the genius ordinarily choose between an examination of the cultural or environmental conditions which affect the great man and a formulation of epistemological theory which will account for his extraordinary gifts. The problem in either case ordinarily remains identical: to explain how a man may know and make without expending effort or submitting to instruction and discipline to acquire technical training. The theoretical core of the argument of primitivism is that the genius is free to produce a beautiful work of art or a work of fine art without the need to relate means and ends. Assertions which derive from these more general suggestions are that products of genius are inexplicable in terms of the means-end relation or that these products are not subject to verifiable and valid judgments.

The more specific assumptions of the theory are sufficiently illustrated in the writings of Addison and Schopenhauer. The English essayist writes that by the " meer strength of natural Parts, and without any Assistance of Arts or Learning," " Prodigies of Mankind " have produced " Works that were the Delight of their own Times, and the Wonder of Posterity." [12] For Schopenhauer, the genius is "contrary to nature," precisely because in him the intellect frees itself from service to the will in order to act on its own account.

Despite the difference in terminology, it is evident that Addison and Schopenhauer both believe in the genius as one endowed with natural gifts. But the latter is more explicit in his description of the great man. Specifically, Schopenhauer argues that the ground for the distinction between the wise man and the genius is that the former retains a practical tendency and is concerned with the choice of the best ends and means, while the latter makes his intellect active on its own account. In order to do so, the genius must have direct and immediate knowledge.

It is not strange that the directness and immediacy of knowledge which Schopenhauer attributes to the genius should bring to mind, within the context of primitivism, the notion of precocity and with it the similarity of the genius to the child, as regards both the latter's life and imagination. And, indeed, Schopenhauer entertains the notion that genius and child are to some extent identical.[13] It is evident, however, that many so-called geniuses develop late in life. It is equally evident that Schopenhauer proposes only a limited identification and that in a somewhat special sense. He argues not so much to establish the identity as to relate the theory of genius to that of play. In childhood man "collects a great store of knowledge for future wants which at the time are foreign to him." The store is brooded over and stored up carefully for the time at which it will be useful. Thus, Schopenhauer emphasizes the notion that the mental powers are presumed to develop earlier than the needs they are designed to serve.

[12] *The Spectator*, No. 160.

[13] *The World as Will and Idea*, Vol. III, Ch. XXXI, p. 161. Cf. Croce, *Aesthetic*, p. 4, who writes that " the child, with its difficulty of distinguishing true from false, history from fable, which are all one to childhood, can furnish us with a very vague and only remotely approximate idea of this ingenuous state."

Over the detailed analysis of the play-theory or with the details of the various conjunctions of genius and childish precocity, we need not delay. It is sufficient to indicate here [14] that this is a theory of imagination's presumed capacity to preform the techniques which are ordinarily evolved and put into effect only as a result of prolonged effort. As an explanation of the manner in which the genius may produce without submitting to training in techniques, it is susceptible, in so far as it is identical with the play-theory of art, to the precise criticisms which have proved fatal to every effort to identify art and play. Here the only criticism which need be mentioned arises from the fact that the play of the child and the precocity of the genius have been regarded both as propaedeutic to serious activities and to the employment of means to ends. If, however, an effort is made to test these implications, what must be made explicit are precisely those aspects of environment and culture, or of epistemological theory in terms of intuition or anticipation, which will account for the knowledge of the means-end relation which primitivism assumes that the genius possesses.[15] The accounts of genius which stress environment and culture may be called theories of cultural primitivism; those which stress epistemological problems, epistemological primitivism.

Cultural primitivism is a less radical venture into the explanation of the genius than is the epistemological form to which we shall later come. Of the variety of its formulations, two are of significance for our present problem. The first is the notion of culture or society as a condition for the emergence of genius. The second is the implication that the artist's intentional reversion for the symbols and techniques of his art pertains to a stage of knowing and making so primitive as to preclude any suggestion of sophistication. One or two historical suggestions concerning the primitive conditions from which it has been assumed the genius emerges will illuminate the point. Sir Francis Bacon, for example, after urging that poetry is a kind

[14] See M. C. Nahm, *Aesthetic Experience and Its Presuppositions*, Ch. VII.
[15] *Ibid.*, particularly pp. 211–13, 222–24.

of learning " unrestrained by laws "[16] which belongs to imagination, remarks that ". . . it makes its own way, so as to have been in high esteem in the most ignorant ages, and among the most barbarous people, whilst other kinds of learning were utterly excluded."[17] John Pinkerton, in his *Letters of Literature,* suggests that " Lord Bacon hath observed that any faculty reduced to an art must of necessity become barren, because art circumscribes it."[18] As is his custom, Pinkerton draws the most radical inference from this suggestion, as he allies it to the genius.[19] Since for him, the genius " needs neither diligence nor assiduity " and disdains to halt along with crutches of application, the stage of society in which the " sun of science " is only beginning to rise accounts for the highest perfection to which poetry attains.[20] William Sharp, in *A Dissertation upon Genius,*[21] presents a less radical interpretation. Intellect only sorts out materials but does not add new ones. The " simple apprehensions " of the savage are " as quick as those of the man raised in a cultivated society." However quick such apprehensions may be, however, genius receives its differences from art, because, Sharp argues, no instances of genius are to be found in any branch of art or science in places where no improvements are sought.

The excessive claims for primitivism and for unrestrained genius tend to be mitigated as we approach the disputed issue of the relation of means-ends to the great artist in the second form of cultural primitivism. In this, it is assumed that the

[16] See *supra,* Ch. I, pp. 9-10.

[17] *de Augmentis,* trans. Devey, II, xiii, pp. 96 ff.

[18] *Op. cit.,* XXX, p. 211.

[19] *Ibid.,* Letter I: ". . . no state of society can be so interesting as that in which the sun of science is beginning to rise, and discover prospects full of splendor and novelty; and in which the mind, vegetating strongly, begins from a vigorous stem to display the buds of elegance."

[20] *Ibid.,* p. 6. But not, however, by anticipation of art: poetry reaches perfection in this stage because ". . . for what it wants in art, in elegance, in harmony, is fully compensated by a wild force in nature, by a simplicity, by a pathos to which every heart is in unison."

[21] *Op. cit.,* pp. 24, 44, 91–92.

artist returns to the past consciously to avoid the appearance of sophistication in his art. The issue is more sharply drawn by those philosophers of art who make an effort to relate Kant's notion of originality to mechanism. It is most clearly delineated in Hegel's examination of the presuppositions of fine art precisely because that examination occurs in a philosophy in which morality conceptually or dialectically precedes the stage of spirit called aesthetic.

Hegel believes that if the artist draws for his material upon contemporary life, " the modifications which the poet can hardly avoid making in it will not readily escape the appearance of a purely artificial and intentional composition." [22] To avoid such appearance and, indeed, to avoid being " shut off from imagination," Hegel maintains that the artist must present " ideal figures of art," for which a search must be made in the " age of mythos . . . in past times, where we shall find the soil most congenial to their growth."

In its Hegelian form, this second form of cultural primitivism may properly be called a cultural analogue to " aesthetic distance." That it but partially frees the artist from need to submit to such requirements as the mechanisms of signs or symbols impose is evident. Furthermore, even were it argued that the theory provides a clue to the interrelation of originality and mechanism and that it is valuable precisely because it does suggest a method by means of which the artist may assure for his product some degree of originality,[23] there must still be accounted for the acquisition of such technical skills as fine art requires. And here the alternative possibilities would appear to be magical powers or epistemological primitivism, neither of which finds its place in Hegel's rational philosophy of art.

The emphasis which Schopenhauer and Hegel place upon the function of the imagination in interrelating nature, art, and fine art, and in bringing together spirit and mechanism, anticipates the most radical and systematic form of the theory of genius as

[22] *The Philosophy of Fine Art*, trans. F. P. B. Osmaston, Vol. I, pp. 254 ff.
[23] Cf. Aristotle's *Poetics* on the poet's use of ancient legends.

a form of primitivism, the epistemological. We have observed in the general tradition of the artist as creator that imagination increasingly bears the burden of the problem of creativity in aesthetic.[24] Its development early in life had not escaped the notice of writers investigating genius. William Duff, in his *Essay on Original Genius,* had remarked that " one who is born with a genius for Poetry, will discover a peculiar relish and love for it in his earliest years," proceeds to infer that " Imagination, which in every man displays itself before any of the other faculties, will be discernible in him in a state of childhood, and will strongly prompt him to Poetry." [25]

It remained for modern aesthetic and the identification of expression, intuition, and imagination to state the problem in its most radical form. It is Croce who, although not gracing the theory of art as expression with this name, makes explicit the epistemological primitivism of the notion of the free genius. But we shall understand Croce's theory more fully if we first make explicit what of it is implicit in Schopenhauer's [26] and Nietzsche's [27] philosophical analyses of art. These in their turn derive from Kant's efforts to reconcile originality and mechanism in the theory of genius. But Kant's reconciliation contains (for reasons which some of his successors made explicit) possibilities for sundering originality and intelligibility and the equilibrium of the notion of genius is made unstable, once Schopenhauer and Nietzsche seize upon the issue of the relations between epistemology and ontology.

The relation of mechanism and originality in the products of genius or the fine artist presents a crucial issue once the post-Kantian philosophies of art attempt to cope with the problems of music. The unique status of this art in the theory of genius is evident, as we compare and contrast Schopenhauer's and Nietzsche's arguments concerning it with their inferences con-

[24] See above, Ch. I, p. 8.

[25] *Op. cit.,* p. 37.

[26] *The World as Will and Idea,* Vol. I, Book III, sec. 52, pp. 150 ff.

[27] More particularly in *The Birth of Tragedy.*

cerning other arts. The principal point is that, as we have suggested, post-Kantian analyses of the fine arts are for the most part examinations, with varying emphases, of the work of art as symbol, as image or feeling, as object made in sensuous media, as a unified form, or as some combination of these analytical aspects. It is notable that the philosophies of Hegel and Schopenhauer do not diverge too sharply as analyses of works of art until the subject is music, at which point the differences are extreme. For Hegel, music belongs to the romantic stage of spirit and so is to be classified with painting and poetry. More specifically, however, Hegel would appear to believe that music is wholly definable in terms of idea and media: " Music has within itself, like architecture," he writes, " a relation of quantity, conformable to the understanding, as the antithesis to emotion and inwardness; and has also as its basis a solid conformity to law on the part of the tones, of their conjunction, and of their succession." [28]

But to Hegel's conviction that music is explicable in terms of mathematics and so is conformable to law and that in it spirit finds the " medium for mental inwardness " and utterance " in its tones for the heart with its whole gamut of feelings and passions," the influential interpretations presented by Schopenhauer and reiterated by Nietzsche are completely antithetical. Schopenhauer maintains that music is the direct expression of the will.[29] As we shall shortly see, the implications of such

[28] *Introduction to Hegel's Philosophy of Fine Art,* p. 207. Cf. *ibid.,* pp. 193, 202, 205, where Hegel, writing of the realization of the ideal in particular sensuous media, argues that " the sensuous element of art has at once to show itself as made particular in itself and as adapted to subjective inwardness." Media in music are sounds. Hegel writes of music that " its medium, though still sensuous, yet develops into still more thorough subjectivity and particularization . . . . Sound [is] the sensuous set down as negated, with its abstract visibility converted into audibility . . . . This earliest inwardness of matter and inspiration of soul into it furnishes the medium for the mental inwardness —itself as yet indefinite—and for the soul into which mind concentrates itself; and finds utterance in its tones for the heart with its whole gamut of feelings and passions."

[29] *The World as Will and Idea,* Vol. I, Book III, sec. 2, pp. 150 ff.

" direct expression " are clear to Schopenhauer's disciple, Nietzsche, but no less influential upon the thought of the author of *The Birth of Tragedy* are the implications of Schopenhauer's theory of genius. For the author of *The World as Will and Idea,* the essence of genius has to do with the perfection and energy of the knowledge of perception,[30] a knowledge which he characterizes as the most original and fundamental.[31] All primary thought, Schopenhauer argues, " takes place in pictures," which he contrasts to the abstractions of thoughts and conceptions.[32] Perhaps most significantly, he holds that knowledge as perception is not only original, but also that it is fundamental: by its means the " peculiar and true nature of things . . . discloses and reveals itself." Finally, it is imagination which, as the indispensable tool of genius, draws fresh nourishment from perception.

In Nietzsche's writing, the strands of cultural and epistemological primitivism begin to be drawn together. " Only in so far as the genius in the act of artistic production coalesces with this primordial artist of the world," writes the author of *The Birth of Tragedy,* " does he catch a glimpse of the eternal essence of art," [33] that essence upon which Schopenhauer had pondered. Culture and theory of knowledge do tend to coalesce in Nietzsche's thoughts concerning genius but, simultaneously, the original interrelating of spirit and mechanism, which for Kant posed the central problem of the freedom of genius, moves toward disruption: " By no means is it possible," Nietzsche maintains, " for language adequately to render the cosmic symbolism of music, for the very reason that music . . . symbolises a sphere which is above all appearance and beyond all phenomena." [34] Nietzsche proceeds, in fact, to generalize this implication: All knowledge of art is " basically quite illusory."

What Nietzsche makes explicit in Schopenhauer's philosophy of music, the inference that language is inadequate to the task

[30] *Op. cit.,* Vol. III, Ch. xxxi, p. 138.
[31] *Ibid.,* p. 141.
[32] *Ibid.,* p. 141.
[33] *Op. cit.,* p. 50.
[34] *Ibid.,* p. 55.

of explaining music and its generalization to all art, indicates the acuteness of his thinking. The argument is fragmentary, however, and the implications of the theory of genius as creator await precise formulation in Croce's aesthetic of expression. In its Crocean form, what we have here called epistemological primitivism is generalized in another way, in the assertion that the genius is "humanity itself."[35] Croce realizes that such extension of free creativity to all humanity is possible only on condition that technique be denied properly to pertain to intuition or expression, the first and aesthetic stage of spirit. For this specific theory of expression, to insist that the artist be able to make is to place both him and his art under alien mastery.[36] As we have observed, for Croce, art is "free inspiration." He now asserts that expression is "the first affirmation of human activity."[37] Poetry is "the mother tongue of the human race."

In so far as this form of epistemological primitivism is argued in specific opposition to a philosophy of art which is intellectualist in nature, Croce's specific target is Hegel.[38] The implications of the opposition of primitivism to a philosophy of art which, as Croce holds "could not discover the first ingenuous theoretic form, which is the lyric or the music of spirit"[39] and which precedes the philosophical problem, become explicit, once we turn briefly to Hegel's theory of genius. For Hegel, the core of the theory of genius is this, that "true originality is . . . identical with true objectivity."[40] It is clear that he means

[35] *Aesthetic,* p. 15: "It has been forgotten that genius is not something that has fallen from heaven, but humanity itself." Croce urges the point in order to insure the identity of genius and taste.

[36] See *supra,* Ch. I, p. 57.

[37] *Ibid.,* p. 26. In contrast (*ibid.,* pp. 111–12), the "volitional fact of externalization is preceded by a complex of various kinds of knowledge. These are known as technique . . . . Expression, considered in itself, is a primary theoretic activity, and as such precedes practice."

[38] Cf. *supra,* Ch. I, p. 53.

[39] *What is Living and What is Dead in Hegel's Philosophy,* p. 122.

[40] *The Philosophy of Fine Art* (E. T.), Vol. I, p. 400. The rational, for Hegel, is the real. The more complete statement which immediately precedes this is Hegel's discussion of originality (Vol. I, Ch. iii, p. 400): "The final result,

that true artistic freedom consists in the objectification of imagination in suitable media and its relation by technical means to the end of art.[41] Presented in this way, Hegel's thesis is no less absolutist than Croce's—and for good reason. It is evident that Hegel's is the artistic analogue to that alternative interpretation of freedom grounded conceptually in Plato's *Timaeus*. Freedom, for both Plato and Hegel, is not freedom to perform miracles but of self-determination within the limits of law.

The antithesis between the creative and the rational genius, who has the " capacity of being completely absorbed in a given subject," [42] turns principally upon the given. Other signposts of the " great analogy " are, however, specified. Whereas for Croce aesthetic is " free inspiration," for Hegel it is " true originality " identical with " true objectivity." Concerning the relation of Hegel's genius to the problem of means and ends, we need recall only the remark that " in a kind of inspired state personal to the artist " the particular subject-matter, which is " essentially rational " is seized hold of.[43] " By virtue of its own resources and quality," the " inspired state," Hegel argues, " re-clothes the same as from within the artist himself . . . ."

We have observed that for Hegel artistic freedom consists in the objectification of imagination in suitable media with refer-

then of our inquiry on this head is that true originality does not consist in merely conforming to the paramount conditions of style, but in a kind of inspired state (*in der subjektiven Begeistrung*) personal to the artist which, instead of committing itself wholly to a mere external manner of composition, seizes hold of a particular subject-matter that is essentially rational, and by virtue of its own resources and quality, re-clothes the same as from within the artist himself and not merely in a way conformable to the essential notion of the art adopted, but also in a form adequate to the universal notion of the Ideal."

[41] See Hegel's discussion, *ibid.*, trans. Bosanquet, Ch. III, Part II, pp. 115–42. It should be noted that for Hegel the imagination is creative but to create is " to apprehend it [i. e. the inner core of reason] clothed in the concrete form of actual existence and individuality." The quotation is from *The Philosophy of Fine Art*, (E. T.) Vol. I, p. 383. See, also, Bosanquet's *Three Lectures on Aesthetic*, p. 62.

[42] *Ibid.*, Vol. I, p. 391.

[43] *Ibid.*, p. 400.

ence to the end of art. The inspired genius is thus intelligible both in terms of imagination and of the power of " technical execution " taken together and operating upon the " immediately presented." It is held that the free personality of the artist and the objective construction of his artistic creation provide the " true explanation " of " artistic originality." [44] It is this identity of free personality and objective construction which gives the work of art, in Hegel's words, " the appearance of being the unique creation of *one* individual mind." [45]

It should be noted at once that there is a specific differentiation in method between Hegel's genius as a maker whose originality is rationalist and Croce's genius as creator whose originality is primitive and intuitive. For the former, the artist fully appropriates objective reason " without mixing up with it, to the detriment of clarity, details he may have borrowed from his own experience." [46] For the latter, " every work of art expresses a state of the soul, and the state of the soul is individual and always new, the intuition implies infinite intuitions . . . particular works of art are infinite: all are original . . . each one unsubdued by intellect." [47]

We have already commented [48] upon the microcosmic conflict which, in the Western tradition of speculation, led to the theological and philosophical controversies concerning universals and the nature of the human soul.[49] We have noted various other differentiations between the Hegelian and the Crocean

[44] *Ibid.*, p. 395.

[45] *Ibid.*, p. 403; cf. *ibid.*, 405. Compare *supra*, Ch. III, p. 105.

[46] *Ibid.*; Hegel adds that " in that case alone will he stamp the material with the genuine mark of his own personal vintage."

[47] *The Essence of Aesthetic*, pp. 56–57.

[48] See *supra*, Ch. II, pp. 74 ff.

[49] A good instance of the rationalist argument in the Middle Ages for the soul's individuality on realist grounds is afforded by Gersonides' differentiation between the active and the actual intellects. All active intellects are identical but the actual intellect acquires knowledge for the individual, thus assuring immortality for each individual, inasmuch as all acquire knowledge through information and learning. See I. Husik, *A History of Mediaeval Jewish Philosophy*, Ch. XV.

conceptions, the most significant of which concern the fine artist and the means-end relation, the problem of what is given to the creative artist, the issue of the objectification of the image in external media, and the awareness or lack of consciousness of the artist while he is in process of creating. We are led now to a more precise specification of the "great analogy" as it explains the tradition of the artistic genius.

The artist's image, for Croce, is immediate and complete. As brought within a system of relations, it becomes knowledge of various kinds. "The toil and the delay recommended by critics," writes Shelley, "can be justly interpreted to mean no more than a careful observation of the inspired moments, and an artificial connection of the spaces between their suggestions by the intermixture of conventional expressions; a necessity only imposed by a limitedness of the poetical faculty itself."[50] We have already noted[51] that the basic difference between the ancient theory of inspiration and the modern theory of expression is that for the latter there is no "controlling force outside the artist." For Plato, the poet inspired is a minister of the gods and a prophet. Within the limitations of what Croce calls "free inspiration," the direct, immediate, and complete image or intuition, the form of epistemological primitivism with which we have characterized this theory of genius, is the analogue to prophecy. The similarity of originality to prophetic utterance is significant of the influence of the "great analogy" upon the theory of genius. No less significant of that influence, however, is the fact that Kant's mechanism suggests the mantic aspect of the classical theory of prophecy. The conflicting influences of inspiration and rationality, which Kant attempted to reconcile and which presented thereafter an unstable equilibrium for Schopenhauer's and Nietzsche's arguments and the ground for the opposition of Hegel's and Croce's theories of genius, express the aesthetic analogue in the theory of genius to this bifurcation in classical theology.

[50] *A Defense of Poetry* (Oxford, 1923), p. 54.

[51] See *supra*, Ch. I, pp. 9, 35.

The Genius and the Prophet

Shelley's suggestion of "a necessity only imposed by a limitedness of the poetical faculty itself," echoes Plato's limitation of the extent of prophecy and inspiration. "No man, when in his wits," Plato writes in *Timaeus,* "attains prophetic truth and inspiration"; but a man "must first recover his wits" in order to understand what he remembers of the state of prophecy or inspiration.[52] The distinction between the two interpretations of the genius, as one "carried out of himself" and as one wholly rational, is analogous to that between the prophet and the mantic. The theory of genius, which naturalizes and humanizes the great analogy of the artist to God, does so by interpreting the artist, as the ancients did the prophet, as one freed from servitude to the means-end relation and from subjection to discipline, technical training, and adherence to rules. But, in its demiurgic tradition, genius is the analogue to the mantic or interpreter.[53]

To clarify the point, let us examine briefly the general implications of the ancient alliance of prophet and inspired poet.[54] At the beginning of this essay, various Platonic inferences con-

[52] *Op cit.*, trans. B. Jowett, 71 e, 72.

[53] Compare, in contemporary literature, E. M. Forster's suggestion in "The Raison d'Etre of Criticism in the Arts," *Two Cheers for Democracy* (New York, 1951), pp. 116–18, that the "critical state is grotesquely remote from the state responsible for the works it affects to expound. It does not let down buckets into the subconscious. It does not conceive in sleep, or know what it has said after it has said it. Think before you speak is criticism's motto; speak before you think creation's." Mr. Forster remarks particularly upon the infectious nature of the work of art, "the power of transforming the person who encounters it towards the condition of the person who created it." But he denies that this is the creation of "co-creators." "Unfortunately," he adds, "this infection, this sense of co-operation with a creator, which is the supremely important step in our pilgrimage through the fine arts, is the one step over which criticism cannot help." Acutely, he holds that it is the freshness of the work of art which is recalcitrant to criticism.

[54] For a study of some portion of the anthropological approach to the problem of prophecy and art, see N. Kershaw Chadwick's *Poetry and Prophecy*. Prophecy is there taken to be (p. xi) "the expression of thought . . . and of knowledge . . . which has been acquired by inspiration and which is uttered in a condition

cerning inspiration were mentioned: that it is a gift to be contrasted to art,[55] that it implies the presence of a divinity, that it is allied to possession and frenzy, and that only when inspired is the poet able to invent. It should also be noted that Plato contrasts the madness produced by human infirmity to the " divine release of the soul from the yoke of custom and convention."

The passage in *Timaeus* concerning prophetic truth which leads to the distinction between the man out of his wits and the interpreter is part and parcel of the notions concerning poetry and prophecy in the earlier Dialogues. It was upon the Alexandrian translators that Plato's words made their significant influence in the historical tradition. Concerning the prophetic state, they separated[56] mantic and prophetic aspects. The latter term was used to refer to " the *ecstatic* utterer," the former to " the *sober-minded* interpreter " of the oracle.[57]

It was Philo whose interpretation of the prophet and the association of prophecy with ecstasy and the passive state influenced the earliest Church fathers,[58] and, it may be added, the

of exaltation or trance, or couched in the traditional form of such utterances." It should be noted, moreover, that the author infers from the survey of material (*ibid.*, p. 41) that " Among the peoples of ancient Europe, and in primitive and backward communities of the present day everywhere inspiration refers not only to the gift of song, and of polished and persuasive speech in general, but also the subject-matter. The association of inspiration and knowledge of whatever kind acquired by supernatural means is ancient and widespread. Inspiration, in fact, relates to revealed knowledge. Revelation covers the whole field of human consciousness. It includes knowledge of the past and the hidden present, as well as the future." The author remarks that revelation of the future is a less important factor than has ordinarily been supposed.

[55] *Ion* 533–34; he writes that God takes away the minds of poets and " uses them as his ministers, as he also uses diviners and holy prophets . . . who utter these priceless words in a state of unconsciousness " since " God is himself the speaker, and . . . through them he is conversing with us." Cf. *Phaedrus* 265; *Symposium* 205–06, 209.

[56] Oehler, *Theology of the Old Testament*, p. 468.

[57] *Ibid.* Oehler maintains that the Old Testament *Nabhi* " is designated by name prophet " and " he may be said to be chiefly characterized not as a *predicter* (a name belonging indeed also to the prophet . . .) but also as *one who declares* what the Divine Spirit has imparted to him, to which function it is essential that it should be consciously and intelligently performed."

[58] Oehler, *op. cit.*, quoting Athenagoras and Tertullian. Wolfson remarks

notion of " divine frenzy " was transmitted to modern thought in Ciceronean writings, and in the books of Varro and Isidore of Seville.[59]

It is helpful for an understanding of the genius in terms of epistemological primitivism to attend to certain suggested distinctions, drawn within the resulting tradition, between the prophet and the genius. Here we may begin with Wolfson's suggestion that prophecy is more than " mere divination " in both Christianity and Islam, because, while prophecy means " prediction," its primary significance lies in " the revelation of certain knowledge for the guidance of men both in their intellectual and moral life." [60] Oehler, in a similar but more specific statement of the implications of the problem, points to the effort to explain Old Testament prophecy " by referring it

that " On his becoming acquainted with Greek philosophy, Philo could not help noticing that these four powers which in Scripture are ascribed to prophecy correspond exactly to the four kinds of inspiration which Plato calls frenzy . . . ." (*Philo,* Vol. II, p. 14). Wolfson adds that Philo " could not have failed to see an important terminological difference between the four kinds of prophecy in Scripture and the four kinds of frenzy in Plato." (Plato subdivides [*Phaedrus* 265] " divine madness " into four kinds, i. e., prophetic, initiatory, poetic, and erotic.) Wolfson holds that the Greek term prophet used in the Septuagint as a translation for the Hebrew term, *nabi'* applies to all four powers alike; in Plato . . . the term prophet is used only " in connection with the frenzy of divination." Cf. Wolfson, *op. cit.,* p. 16. See Bigg, *The Christian Platonists of Alexandria,* p. 22: " The idea of a personal Revelation comes to Philo from the Prophetic Vision of the Old Testament." Bigg adds that Philo gave the notion of personal Revelation " systematic form and scientific grounding."

[59] See Courtland D. Baker's " Certain Religious Elements in the English Doctrine of the Inspired Poet During the Renaissance," *E.L.H.,* Vol. VI (1939), pp. 300–25. The Ciceronean writings were principally *Pro Archia Poeta* 18, *De Divinatione* 1, 80, and *De Oratore* II, 46, 194. Isidore's *Etymologiarum,* VIII, Ch. 7, is ordinarily cited. Baker holds, *op. cit.,* p. 301, that " Even if the entire literature and thought of antiquity had perished, it is entirely conceivable to suppose that the poetry of the late Middle Ages and of the Renaissance would have contained, nonetheless, an avowal of belief in the divine participation of the human creative mind with that of Deity, so firmly rooted is this belief in certain characteristic modes of thought inherent in Christian doctrine." The significance of the argument is small, however, in the face of the fact that the Greek elements did survive. Baker's view does suggest, however, the force of the analogy we have been discussing.

[60] *Philo,* II, p. 63.

to *prophetic powers inherent in the human mind,* and manifesting themselves also in the *conceptions of genius,* whether of the poet, the artist, the hero, etc." [61]

To the theory of " natural divination," Oehler objects, arguing that there is no evidence that the natural genius knows anything " positively respecting the purposes of God's ways upon earth." [62] To a consideration of this objection we shall shortly come. It is evident, however, that whether the prophet and the genius are identical in the specific respect of knowing " the purposes of God's ways upon earth," the general grounds for their identification are made clear. The prophet may be the unconscious instrument for the divine word but it is evident that what he knows is not the result of prior training, discipline, education, or art. And so with the genius, who even in Croce's naturalist interpretation provides by aesthetic intuition the individual images which serve as content for all later moments of spirit. And the intuition is not, in the strictest sense, presupposed by science, ethics, practice, causal relations, means-end relations, or the principle of contradiction. Epistemological primitivism in aesthetic in the terminology of the genius is thus the naturalist correlate of prophecy. For the artist, however, there is freedom as autonomy.

But the differentiation between prophet and genius is no less clear. Oehler states the latter portion of the distinction between prophet and " natural genius " as an article of faith. There need be little doubt that the content of presumably true prophecy, got by the prophet and expressed by the mantic, has been interpreted to relate principally to the " guidance of men both in their intellectual and moral life." It is nonetheless true, however, that the theory of the artist as genius may include such content. For if we limit our interest in the work of art to *what* is expressed by prophet and poet, it is not easy to distinguish on this ground into which category Dante would be placed, or the Michelangelo of " The Last Judgment," the Blake of *The Book of Thel* or Milton writing his " unpremedi-

[61] *Theology of the Old Testament,* p. 481.

[62] *Op. cit.,* p. 482.

ated verse " concerning the " ways of God to man." It is evident, certainly, that the theory of genius is intended to account for the artist who includes not only this but also content in his art other than what reveals " the purpose of God's ways upon earth." Prophecy has for the most part restricted its subject to the field of religion and morality, while the scope of the artistic genius extends to nonreligious and nonmoral symbols.

That centuries of thinkers have identified certain characteristics of the prophet and the fine artist as genius, as well as some coincidence in the symbols they employ, implies only that epistemological primitivism as a theory of the capacity to preform knowledge suggests the generic identity of prophet and genius. In examining the main inference to be drawn from this suggestion, the history of the theory of inspiration and imagination proffers the profound observation of a shrewd and acute mind to aid us. " No poet," wrote Shaftesbury in " A Letter Concerning Enthusiasm," ". . . can do anything great in his own way without the imagination or supposition of a divine presence." [63] Shaftesbury goes to the root of the problem: the need is to transport or inspire the mind, " with more than I feel at ordinary hours." [64] And he adds, sagely enough, that whether the " divine presence " be spectral or real is of no consequence. The import of Shaftesbury's remark concerning the inspiration of the poet becomes clearer for our understanding of artistic creativity as we turn to Bergson's religious philosophy. For Bergson, the prophet is the mystic, free of " closed communities " and endowed with intuition. Mysticism is itself " the establishment of a contact . . . with the creative effort which life itself manifests." [65] How is the " radical transformation of humanity " which Bergson believes to be the task of the

[63] *Op. cit.* Anthony, Earl of Shaftesbury, *Characteristics of Men, Manners, Opinions, Times,* etc., ed. John M. Robertson (1900), Vol. I, p. 36.

[64] *Ibid.*, pp. 8–9.

[65] *The Two Sources of Morality and Religion*, pp. 209; cf. 228. (italics mine) An interesting illustration of the naturalist interpretation of inspiration is Castelvetro's explanation (*Poetica d'Aristotele vulgarizzata et sposta,* trans. Allan H. Gilbert, Ch. IV, 65, 11): " Anything done by someone else is highly regarded,"

great mystic effected? It is a creation and the mystic brings it about " *by setting an example.*"

Psychologically, the points of Shaftesbury's and Bergson's statements, the first concerning the stimulus to inspiration, the second the source of creativity, suggest the compulsion to which may be traced both the figure of the prophet-mystic and the genius. Psychologically, both figures are understandable in precisely the way in which the old saying, that history is what Alcibiades said and did, is understandable to the historian. The issue of the artist as creator concerns techniques, rules, inspiration, and souls. That of the genius and the prophet concerns original knowledge, interpretation, and the contact with " the creative effort which life itself manifests," i. e., with freedom. Men do not, however, ordinarily think in terms of souls, techniques, or rules, or, indeed, of abstract freedom. They cherish images of personages, of heroes, of saints, and of geniuses in art, images which embody unparalleled valor, virtue without stain, constructions of supreme excellence and originality, and knowledge without error.

All such imagined embodiments appear to serve as grounds for inspiration. As, in Lord Rosebery's words, " France in chill moments of disaster . . . will turn and warm herself at the glories of Napoleon," so men will be inspired by images of Leonardo, Dante, Shakespeare, Giotto, St. Francis, Beowulf, Charlemagne, and their fellows. Psychologically, such images inspire men in moments of frustration, despair, or discouragement. In them, men discover a source of courage, needed to sustain them in the eternal task of creating.[66]

Castelvetro remarks in explaining that the notion of " divine madness " had its origin in the ignorance of the common people, " and seems marvelous to those who have not the power to do it themselves, and because men commonly measure the forces of the body and of the ability of other men by comparison with their own, they reckon as a miracle and a special gift of God that which they do not know how to attain by their own natural powers, and see that others have attained. Hence the first poets were thought by the ignorant people to be full of the spirit of God and to be aided by God. For the people admired beyond measure the invention . . . .

[66] See M. C. Nahm, *Aesthetic Experience and Its Presuppositions,* Ch. XVIII.

The genius is, in this sense, one specification of the image of the leader,[67] of which the prophet is another. More specifically, however, and in terms of epistemological primitivism, the grounds for the affinity of the genius and the prophet become more evident. The more inclusive subject-matter with which the genius works indicates this by suggesting also the limitation of the prophet-saint's interest to morals and religion. Prophetic insight endows the saint with knowledge which frees him to act without sin. The saint, in Augustine's classical statement, " is unable to sin." The hero, facing dangers mortal to lesser individuals, is free to overcome insurmountable odds. The genius in art is free to imagine and to know in some manner unconditioned by the possibility of error.[68] And all are free in specific ways without the conditioning and training of art.

The genius is, thus, a species of the free man, of which the leader is in all likelihood the primordial image and genus. The notion is thus the product of the imagination, a work of art. If the image as a work of art comes under the rules of technique —and the likelihood is great that it will do so, inasmuch as it pervades myth, folklore, and cult-worship,—this fertile source of symbolism may yield a work of fine art.

There meet—and separate—in this tradition of the genius, two images, that of the miraculous creator of unique individuals and that of the wholly rational demiurge. These products of imagination are personifications or hypostatizations of the extreme limits to which speculation carries the notion of men's powers and freedom.[69] The limits are converted by imagination into creator and maker. It is evident, however, that the genius, as a specification of the generic symbol of the leader, is not merely a personification or hypostatization of the extreme limits

[67] I have argued elsewhere, *Aesthetic Experience and Its Presuppositions*, Ch. XIII, that the leader is one of the primordial cutural generic symbols toward which man is predisposed by feeling. I have there related the symbol of the leader to the reproductive imagination and have attempted to account for the recurrence of the theme of the great man in the various arts.

[68] See *supra*, on Plato and Longinus, Ch. IV, p. 134.

[69] See the next chapter.

of men's freedom nor is it only an example serving to personify ideals and stimulate men to creativity. The philosophical problem, implicit in the image of the producer of what is unique and perfect, centers upon the status and meaning of the philosophical abstractions, unconditioned creativity and wholly conditioned rationality. We shall argue that these abstractions are required for our understanding of the artist as creator. They contribute to an intelligible statement concerning the structure of art. This they do as limiting conceptions or regulative principles of human freedom.

The course of the argument concerning the artist as creator in terms of the genius and, more specifically, by reference to the theory of epistemological primitivism is already conditioned by the distinctions implicit in the freedoms of the hero, the genius, and the prophet. The meaning of genius has already been made more specific by relating it and the other species of the image of the leader to the structures of art, of deeds, and of sin. In the following chapter, we shall argue that it is his attention to the " beautiful " and " sublime " which in fact distinguishes the artist from the saint, the prophet, or the hero.[70] It is in the aesthetic usage of these and associated terms, rather than in the indiscriminate use of " inspiration," " freedom," or " creativity," that the meaning of epistemological primitivism may be ascertained. By examining the terminology in relation to the theory of genius, we advance toward answers to two questions formulated within the tradition of the "great analogy ": How can a structure for a work of genius be designated if the means by which it is made are " invisible "? How can a critical term be got to the work of fine art if criticism and judgment are judged to be the correlatives to a nontechnical creativity?

[70] The distinction must, however, await its fuller validation in terms of the structure of art, in which the theory of epistemological primitivism is shown to be complementary to theories of making and symbolizing in " concrete significant form." See *infra*, Ch. VII and VIII.

6 Genius, Its Philosophical Significance: The Sublime and the Beautiful

> At the same time, I could not help thinking that Mr. Johnson showed a want of taste in laughing at the wild grandeur of nature, which to a mind undebauched by art conveys the most pleasing awful, sublime ideas.
>
> *Boswell's London Journal* 1762–1763

In the preceding chapter we have followed the development of the theory of genius in the philosophy of art and have concluded that in it we come upon the humanization and naturalization of the great analogy of the artist to God the creator and maker. Psychologically, this development indicates the compulsion which leads men to imagine abstract ideas and ideals in concrete images and suggests the grounds for the recurrence of the analogy and of inspiration in the history of the Western tradition. The ideas and ideals, the humanization of which has produced the figure of the genius as fine artist, are perfection and novelty, the former the limiting conception of technique, the latter that of creativity. Both express the ideal of autonomy.

The philosophical significance of the theory of genius for aesthetic, in contrast to the psychological, is to be sought in the specifications of the ideas of perfection and creativity or originality in the objects and events the genius is presumed to make or create. At this point, the historian of ideas and the aesthetician encounter some obscurity, owing in part to the interest displayed by eighteenth-century thinkers in the merits of artistic objects as objects or events produced either by imitation or imagination. Were mimetic or imagined objects and events in fact the principal structures which eighteenth-century thinkers judged to be those correlative to the artist in the theory of genius, the controversy between the ancients and the moderns could be stated in its entirety as George Puttenham had stated it at the end of the sixteenth century.[1]

The dogma firmly held and widely received in the history of criticism that the controversy in the century in question does primarily concern imitation and imagination has a basis in the terminology of the period. As we have observed,[2] however, the tradition of creative freedom which had been built in the writings of Muratori, Bacon, Hobbes and Addison slowly eliminated the issue of imitation, the vestiges of which are no longer the center of interest for the dominant epistemology of the period of genius. The bondage or freedom of the artist is argued on grounds of rationality or originality in the context of the theory of the association of ideas. Despite the change to association-psychology from a discussion of universals internal or external to the agent,[3] the fundamental issue of freedom remains. The rival claims of freedom of choice and of free originality are tested by reference to the structure of the work of art. Proponents of freedom in terms of natural choice come, under the influence of the theory of genius, to concentrate attention upon the beautiful. Proponents of the theory of freedom in terms of nonnatural originality attempt to specify the structure of the sublime.

Speculation upon the beautiful or the sublime as structures of the work of art produced by the genius, follows Platonic and Aristotelian theories of rational technique and develops hints got from Plato's *Ion* and Longinus' *de Sublimitate.* As we have observed, Kant's *Kritik of Judgment* is the philosophical repository of a century's speculation. It is, of course, more than this. Kant's systematic reordering of the problems of mechanism and originality under the influence of the theory of genius suggests the philosophical meaning of the theory itself, although that meaning awaits clarification by the correction of an error

[1] *The Art of Poetry.* See *supra,* Ch. I, p. 12 n.

[2] See *supra,* Ch. I, pp. 8 ff.

[3] See *supra,* Ch. II, pp. 69 ff.

implicit in Kant's own speculation. Precisely what that meaning is we discover not alone from Kant's philosophy but also from the thought of Burke and " many clear-headed men among us " whose writings Kant knew and with whose " physiological " approach to aesthetic theory he compares and contrasts his own " Transcendental Exposition of aesthetic judgments." [4] This he does " in order to see whither a merely empirical exposition of the Sublime and Beautiful leads." How empirical the expositions were concerning the sublime and the beautiful written by men who—principally with the exception of Burke—had fallen under the spell of the theory of genius is in itself a controversial matter. More significantly, if compatibility be the criterion, Kant's " Transcendental Exposition " succeeds no better in the task of relating the sublime to the beautiful than do the methods of the empiricists. Kant maintains that the judgment of taste concerning the beautiful depends upon the relation of the imagination to the understanding, while our experience of the sublime is grounded on a relation of the imagination to reason. For reasons which we shall suggest,[5] Kant regards the beautiful and the sublime, species of the aesthetic genus, as incompatible, although judgments of both are recognized to be best stated in terms of " ought " rather than of " how," a terminological distinction which, perhaps, may be best interpreted to differentiate a judgment of value from a judgment of fact.

This incompatibility in Kant's speculation upon aesthetic reflects the ancient conflict between creating and making. It reflects that conflict, however, in terms of the particular heritage interpreted by intelligent writers who sought to free art from the domination of Aristotelian rhetoric and poetic and who, once successful, tried to formulate an aesthetic specification of the product of genius. They sought a structure for the original, judged to be either inexplicable or not wholly explicable in terms of art or technique.

[4] *K.d.U.*, sec. 29, p. 147.

[5] *Infra*, this chapter, pp. 201 ff.

The burden of the requirement of perfection is sufficiently illustrated by the remark of Martelli: "One must not desire from a thing the perfection, which would destroy it." [6] Martelli "repents" of having tried "to conform tragedy to the idea" which he had of it, "by imitating those examples which approximated most to the idea." He had more particularly in mind the rigorous unity of place which he believes is "inconsistent with verisimilar representation." It is, however, one thing to recognize the difficulties inherent in a theory and quite another to provide an adequate framework of reference for what one desires, the cause of forsaking what one forsakes.

Addison, whose writings much influenced Kant, had attempted to explain the freedom of the artist as creator from external objects and ideas, whereas Martelli had sought to imitate "those examples which approximated most to the idea." Addison breathes the spirit of the "new freedom" in his remark apostrophizing "how great a power then may we suppose" the artist to possess which "might suffice to make up the whole of heaven or hell of any finite being." [7] This power, he continues, "bestows a kind of existence, and draws up to the reader's view several objects which are not to be found in being. It makes additions to nature, and gives a greater variety to God's works. In a word, it is able to beautify and adorn the most illustrious scene in the universe, or to fill the mind with more glorious shows and apparitions than can be found in any part of it."

Longinus had, not dissimilarly, maintained that "sublimity," that "echo of a great soul," may produce what transcends not only nature but the divine and may raise inspired men "almost to the intellectual greatness of God." [8] Arguing as he did both

[6] *L'Impostore,* quoted by J. G. Robertson, *Studies in the Genesis of Romantic Theory in the Eighteenth Century,* p. 132.

[7] *The Spectator,* ed. Tegg, No. 421, p. 485.

[8] *de Sublimitate* IX: "Homer can magnify even what is divine: As far as a man's eye may pierce the haze, who stands on a cliff-top gazing over the wine-dark sea, no less was the resounding leap of the God's horses. He measures their leap by the standard of the universe." Compare *ibid.,* XXXV: "Not even

that "precision in every detail" may come "perilously near littleness" and that the great orator may be "far removed from flawless perfection, yet rise above all that is mortal," Longinus suggests, as we have observed, that there are two kinds of genius.[9] More significantly, he writes of the work of art as an organism.[10] The suggestion which follows, that "the limits which encircle" great passages afford them "a new voice" provided that "they are formed by partnership into a body, and also enclosed by the bond of rhythm," does not escape the critical attention of the eighteenth century.[11]

To some of the many elaborate attempts to develop Longinus' suggestion that novelty is explicable in terms of organic wholes—a suggestion in itself foreign neither to Plato's nor Aristotle's philosophies of art—we shall shortly turn. The more general problems of the philosophical meaning of the genius are, however, of more immediate interest. We have observed that imagination had become an increasingly flexible and controlled instrument for critical and aesthetic uses, as we have likewise indicated instances of efforts to employ it to search out the uttermost limits of novelty.[12] The temper of the instrument is severely tested by the theory of association of ideas. If, as Addison insists, this "talent of imagination . . . has something in it like Creation," and if to the new or uncommon, as he holds, God "has annexed a secret pleasure," it may possibly be

the whole universe can suffice the reaches of man's thoughts and contemplation, but oftentimes his imagination oversteps the bounds of space." (A. O. Prickard, *A Treatise concerning Sublimity*)

[9] See *supra*, Ch. IV, p. 131. Cf. p. 141.

[10] *de Sublimitate* XL. "Language is made grand in the highest degree by that which corresponds to the collocation of limbs in the body, of which no one, if cut off from another, has anything noticeable in itself, yet all in combination produce a perfect structure."

[11] See Shaftesbury and Kant on the analysis of the beautiful, *supra*, Ch. IV, p. 147 and *infra*, this chapter, pp. 194 ff.

[12] See Robertson, *The Genesis of Romantic Poetry*, p. 87, for the relation between Muratori and Longinus. Robertson maintains that Muratori "established in unambiguous terms the imagination as the essential factor in artistic creation." On the origins of the imaginative theory of art, see Croce's *Aesthetic*, pp. 193 ff. and pp. 480–81.

that the " secret pleasure " is owing to its introduction by a precedent idea. There would appear to be little place for the novel in a theory so rational as that called association of ideas.

Of the speculative critics who not only advocated but advanced the theory of genius, William Duff and Alexander Gerard most clearly suggest the difficulties presented to speculation by association and novelty. Duff makes of imagination a kind of *omnium gatherum,* a faculty by which the mind, explicable in terms of Lockeian epistemology, is filled with simple ideas and reflects upon its own operations.[13] Imagination, however, also possesses a " plastic power of inventing new associations of ideas, and of combining them with infinite variety," a " plastic power," Duff argues, which indicates the imagination's ability to " present a creation of its own." His own suggested solution to the problem is that the " vigorous exertion " of this faculty distinguishes the genius from the man of talent.[14]

Gerard, writing in *An Essay on Genius,* enunciates a not dissimilar point of view. The principles of association while " never perhaps entirely dormant or impotent " do not exert themselves with the same ease or with the same force all of the time.[15]

Duff and Gerard clearly hope to rationalize the theory of genius and that of the emergence of novelty. Their use of the ambiguous word " inspires " does not necessarily argue a lack of success. There are, however, hints that neither writer is

[13] *An Essay on Original Genius,* pp. 7–8 ff. It " assembles the various ideas conveyed to the understanding by the canal of sensation, and treasured up in the repository of the memory, compounding or disjoining them at pleasure."

[14] It is interesting that Duff contrasts the genius with wit and humour, all the " offspring of imagination." The latter " neither invent nor create," their " proper province " being " to assemble with alertness those sentiments and images, which may excite pleasantry or ridicule." (*Ibid.,* p. 47.)

[15] *Op. cit.,* pp. 237–38. Genius, Gerard holds, is " extensive and vigorous " and " can with ease perfect inventions " when the principles are active " and ready to run from any idea that occurs, through a long train of other ideas related to it, without a possibility of our resisting their influence, or cooling the ardour which their activity inspires."

wholly satisfied that the genius and his originality may be brought within the confines of the theory of association of ideas. Gerard remarks upon the fact that the ability of the imagination to " perfect inventions " with ease is like " a lucky and unaccountable hit, in pursuing which it has formerly toiled in vain." Gerard also provides prescriptions for the production of " this vigour and alertness of invention," so fundamental to the notion of the genius.[16] Still, neither diligence nor acquired abilities assist or improve genius. Only a vigorous imagination can produce it. Mere labor can but mimic genius and the latter's work " will always bear evident traces of unnatural force and awkward straining."

Duff, too, tends to doubt the adequacy of his own assumptions concerning the principles of association. His conception of the nature of the problem is precise. Speculation must account for the " new " in the " peculiar character of original genius." [17] Gerard's doubts get to the core of the problem of the genius, his originality, the novelty of his product, and the relation of the two to the theory of association. He is somewhat sceptical of the possibility that novelty by itself is sufficient recommendation for what we may call aesthetic value;[18] nor does he hold it a reproach to genius that it receive materials " wholly prepared, from sense and memory." He tends to interpret the function of the faculty of invention not in terms of

[16] *Op. cit.*, pt. 2, sec. viii, pp. 237–38. ". . . it is necessary that there be some present perception connected with many others, from which it may set out; that the associating principle to which that connexion corresponds be strong; that the mind be not deeply engaged in any other train of thinking which might lead off from this track; and that we have a strong association of design."

[17] *An Essay on Original Genius*, p. 89. Duff adds that this peculiar character is " to strike out a path for itself whatever sphere it attempts to occupy; to start new sentiments, and throw out new light on every subject it treats . . . . It is distinguished by the most uncommon, as well as the most surprising combinations of ideas; by the novelty, and not unfrequently by the sublimity and boldness of its imagery in composition."

[18] *An Essay on Genius*, p. 77. ". . . the face of novelty which infant conceptions wear, fails to recommend them promiscuously, till reason has had time to survey and examine them."

the production of ideas but, rather, in its application and arrangement of them. "The power of fancy" is subject to the same limitation as our power over the natural world. It cannot create.[19]

Gerard may with some justification be said to represent the soberer advocates of the theory of genius. "As we can create no new substance," by our imagination, so our capacities to receive novel ideas are likewise limited. Gerard's words might well be a monument to the rationalist theory of genius:

> . . . The boldest fictions of the poets, which least resemble any thing in nature, are yet composed of parts which really exist in nature . . . . Indeed though it were possible for fancy to create ideas wholly unlike to those things which men have access to observe, the attempt would prove entirely useless. The artist might amuse himself with the forms of his own creation, but they would produce no effect either on the taste or on the passions of others. Men can be touched only by ideas which they are able readily to conceive; and they can conceive only those ideas, the members of which sense has already deposited in the memory.[20]

No little ingenuity had been expended in the eighteenth century in an attempt to escape the dilemma of original genius and association of ideas by reformulating Longinus' assumption that there are two kinds of genius, the natural, "far removed from flawless perfection," and the lesser, whose powers derive from art. Gerard's statement of the problem appears to place it beyond possibility of solution in terms of the correlative Longinean theory of organic wholes."[21] To urge that "men can be touched only by ideas which they are able readily to conceive" is to emphasize, within the theory of association of ideas, the

[19] *Ibid.*, pp. 99 ff. "Give it a stock of simple ideas, and it will produce an endless variety of complex notions: but as we can create no new substance, so neither can we, except in perhaps a very few peculiar instances, imagine the idea of a single quality which we have never had access to observe."

[20] *Ibid.*, p. 102.

[21] See *de Sublimitate* XL, where it is suggested that "a new voice" is given to separate parts "when formed by partnership into a body, and also enclosed by the bond of rhythm."

hypothesis that the perfection of art implies intelligibility. Novelty then becomes a strict alternative to intelligibility, as creativity does to art. Philosophers of art are presented, at least ostensibly, by the eighteenth-century theory of genius with a strict alternative, to be understood in terms of the dominant epistemology of their times: either they must deny that novelty is the essential problem of aesthetic, the alternative chosen by Burke; [22] or deny that the theory of association is relevant to artistic and aesthetic processes, the alternative chosen by that greater thinker, Kant.[23]

Let us examine the consequences of the presentation of this presumably strict alternative for the theory of the structures of the beautiful and the sublime. We shall note, as we proceed, certain general tendencies. Among these are the increasing dependence upon description in negative terms of objects and events called sublime; the augmented importance in theory of the mind's reflections upon its own operations; and the increased interest in the possibility that the uniqueness sought as the correlative to originality is discoverable rather in a novel state of mind than in natural or artistic events. The increased emphasis upon the autonomy and uniqueness of the experiencing mind, evident in Burke's resort to " self-preservation " and Kant's use of ideas of reason, suggests a reordering of the " great analogy " for the aesthetic of the period of association of ideas. So far as freedom is concerned, it brings to the subject a con-

[22] Burke begins *A Philosophical Inquiry into the Origin of Our Ideas on the Sublime and the Beautiful* (part 1, sec. 1) with mention of the problem of novelty. Men's minds do have a creative power of their own, he grants, but can only " vary the disposition of those ideas " which have been received from the senses. Burke does not deny that " some degree of novelty must be one of the materials in every instrument which works upon the mind." Curiosity is, indeed, interpreted to be " the first and simplest emotion which we discover in the human mind " and its primary desire is for novelty. Rather, Burke emphasizes the fact that " as those things which engage us merely by their novelty, cannot attach us for any length of time, curiosity is the most superficial of all the affections." (The references, except where otherwise noted, are to the Bohn edition.)

[23] *K.d.U.*, secs. 22 and 49. See *infra* (this chapter), pp. 191-92, 202-203.

ception of the artist not unlike the assertions concerning God made by Augustine and Anselm.

Burke, whom Kant judged to be the most important author among those who adopted the empirical method in explaining the beautiful and the sublime, presents his argument in a way designed to leave little room for mystery and none for unintelligibility or vagueness. He denies the importance of novelty but does not deny that men do have a sort of creative power of their own. Mental processes consist, however, largely in the varying dispositions of data provided by the senses. We do, indeed, produce "new images," Burke argues, but we do so principally by "making resemblances . . . . we unite, we create, we enlarge our stock." [24] As regards taste, Burke grants that error is possible. It is explained on grounds of defect in judgment, a faculty which Burke holds to be "for the greater part employed in throwing stumbling blocks in the way of imagination." [25]

Burke's specific analyses of the structure of the beautiful are congruent with so rational a presentation of general principles of taste and belong almost wholly to the classical tradition of rational technique. He offers, for example, a notably Aristotelian description of the beautiful.[26] It is "small, smooth, gradually varied, delicate." Equally notably, the description of the experience of the beautiful is appropriate to the object.[27]

Burke's analysis of the limited and definable structure of the beautiful, with its inheritance from Aristotle and Aristotelianism, is in marked contrast to that which he offers of the sublime. An evident reliance upon negative characterizations of the latter's structure in art or in nature provides theorists of the associationist school of ideas with an obvious alternative to the

[24] *Op. cit.*, Introduction, p. 58.

[25] *Ibid.*, p. 65. Compare Burke's remark, Introduction, "So far as Taste is natural, it is nearly common to all."

[26] *Ibid.*, part III, secs. XIII ff.

[27] "The head reclines something on one side, the eye lids are more closed than usual and the eyes roll gently with an inclination to the object; the mouth is a little opened, and the breath drawn slowly, with now and then a low sigh."

task of describing the novel, the unique, or the original. Burke urges that "a clear idea . . . is another name for a little idea," whereas "hardly anything can strike the mind with its greatness, which does not make some sort of approach towards infinity; which nothing can do whilst we are able to perceive its bounds; and to see an object distinctly, and to perceive its bounds, is one and the same thing." [28]

The consequences of a distinction between the beautiful and the sublime, in which the former is analyzed precisely and affirmatively, while the latter is presented in terms of an approach to infinity, boundlessness, lack of clarity, great size and similar indefinite and negative terms, are at once evident in Burke's writing. The attempt to remedy the latter description becomes increasingly difficult, and a definable or analyzable structure for the sublime work of art or event in nature is less the object of speculation than is the determination of the state of mind in the experience called sublime.

How consistent Burke is in denying to novelty an eminent position in his philosophy of taste the reader of *A Philosophical Enquiry into the Origin of our Ideas of the Sublime and Beautiful* may judge upon learning that the sublime in nature causes "astonishment," a state of soul "in which all its motions are suspended, with some degree of horror." Moreover, the direction of interest from the indefinable object or event called sublime toward the specific and specifiable state of mind is no less clearly indicated in Burke's emphasis upon the power exerted by the mind in its contemplation of ideas which in other contexts induce pain and terror. Nothing, Burke argues, is sublime which is not some "modification of power." Pain is always inflicted by a power in some way superior.[29] "The sublime is an idea belonging to self-preserva-

[28] *Ibid.*, p. 92. Burke remarks that the idea has been opposed but he still maintains that "in nature, dark, uncertain images have a greater power in fancy to form the grander passions, than those have which are more clear and determinate."

[29] *Ibid.*, part II, sec. V, p. 94: ". . . we never submit to pain willingly. So that strength, violence, pain, and terror, are ideas which reach in upon the mind together."

tion "; [30] an idea which when associated with pain and terror makes the object sublime and the experience that of " astonishment," " a sort of tranquillity tinged with terror." [31]

As we turn to Addison, we find that he employs a phrase which justly characterizes not only his own conception of sublimity but that of Burke as well: " If we consider, therefore, the nature of this pleasure, we shall find that it does not arise so properly from the description of what is terrible, as *from the reflection we make on ourselves at the time of reading it*." [32] The structure of the external incitements to the experience of sublimity are less significant than is the freedom of the mind exerted in asserting its own powers. Indeed, Addison goes so far as to maintain that " the more frightful appearance they make, the greater is the pleasure we receive from the sense of our own safety." [33]

Burke probably develops the conception of the sublime to the limits imposed by novelty and creativity upon an empiricist whose epistemological theory is based on Locke's philosophy. The attention he pays to the mind's reflections upon its own operations no doubt influenced Kant, who carried to its logical conclusion its implications in his own conception of sublimity.[34] For Kant, there are no sublime objects or events. What is novel

[30] *Ibid.*, part II, sec. XXII, p. 112.

[31] *Ibid.*, part IV, sec. VII, p. 149. ". . . if the pain and terror are so modified as not to be actually noxious; if the pain is not carried to violence, and the terror is not conversant with the present destruction of the person, as these emotions clear the parts, whether fine or gross, of a dangerous and troublesome encumbrance, they are capable of producing delight; not pleasure, but a sort of delightful horror, a sort of tranquillity tinged with terror, which, as it belongs to self-preservation, is one of the strongest of all the passions. Its object is the sublime. Its highest degree I call *astonishment*."

[32] *Op. cit.*, No. 418, p. 482. (Italics mine)

[33] *Ibid.*, No. 418.

[34] Compare Alison's statement (*Essays on the Nature and Principles of Taste*, p. 115) : " The conclusion, therefore, in which I wish to rest is, that the Beauty and Sublimity which is felt in the various appearances of matter, are . . . to be ascribed to their expression of mind; or to their being, either directly or indirectly, the sign of those qualities of mind which are fitted, by the constitution of our nature, to affect us with pleasing or interesting emotion."

is not the sublime as an external event but the state of mind. What is free is an autonomous structure of the mind, analyzed in terms of its operation in producing ideas of reason, ideas which provide a ground for freedom from relations both to sensuous and to external conceptual events.

Burke does not rely upon the theory of genius in the presentation of his aesthetic. Addison, on the other hand, is much influenced by it. His writings, as do Burke's, not only affect Kant but the latter's philosophy is influenced by the tradition of the English school concerning genius.[35]

[35] See Schlapp, *Die Anfänge von Kant's 'Kritik des Geschmacks'* and *Kant's Lehre vom Genie und die Entstehung der Kritik d. Urtheilskraft.*

It is not amiss to recall that the theories of the structure of the sublime in nature and art, as well as the structure of the beautiful, run parallel to those of Burke. A selection of instances will illustrate the point. Duff, writing *An Essay on Original Genius,* maintains (pp. 178–79) that "the Imagination of a Poet, whose Genius is truly Original, finding no objects in the visible creation sufficiently marvellous and new, or which can give full scope to the exercise of its powers, naturally bursts into the ideal world, in quest of more surprising and wonderful scenes, which it explains with insatiable curiosity . . . and depending in its excursions wholly on its own strength, its success in this province of FICTION will be proportionable to the plastic power of which it is possessed." It is notable that he adds (*ibid.*, p. 283) that "Every species of original Genius delights to range at liberty . . . . This noble talent knows no law, and acknowledges none in the uncultivated ages of the world, excepting its own spontaneous impulse, which it obeys without control, and without any dread of the censure of Critics." In contrast, Gerard, in *An Essay on Genius,* p. 84, remarks that "Every work of Genius is a whole, made up of the regular combination of different parts, so organized as to become altogether subservient to a common end . . . . Fancy forms the plan in a sort of mechanical or instinctive manner: judgment, on reviewing it, perceives its rectitude or its errors, as it were scientifically . . . ." He continues (*ibid.*, p. 86) ". . . Fancy could not have formed the regular plan of an epic poem, though Homer had had the strongest and most constant perception of the end at which it aimed, if judgment had not, for the consideration of this end, and the repeated comparison of it with the means which imagination proposed for accomplishing it, discovered, in what situation every incident would produce the greatest effect." Judgment, on his view (p. 90) may supply genius with new material.

Henry Home in *Elements of Criticism* (Ch. I, p. 23) remarks upon his assumption that "Every work of art that is conformable to the natural course of our ideas, is so far agreeable; and every work of art that reverses that course, is so far disagreeable. Hence, it is required in every such work, like an organic

We have suggested that, in part as a result of his heritage from eighteenth-century and from Longinean speculation upon the notion of the genius, in part in consequence of his own systematic approach to aesthetics, Kant's writing upon the beautiful and the sublime reveals most clearly the philosophical significance of genius. In all probability, this result is also in part owing to the fact that his heritage from the writers upon the original genius presents a strong compulsion to specify beauty and sublimity, a compulsion measurable in fact by examining the systematic conception of reason and of its ideas. This is argued consistently in the moral and metaphysical fields. It is distorted, however, in its application to a field in which the presentation of objects and events to imagination would appear to be so essential that to rely solely upon the nonempirical regulative principles or limiting conceptions of reason must have appeared absurd even to Kant. In any case, the aesthetic speculation is in striking contrast to what Kant does argue in his ethical theory. In the latter he maintains that the moral law holds categorically even if no individual moral action were free from secret motives of self love. The aesthetic theory is at least designed, on the contrary, to specify beautiful objects and events, as well as the occasions for judgments of taste in the sublime.

Freedom is no less the core of the aesthetic than of the moral problem for Kant. The judgment of taste is disinterested and

system, its parts be orderly arranged and mutually connected, bearing each of them a relation to the whole . . . ." He suggests (*ibid.*, pp. 201–02) that "the beauty of figure . . . arising from . . . regularity, uniformity, proportion, order, and simplicity . . . contribute each of them to readiness of apprehension; and enable us to form more distinct images of objects than can be done with the utmost attention where these particulars are not found." "Grandeur" and "sublimity" on the other hand are not essentially dependent on these qualities. Indeed (p. 216), "the spectator is conscious of an enthusiasm, which cannot bear confinement, nor the strictness of regularity or order . . . ." Home holds (*ibid.*, p. 258) that novelty has the most powerful influence in raising emotion. A new object arouses instantaneous wonder, the highest degree of which arises from "unknown objects that have no analogy to any species we are acquainted with . . . ." (*Ibid.*, p. 269)

free satisfaction, differing from that of moral law in that it is imputed and not commanded. Art is described, as we have observed, as " production through freedom, *i. e.* through a will that places Reason at the basis of its actions." [36] Beautiful art—which " cannot itself devise the rule according to which the product is possible " [37]—is only possible as a " product of Genius." The first property of genius is originality,[38] entirely opposed to the spirit of imitation, whose mental powers are constituted of a " union (in a certain relation) " of imagination and understanding.[39] Genius itself is " the exemplary originality of the natural gifts of a subject in the *free* employment of his cognitive faculties," inspired and described also in terms of ineffable spirit.[40]

In the establishment of the artist as a creative, original and free producer, Kant not only commits himself to the tradition of genius but to that of imagination, as well. Imagination, in its aesthetic function, is a productive faculty of cognition. As we have observed, it is very powerful " in creating another nature, as it were, out of the material that actual nature gives it." [41] Kant strives, however, to make its products intelligible as well as uniquely aesthetic. For him the freedom of the genius cannot be interpreted, as it was by Duff, as a " noble talent " which " knows no law." Its law is provided by the understanding. As we have suggested, Burke accepts the theory of association of ideas and ostensibly reduces the value and significance of novelty for aesthetic, while other associationists hold to the importance of novelty at the expense of a consistent epistemology. Kant on the contrary, denies the relevance of the association of ideas

[36] See *supra,* Ch. IV, p. 136. See, specifically, *K.d.U.*, sec. 43, trans. Bernard, p. 183. See also *infra,* this chapter, p. 195.

[37] *K.d.U.*, sec. 46, p. 189.

[38] *Ibid.*, p. 189.

[39] *Ibid.*, sec. 49, p. 201.

[40] *Ibid.*, p. 203.

[41] See *supra,* Ch. IV, p. 148. " Spirit " ensures originality and must be free in art. Kant argues that, while it is true that spirit alone inspires the work, without " mechanism " it would have no body and would evaporate altogether.

to the judgment of taste by distinguishing productive and reproductive imagination, thus enabling us " to assert our independence as against the influences of nature." [42]

As we proceed to examine Kant's aesthetic of freedom in detail, more particularly with reference to the problems of genius and the structures of the beautiful and the sublime, it should be observed that, in the present writer's opinion, the clarity with which Kant delineated the issue of a reconciliation of freedom as comprehending law or intelligibility and originality or uniqueness is not paralleled by the solution he gave to the problem. His feat in systematizing the poetic and often inexact suggestions of those writers who influenced him is one to be reckoned with, as is the economy with which he brought within the scope of the earlier Critiques the central problem of aesthetic.

One may venture the suggestion that history proved too much for Kant. His account of natural beauty and of the product of the genius, while ostensibly free of theology, bears the mark of the long speculation which assumed that the artist is analogous to God the creator and God the maker. Kant's analysis of the structure of beautiful objects and events subject to the judgment of taste is in the tradition of freedom of choice. His analysis of the sublime is in the tradition of creative freedom. Originality is denied the first, intelligibility escapes the second. The novel or the unique is product of the creation of a state of mind, not in the making of an external object or event. And the reconciliation of freedom of choice and freedom of creativity, which had it been philosophically sound would have meant

[42] The empirical employment of imagination, as reproductive and to which are attached the associating powers, will not ensure originality. " The Imagination," Kant writes (*K.dU.*, sec. 49, p. 198) , " (as a productive faculty of cognition) is very powerful in creating another nature, as it were, out of the material that actual nature gives it. We entertain ourselves with it when experience becomes too commonplace, and by it we remould experience, always indeed in accordance with principles which occupy a higher place in Reason (laws too which are just as natural to us as those by which Understanding comprehends empirical nature) . Thus we feel our freedom from the law of association . . . ."

a reconciliation of the beautiful and the sublime, remains an insurmountable obstacle. Kant's own system provides the ground for the reconciliation, a fact which he himself fails to apprehend, perhaps because of the obscuring image of the inspired genius. Finally, the beautiful product of the genius' art remains ineffable, incomparable, and indefinable.

Let us turn to Kant's analysis of natural beauty and of beautiful art, in which, if we are correct, the theory of freedom of choice is implicit and in which the influence of the demiurgic hypothesis of making leads to an absolutist point of view, explicable in terms of religious and psychological compulsions. Kant's analysis of the objects of the judgment of taste called beautiful falls within the rational Aristotelian tradition, and does not deviate in detail too radically from the inferences drawn by Burke, Addison, and others of the English school of writers [43] traceable to similar demiurgic sources.

For Kant, the formal characteristics provide the principal, if not the exclusive criteria of beautiful objects and events,[44] while the experience of such forms as have " definite boundaries " is one in which the faculties of imagination and understanding are in harmonious and free interplay. As forms, beautiful objects and events are easily perceptible and their representation is easily maintained.[45]

If, as Kant holds, the judgment of taste is " disinterested and

[43] Burke's description we have noted. Addison held that the pleasures of imagination are not so gross as those of sense, nor so refined as those of understanding. Kant holds that the judgment of taste is aesthetical, meaning negatively that it is neither sensuous nor intellectual. Kames and Hutcheson had remarked the subjectivity of the experience of beauty, as well as its immanent teleology, problems which much affected Kant's thought. From Kames and Hutcheson, Kant likewise derived his distinction between free and dependent beauty.

[44] Kant tends to rely upon the abstraction of form from matter in his systematic theory. See M. C. Nahm, *Aesthetic Experience and Its Presuppositions*, pp. 119 ff.

[45] " We *linger* over the contemplation of the beautiful, because this contemplation strengthens and reproduces itself . . . ." (*K.d.U.*, sec. 12, pp. 71–72) This is an interesting analogue to the doctrine of continuous creation. Compare Descartes' *Meditations*, III.

free" with reference to beautiful formal objects and events and if, as he further argues, they must be considered "as if" they were made by a will, i. e., as if they fell under laws which produce a unity "as they would have if an Understanding (although not our Understanding) had furnished them to our cognitive faculties,"[46] we may ask what *in the structures* of natural beauty under consideration provides the grounds for the free interplay of the faculties which for Kant is central to his doctrine of an *a priori*, universal, and singular judgment of taste. Kant certainly regards them as unique to the aesthetic judgment, although the argument is unsound.[47]

Beautiful objects appear to be distinguished from empirically definable objects and events by formal characteristics and are set off from other objects and events principally by "delineation" but, by implication, also by the principle of variety in unity. But whether we take "*delineations à la grecque*," as illustrative of the first, or "isochronous vibrations (*pulsus*) of the aether" as illustrative of "the form of the combination of different representations,"[48] whether we take free or dependent as illustrative of simple or complex forms or unities, we discover in Kant's examples only the reiteration of the ancient doctrine that what nature presents as an aesthetic object is the function of the unity, form, or whole.[49] If, as appears to be implied, there is an analogy to an "original faculty,"[50] certainly the need to resort to the term "ineffable" is not evident with reference to these formal objects and events. What is common to such beautiful objects is the form. As Bosanquet suggests, Kant's theory is that a form of beauty has "a content which can be analysed."[51] We may speculate concerning the nature of the process implied in the phrase that the objects are "as if they

[46] *K.d.U.*, Introduction IV, p. 18.
[47] Cf. M. C. Nahm, *Aesthetic Experience and Its Presuppositions*, pp. 127 ff.
[48] *K.d.U.*, sec. 14, p. 74.
[49] Cf. *supra*, on Longinus, Ch. VI, p. 181.
[50] *K.d.U.*, sec. 17, p. 85.
[51] *A History of Aesthetic*, p. 278.

fell under laws which produce a unity as they would have if an Understanding . . . had furnished them to our cognitive faculties." This means that we attempt to discover the metaphysical ground for the notion of "purposiveness without purpose," which is a statement of immanent teleology. We may only infer that the process, manifest "as if it were one of will," is one characterized by rational freedom of choice, and that it is manifested in intelligible objects or events analyzable into simple or complex forms or unities, abstracted from content.

But if the natural objects and events called by Kant beautiful do not satisfy his own criterion of originality, they do succeed in satisfying that of technical perfection. Their potentialities for analysis parallel those of their formal structure. The hypothetical will which acts as if it were an understanding presents for our perception objects and events of so beautiful and formal a kind that Kant believes them to be objects of an universal, if subjective, judgment of taste. Vestiges of power and knowledge adhere to this postulated will; one consequence is that we are not fully informed concerning what the ground for the singular judgment is.

Kant faces up to the problem of originality and creativity in the theory of genius and of beautiful art. In view of the emphasis in his theory upon the formal and rational structure, his use of the word "genius" promises little. For art must appear like nature in order to endow it with that freedom "from all constraint of arbitrary rules as if it were a mere product of nature." [52]

In discussing art in general, Kant amplifies his suggestion that it is production through freedom, through a will that places reason at the basis of its actions, by referring to bees' cells of wax. This, he holds, we call a work of art, but only by

[52] *K.d.U.*, p. 187. The analogy between the genius and the hypothetical will which makes it in aesthetic experience appear as if the objects and events were the product of an understanding is clear: art is described as "production through freedom, i. e., through a will that places Reason at the basis of its actions." *K.d.U.*, sec. 43.

way of analogy.[53] If, as Kant argues, " we call anything absolutely a work of art in order to distinguish it from a natural effect, we always understand by that a work of man," [54] we should then be able to proceed from his own presentation of beautiful arts in order to determine what kind of creator is that genius who " is the exemplary originality of the natural gifts of a subject in the *free* employment of his cognitive faculties " [55] and who through his exercise of art in freedom gains a new rule for art.

The genuinely illuminating phrase which Kant employs and which provides the clue to the nature of the producer of beautiful arts of genius is " proper rational deliberation." [56] We learn that the work of beautiful art is a representation [57] and that, as we have noted, as such it is superior to nature because it " describes as beautiful things which may be in nature ugly or displeasing." [58] It is expression for purposes of communication,[59] which lead to the arts of speech, the formative arts, and the art of the play of sensations. Kant's further speculation amplifies this by analysis of the arts of speech into rhetoric and poetry, in terms of the free play of the imagination; [60] the formative arts, " or those by which expression is found for Ideas in *sensible intuition* (not by representations of mere Imagination that are aroused by words) , and the art of the Beautiful Play of Sensations (externally produced) ." [61]

[53] *Ibid.*, sec. 43, p. 183. " As soon as we feel that this work of theirs is based on no proper rational deliberation, we say that it is a product of Nature (of instinct) , and as Art only ascribe it to their Creator."

[54] *Ibid.*, sec. 43, p. 183.

[55] *Ibid.*, sec. 49, p. 203.

[56] *Ibid.*, sec. 43, p. 183. It should of course be noted that Kant regards " beautiful art " as " a mode of representation which is purposive for itself, and which, although devoid of definite purpose, yet furthers the culture of the mental powers in reference to social communication." (*Ibid.*, sec. 45, p. 187) This is to be understood principally in terms of Kant's inference that the judgment of taste is universally communicable.

[57] *Ibid.*, sec. 48, p. 193.

[58] *Ibid.*, sec. 48, pp. 184–95.

[59] *Ibid.*, sec. 51, pp. 206–07.

[60] *Ibid.*, sec. 51, pp. 207–09.

[61] *Ibid.*, sec. 51, pp. 208–09, 212.

It is unnecessary for us to examine in detail this statement concerning the beautiful arts—painting, sculpture, architecture, rhetoric, poetry, and drama. What is important is the fact that Kant proceeds as if the beautiful arts were completely analyzable: ". . . in all beautiful art the essential thing is the form "; [62] the expression of intuition and sensation; the spatial [63] character of the formative arts; and the temporal [64] character of such arts as music.

We appear to have reached, once again, a conclusion which accords with that which followed from our mention of Aldous Huxley's statement concerning the concert at Tantamount House. Beautiful art for Kant would appear to be describable in terms of technique (spatial and temporal elements), symbols or representations, forms, and expressions, including those of intuitions and feeling. Thus far, one may only infer that the artist deliberates and expresses his freedom of choice, precisely as does an artisan or a technician in producing what Kant calls in contrast to beautiful, mechanical, pleasant or mercenary arts.

The general tenor of Kant's writing concerning the genius, grounded on spirit and mechanism, does tend to emphasize the importance of law, judgment, and taste.[65] But for all his insistence upon comprehensibility and intelligibility, Kant sees clearly that beautiful art poses the problem of originality. "*Originality* must be its first property," [66] Kant writes of genius, although taste must be the *conditio sine qua non* of the beautiful work of art. And Kant insists upon the inspired character of the genius, his inability to learn by rule or teach by rule, and

[62] *Ibid.*, sec. 52, p. 214.

[63] *Ibid.*, sec. 51, p. 209.

[64] *Ibid.*, sec. 51, p. 212.

[65] See, for example, his answer to the question " whether it is more important for the things of beautiful art that Genius or Taste should be displayed." (*K.d.U.*, sec. 50, p. 205) " Abundance and originality of Ideas are less necessary to beauty than the accordance of the Imagination in its freedom with the conformity to the law of the Understanding. For all the abundance of the former produces in lawless freedom nothing but nonsense; on the other hand, the Judgment is the faculty by which it is adjusted to the Understanding."

[66] *Ibid.*, sec. 46, p. 189.

upon the fact that the genius " does not know himself how he has come by his Ideas." [67] Are we then justified in regarding freedom of choice as adequate to Kant's explanation of the beautiful arts and so ignore his references to the genius' powers of creation and originality? Do we correctly attribute the ineffability of the process and the product of genius solely to the influence of centuries of speculation on the analogy of the artist to God?

There is one point at which Kant's analysis of beautiful objects and events, both natural and artistic, goes beyond the possibility of explanation in terms of rational theory of freedom of choice to offer us the clue to his use of the word genius. That point relates to the perfection of beauty achieved by nature and the genius. Kant has argued that the correlative to a will is an absolutely beautiful form. The correlative in art to that will is the genius. The difficulty in the theory and the need for resort to the theory of genius are traceable to the fact that the argument should have been that, correlative to an experience explicable on grounds " as if " there were a will, the forms should have been described " as if " they were absolutely beautiful, and the artist similarly, " as if " he were a genius.

The error is illuminating. Kant has argued that the beautiful object is structurally rational, analyzable, and, by implication, the product of free choice. What transcends rational explanation and requires the use of genius can only be the notion of complete perfection, which in turn can only be the product of omniscience or omnipotence employing wholly intelligible technique. Kant should have argued that the absolutely beautiful object of the universal judgment of taste is an idea of reason, a limiting conception or a regulative principle. Only by proceeding from the conditioned to the unconditioned can the beautiful as such emerge. Kant does refer to the idea of

[67] Cf. *K.d.U.*, sec. 43, pp. 183–84: ". . . what we *can* do, as soon as we merely *know* what ought to be done and therefore are sufficiently cognisant of the desired effect, is not called Art. Only that which a man, even if he knows it completely, may not therefore have the skill to accomplish, belongs to Art."

reason but he also specifies the wholly formal object as what is experienced. He fails to observe what is implicit in his system of philosophy, namely, that were the beautiful considered as an idea of reason, the demiurgic aspect of the genius would have been clarified in that the genius, like the will, is an hypostatization or personification of the limiting conceptions of intelligibility and perfection by means of technique.

Kant insists, it is true, upon originality in the art of genius but originality is correlative to the ineffable. There is, however, another answer in Kant's theory of genius to questions concerning originality and the emergence of the novel and unique, even under the *conditio sine qua non* that judgments are made in terms of law and intelligibility. Its implications, as well as the more general implications of the theory of originality or creativity, become explicit in the analysis of the sublime. We have observed that, for Addison, the implication of the statement that " imagination . . . has something in it like creation " is made explicit in the suggestion that there is a " new principle of pleasure, which is nothing else but the action of the mind." For Kant, it may be argued as we have already implied, the contribution by the genius of what is original does not manifest itself in works of beautiful art–if it does so, it remains ineffable –but, rather, it manifests itself as the novel state of mind created by genius in another genius. Such creation is got neither by the first genius laying down a rule nor by the second artist imitating the product of the first.[68]

It is this creating of an unique creator, of genius by genius, reminiscent of Sir Philip Sidney's remark concerning that maker who bestows " a Cyrus upon the world to make many Cyruses," which must be kept in mind as we turn from the analysis of the beautiful to that of the sublime in Kant's aes-

[68] *K.d.U.*, secs. 48–49, pp. 192, 203. Kant maintains that " the Ideas of the artist excite like Ideas in his pupils if nature has endowed them with a like proportion of their mental powers." The product of genius, not to be imitated, " awakens to a feeling of his own originality " another genius " whom it stirs so to exercise his art in freedom from the constraint of rules, that thereby a new rule is gained for art . . . ."

thetic. But, as we do so it is also well to recall the contrast between the demiurgic theory of the beautiful and the creative theory of the sublime. Beautiful art awakens to a feeling of his own originality another genius by means of an externally produced object or event. In contrast, for Kant, there are no objects or events natural or constructed which may be called sublime. As Bosanquet remarks, the sublime has no analyzable content. Kant is prepared here to abandon not only the law of association but also the intelligible structure of the sublime in nature upon which many writers of the eighteenth century had relied. He does this in order to secure complete creativity for his aesthetic.

The detailed influence of those writers upon the sublime whom Kant read need not detain us.[69] The significant contributions to the theory which clarify the meaning of genius are the facts that Burke's theory offers Kant the notion of the limitations of the powers of the imagination,[70] and that Addison (and perhaps Home) suggests the *bewegung*, the movement or action of the mind, which appears to be the ground for the feeling of sublimity. We do well to recall, also, that Addison had argued concerning the sublime that the " nature of this pleasure . . . does not arise so properly from the reflection of what is terrible, but as from the reflection we make on ourselves." The sublime is great beyond comparison; its final

[69] It is enough to point out the following facts. Addison employs the notion which, in Kant's writing, becomes the mathematically sublime, a notion primarily based on size. Burke's writing suggests the dynamically sublime, primarily based on power. It should be remembered, however, that Kant differentiates the mathematical and the dynamical as terms characterizing the categories in *K.d.R.V.* (B 110) and discusses, in these terms, how far these concepts of the understanding " are adequate to the idea of reason." (*Ibid.*, B 57) Both Burke and Addison use the conception of the infinite in their writing on the subject.

[70] Burke had argued that the imagination is a process which traces power through its various gradations " unto the highest of all, where our imagination is lost." Addison held that " fancy " which finds itself in a " chasm " is brought to a stand, after the understanding " opens an infinite space on every side for us; our reason can pursue a particle of matter through an infinite variety of divisions." *The Spectator,* No. 420.

cause, that we are destined to find satisfaction in the infinity of God alone.

As we have observed, Kant's theory of beautiful art, produced by the exercise of freedom of choice by the genius, ostensibly transcends definition and rule to the ineffability which is owing to spirit. The search for the originality in the product of beautiful art which differentiates it from the product of mechanical art ostensibly is that for representations in free employment for which " no expression marking a definite concept can be found." It may be pointed out, however, that the perfection of beautiful art does produce an object or event analogous to such natural objects as the rose, which Kant maintains is an object of singular judgment.[71] While, on his argument, we cannot in aesthetic experience generalize the singular judgment, it is none the less true that we can pronounce each rose beautiful as nature presents it. In other words, the judgment of the beautiful is intelligible to the unique instance (should we grant that we can differentiate the immediate judgment, " this rose is beautiful," from the mediated judgment and still give a name to the object of the aesthetical judgment) and corresponds to that presumed perfection of technique which Kant's theory of genius attributes to the powers of the artist.

There is evidence that Kant was aware of a systematic difference in the ground for judgments of the beautiful and the sublime. With some of the incompatibilities we are not here concerned.[72] The significant incompatibilities for our essay of freedom arise from the fact that in a formal sense the free art

[71] *K.d.U.*, sec. 8, p. 61: ". . . I describe by a judgment of taste the rose, that I see, as beautiful. But the judgment which results from the comparison of several singular judgments, 'Roses in general are beautiful' is no longer described simply as aesthetical, but as a logical judgment based on an aesthetical one." A singular judgment takes into account the particular nature of the subject and has no extension.

[72] Kant argues that beauty is compatible with charm and the play of imagination but that it is incompatible with the furtherance of life. The sublime is emotional and " incompatible with physical charm." Bosanquet remarks, *op. cit.*, pp. 275–76, that " For Kant, as for Burke, there is no acknowledged synthesis of the sublime with the beautiful . . . . We cannot say, therefore, that he makes

of the genius does not produce what is original, whereas Kant's analysis of the sublime rests upon the hypothesis of originality or creativity. The flaw in Kant's aesthetic derives from his incapacity to relate mechanism to orginality, i. e., to relate what he calls the beautiful to what he calls the sublime.

Kant's account of the judgment of taste in his analysis of the beautiful rests upon the relation of the imagination to the understanding, in his analysis of the sublime upon the relation between imagination and reason. The latter faculty is that to which Kant constantly refers in his discussions of freedom of the noumenal self.[73] The extent of the freedom of the mind experiencing sublimity is indicated by the fact that Kant conceives the intelligible freedom of the experience of the beautiful in terms of the extension of the imagination under the laws of understanding as a whole.[74] This kind of freedom is, however, inadequate in explanation of the sublime. The sublime "in the aesthetical judging of an immeasurable whole like this" he remarks, taking the illustration of the universe, lies in the "fact that in our progress we ever arrive at greater units"[75] while yet even this systematic division of the universe "represents our Imagination with its entire freedom from bounds, and with it Nature, as a mere nothing in comparison with the Ideas of Reason, if it is sought to furnish a presentation which will be adequate to them."[76]

We have noticed that Kant denies the relevance of association of ideas to the judgment of taste. He also emphasizes productive, rather than reproductive imagination in developing his theory of beautiful art. In the analysis of the sublime, like-

the sublime a species of the beautiful. Both, rather, are species of the aesthetic judgment, but only beauty belongs to the judgment of taste, while the sublime is rooted in an emotion of intelligence. (Geistesgefuhl)."

[73] In his analysis of the sublime, Kant goes so far as to urge that the "formlessness" of the objects which occasion the experience of sublimity may indicate a purposiveness in the subject in respect of the object "in virtue of the concept of freedom." (*K.d.U.*, Introduction VII, pp. 33–34)

[74] *K.dU.*, sec. 35.

[75] *Ibid.*, sec. 26, p. 118.

[76] *Ibid.*, sec. 26, pp. 118–19.

wise, it is argued that the reproductive imagination is inadequate.[77] More significantly, however, in describing sublimity, Kant appears to regard this sensible faculty, imagination, whether in its productive or reproductive operations, as inadequate. It is inadequate in comprehension, yet it shows that its destination is to make itself adequate to the idea of reason.[78]

Little more is required, in fact, to assure us that Kant has here provided an aesthetic specification of the theory of free creativity and that the core of the " great analogy " concerning freedom unconditioned by external relations remains. That little more can be supplied at once. First, the sublime is, in contrast to the beautiful, formless.[79] As Plato implies that the inspired poet is freed from the need to have knowledge of art or to validate judgment, so Kant frees the mind which experiences sublimity from the restrictions imposed by a relation to *sensibilia*,[80] i. e., as God is said by Augustine to be free from external relations to the matter which He creates. Moreover, the inference is drawn at once that there are no sublime objects in nature.[81] The conclusion correlative to that of omnipotence is arrived at in the inference concerning omniscience, i. e., the autonomy of the thinking self.[82]

[77] See, for example, the illustrations Kant gives of the Pyramids and of St. Peter's at Rome, *K.d.U.*, sec. 26, p. 112. He remarks that " there is here a feeling of the inadequacy of his Imagination for presenting the Ideas of a whole, wherein the Imagination reaches its maximum, and, in striving to surpass it, sinks back into itself, by which, however, a kind of emotional satisfaction is produced."

[78] *Ibid.*, secs. 28–29.

[79] *K.d.U.*, sec. 23, pp. 101–102: " The Beautiful in nature is connected with the form of the object, which consists in having definite boundaries. The Sublime, on the other hand, is to be found in a formless object, so far as in it or by occasion of it *boundlessness* is represented, and yet its *totality* is also present to thought." Cf. *ibid.*, sec. 24, p. 105.

[80] *Ibid.*, sec. 23, p. 103: " No sensible form can contain the sublime properly so-called."

[81] *Ibid.*, sec. 25, p. 109: The sublime is " not to be sought in the things of nature, but only in our Ideas."

[82] In the sublime there is " totality of intuition, with no comparison and contrast, which is explicit in all measurement." The sublime is possible through

Kant's theory of the beautiful is, with the exception of the suggestion that it is possible to produce a technically perfected work of beautiful art, a natural one. His theory of the sublime is, in almost every aspect, nonnatural. Reason is self-subsistent and transcendent. Taken literally, Kant admits that the ideas of reason, in natural terms, are impossible.[83] A relation to the infinite, expressible in numbers, is impossible; our physical power compared to that of nature is impotent. What Kant requires of the reason is, in fact, judged by him to be a self-contradictory conception, which places judgment beyond the reach of comparison and contrast, and carries " our concept of nature to a supersensible substrate . . . ." [84]

The miracle of God's creative powers is thus, in aesthetic, stated in terms of the self-contradictory idea of totality. God's autonomy, specified in terms of matter, is paralleled in the mind's freedom from *sensibilia.* His omniscience, specified in freedom from uncreated ideas,[85] finds its analogue in Kant's

the law of reason, " which recognises no other measure, definite, valid for every one, and invariable, than the absolute whole." (*K.d.U.*, sec. 27, p. 119.) Cf. *ibid.*, sec. 26, p. 111 on the mathematical estimation of magnitude and of absolute magnitude.

[83] *K.d.U.*, sec. 26, p. 115. Writing of the mathematically sublime, Kant maintains that " the voice of Reason . . . requires totality," comprehension in one intuition, from which not even the infinite " space and past time " are excepted. But the " infinite is absolutely . . . great . . . ." To think as a *whole* indicates a faculty of mind which surpasses every standard of Sense. For [to represent it sensibly] would require a comprehension having for unit a standard bearing a definite relation, expressible in numbers, to the infinite; which is impossible.

[84] See *K.d.U.*, sec. 26, p. 111. Kant contrasts the unit of a standard bearing a definite relation, expressible in numbers to that of our comprehension of the sublime. See also, *K.d.U.*, sec. 26, p. 117: " Now the proper unchangeable fundamental measure of nature is its absolute whole, which, regarding nature as a phenomenon, would be infinitely comprehended. But since this fundamental measure is a self-contradictory conception (on account of the impossibility of the absolute totality of an endless progress), that magnitude of a natural object, on which the Imagination fruitlessly spends its whole faculty of comprehension, must carry our concept of nature to a supersensible substrate . . . ."

[85] Cf. *supra*, Ch. II, p. 70. See, also, *Monologium*, Ch. XI. Anselm points out that the " supreme Substance took absolutely nothing from any source, whence it might either frame a model in itself, or make its creatures what they are."

argument that the sublime is " not to be sought in nature, but only in our Ideas." Things and events become in the theory of sublimity mere occasions for the process in which the mind expresses its free powers. Only by " subreption " may nature be called sublime. The mind's power is declared in terms of ideas of the unconditioned and the infinite. It is manifested in the " dynamically sublime," in that, in contrast to our physical impotence " considered as beings of nature," we have a faculty of judging independently of, and a superiority over, nature, wherein " nature is regarded as small in contrast to our ' personality.' " In this sense, Kant's conception of sublimity is a statement of our omnipotence and omniscience in contrast to our state as creatures of nature.

It bespeaks the strength of the compulsion implicit in the image of the genius in its association with the conception of sublimity in the eighteenth century, that Kant should have formulated as part of his aesthetic a theory of the autonomous and unconditioned freedom of the judging mind. The existence of God, as well as the possibilities of freedom and immortality are problems which in his systematic philosophy give rise to dialectic. Reason leaves in speculation upon them the conditioned for the absolutely unconditioned. The original state of the mind achieved in the experience of sublimity, as well as presumed perfection of the beautiful, suggests an experience of unattainable absolutes. God, freedom, and immortality remain postulates in Kant's ethical system. Similarly, an act performed on motives of pure duty may, Kant admits, never have been performed. In aesthetic theory, in contrast, it is assumed that both perfection and originality are achievable and achieved.

If, now, we recognize that the compulsion so to speculate upon the sublime and the beautiful is integral to what produces the image of the genius, which is in turn the humanization of the analogy of the artist to God the creator and the maker, we are prepared also for the reiteration at the level of the sublime and the beautiful of the incompatibility of theories of creating and making, of expression and making and symbolizing. The philosophical meaning of genius is clear. Psychological compulsions lead to the personification of notions of perfection of technique in producing the wholly intelligible, and of originality in producing novelty. Although Kant errs in specifying the products of genius—which are ideas—his systematic account of philosophy suggests both a sounder hypothesis for products of beautiful art and for the interrelations of perfection and originality. What Kant did was to commit what Whitehead was to call the fallacy of misplaced concreteness. Had Kant been content to maintain that regulative ideas of reason are beyond attainment (precisely in that they do not give constitutive knowledge) and that the ideas are goals or limiting conceptions which we approach without limit but to which we never attain, he would have avoided error.

Kant's speculation concerning aesthetic is thus influenced by the "great analogy." The proper study of the artist as creator relates to the *direction* of an imagination which presents to itself alternative possibilities for making within the context of the "limiting conceptions" which mark its *destinations.* The destinations are the wholly intelligible as product of perfection of technique and the unique as product of unconditioned originality. Every work of art is a product of the imagination as it operates within the continuum marked off by these limits. The work of fine art is the product of imagination. As product of art it is made by the artist who sets goals of perfection and originality and it is both intelligible and novel.

Perfection and originality as destinations of the imagination are not merely limiting conceptions. They are also regulative principles and, as we shall argue, aesthetic values.[86] The explanation of the work of fine art as intelligible object has for its framework of reference the idea of perfection; that for originality comes within that framework, but it comes within that of the total structure of the work of fine art, as well.[87] Both conceptions pose the problem of immanent teleology.

[86] See *infra,* Ch. XI.

[87] Kant's aesthetic expresses the following important notions: the freedom of

It has been maintained in the argument just presented that the incompatibility with which the eighteenth century in general and Kant in particular labored has its origin in the analogy of the artist to God as creator and maker. Kant fails to relate mechanism to spirit. His failure is owing not alone to the inheritance, sustained in the theory of art as inspiration, of the belief that originality implies ineffability. On his own showing, the area of ineffability is reducible *ad infinitum,* although it can not be wholly got rid of. Had he argued this consistently, i. e., had he taken originality as the limiting conception, an empirical approach to it as the goal of the fine artist's search might have been forthcoming. The obstacles to such an approach become insurmountable for Kant precisely because he does not recognize the fact that his conception of the sublime is an assertion of the mind's complete originality or freedom and that, had he been consistent with his own principles, the mechanisms of art must be related to spirit by interrelating the beautiful and the sublime.[88]

We may state the problem more clearly in terms of freedom. What Kant and the critical and philosophical essayists of the eighteenth century were embroiled in was the controversy concerning freedom of choice and freedom of originality. If we assume, as we shall do, that the limiting conceptions of perfection and originality are values, the problem in the artist as creator becomes one of relating the work of art as product of free choice to the work of fine art as product of free choice *and* free originality. The work of art thus becomes what we judge; the work of fine art, what we judge and what we ought to

the genius, the limiting conception, the movement of the imagination and its destination, and the creation of an original state of mind. See *K.d.U.*, p. 126 and sec. 49, pp. 198–99. Kant describes there "such representations of the Imagination" as *ideas,* "partly because they at least strive after something which lies beyond the bounds of experience, and so seek to approximate to a presentation of concepts of Reason . . . ."

[88] The difficulty is, of course, partly terminological. In a sense, the work of art is not beautiful until it is related to concepts such as the tragic, comic, and sublime. See *infra,* Ch. XI.

judge. The aesthetic problem thus becomes not an aspect of the "great analogy" but that of the interrelating of mechanisms and means to the end of fine art.

The assumption of the remainder of this essay of the artist as creator is that the work of fine art is intelligible.[89] If we are correct, the principal difficulty which has led to such an assumption as Foster's that the artist "has no clear knowledge of what he is going to achieve before he has achieved it,"[90] has its source in theological implications introduced by the "great analogy" into aesthetic theory. The argument that "if God is a Creator, natural objects can have no form distinguishable as the object of the intellect," inasmuch as "the form of natural objects would be distinguishable (and the objects therefore definable) only if the activity of God were purposive, *i. e.*, directed upon an end whch is not itself the product of his activity," is a statement concerning creativity inapplicable to the fine artist. Whatever significance the statement has if applied to God, its implications of artistic omniscience and omnipotence for fine art remain mere analogy.

To urge the contrary to the statement, "the meaning of a painting is not intelligible in the sense in which the purpose of a wheelbarrow is,"[91] is not to argue that the purpose of Titian is identical to that of the maker of a farm implement. It is to maintain at the outset, however, that Titian's "Assumption" is a religious painting, that it is a symbol, a sign, a form, an expression, and a product of technique. What more a work of fine art may be, our argument will attempt to show. In any case, that more may not with impunity be dissociated from the fact that it is the product of an artist whose freedom is conditioned by nonaesthetic presuppositions. Whether, as a work of fine art it is also explicable in terms of an aesthetic purpose, remains the central problem for this essay.

[89] Not specifically "in the sense in which the purpose of a wheel-barrow is," to use M. B. Foster's phrase, but certainly generically in this purposive sense. See M. B. Foster, "The Christian Doctrine of Creation and the Rise of Modern Science," *Mind*, N.S., Vol. 43, p. 462.

[90] *Ibid.*, p. 462.

[91] *Ibid.*, p. 462.

We propose to examine next the aesthetic problem of the artist as free creator, as one whose originality produces a unique work of fine art and whose technique makes that unique work of fine art intelligible. Were we to learn no other lesson from the "great analogy" and its history, it would be of value to have discovered the truth of the proposition that if by real creation is meant creation without presuppositions, "even the finest accomplishment of the human spirit is not real creation."[92] We accept the conception of creation under the conditions which make it philosophically meaningful: "to give this material a new shape, the form of his [the artist's] own mind or imagination."[93] What the new is, remains our problem; but it is certainly new under such conditions as render the term intelligible. It may be added that we do learn lessons other than this from the "great analogy," as we shall observe[94] in examining within the context of art the significance of such value-terms as sublimity and beauty which the "great analogy" sustained in history.

[92] E. Frank, *Philosophical Understanding and Religious Truth*, p. 57.
[93] *Ibid.*, p. 57.
[94] See *infra*, Ch. XI.

II The Structure of Art and Fine Art

Genius and taste no longer mean for us what they meant to the poets and critics of the Romantic period. Their halo, their mystery, their power are gone. By genius is now merely meant the creative faculty, the power of self-expression, which we all share in varying degrees. By taste is meant the power to see and understand and enjoy the self-expression of others, a power which all of us must in some measure share or no art would be intelligible . . . . We are all geniuses; we are all possessed of taste.

SPINGARN, *Creative Criticism*

7 The Structure of the Work of Art

> . . . awakens to a feeling of his own originality . . . stirs to exercise his art in freedom.
>
> KANT, *Kritik of Judgment*

Walter Pater once wrote that " nothing which has ever interested living men and women can wholly lose its vitality . . . no dream which has once been entertained by actual human minds . . . ." Men's intimations of divinity have brought within the scope of speculation problems of the provenance, nature, and province of their own creative powers. The speculation has been stimulated and sustained, as we have observed, by " genius," " inspiration," the " corruption of beauty," " means-invisible," and similar words and phrases recurrent in the tradition of the artist as creator.

If we are to believe Benedetto Croce, who perhaps of all aestheticians most eloquently voices the conviction that artistic and aesthetic expression is free creation, the production of physical beauty implies a will which persists in " not allowing certain visions, intuitions or representations to be lost." [1] Raphael's " The School of Athens " portrays Neoplatonic philosophy. Van Dyck's " Portrait of a Gentleman " offers us the likeness of an unknown man. The " Colleoni Monument " is a spectacular presentation of a condottiere. The temple at Segesta celebrates a victory never won. Each representation preserves a specific nonaesthetic meaning. If something other than this is not lost, the explanation of its persistence must be consonant with the theory that the artist is free and that " fine art " is more than a mere phrase. For the moment, however, it is sufficient in an essay of the artist as creator to assume that, in addition to the unique perception Monet affords us in the " Rouen Cathedral," the style embodied in della Robbia's " Visitation," and the

[1] *Aesthetic*, p. 111.

feeling which gives title to El Greco's "Ecstasy in the Garden," these works of fine art also embody the two principal values which the tradition of the artist as creator has sustained and which its great thinkers have sought to define in terms adopted from theology. The first is intelligibility, the product of power and knowledge achieved through the application of technique and directed toward perfection; the second, individuality, the product similarly of knowledge and power, achieved presumably by means of technique and directed toward originality, interpreted in terms of the production of unique individuals.

Should we, however, succeed in describing how the inspired poet or the great architect objectifies the artistic estimate of life's excellences, perfection, and values in the work of fine art, we should not yet be at the end of the inferences which may be drawn. The tradition of the artist as creator informs us not only concerning the *what* that men have believed to be of supreme value in creativity; it likewise tells us *how* men have tried to explain the transmission of these values from artist to man of taste by means of the work of fine art. As we have argued, the theory of the genius is the aesthetic specification of the great analogy between God as creator and maker and the artist. It is from this aesthetic specification that contemporary aesthetic has proceeded to abstract, as the most significant element, the identity of genius and taste.

To urge, as Spingarn does, that the identity of genius and taste is "the final achievement of modern thought on the subject of art" [2] is hyperbole and tends to obscure two important facts. In the first place, the statement does not sufficiently emphasize the fact that the identification of artist and aesthetic perceiver is explicitly suggested in speculation upon art as early as Plato's image of the magnetic rings [3] and in Aristotle's statement that poetry seems to spring from two natural causes,

[2] *Creative Criticism*, p. 42.

[3] *Ion*, 533 ff. See M. C. Nahm, *Aesthetic Experience and Its Presuppositions*, Ch. x.

the instinct of imitation and delight in imitations,[4] and that it is the central problem of eighteenth-century theories of genius. Secondly, "final achievement" too readily suggests that the implications of the identity have been made fully explicit. Croce does not err, certainly, in arguing that we are revealed to ourselves by great artists only because there is an "identity of nature between their imagination and ours."[5] Rather, too much is taken for granted in such a statement. If, as we have intimated, the work of fine art does embody men's conceptions of supreme value, i. e., perfection and originality, expressed as intelligibility and individuality, the assumption that there is a relation between the fine artist and the perceiver who re-creates the values the fine artist has embodied must take account of the fact that what has been objectified by the one for the other has received its intelligible form in a medium available for but different from imagination. This, in turn, implies that works of art and fine art are interrelated, that the latter, no less than the former, is a product of technique, and, finally, that corresponding to this technique, the judgment made by the perceiver of the work of fine art is a rational correlate to the technique.

It is in the investigation of areas of speculation in which the problems of the relations of technique and judgment, of work of art and work of fine art, and of value and fact, converge that the aesthetic issues—in contradistinction to the theological, which sustained them until they were specified and self-subsistent—emerge. How complicated the issues are is sufficiently indicated by a brief anticipation of the argument we shall present in the remainder of this essay. We shall maintain that the work of art is a limited structure within a total structure and that the limited structure is explicable in terms of the artist's freedom of choice employed as technique upon such matter or

[4] *Poetics*, IV. For the general problem, see M. C. Nahm, *Aesthetic Experience and Its Presuppositions* and M. C. Nahm, Introduction, *Aristotle on Poetry and Music*.

[5] *Aesthetic*, p. 14. Compare Spingarn, *Creative Criticism*, p. 138.

mechanisms as colors, tones, silences, presupposed signs or symbols, feelings or images. We shall argue that the work of fine art, the total structure, is also a product of artistic technique, but that, while it is describable in terms of freedom of choice, such description is incomplete without reference to freedom of originality. The latter, we shall argue, is explicable by reference to regulative conceptions of perfection and originality. The product of creativity, i. e., of these two freedoms, is an intelligible and individual work of fine art, re-created by the aesthetic perceiver. The aesthetic problem is posed by the need, on this hypothesis, to specify the means-end relation employed by the fine artist to produce the unique and intelligible work of fine art, that relation being susceptible to correlative judgment.

If, as we maintain, this is the problem of the artist as creator for aesthetic speculation, we are led again to ask the question, what is the work of art? [6] The incompatibility of the answers, on the one hand that the work of art is an object or event made and a sign or symbol signified, and on the other hand that it is an image or intuition expressed, led us to examine the great analogy between the artist and God. With the theological background of the artist as creator now explicit, let us examine in detail these three traditional answers to the question asking again whether there is a relation among them at the level of philosophy of art and what that relation is.

It will be recalled that Aldous Huxley, in his description of the recital at Tantamount House, expressed interest in the tools and materials of art—the snout and rosined horsehair—which suggest the theory of art as making; in the " grand things in the world," which implies the theory of art as a symbol; and in the Rondeau, which provokes in the poet " a slow meditation upon beauty " and in turn evokes the theory of art as creative imagination, called expression.

In each of these analytically distinguishable philosophies of art, that of making, of symbols, and of expression, it is assumed

[6] See *supra*, Ch. I, pp. 26 ff.

that the real, i. e., the product of the artist's constructive or creative powers, is the structure of the work of art, respectively as object made, as sign symbolized, and as image expressed. As we have observed, in the history of aesthetic speculation, autonomy has been claimed for each hypothesis concerned with the work of art's morphology.[7] We propose to argue, on the contrary, that the theories are not mutually exclusive but, rather, that they are complementary and that judgment may be made and validated if we consider the work of art to be a structure of such kind that, in terms of these complementary theories, it is describable as a concrete significant form. Finally, we shall maintain that the work of art as concrete significant form is the ground for the aesthetic specification of the demiurgic theory of making and for the inference of the maker in the most generalized sense of the term, i. e., as one who employs techniques in terms of freedom of choice.

Let us proceed to an examination of these complementary theories of the work of art and the philosophical problems concerning the artist as maker and the product of his art which are raised.

The Demiurgic Theory of Making: "Concrete Significant Form" and the Artist's Freedom of Choice

Plato, as we have noted held that the craftsman must proceed rightly and, by implication, that he should acquire "a knowledge of a whole art." [8] By contrasting the inspired poet to the artisan and by freeing the former from the requirement that he pass judgment upon his art, Plato implies that making provides the sound ground for the judgment of the work of art. This is, likewise, the speculative ground for the theory of demiurgic and artisan making.[9]

[7] See *infra*, Ch. I, pp. 29 ff. [8] See *supra*, Ch. I, p. 43.

[9] See also his distinction between the technician and the maker of copies of products of technique in *Republic* x. Plato constantly argues that measure, i. e., judgment in mathematical terms, is the highest form of knowledge of art.

We have also remarked upon Aristotle's suggestion, in one of the three classical statements concerning the meaning of freedom in art and its matter, that art is concerned with " coming into being, i. e., with contriving and considering how some thing may come into being which is capable of either being or not being." [10] It is notable that while the reasoned state of capacity to make has its origin in the maker and " not in the thing made," what is in fact produced by tools and techniques is a structure, ordinarily referred to as an artifact, and an object or event separated from the maker. Technique transfers the form in the mind of the artist to the material. The general assumption of the theory of making is that an intelligible form is produced in the matter upon which the artist operates by means of technique. It is inferred that, because the artifact or work of art is spatially and temporally independent of the maker, it is an object subject to objective judgment.

The recurrent claim that making and the object made are grounds for meaningful and objective judgment is persuasively put forward by Rhys Carpenter: " Out of materials which—artistically—are nothing at all," Carpenter writes in his analysis of the basis of artistic creation, " the artist creates the work of art . . . . Works of art are stamped, through and through, over and over, with their specific phase in the long evolution of style . . . . Style is all that structure and articulation by which a painted picture or carved marble becomes emotionally intelligible." [11] Style it is, therefore, which, according to Professor Carpenter, in " that broader discipline " converts " the layman's ordinary world of vision into the painted world of pigment, the cast world of bronze, the carved world of wood and stone," [12] and which is not only central to the theory of art as making but would appear to be its essence as well.[13] There would appear to

[10] Cf. *supra*, Ch. I, p. 36.

[11] " The Basis of Artistic Creation in the Fine Arts," *The Basis of Artistic Creation*, pp. 30–32.

[12] *Ibid.*, p. 41.

[13] *Ibid.*, p. 36.

be little doubt that the real as object of our judgment is, on this view, the object made and stylized.[14]

It is evident, in Carpenter's argument, that the adoption of the theory of art as making precludes and is intended to preclude the artist's free originality in order to establish the prior values for the work of art of intelligibility of style and potentiality for proper classification.[15] It is no less clear that the artist is not deprived, in so far as the argument may be considered complete, of freedom of choice. He chooses from " the layman's ordinary world of vision " the materials he will work upon, namely, pigment, bronze, wood and stone; and, quite as clearly, he may choose to stress the capacity of metal to express vital power as does Verrocchio in the " Colleoni Monument," the geometry of extreme foreshortening, as does Tintoretto in " The Vision of Ezekiel," or illumination by contrast to darkness, as in Rembrandt's " The Night Watch."

It is notable that the artist's freedom of choice is effectuated by means of technique operating upon materials to produce a specification of style which, in turn, renders the work of art " emotionally intelligible." But it is clear that this is implicit at every level of analysis of the theory of making and, in this, that the theory of technique is complementary to the theory of the work of art as a symbol. Thus, a distinction between such stylistic symbols as Carpenter mentions, e. g., the evidence of Mantegna's " comprehension of the correct geometric solution of extreme foreshortening," and, by way of illustration, the

[14] In his emphasis upon the processes of construction, Carpenter's form of the theory resembles that of Samuel Alexander, to which we shall later refer. It is, moreover, not uninteresting that Maritain's philosophy of the art of making, one with its source in Aristotle, lays stress upon the artist who works in *sensibilia* and produces in every making a product in which the form shines " on the proportioned parts of matter." Nor is it without significance that precisely as Carpenter denies to the artist all but the illusion of freedom, so Maritain maintains that " the production of beauty belongs to God alone as His true property," and that the artist must accept the postulate of art's " essential being." See Jacques Maritain's *Art and Scholasticism,* (E. T) pp. 25, 35, 93. See M. C. Nahm, *Aesthetic Experience and Its Presuppositions,* pp. 58. 59, 60.

[15] See *supra,* Ch. I, pp. 21 ff.

symbolism of imperial power in the equestrian statue of Marcus Aurelius, is one of degree of representational specification. In the first, the geometrical solution symbolizes the complex theory of perspective and an augmented interest in a mathematical interpretation of the universe. In the second, the symbol is of Stoicism and imperium, less specified now simply because the barbarian under the bronze horse's hoof has disappeared.[16] The symbol of both the less and the more specified representation is the form imposed by the artist upon the material. The abstract presentation of the theory of technique assumes that by the use of tools and a relation of means, including techniques, to ends, artifacts are produced. It is but another level of speculation which generalizes and maintains that a form has been imposed upon the material of art, that the material embodies this form, and that what the artist conceives as the end of his art, the perceiver knows as an intelligible form.[17]

Differentiations between the theory of the work of art made

[16] The fact that the statue was taken to be a representation of the Emperor Constantine and, it is assumed, escaped destruction as a pagan monument on that account, indicates the difficulties of interpreting specific symbols and the value of iconology.

[17] The complementary nature of the two theories of the structure of the work of art is evident even at the level of what might be called "unconscious symbolism." Piero Pollaiuolo, in "Portrait of a Young Lady" and Domenico Veneziano, in "Madonna and Child," appear to represent the ladies of the period with hair plucked from the forehead with as little consciousness that they are portraying, as well, an Italian court-custom, as did the Pueblo Indians who, in their use of sea shells for ornamentations, symbolized trade with the Pacific or Gulf tribes. See V. Gordon Childe's *Man Makes Himself*. Childe remarks, *op. cit.*, p. 7, that "The archaeologist collects, classifies, and compares the tools and weapons of our ancestors and forerunners, examines the houses they built, the fields they tilled, the food they ate (or rather discarded). These are the tools and instruments of production, characteristic of economic systems that no written document describes. Like any modern machine or construction, these ancient relics and monuments are applications of contemporary knowledge or science existing when they were fashioned . . . . The tools employed . . . symbolize a whole economic and social system." See also, Stanley Casson on the use of emery in ancient sculpture and the implications of trade and transportation. (*The Technique of Early Greek Sculpture*, pp. 19 ff.) See also, E. M. W. Tillyard's *The Elizabethan World Picture*, for what the Elizabethan took for granted and what appears in the drama.

and the work of art symbolized disappear in the separation of the embodied form from the maker by the act of making. That the work of art made and separated from the maker is yet taken to be intelligible in terms of the artist's intention, the history of aesthetic has correctly come to regard as a ground for judgment of the work of art as a symbol.[18]

It is immediately apparent, however, that, so far as our central problem of the artist's freedom is concerned, the separation of object or event made and form or sign symbolized does serve merely as a ground for freedom and, in fact, states the problem of freedom itself in the constantly reiterated fashion of negation, i. e., free from something. And there is immediately suggested the possibility that while the theory of the artist as maker is compatible with that of the artist as symbolizer the relation may in fact be nonreciprocal in precisely that aspect of freedom of choice which is our principal interest. It is an assumption of the theory of making that the artist does exercise freedom of choice but not of originality in the construction of the work of art and in its elaboration and perfection as a finished object or event. It is not so evident that the theorists of the work of art as a sign of symbol pay more than lip-service to the hypothesis of freedom of choice.

The issue of freedom is raised in the structural theory of the work of art as a symbol by the name, iconology, used to designate the most influential methodology employed in contemporary studies in the history of art. It is significant that to " icon " or sign, the word " ology " is added, inasmuch as this implies that the method is a science. The theory of making,

[18] I am not here concerned with the question, whether or not Aristotle had got to the stage of speculating upon works of art as symbols—an historical question of importance under other circumstances—inasmuch as it is the Stagarite's theory which served as the basis for the theory of the work of art as symbol. Bosanquet, in *A History of Aesthetic*, pp. 56 ff., and Butcher, in *Aristotle's Theory of Poetry and Fine Art*, Ch. II, are in agreement that he has not done so. It is my concern, however, to point out that the embodiment of the form in the material is recognized by Aristotle to alter the *meaning* of the form, as well as its effect upon the perceiver.

on the contrary, is a theory of art traceable as such to the Aristotelian distinction between the object of scientific knowledge, which is, as he writes, "of necessity," and the object of art, "*which is capable of either being or not being* . . . neither with things that are, or come into being, by necessity, nor with things that do so in accordance with nature . . . ." [19]

The general tenor of the theory of iconology is almost precisely summed up in the Aristotelian phrase that "what we know is not even capable of being otherwise." This is most evident in the specific reference in this theory of the work of art as a symbol to meaning, rather than to the form (e. g., as style) as the important structural factor in the work of art. It is meaning which has been selected as the ground for the judgment of the real and to the examination of the intrinsic meanings of works of art we shall now turn in our search for an answer to the question, what is the work of art? The theory of intrinsic meanings is argued in perhaps its most cogent form by Erwin Panofsky in his *Studies in Iconology.*

Panofsky carefully lists such meanings as "political, poetical, religious, philosophical, and social." [20] The question is raised at once: do we here, in the extensive studies of signs and symbols, in iconography which explicitly marks out its field as "subject matter or meaning of works of art, as opposed to their form," do we here come upon the structure which is the real object of judgment?

As regards the work of art in general, it is well to note, in answer to the question, that Panofsky remarks of the "*three strata of subject matter or meaning*" in the work of art that they are not merely neatly differentiated categories which seem "to indicate three independent spheres of meaning." On the contrary, these strata "refer in reality to aspects of one phenomenon, namely, the work of art as a whole." [21]

[19] Aristotle, *Nicomachean Ethics*, 1139 b 23; 1140 a 13. (Italics mine)

[20] *Op. cit.*, p. 16.

[21] *Ibid.*, pp. 16–17. The methods of approach, it is urged, "which here appear as three unrelated operations of research merge with each other into one organic and individual process."

It is the statement concerning the " work of art as a whole " which poses the significant problem for the theory of symbols as a sufficient explanation for the structure and judgment of art. It is here that the issues of the freedom of the artist, either in terms of choice or originality, are implicit, as is the correlative problem of the intelligible and unique work of art. It is not easy to ascertain precisely what Panofsky means by the " work of art as a whole." He draws the distinction between " form " and " subject matter or meaning " and this suggests that the " work of art as a whole " does not mean the whole work of art.[22] Yet the inclusion of the " expressional " as one of the two factors belonging to the " primary or natural " class of meanings suggests that he does mean this.[23] The general tone of his *Studies in Iconology* makes the latter the more likely possibility, the more so because in his account of the work of art is included, within the general description of the strata of meaning, " empathic " and " psychological nuances." The controlling principle of expressional strata of meaning is held to be the history of style.[24] It appears probable that by " empathic " and " psychological " as parts of the expressional, are meant " individual " and, possibly, " creative." [25]

What happens to art as a discipline classically interpreted in terms of freedom of choice once it is limited by a methodology intended to provide a scientific procedure is most evident in Panofsky's argument that a painting by Maffei represents Judith and not Salome.[26] We are told that there are " several sixteenth-

[22] *Ibid.*, 16–17.

[23] *Ibid.*, pp. 3–4.

[24] *Ibid.*, pp. 14–15.

[25] The latter assumption is made in the light of a more general context of the study of art than is made explicit in *Studies in Iconology*. But it is within that more general context that the implications pertinent to the present essay of the theory of the work of art as a symbol may be made explicit. There are, in fact, relevant to the theory of the artist as creator two familiar issues, namely, the artist's freedom of choice in a " science of icons," and the artist's creative and originative powers with reference to the " expressional " stratum of meaning. See *infra*, the present chapter, pp. 224 ff.

[26] *Studies in Iconology*, pp. 12 ff.

century paintings depicting Judith with a charger; there was a *type* of ' Judith with a charger,' but there was no *type* of ' Salome with a sword.' " Professor Panofsky is, no doubt, correct in his conclusion that the painting in question " represents Judith and not, as has been assumed, Salome." It is, necessary, however, to distinguish between the specific accomplishment and the general theory. The reader of the Apocrypha would encounter no difficulty in associating either Salome or Judith with a sword. Nor is it likely that he would fail to continue to associate them by a deficiency in the surviving material of the notably fragile art of representation. Neither is there a logical contradiction in assuming that an individual artist proceeded to the rather obvious association of Salome with a sword. If, indeed, this act of imagination be put out of court by high priori and categorical decree, it is still not beyond belief that the structure of the made work of art may have suggested to an artist that a sword be represented. The weapon as symbol of Salome would require rather less inventiveness on the part of the artist than that which gave seacoasts to Bohemia and far less than that which gave " blind mouths " to ecclesiasts. Should the emphasis fall upon the theory of types, it may well be asked whether the genus of icons may with impunity exclude morphological species in order to limit the work of art to intellectual or literary signs. As we have seen, style as " structure and articulation " becomes or may become symbolic in the work of art, as the more specific presentations of the halo, the nimbus, and the mandorla indicate.[27]

The argument of theorists of the work of art as a structure of signs or symbols tends to concentrate interest in the genus or type to which the specific painting belongs. It thus threatens to limit, if not exclude, the possibility of the artist's freedom of choice and, hence, to deny the ground for distinguishing art from science. There is in a theory of this kind no adequate answer to questions concerning the value of the work of fine art, the explanation of the single instance of an icon, or the

[27] Compare Aristotle's *Poetics* and the " ideal " Achilles.

origin of a type. The theory of making, as presented by Carpenter, and the theory of signs, as presented by Panofsky, emphasize the intelligibility of the work of art.

It may be urged, however, that both Carpenter and Panofsky mean by the work of art more than this in theory, and this must be granted. The former insists upon the " emotional intelligibility " of the object or event; the latter introduces, as we have seen, such words as " empathic," " psychological," and " expressional." But one may ask several questions which appear to remain unanswered, at least in *Studies in Iconology*. In the first place, what does become of the expressional meanings included in the synoptical table in Professor Panofsky's study?[28] Secondly, what precisely is the " work of art as a whole " ? It is evident that the inclusion of these terms indicates that the theory of the work of art as symbol requires not only the theory of the work of art as making as its complement, but that of the work of art as expression, as well. As we shall see, the theory of the work of art as expression is a theory not of freedom of choice but of freedom of originality. The reluctance to elaborate upon its implications in a theory either of making or symbolizing is easily understood.

That the mature theory of making does require reinforcement from the complementary hypothesis of expression is evident the moment one touches upon the problem of judgment of the work of art as made. Few better illustrations of this fact may be found than in Samuel Alexander's aesthetic theory in the realist tradition, an interpretation which places emphasis upon construction and making. Alexander assumes, in tracing the development of the " instinct for constructiveness " into " object of contemplation," that he has offered a sufficient analysis of the emergence and character of fine art. The account, however, does go beyond the author's initial postulates, which are that the ultimate basis for the aesthetic sense is this " instinct for constructiveness,"[29] and that the

[28] *Studies in Iconology*, pp. 14–15.
[29] As given in *Art and Instinct*.

aesthetic impulse and the aesthetic emotion which goes with the impulse are an outgrowth of that instinct " when it has become first human, and next contemplative." [30] In order to relate the making of the work of fine art and the experience of making, i. e., the judgment upon it, Alexander converts the *process*, making, into the object of judgment. In aesthetic experience, however, no external object or event corresponding to the object or event made or constructed is in fact made or constructed. The contemplation of the process, i. e., our judgment or aesthetic experience,[31] must therefore be regarded as an event, and as an event meaningful in large part as our reconstruction in imagination of the maker's original and successive mental and physical processes as these were directed to the production of the work of art.[32]

It would be an error to conclude, however, that the real as object of judgment in Alexander's theory is the imagined event alone and without consideration of the object or event made. By " the simple process of imputation," Alexander writes, the object brought before the mind " forms part of the whole perceived external object because the conation to which it corresponds is linked into a unity with the conations evoked by the presented external thing." [33]

The significant reasons for retaining, even by " imputation," the " presented external thing " in examining the judgment of

[30] *Ibid.*, p. 6.

[31] Alexander appears to identify these. See, for example, his statement concerning evaluation, *Beauty and Other Forms of Value*, p. 7, and his agreement with Croce, *ibid.*, p. 29.

[32] *Ibid.*, pp. 29–30. ". . . we can proceed from creation to appreciation . . . . The work of art throws the spectator back into the frame of mind in which the artist produced it . . . . The picture sets the spectator following the artist's hand, the poem read aloud sets the reader constructing the words into their perfection of unity, and, incidentally . . . may induce in us the passions which supplied the poet with his words."

[33] *Ibid.*, p. 26. He adds that " the imputation characteristic of the work of art is precisely of this nature. The mind is mixed in artistic creation with its materials because the impulses initiated in it in the course of construction are reflected in the materials as worked up into their artistic form."

the real in aesthetic is matter for later consideration.[34] Our immediate concern is to point out that it is precisely on this issue of the reality of the external object that the expressionist attacks both the theory of the structure of the work of art as made and as a symbol. We shall turn to the third theory of the work of art as a structure, that of expression, to examine more particularly the reasons for its ostensible incompatibility with the theories of the work of art as symbol and object made. The compatibility of the two theories of the structure of the work of art derives, as we have seen, from the common assumption that art is a state of capacity to make, to impose a form which has its origin in the maker, upon a material external to the maker. The theories are explicable in terms of natural freedom of choice and may be interpreted [35] in more modern terminology as hypotheses in which the imagination is assumed to be able to select among alternative images or modes of action. It is implied in both theories, moreover, that a means-end relation is demonstrable between the technique of the artist and the end he intends to produce in the work of art, and that this intention is evident in the intelligible form, i. e., the work of art, he produces.

The divergences between these theories of the artist's freedom of choice and the theory of expression, as it is presented in its most influential statement by Croce, are at once evident. Croce denies that the artist is to be understood in terms of intention,[36] that there is a means-end relation,[37] that objective judgment is possible,[38] and that art is technique.[39] To assert the possibility, as we have done, that one may interpret the work of art as a structure in which what is made, what is symbolized, and what is expressed are complementary aspects of the

[34] See *infra,* this chapter, pp. 233 ff. and Ch. VIII, p. 255.

[35] See *infra,* this chapter, pp. 235 ff. See also, M. C. Nahm, *Aesthetic Experience and Its Presuppositions,* Ch. XV.

[36] *Aesthetic,* Ch. VI and VII.

[37] *Ibid.,* p. 51.

[38] *Ibid.,* Ch. IX.

[39] *Ibid.,* Ch. VII and XV.

same object or event, encounters perhaps its crucial test in Croce's theory of the artist as one who exercises free originality.

Croce denies that art is explicable in terms of either mechanism or of freedom of choice. For him, matter approximates to nonexistence and the mind's activity at the aesthetic or expressive level, as we have observed, is prior to the stage of practice in which the means-end relation emerges.[40]

Croce's principal effort in aesthetic is directed toward the establishment of the work of art in its autonomous state. To succeed, he must argue an aesthetic of unconditioned free creativity or originality. Freedom of choice implies that the artist's making is conditioned by external objects and events, and the rules of art which may be formulated for its operation owe their effectiveness only in part to the maker. The theory of making and the theory of symbols are, therefore, denied relevance and significance in Croce's aesthetic. A separate examination of these two denials, upon which rests the incompatibility of the work of art as expression of feeling with the work of art as object made or sign symbolized, will serve as an introduction to the theory of the artist as one endowed with free originality.

In examining briefly Alexander's mature theory [41] we have observed that the theorist of making, in order to reconstruct the process of making in judgment, has recourse to the theory of art as imagination. The expressionist, in contrast, not only denies the identity of expression and making; he denies that they complement each other as grounds for judgment.[42] The expressionist asserts rather, that the real is the imaginative reforming of the artist's mode of expression or imagination. Croce, by way of illustration, asks, " How could we judge what

[40] See *Aesthetic,* p. 4.

[41] See *supra,* this chapter, p. 225 ff.

[42] See Collingwood, *The Principles of Art,* p. 149, on the position of the " realistic " philosophers, including Alexander, who regard " the peculiar value which belongs to an experience such as that of listening to music " not to arise from " getting out of these things what is really in them . . . but from our being stimulated by contact with them to certain free activities of our own."

remained external to us?" [43] and prefaces the question with the warning that "If by art be understood the externalization of art, then utility and morality have a perfect right to enter into it; that is to say, the right to be master in one's own house." [44]

The mastery in one's own house, made precarious in Croce's opinion by the externalization of the image by means of making, is properly understood to be correlative to the central proposition concerning images, i. e., that "expressions . . . are not divisible." [45] It is by inference and argument in support of the latter proposition that Croce intends to exclude both the theory of making and of symbols from his aesthetic and to establish the autonomous aesthetic image, the "individual," "individual things" in contrast to relations, and images in contrast to concepts.[46] This exclusion, intended to establish the novel and original product of "free inspiration," is designed to exclude making and symbols at different levels of analysis of artistic and aesthetic experience. The indivisibility of expression is an hypothesis designed to undercut the theory of making in order to establish the creative character of aesthetic activity. It is intended to undercut the theory of symbols in order to establish the derivative argument that the work of art is an intelligible individual.

If we consider the first level of making, we discover that on Croce's view, it is the material upon which the technique of the artist is presumed to operate in the theory of making which

[43] *Aesthetic*, p. 121. Compare Collingwood, *op. cit.*, pp. 150–151: "There is no justification for saying that the sensuous part of it [the experience] is something we find and the imaginary part something we bring, or that the sensuous part is objectively 'there' in the 'work of art', the imaginary part subjective, a mode of consciousness as distinct from a quality of a thing . . . . We bring our powers of vision with us, and find what they reveal. Similarly, we bring our imaginative powers with us, and find what they reveal: namely, an imaginary experience of total activity which we find in the picture because the painter had put it there."

[44] Croce, *Aesthetic*, p. 116.

[45] *Ibid.*, p. 70. Cf. *ibid.*, p. 20 on the indivisibility of the work of art.

[46] Cf. *ibid.*, p. 1.

common sense ordinarily interposes to hamper aesthetic in conceiving art as unconditioned originality. Croce writes, however, that expression or intuition is art or aesthetic experience precisely because, as form, it permits us to distinguish freedom from that which "the spirit can never apprehend in itself as simple matter," from "mechanism" and "passivity" which the spirit of man "suffers, but does not produce." [47] The identification of expression with freedom and creativity leads Croce to hold that the structure of the work of art as image is the product of "free creation."

The hazards which this identification of the artist with the free creator entail for the judgment of the work of art are soon evident. It is not only a declaration of freedom from making; it also argues for the complete freedom of art and aesthetic experience from public, valid, or objective judgment, inasmuch as Croce identifies art and aesthetic judgment, genius and taste.[48] If, therefore, art is in this negative sense free and private because it is not made, judgment is, in aesthetic theory, similarly free, private, and nominal. Any form of classification which pretends to be precise claims objectivity as judgment. It follows that in Croce's theory, any such public and valid judgment of the image will be denied validity. Consequently, "the sublime (or comic, tragic, humorous, etc.) is *everything* that is or shall be *called* by those who have employed these *words*." [49]

The presumed justification for this privacy and nominalism of judgment is the individuality of intuitions. Artists and aesthetic perceivers alike imagine "the individual expressive fact," [50] and of such facts Croce urges, "not one . . . is interchangeable with another, because every impression or content differs from every other content." [51]

[47] *Ibid., Aesthetic,* pp. 5–6. See *supra,* Ch. II, p. 65.

[48] *Ibid.,* p. 120: ". . . the activity of judgement which criticizes and recognizes the beautiful," he writes, "is identical with what produces it . . . ."

[49] *Ibid.,* p. 90.

[50] *Ibid.,* pp. 67–68.

[51] *Ibid.,* pp. 67–68.

In Croce's assertion that the image as the structure of the work of art is " the individual expressive fact," we arrive at one of the basic conflicts between the theory of the artist as maker and the theory of the artist as free creator. Correlative in judgment to free choice in artistic making is the proposition that meaningful judgments are meaningful only if they are " capable of confirmation or refutation from an indefinite series of other points of view." [52] It is, by implication, this kind of stipulation that is denied to art by Croce and it is denied on the grounds that neither comparison nor contrast of intuitions or expressions " considered directly or positively " can be made.[53]

Croce admits that intuitions do resemble each other. The relation that holds among them is not one of identity but, rather, of " likenesses such as are observed among individuals which can never be rendered with abstract determinations." The consequence would seem to be that aesthetic judgments are absolutely free because they are wholly meaningless.

There would appear to be at least two tests to which the soundness of this theory of the artist as a free creator imagining without relation to external conditions may be submitted. The first is to determine whether or not it leads to paradox; the second, whether the argument intended to substantiate it is consistent. The crux of the latter test is whether, in its elaboration, expression does or does not reduce to the theory of the artist endowed with freedom of choice rather than of originality. As regards the first test, it would appear obvious that Croce has written an aesthetic which is itself a paradox. Patently, the terms " art," " image," and " intuition " are no more applicable to the expressive facts than are the terms " sublime " or " comic." The fundamental paradox, however, is that even for intuitions " considered directly or positively," there *are* " abstract determinations." In considering intuitions defined as

[52] E. A. Singer, Jr., *Mind as Behavior*, p. 197. See *infra*, this chapter, pp. 236 ff.

[53] *Aesthetic*, p. 70: Intuitions, he maintains, are " not divisible into classes." " How " he asks " can a comparison be made where there is no comparative term? "

wholly individual, Croce himself holds that the expressive facts which " are so many individuals " are interchangeable with one another in the " common quality of expression." [54] This means that they have in common not only the " abstract determinations " of expression and art and intuition but also of individuality or novelty. In consequence, we find that the same word is characteristic of the individual and of the common.

Paradox is not, however, the sole consequence of the implication that the artist is a free creator and that the image or intuition belongs to no class but is rather an individual without relations. It is instructive that nominalism is not the final outcome of Croce's speculation upon judgment in art. Indeed, it is doubly instructive because it is precisely the same proposition, " expressions . . . are not divisible," which, applied in the attack upon theories of technique and matter, is now turned upon the theory of symbols. It is the latter theory which, from Aristotle to the iconologists, has provided with genus or class these same individuals and so has rendered them intelligible as objects of public or valid judgment. " We find our own impressions fully determined and realized," Croce writes, " in the expression of a poet . . . ." [55] And he argues that " if the symbol be conceived as separable—if the symbol can be on one side, and on the other the thing symbolized . . . the so-called symbol . . . is science, or art aping science."

Yet, although Croce maintains that the image is not a symbol in this commonly received sense of the word, we do well to examine certain significant statements which do bear upon the objective judgments presumed to be possible in his theory, as well as complementary statements which enlighten us in the matter of the structure of the work of art in the theory of art as expression. It is significant, in the first place, that Croce should assume that although " we are not Dante, nor Dante we," yet, " in that moment of contemplation and judgment, our spirit is one with that of the poet, and in that moment we

[54] *Ibid.*, p. 68.
[55] *Ibid.*, p. 34.

and he are one thing." [56] It is significant, secondly, that in this derivative argument, the correlative in the theory of expression to Alexander's " presented external thing " now appears as the reproduction induced by " physical beauty " or " stimulus." [57] Finally, it is significant that while there are in this theory no " natural signs," [58] and that it is asserted that no two expressions can be identical,[59] Croce still believes he is posing a meaningful question when he asks, " How are we to succeed in causing the expression to be reproduced by means of the physical object? " That such reproduction does occur is taken to be the fact: we are assured that it " always occurs when we can replace ourselves in the conditions in which the stimulus (physical beauty) was produced." [60] Not only does it occur; we are told how to induce this reproductive experience: " with the help of memory we surround the physical stimulus with all the facts among which it arose; and thus we enable it to act upon us as it acted upon him who produced it." [61]

Now this is in evident contradiction to Croce's assertions that between expressions only resemblances exist and that there is only a relative possibility of translations. It is, in addition, an explicit admission that by means of palaeography, philology, and history we can and do separate off from the physical stimulus that " symbol on one side " from the " thing symbolized," i. e., the " facts among which " the stimulus arose. This must be the case, inasmuch as the facts which memory and science relate to the physical stimulus in the reproduction of the artist's expression do in fact relate to it, and it, as physical stimulus, must be a sign for the facts which it signifies and which we relate to it, by replacing the facts among which it arose.

It is significant that Croce's identification of aesthetic and artistic processes implies that the physical stimulus is not merely

[56] *Aesthetic*, p. 121.
[57] *Ibid.*, p. 125.
[58] *Ibid.*, p. 125.
[59] *Ibid.*, pp. 67–68.
[60] *Ibid.*, p. 125.
[61] *Ibid.*, p. 126.

an isolated image but a sign for the artist's, for tradition's and for history's meaning. The identity of souls which, it is argued, is the consequence of this could result only if the individual work of art incorporates the classes which make the image intelligible and which permits judgments to be made objectively. If, however, the image is thus intelligible, Croce is in fact urging that expression needs as its complementary hypothesis the theory of symbols which places emphasis upon the type, the class, or the genus to which the individual belongs. Consequently, we must examine the work of art not only as a form but as a meaning. And we do well to recall that the theory of symbols is, as we have observed, an elaboration in terms of emphasis upon meanings, of the theory of making. This, too, is implied in the use of Croce's theory of the physical stimulus.

The argument presented thus far suggests that Croce's theory of art as expression is identical in certain respects with the structural theories of making and symbolization. In consequence, his use of the word " image " needs, in order to account for aesthetic experience, i. e., for the actual identification of genius and taste, some modification of the hypothesis that the image is produced by an unconditioned and wholly original creator. There yet remains to be considered, however, the central assumption of the theory of art as expression, namely that art is imagination. The nerve of Croce's interpretation is, as we have observed, in examining the relation of the genius to the prophet,[62] a form of epistemological primitivism. What Croce intends is clear in his relating of the particular work of art and the individual state of the soul.[63] Each state of soul expresses impressions, while what is expressed in imagination, intuition, or art is knowledge " free from concepts and more simple than the so-called perception of the real." [64]

[62] See *supra*, Ch. v, pp. 162 ff.

[63] Particular works of art express " a state of the soul, and the state of the soul is individual and always new . . . particular works of art . . . are original . . . each one unsubdued by the intellect." (*The Essence of Aesthetic*, pp. 56–57)

[64] *Aesthetic*, p. 17, and *What is Living and What is Dead in Hegel's Philosophy*, p. 123: Art as imagination is " the first ingenuous theoretic form . . . the lyric

It is important to recall that Croce sharply distinguishes conceptual and aesthetic knowledge. The most important aspect of that distinction is that knowledge of concepts is knowledge of relations of things, while knowledge by intuition or imagination is knowledge of the individual thing.[65] It is upon the pivot of this distinction that the problem of the work of art as a product of freedom of choice revolves. If Croce is correct in forcing the distinction, the structure of the work of art as an image falls outside the universe of discourse of art and within that of free originality. The strength of the traditional conflict between mimesis and imagination,[66] tends to make of the latter a wholly originative faculty and lends force to Croce's assumption. It will be recalled, however, that the differentiation between the genius and the prophet, which theorists in the " great analogy " took to be identical principally on grounds of epistemological primitivism, turns upon the divergence between the structure of art and the structure of prophecy, whether that of the predicter or of the interpreter.[67]

If it be assumed, however, that the philosophical problem of the wholly creative imagination is to be argued in terms of the work of art *in suo genere*, it must be clear that we can and must distinguish between imagination as an instrument which produces the work of art as a made and symbolical structure possible in terms of freedom of choice and the work of art as image in which freedom of choice is exercised.

To illustrate the need in the theory of the artist for the imagination as a condition for the technique which makes effective freedom of choice, we need first but recall that the traditional conception asserts that the province of art is " with con-

or music of the spirit . . . in which . . . the philosophical problem has not yet emerged."

[65] Croce distinguishes between the intuition and " the so-called concept of the individual which is always a universal or general concept . . . incapable of attaining to that individuality to which historical knowledge, as aesthetic knowledge, alone attains." *Aesthetic*, pp. 27–28.

[66] See *supra*, Ch. I, pp. 8 ff.

[67] See *supra*, Ch. V, pp. 171 ff.

triving and considering how something may come into being which is capable of either being or not being." This is but to assert that if there be choice in either the process of making or of symbolizing, the imagination must present itself with alternative stimuli as alternative modes of possible making and signifying. As concerns judgment, the correlative to the operation of imagination, this implies comparison and contrast of the work of art with what it was, i. e., with the nonaesthetic mechanisms from which it is formed.[68]

We have observed that difficulties implicit in the theory of the work of art as symbol, as interpreted in iconological terms, are owing precisely to a failure to recognize possibilities for freedom of choice among signs. Yet it is not difficult to indicate the series of arts and sciences by comparison to and contrast with which meaningful judgments directed to works of art may be made. The confirmatory series, sufficient for a working hypothesis, the " indefinite series of other points of view," follow. The first specification of what may be taken to be the generic term is the natural instinct to imitate. It occurs in the philosophical science of logic. It is followed by the transformation of logical signs into symbols, as logic becomes iconology in the application of the science of signs to the philosophy of art. Iconology is correlative, as a study of the grounds for meaningful judgments from an indefinite series of points of view, to art, the generic term, in which the products made by man's tool-making capacity are first specified in the philosophical analysis of teleology, which relates means and ends. More specifically, the sequence is sufficiently indicated by Samuel Alexander in the following natural order: the instinct for construction, making, craft, skill, technique, and, finally, object of contemplation.

May a similar series be set up for the work of art as expression, so that what Croce implies is a free and nominal judgment may be brought within the limitation of comparison and con-

[68] It implies as well the fundamental correlate to the theory of freedom of choice, namely that " meaningful judgments are meaningful only if they are capable of confirmation from an indefinite number of points of view."

trast and so that we may approach the absolutely limited judgment, i. e., a judgment completely restricted to the experience of the work of art as image after the fullest comparison and contrast of the art-object in its various levels of meaning? This may be done if we know from what image presented by the imagination the work of art derives, i. e., if we know not only what the image is but what it now is not or what it has been. Croce himself suggests that such reconstruction is possible,[69] and we have indicated, as a result, that the theory of expression is in consequence not incompatible with that of making or of symbolizing. But in the strictest sense, such comparison and contrast as are necessary for meaningful judgments appear impossible. Art, intuition, feeling, and imagination are the first moments of spirit and have neither mechanisms nor presuppositions analogous to those present to the theory of signs and making. Matter in contrast to spirit is a " limit." There are no ends of art. There are no degrees of beauty.[70] Nor, presumably, are expressions genuinely in contrast to impressions, inasmuch as the stage of impressions is not a stage of spirit but its contrary.[71]

It would appear difficult, if not impossible, to suggest that Croce's theory of expression reduces to a theory of free choice with a correlative hypothesis of meaningful judgment. But, while these specific suggestions meet obstacles, the general theory of imagination upon which the theory of art as expression is grounded is vulnerable at two points. It is logically in error and, secondly, it ignores certain mechanisms, the " something compulsory," which makes the life of feeling or imagination intelligible.

The first point, that of logical error, is best indicated by the suggestion of paradox in Croce's use of the word individual

[69] See *supra*, this chapter, p. 233.

[70] *Aesthetic*, p. 79. " It is in fact impossible to enumerate the merits or to point out what parts of the latter [i. e. works of art that are more or less complete failures] are beautiful, because being a complete fusion they have but one value . . . . The beautiful does not possess degrees . . . ."

[71] *Ibid.*, pp. 5–6; cf. pp. 19–20.

and his denial that there are "abstract determinations" between intuitions. This, as we have observed, leads to the conclusion that "individual" intuitions possess in common "individuality," [72] a conclusion of interest in that in it is implied the fact that thinking requires the common as well as the individual. The consequence is that we find the same word used to designate the individual and the common. The fact is significant. It suggests, in the first place, that the words "individual" and "common" mutually imply each other, precisely as do such terms as "husband" and "wife," "right" or "left," and that each term of the pair is meaningless except in such context, implicit or explicit. Secondly, it suggests that the implications in the theory of art as expression that the individual is of superior aesthetic value to the common is mere assertion. More significantly, such assertion is irrelevant at the level of discussion of the structure of the work of art, at which the terms in question are not evaluative. They function here only at the level of meaning, at which there *is* one relevant problem: the logical priority or posteriority of the terms "individual" and "common." If we seriously consider the question, which of these terms, "common" or "individual," is not aesthetically more valuable, but logically prior or posterior, there is no doubt what our answer must be: in knowing, the common factor is antecedent not only to specification but to individuality. To recognize what an individual feeling, image, or work of art is, precedes knowing whether it is either novel, individual, or a distinguished individual of its class. Even to denote presupposes knowing the *what* to which one is pointing. It may be that El Greco's "Toledo" is unique but what that individuality means is intelligible only in terms of the art of Tintoretto and the Venetian painters.[73]

What is evident for the individual image is no less so concerning the general theory of imagination or feeling or intuition. The mechanism, the "something compulsory" presup-

[72] See *supra*, this chapter, p. 232.

[73] See *infra*, Ch. XII.

posed by the most specific structure of imagination or feeling which for Croce is identified with art, is the entire " life of feeling " which includes not only reproductive imagination but stages of productive imagination anterior to the aesthetic mood.[74] In Croce's contrary hypothesis, we discover the basic fallacy of epistemological primitivism as a theory of genius and art.

Precisely, therefore, as generic symbols and generic techniques are the presuppositions of specific symbols and specific artistic skills, so a generic life of feeling is the presupposition of artistic creativity. In general, the series which provides comparison and contrast proceeds from generic feeling as apperception, instinct, emotion, and mood. These are the ranges of feeling from reproductive to productive imagination. As there are sciences, i. e., most generalized systems of meaningful judgments, of logic and of art, so there is a science of psychology. Man is not only interested in connotations and in the construction of tools and instruments for the control of environment

[74] See M. C. Nahm, *Aesthetic Experience and Its Presuppositions*, p. 326: " The ' life of feeling ' is . . . therefore, in distributive terms . . . ' instinct,' ' emotion,' and ' mood.' It is to be regarded collectively, as a *continuum* constituted of observable behavior. Two significant variations characterize the observable behavior within the extreme ranges of the *continuum* of feeling. The behavior varies directly in intensity from overt action in the instinctive range to peripheral reaction in the range of ' mood.' Within these same ranges, however, the behavior varies in overtness or intensity in inverse proportion to the alternative stimuli or modes of possible action which the organism ' imagines ' or presents to itself. In the present usage, an ' image ' is a stimulus effective for the production of effective behavior in an organism. The behavior evidenced in the *continuum* of feeling is interpreted as the organism's capacity to present effective stimuli to itself. The *continuum* is, moreover, susceptible of further interpretation in terms of two diverse but interrelated operations: It is throughout the entirety of its dimensions an inherited biological and a derived cultural *Apperceptionsmass*. This aspect of feeling may properly be called ' reproductive imagination.' In addition, the behavior of the individual who ' feels ' evidences a capacity for the presentation of alternative stimuli or ' images.' This capacity is minimally operative in the range of the *continuum* called instinct. It is present, but less evident in reflex and tropistic action. This characteristic of feeling,—the organism's presentation to itself of alternative stimuli—may properly be called ' productive imagination.' "

and of himself. He is also a creature moved by certain signs, configurations, and techniques. He reacts in generic ways to the images and representations and these he has the power to symbolize and by means of technique to embody in media.

We shall now assume that, with reference to the work of art, the traditional structural terms, " image," " symbol," and " object made," may be considered on the same level, i. e. solely in terms of the " limited structure of the work of art," and that we may proceed in terms of making and, by analogy, of symbols and feelings. We shall attempt to show in the next chapter the complementary relatedness of these aspects of the work of art in the work of art. We shall attempt to suggest this within the context of the theory of the artist endowed with freedom of choice. We shall attempt to indicate the meaning of the " something compulsory " as mechanism by which Kant tried to indicate what was intelligible in the product of genius. We shall do this first in terms of the nonaesthetic symbols, crafts, and feelings which provide for the degree of productivity implicit in making. We shall then proceed to show how the products of such making in their turn provide the " something compulsory " for the individual and original work of fine art.

We shall examine the former problem in terms of the structure and judgment of the work of art as a " concrete significant form."

8 Structure and the Judgment of Art: Concrete Significant Form and the Freedom of Making

> A tremendous effort is necessary in order to work towards it [the goal]; not merely a technical effort, but a moral effort, too,—the effort to subject all considerations of technique, style, and purpose of this one ideal: congruence.
>
> PAUL HINDEMITH, *A Composer's World*

We have argued in the preceding chapter that the three principal theories formulated in the history of the philosophy of art to describe the structure of the work of art, and, possibly, the real object of judgment, do in fact complement each other. We shall now proceed to inquire whether from what is as yet largely an aggregate of three hypotheses there may be formulated a single theory relating to the morphology of art. In this inquiry, we shall have recourse to the contributions of the three theories taken together and, if the undertaking prove successful, the resulting analysis of the artist as maker should prove valuable as a ground for our understanding of the artist as creator. If this, in turn, informs us concerning the nature of the freedom with which aesthetic theory has endowed the artist, we may expect to show how judgments upon works of art are meaningful and that judgments upon fine art are evaluative and objective, not merely generic and nominal.

The work of art is, in morphological or structural terms, a "concrete significant form." As concrete, it is made by means of technique directed upon material; as significant, it embodies a sign; and, as form, it is expressed. Symbolization brings into the work of art and, ultimately, into the work of fine art, signs derived from men's experiences of non-aesthetic objects and events. The artist imagines and expresses such signs as possible modes of making in material or media with potentialities for the signs' objectification. By means of making, this subjective process is objectified and embodied in the material. In this technical process the potentialities of the material are actualized.

To state the problem of the structure of the work of art in terms of concrete significant form is to state it in terms of artistic freedom of choice. We have argued in the preceding chapter the impossibility of the theory of art as image or expression to exclude symbolism and making. It is sufficient at the moment to maintain that it is making that establishes art in its public nature, in contrast to the privacy and nominalism of expression. In terms of freedom of choice, the capacity to make an object or event external to the maker is basic to the actualization of such freedom. Making it is that separates the object or event in space and time from the agent. The artist is free, also, within the limitations placed upon his imagination and technique by the material with which he works, to impose a form upon the object or event made, a form intelligible either in terms of style or of representational symbols.

To the relations of imagination and technique we shall return. It is necessary to point out at this juncture, however, that art produces not only an object or event. It produces more, in fact, than a significant and intelligible form separated from the artist. In the work of art, the artist expresses feeling in the separate medium, an *idem in alio,* as De Quincey called it. De Quincey described this as " the same impression . . . restored in a different material . . . by means of a different instrument." Art as making produces, in a word, a sign made by technical processes by means of which the artist objectifies his feelings in the media of art.

In a consideration of freedom of choice in making, it is feeling as reproductive imagination that is of primary significance.[1] It is this recognitive function of experience which conditions the basic intelligibility of signs and symbols in art. Its two principal aspects are, in Kant's terminology, " reproduction of representations " and that connection of representations in the imagination " with some one representation in preference to another." [2] We may tentatively suggest that the regulative principle provided by perfection of technique is the governing principle for the direction of the preference. Our immediate interest is in the fact that reproduction and preference constitute the primary conditions under which artistic choice operates.

Feeling, as reproductive imagination, is for the organism the predisposition which endows it with sufficient familiarity of the specific aspects of the imagined—as reproduced and self-presented—world to make possible experience of that world. In feeling, we come upon that aspect of mind described by Bergson as " pure memory," the memory " fixed in the organism " which is " nothing else but the complete set of intelligently constructed mechanisms which ensure the appropriate reply to the various possible demands " and " enables us to adapt ourselves to the present situation." [3] We know this predisposition normally under the names of tropism or instinct in which such actions as panic-fear or rage are constituted of what the mechanist calls " trigger-like " reactions to stimuli. In feeling, we react in part as a preorganized nervous and physiological structure to extrinsic stimuli.

It has been indicated that one condition for the artist's freedom of choice in making is the fact that imagination prefers one stimulus or set of stimuli to another. Such preference is possible at all levels of feeling but emotion and mood are the ranges among these various modes of which the artist principally

[1] See M. C. Nahm, *Aesthetic Experience and Its Presuppositions*, Ch. XI. It is necessary for the argument of the present chapter to present in summary form a portion of the theory of the above-mentioned book.

[2] *K.d.R.V.*, A 121.

[3] *Matter and Memory*, p. 195.

avails himself in his preferential use of feeling operating epistemologically to make familiar the world of experience.

To feeling, as a form of primitive predisposition, we owe the familiarity experienced in the realm of art, as well as the occurrence and recurrence in art of generic symbols. Art cannot symbolize feelings in abstraction, simply because what is felt is not a mere abstraction. Moods, emotions, and instincts, constitutents of the life of feeling, are attached to and aroused by incidents, events, ideas, and objects which the artist does not create but which are, rather, a portion of the nonaesthetic framework of reference, the mechanisms for the process of symbolization. That framework of reference is man's racial and cultural background, " a simple produce of the common clay," providing symbols to which the artist's feelings attach and by means of which the artist evokes the perceiver's feelings. The signs and symbols of art derive from the common framework of reference of religion, art, science, and morality. It is by means of the art of generic symbolism, in primordial images, that

> The fair humanities of old religion,
> The Power, the Beauty, and the Majesty,

are revived.

These images live, not in the " faith of reason " but in the reproductive life of feeling. It is because this is their cognitive ground that the signs embodied in works of art are familiar and that the history of art is in large part a history of the recurrence of symbols—symbols of the hunt and the chase, of danger and vengeance, chicanery, death, old age, change, tales of marriage of spring and winter, the passage of time and of the seasons, chance and love, the ladder and the tree of life, the isles of the blest, the demons and the werewolves of a hundred Beowulfs and Homers, tales of horror, the storied fables of the beneficence of warm sun and soft rain, of the mating of earth and heaven, the havoc of storm, hurricane, earthquake, tidal wave and typhoon, of plague and pestilence, of starvation, of war, of magic and of witchcraft. From these primordial and generic signs, the artist fashions symbols of the "old and universal arousers," and from them derive the attributes in art of familarity, communicability, and intelligibility.

The framework of reference for the meaning of these generic signs is the race of men and the culture of man. The symbols of art draw their sustenance from race and culture, the former providing grounds for intelligibility general in scope, the latter, for intelligibility limited to different and differing cultures. There are, therefore, two classes of generic symbols in art which are explicable principally in terms of reproductive imagination. Racial generic symbols in art have their presuppositions not solely in the context of human experience but also in that heritage that man shares with the brute. We need mention here but two such symbols, those of the leader and of the mother. The leader is the "wintry slayer" of epic, romance, and tragedy. His meaning is known to all men, whatever may be the divergences of their cultures, because men are social animals and because the leader evokes feeling. Hamlet and Orestes derive from the self-same source as do Pericles, Genghis Khan, Napoleon, and Lincoln. But so, too, do those geniuses in art, like Leonardo and Michelangelo, Shakespeare, and Pheidias, in whose images are signified the artistic genius, the specification in the "great analogy" of the leader, like its analogues, the hero and the saint.[4] Diverse arts offer constantly the symbol of the great man because the relation of men to the great man is comprehensible to all men, precisely as they present constantly the specifications of the mother, the symbol of fertility.

In practice racial generic symbols such as leader and mother are specified both in terms of field of interest, as in the instances of genius, hero, and saint and in terms of culture, as in Demeter and Madonna. The point is of consequence here principally because it suggests what is in fact the case, that the most significant level of artistic symbols, that of cultural generic symbols,

[4] See *supra,* Ch. v, pp. 175 ff.

may be examined either as a specification, an extension, or a redirection of feeling as it is attached to and evoked by signs. What, in Rebecca West's fine phrase " has been slowly bred in our kind . . . has now the force of an instinct."

Cultural generic symbols of art derive principally, however, from situations, ideas, events, and incidents meaningful to men alone. The conception of immortality may be, as Bergson judges it to be, the extension of experience that lies beyond the brute's powers. A similar extension is evident, to cite another illustration, in so-called Platonic love, which so vividly affected Renaissance art and poetry. In any case, at the level of feeling directed to and evoked by culture, it is the codes of law, the theologies, the moralities, and conditions of family, society, and individual which profoundly affect men emotionally. The signs of this feeling, transferred by art into the media of the various arts, are discovered in the generic cultural symbol. The specifications of the symbolism may vary as greatly as do the divergences explicit in theories of metempsychosis and of personal immortality; of Dante's and Milton's symbols of light; of the Egyptian conception of the " luminous Khu " and of artistic interpretations of Plato's comparison of the good to the sun and the Neoplatonic image of the stream of light. We note the specific uses of such symbols of immortality or divinity as the nimbus or the halo or the streams of light emanating from the fingers of Aten, the " lord of the beams of light." What is of primary interest for the intelligibility of art is the generic symbol common to all instances and possibilities. The iconologist's interpretation of the significance of the symbol, the archaeologist's knowledge of the development of tools and styles, of the elements in art which are indigenous to a culture and those drawn from adjacent cultures, the historian's skill in making manifest the industry, commerce, and conquest signified in the work of art, present " indefinite series of other points of view " which help us to validate judgment.

If we are to understand what the work of art is as a concrete significant form, however, it is no less important to recognize that making serves as the necessary but insufficient criterion of art. Making is the artist's imagination freely at work under conditions requiring choice. Neither symbolism, feeling, nor feeling attached to or evoked by symbols is uniquely characteristic of art. What is unique to the art which is potentially fine art is the conjoining of feeling and symbols in the process by which the artist signifies the generic symbol in a medium external to him. This means simply that, in abstraction, technique is the carrier of the values of sign and feeling.

The consideration of technique as the artist's imagination is sufficiently illustrated, for the moment, by a reference to the sculptor's art. In working upon marble, the technique does not separate out into making, symbolizing, and feeling. The sculptor, working in relief, imagines the sign of his feelings in the marble, precisely as the projective geometer envisages bodies in space and as the surgeon anticipates in performing an operation. Were this not the fact, the sculptor's first strokes would eliminate the pattern drawn upon the stone and eliminate, as well, the image. Technique is a process in which are amalgamated the correlative symbols and feelings, specifying both in a style selected by the artist and conditioned by the medium. Objectively, it functions as productive imagination in discovering and making explicit the implicit capacities of media upon which the signs, whether forms of techniques or specific representations as signs of feeling, are impressed and in which they are made intelligible.

The most important inference to be drawn from the interrelating of the processes in making of constructing, symbolizing and feeling is its invalidation of the expressionist theory, as formulated by Croce, that the artist expresses the unique and individual image. The artist does not express the work of art alone, a symbol of aesthetic experience alone, or a technically produced object or event alone. The proposition that he does express any one of these is but partially valid. What he does express—and the processes are the vehicle for that expression—is the potential aesthetic experience. Croce's theory, with its identification of genius and taste, suggests if interpreted narrowly that the experience of art begins *ex nihilo.* The same point is made in the words that the artist presents the perceiver with a "vacuum" which the latter in turn must "enter and fill up to the full measure of [his] aesthetic emotion."[5] On the contrary, our experience and our judgment upon it in relation to the work of art begin with generic signs, feelings, and techniques which are actualized in the work of fine art and in aesthetic experience. In the sense in which the work of art is a presupposition of the work of fine art and the factual experiences of signs, feelings, and techniques are presupposed in the experiences of aesthetic values, the work of art is not a vacuum. What, however, is required to evoke aesthetic experience after the recognition of the generic symbol, after the analysis of the techniques and materials used, and after insight into the feelings, both general and specific which the symbols evoke, is not implausibly likened to a vacuum. The reason for this is crucial for an understanding of the artist as creator and may be stated succinctly: aesthetic experience is a creative act of the same order as the act of artistic creation.

This proposition, that aesthetic experience is no less a creative act than is the initial act of producing the work of art, is implicit in much that poets, critics, and philosophers have hinted concerning the relation of the artist and the perceiver of the work of art.[6] The assertion is explicit in remarks concerning the

[5] Okakura-Kakazu, *The Book of Tea,* p. 61. Compare O. Sirén, *The Chinese on the Art of Painting.*

[6] Schiller, certainly one of the most sensitive and perceptive writers in aesthetic, remarks that aesthetic experience "will endeavor to receive as it would itself have produced, and to produce as it aspires to receive." Keats writes, in *The Fall of Hyperion* (i, 7–15):

> But bare of laurel they live, dream and die;
> For Poesy alone can tell her dreams,
> With the fine spell of words alone can save
> Imagination from the sable chain

identity of genius and taste, such as those with which the present chapter began. It remains, however, to make the grounds for this identity explicit. That these are complex, we discover if we test the adequacy of the true but misleading proposition that " the artist expresses the work of art." This proposition is true but it is true only in the limited sense in which the work of art is taken to be an instrument for the image the artist must objectify in order to permit the aesthetic transaction to take place. However, the conditions under which the work of art acts as an instrument in the transaction between artist and perceiver are, first, reproduction of the generic signs in the work of art, as well as of the material and technique which bear those signs; specification of the generic signs into specified symbols; creativity, displayed in the individualization of the symbols, technique, and material; and, finally, self-produced originality, the end achieved of the work of fine art as an instrument in the process described in terms of the originality of the artist as creator.

As this essay proceeds, it will be argued that in spite of the reversal of the temporal order of the two acts of making and aesthetic remaking in experience and judgment, identical conditions hold and must hold for artist and aesthetic perceiver. Preliminary to the examination of the factors needed for an understanding of the artist as creator, we shall mention two points which follow upon the hypothesis that aesthetic experience is no less creative than is artistic making. First, the work of art is so made that although its generic symbolism is actualized, some portion of its meaning remains merely potential for the perceiver. This statement holds, too, *mutatis mutandis,* for the generic making and the generic feelings which technique as imagination presents. Secondly, the relation between artist

---

And dumb enchantment. Who alive can say
" Thou art no Poet—mayst not tell thy dreams? "
Since every man whose soul is not a clod
Hath visions, and would speak, if he had loved
And been well nurtured in his mother tongue.

and perceiver is achieved only as these potentialities within the work of fine art are actualized in aesthetic experience. They can be actualized only at the level of cultivated taste. The work of fine art is a bare and generic—though powerful—symbol, a mere product of technique or an abstracted utterance of feeling, for the natural man. For the trained taste it is a symbol at once intense and profound, inexhaustible, and imaginatively allusive. The reason is both clear and important: the artist, in the process of making the work of art, actualizes the potentialities of symbols, feelings, and media by specifying and individualizing. We may approach the temporarily reversed but, for the purposes of our analysis, generically identical processes of specification and individualization, either by an analysis of artistic making or aesthetic experience or criticism. In this approach to what is made and created, in the theory of the artist and the perceiver as creators, we are engaged in two tasks. The first has as its goal a completely meaningful judgment. The second has as its ideal completion the endless approach to that limit of our own creative efforts in which we are, at least analogously, productive and original minds and artists. We may indicate the nature of this approach by examining the education of taste.

As may be recalled, Croce's theory implies that the absolutely free judgment is possible in aesthetic precisely because aesthetic taste, as exemplified in judgment, in criticism, and in classification, is wholly meaningless. The wholly meaningful one will be, therefore, the absolutely limited one, i. e., one completely restricted to the aesthetic experience of the work of art after the widest comparison and contrast of the art-object at the various levels of meaning through which our analysis leads. By ascertaining the levels through which the generic symbol, the generic technique, and the generic feeling are carried in their public and nonaesthetic character, we proceed through orders of as yet nonaesthetic fact, by means of specifying processes of making, as the condition but not the determination of our approach to the individualized and unique symbol of fine art and aesthetic value. We learn what an individual of a class is (in this instance, object or event belonging to the class, work of fine art), if we know not only what it is as work of fine art but what it is not as specific work of art and what it has been as generic work of art, i. e., how it differs from other members of its kind and by what processes the general has been made, first, specific and, finally, individual or unique.

As for our second task, the explanation of the education of taste, we discover that this is but a specific form of all education, the " second creator," which reforms and sustains man's natural gifts, virtues, and skills by presenting alternative modes of thoughts, actions, and makings unknown to natural man, and supplying the tools with which he exercises power and secures control over what his imagination becomes increasingly well trained to present.

We begin with the natural values explicit in fine art for aesthetic experience, for the most part with the explicit generic symbols, and proceed toward their individualization as aesthetic values. We do not begin *ex nihilo,* inasmuch as the work of art is made with symbols initially selected for the expression of the artist's feelings in media upon which has been imposed the discipline of making. We have already observed [7] some of the steps in the series, i. e., in logic, philosophy, and psychology, in which the natural values explicit in art are presented in the work of art through freedom of choice for our judgment.

It is, however, in the more specific fields derived from this general level of natural values, i. e., in fields in which these natural values are specified, that we are now interested. Aesthetics, which brings to the more circumscribed world of art and aesthetic experience immediate specifications of philosophy, may convert, for example, the general problem of form and matter into significant form and thus examine together the speculative problem of form and matter and the means-end

[7] Cf. *supra,* Ch. VII.

relation. The latter characterizes man as having an art which manifests itself in making or constructiveness. Aesthetics also specifies general psychological theories, such as that of feeling, into hypotheses like empathy, tactile values, and *katharsis*; directs anthropology toward archaeology and ethnology to provide us with the history of developing tools, the chronicle of available materials, transportation, and cultural values.

From these more general approaches to art and from the still natural level of values, we proceed to more specific levels. We do so and can do so, however, because all education comprises two factors, a knowledge of tools, i. e., the instruments by means of which man controls and understands nature and human nature; and the acquisition of experience, i. e., the means by which he makes that knowledge his own. In the education of taste, our first interest is in tools, an interest which may be satisfied because the work of art derives from the nonaesthetic framework to which its symbols refer and from the nonaesthetic realm of making which is the manifestation of the instinct for the use of instruments. In consequence, the work of art is a tool for the understanding of a culture, a veritable microcosm of the macrocosmic culture. As such a signifying tool—or " unconscious symbol "—, the work of art is susceptible to precise analysis in its context of meanings or symbols by the iconologist, who specifies philosophy's organon of logic, and by the archaeologist and historian of art who bring their science to the instruments and materials available for the making of the work of art.

The work of art is not, however, merely a microcosm of man's experience in general and of the culture in which it is produced. It is a tool by means of which we discover the more specific nature of art implicit in art's morphology or structure and are placed by that discovery on the way to an understanding of the unique work of fine art. Signs and symbols are presented in specifiable material structures. The natural values of form and matter, having been superseded by significant form, may give way, in turn, to concrete significant form. The natural values implicit in making as a process or technique, having been explicit in the externalization of symbols by the principle of *idem in alio,* may now become objects for contemplation in their own right. But the historian of art and the critic are at this level interested in the interrelation of meanings and forms in the conjoining of generic symbols and generic techniques, not, however, in isolation but in morphological terms,—modes, styles, stylizations which operate variously in divergent media, in various arts, and in various eras.[8]

The stage in which signs and symbols are presented in specifiable material structures and in which the problems of style and modes arise, is the forecourt of that in which art is conjoined to fine art: the transition stage in the education of taste from art judged as a tool to art regarded as experience, from generic rules of art to the art of the individual maker. Paradoxically enough, the study of art as a tool shows that the study of tools transcends tools. Not only are we freed to realize objectively the constant contribution of these nonaesthetic values to aesthetic experience; we are also and more significantly initiated, through their agency, into the creative imaginative experience.

Briefly, the ground for the process which culminates in the conjoining of the fine artist and the aesthetic perceiver appears to be as follows: the transition in the education of taste from tools to experience occurs because it is vital to attain to the succeeding level of value, the condition for which is the experiencing, i. e., the living through and rethinking under the discipline of the artist, the knowledge, information, and technical skill which have been objectified in the work of art. Experiencing and experience mature us and, in fine art, this maturation

[8] Many problems of a general character arise at this level of analysis: Is Schopenhauer correct in formulating a theory which separates music from the other arts? If Dali and Eliot disagree concerning the nature of the initial stimuli which caused the artist to produce, is the difference in theory the consequence of a difference in the arts, in the precision of the symbols available in the arts, or in the unique differences which hold among artists?

marks the growth of the creative life of the imagination as it operates in the realm of conscious, individualized, and selected symbols, in contrast to unconscious, generic, and at least at times inadvertently used symbols and techniques.

The means by which this succeeding level is achieved is the process of making, the process discarded by Croce to ensure art's privacy and novelty. By the instrumentality of making, sign, symbol of feeling, and morphology are united. Making at this level is neither merely craft, style, technique, nor object for contemplation. Rather, it becomes a process integral to the morphology of art. In consequence of its operation, there open for the aesthetic perceiver and for his judgment avenues which the imagination of natural man never makes evident. What for the uneducated taste or imagination may be merely mimetic, realistic, evidence of adeptness with tools, proof that certain materials are sensuously attractive or repulsive, or, indeed, all of these in separation, is for the educated taste the specified rendering of each of these " natural " values in a morphological whole which sustains them restored both in specification and, perhaps if the process continues as one of fine art, in uniqueness as well. This means restored in the sense that the merely potential sign for technique, symbol, and feeling presented by the artist is now made explicit by knowledge and imagination, brought to that sign by the aesthetic perceiver.

We shall return shortly to a study of more explicitly artistic specifications possible in terms of freedom of choice. There are, however, more immediate problems which condition the duality of freedom of choice and freedom of originality. The first of these problems concerns the inferences to be drawn from this interpretation of the morphology of art in the domain of freedom of choice, in which it is assumed that the artist does not merely express the image but the potential aesthetic experience. The immediate inference is that the work of art is not a static product but, rather, an event in the total structure of the work of fine art. It is this structure which relates artist and aesthetic perceiver and which, as event, is made actual by the productive powers of the latter. As Alexander correctly points out, " the picture sets the spectator following the artist's hand, the poem read aloud sets the reader constructing the words into their perfection of unity . . . ."[9] As we have observed, in order to relate the making of the work of art and the experience of making, i. e., the judgment upon it, Alexander converts the *process*, making, into the object of judgment.[10] The event thus becomes meaningful in large part as our reconstruction in imagination of the maker's original and successive mental and physical processes as the latter were directed to the production of the work of art.

The phrase, " in large part," will require modification as we proceed. The inference concerning the work of art as made and the grounds for valid judgment may be drawn at once. The grounds for comparison and contrast, required for meaningful judgments, those " capable of confirmation or refutation from an indefinite series of points of view," are principally provided for the work of art as product of free technique at two levels. Generically, there is comparison to and contrast with the work of art as object or event produced and the limiting conception of technically perfected structure, the latter extrapolated from the event called work of art. The limiting conception is the postulated end of making. The judgment is a judgment of value in the area of artistic free choice and is the specific judgment in terms of intelligibility. Specifically, the differentiae for judgments of value within the realm of freedom of choice are provided by the three functions of the structure of art serving as mechanisms, i. e., making, expressing, and symbolizing.

[9] *Beauty and Other Forms of Value*, pp. 29–20. See *supra*, Ch. VII, pp. 221 ff., on the complementary natures of making and expression.

[10] See *supra*, *ibid.*, and *Beauty and Other Forms of Value*, p. 26: " The mind is mixed in artistic creation with its materials because the impulses initiated in it in the course of construction are reflected in the materials as worked up into their artistic form."

The direction of the analysis in judgments of value conditioned by freedom of choice is toward the work of art as a wholly specified event, i. e., as that which progressively approaches *ad infinitum* but is never coincident with the limit of perfection. The three processes, making, expression, and symbolization, lead from the mechanisms provided by nonaesthetic materials (colors, sounds, stone, bronze, words, signs, feelings, and techniques, etc.) into the structure of the work of art as a concrete significant form. In correlative terms, judgment moves from the discourse of factual judgment in philosophy, logic, psychology, and technique into that of iconology, imagination, and craft. As directed by the artist and by us as percipients in our imaginative reconstructions, i. e., in our judgments, the processes provide us with " what the work of art has been but is not." In conjunction, as concrete significant form and as directed from the limited structure of the work of art toward the limit of technical perfection and, for the perceiver, of wholly meaningful judgment, the three processes provide the ground from which we postulate the work of art as what " ought to be " but " is not." What the work of art is is thus a process of becoming, judged within the limits of its past as mechanism, compared to and contrasted with its future, as postulated limit of perfection.

The movements of the analysis toward the intelligible work of art and from the work of art toward the extrapolated limit of perfection provide us with a framework for meaningful judgments, judgments which are in ideal terms wholly limited and, therefore, ideally, entirely free in terms of choice. In theory, this means that the possibilities implicit in the making of the symbol of feeling in the media have been made explicit. Such is the ideal consideration of the concrete significant form as wholly restricted to the artistic and free making, the work of art, the free experience of the work of art, and the end of art. Such judgments are made after the most complete possible comparison and contrast of the interrelated structures in the various levels of meaning through which our science and reflection inform us that the work of art has passed in its emergence from mechanism to concrete significant form and from concrete significant form to technically perfected work of art.

The limiting conception of perfected work of art in the universe of discourse called freedom of choice is the postulated wholly specified and wholly intelligible work of art, i. e., the extrapolated limit of specification of the generic processes of symbolization, making, and expressing, and their unification in a concrete significant form.[11] The process of making, as the

[11] The unification, i. e., the work of art as " concrete significant form " is not a product of the three processes themselves. It is produced by technique but by a technique which relates not so much to the specifying as to the direction of the specification in relation to the extrapolated limit, perfected technique. It therefore concerns the " destination of the imagination," which is examined in the next chapter. An interesting comment upon the problem is presented by Thomas Mann in *Dr. Faustus,* p. 180: " What Kretschmar did was to point out weak places, recommend corrections of tempo, the enlivening of a stiffish rhythm, the better articulation of a theme. He pointed out to him a middle part that came to nothing, a bass that did not move. He put his finger on a transition that was only a makeshift, not organic, and compromising the natural flow of the composition . . . ." Mann writes, however, that in fact Adrian basically needed no mentor. Adrian had the " artistic sense." This Mann describes as " the understanding which is the actual agent of the work-idea—not the idea of a particular work but the idea of the opus itself, the objective and harmonic creation complete, the manager of its unified organic nature; which sticks the cracks together, stops up the holes, brings out that ' natural flow '—which was not there in the first place and so is not natural at all, but a product of art—in short, only in retrospect and indirectly does this manager produce the impression of the spontaneous and organic."

An eloquent statement of the identity of inspiration and the structural conception of the whole work of art is Paul Hindemith's interpretation of musical vision in *A Composer's World.* Hindemith argues (*op. cit.,* pp. 61–63) that " If we cannot, in the flash of a single moment, see a composition in its absolute entirety, with every pertinent detail in its proper place, we are not genuine creators. The musical creator, like any other creative individual, is permitted to share with the demiurge the possession of vitalizing visions; but it is the privilege of the demiurge to transform them into concrete existence without any interfering technical obstacle, whereas the creative musician, by reason of his earthly heritage, has to overcome many hurdles between them and their realization. If he is a genuine creator he will not be disturbed or discouraged by this fact. Not only will he have the gift of seeing—illuminated in his mind's eye

carrier of value for the work of art, specifies these generic factors in the work of art. Our judgments ascertain the levels from and by means of which the generic feelings, symbols, and techniques are borne in the direction of complete specification. Each instance of such ascertainment is a comparison and contrast of " what becomes," i. e., of the event called the work of art, with its prior and posterior stage. This process provides the condition for judgment which is the subsumption of the particular level under the general morphological level. It also provides grounds for comparison and contrast of one stage of the emerging process within the work of art to and with the other two stages.

Judgments of this kind are " horizontal " rather than " vertical." They serve for evaluation of such general aspects of the work of art as the artist's predilections and the limits imposed by material, sign, and feeling. Some artists feel more deeply than they think and their work displays powers of expression superior to its intellectual content; others, more intellectual, present us primarily with products of their mood, while still others emphasize craftsmanship, which may dominate both sign and feeling. Thus Debussy's *La Mer* is predominately an expression of feeling, as is Cezanne's " The Bathers," while Picasso's " Woman with Mandolin," Brancusi's " Bird in Space," Epstein's " Mother and Child " and Barlach's " Old Woman with a Stick " principally display craftsmanship. In Rodin's " Gates of Hell," Raphael's " The School of Athens," and Shakespeare's *Troilus and Cressida,* significance is predominant.

as if by a flash of lightning—a complete musical form (though its subsequent realization in a performance may take three hours or more) ; he will have the energy, persistence, and skill to bring this envisioned form into existence, so that even after months of work not one of its details will be lost or fail to fit into his photomental picture . . . . In working out his material he will always have before his mental eye the entire picture . . . . It is in those few uncontested masterpieces that we feel the breath of universality and eternity, because their particular kind of perfection, the absolute coincidence of intention and realization, is almost superhuman."

It is evident, also, that each specific process of making, expressing, and symbolizing may be placed with some accuracy within the bounds of general levels for purposes of comparison to and contrast with each other as the analysis approaches the limiting conception of intelligibility as correlative to technical perfection. This provides, in terms of the work of art, what it "ought to be" when judged in evaluational terms.[12] Such general comparisons and contrast, however, are likely to be retrogressive in the sense that, for example, one poet's product is judged to be more intellectual, psychological, or technical than another's. In terms of the work of art, however, the "horizontal" judgment in most instances is better made in terms of the conditions confronting the artist within the context of the work of art, the requirements laid down by sign, feeling, and materials employed for technical purposes. These more adequate criteria are directed to the specific work of art within the end-product of the process of making, i. e., in the building made, the painting painted, the sculpture completed, the dance and the symphony. These specifications are or may become [13] genuine aesthetic criteria. In the context of the present discussion, however, they are principally to be regarded as such additional specifications of general processes as are possible within the area of the artist's free choice and objects of judgment in terms of increasing intelligibility.

The criteria for specification within the work of art which indicate the course of development toward the perfection of the object or event made as a limited structure called a concrete significant form are here presented abstractly. As they are not only factors conditioning the specification of the work of art but are also conditions for the individual and unique work of fine art, we shall defer [14] presenting the illustrations and details which will function in making specific a kind in terms of perfection. The criteria are: first, *complexity*,—the direct conse-

[12] Incompletely, as we shall see.

[13] See *infra*, Ch. XI, on these criteria as aesthetic values.

[14] See *infra*, Ch. X–XII.

quence of the conditioning of the work of art by the three structural processes, introduced into the work of art by means of tools. Secondly, *temporal spread,* the subjective aspect which corresponds to complexity, the specification of the fact that the work of art is an event or a becoming. Temporal spread may be regarded as the structural precondition for all other structural criteria. Its use permits productive imagination to select from the variety of stimuli presented in the nonaesthetic aspects of art those which the artist prefers in the particular specific structure being made, i. e., permits the necessary scope for the imaginative process. Thirdly, the natural value of *unity,* which initially marks off the work of art from the universe of meanings and objectifies the symbols of feeling by means of the artist's imposition of form on media, is converted in the structure of art into *internality. Internality,* a criterion for judgment of structure, in its turn functions as an instance of the *law of organic wholes.* By its means are excluded the accidental and irrelevant in even such ostensible instances of externality as the site of the building in relation to the building's structure. Fourthly, both temporal spread and internality are additionally specified to become conditions for *diversity in unity.* Fifthly, there emerges the *order of specific intervals,* at which juncture what on the nonaesthetic level is natural craft or technique, signs, or feelings, becomes in structural terms the process by means of which the artist controls the order and frequency of expressed images, i. e., the order, frequency and recurrence of symbols, of stylistic phenomena, and of expression of feeling within the work itself, providing subordinate limiting criteria for intelligibility and economy within the structure of the work of art.

At this specific level, the technical artist can at once clarify theoretical problems implicit in the meaning of symbols by specifying them within a context, as well as display technical mastery over media and objectify feelings which he shares with his audience. The factors manifest, as well, the aesthetic potentialities in the media of the arts themselves of the event called the work of fine art. Such potentialities are variations in theme and motif within the style or mode, the balance of masses of figures and shades, and the organization of the sensuous and symbolic aspect of the work of art in terms of form. It is from the rhythm which emerges that the specific functions of the work of art as object or event technically produced are made explicit in technical terms, in repetition, harmony, and diversity in unity. It is here that art approaches most nearly to complete intelligibility, to the perfection of the event called concrete significant form.

Similarly, these criteria function as conditioning technical factors for the judgment, "this is a work of fine art," providing as they do the condition for the operation of productive imagination in presenting to the aesthetic perceiver the alternative possibilities for free choice latent in the images introduced by the artist into the work of art by means of the three generic processes of making, symbolizing, and expressing. The latter are the specifications of the original formula, *idem in alio*. The painting, building, musical composition, poem, dance, or sculptured figure is then analogous to an organism and is presumably describable in terms of a single function, while preserving complexity and diversity of parts. At the perfected level of art, the disciplined, differentiated, and specified application of the formula forces the attention of the perceiver to the specific characteristics of the event.

"Where the structure forces us to appreciate" each specific part, "it is natural," writes Gerard Manley Hopkins, "and in the order of things for us to dwell on all modifications affecting the general result or type." [15] In the specific concrete significant form, attention to symbol, media, technique, and the relation of parts makes intelligible the work of art. The problem remains, however, whether making in its specifications and education of taste in its specifications as criticism and judgment do or do not exhaust the potentialities of the work of

[15] *The Note-Books and Papers of Gerard Manley Hopkins*, p. 94.

art as work of fine art. The interrelations of processes in organic wholes called buildings, painting, poems, and other works of art are extraordinarily diverse and complex. Media are recalcitrant, significance ambiguous, and feelings intermixed. And if the perfection sought is by definition an unattainable norm, it would appear to be difficult, indeed, to urge that the concrete significant form is insufficient for the task of providing grounds for inferences concerning the nature of the artist as creator.

Would it not be possible, selecting for brief illustration two of the works of art which we at the outset judged to be works of fine art, to satisfy the requirements for freedom in the fine artist by tracing the specifications of genera which we discover in Verrocchio's "Colleoni Monument" and della Robbia's "Visitation"? These, in terms of the significant in concrete significant form, are generic symbols, the one of the leader, the other of the mother. The first, in Venice, is specified in a bronze, equestrian statue, judged by some to be the finest of its kind in existence; the second, in Pistoia, in the Church of S. Giovanni Fuorcivitas, a relief of two female figures, in glazed terracotta, suggests the "maturest time of the artist's powers." We know specifically that the horseman is Bartolomeo Colleoni of Bergamo, a condottiere general of Venice, who died in 1475; that Vellano of Padua and Leopardi of Ferrara, as well as Verrocchio were given commissions for equestrian statues; and that the latter's model was completed in 1481. We know that the statue expresses in both horse and rider the audacity and individuality of the Renaissance which is the theme of Burckhardt's *Civilization of the Renaissance*; that the specification of Colleoni upright in the saddle is in unity with the warhorse, while providing variety; that there is an extraordinary illusion of movement in the animal and of vitality in the rider, owing principally to the diversification of planes in modeling and in the consequent play of light and shade. Mannerisms which specify the genus appear in the ornamentation of the mane and tail of the horse, in the arrogant set of shoulders and head and in the force of the countenance of the horseman.

In contrast, the " Visitation " is a grave and tender study of great simplicity and depth of feeling. Reverence and pity, piety, grace, and the hardihood that comes from suffering are here in extraordinary combination. The terracotta has considerable potentialities for the presentation of delicacy of color and is evidently equally suitable to the task of embodying the less strenuous expressions of feeling. Whereas the unity of the Colleoni statue is one of arrogant pride and the manifestation of virile power, got in part by the extraordinary unification of horse and rider, while yet marking the inner conflict by placing the rider imperiously erect in his stirrups, the " Visitation " is of gentle mood, in which color combines with confluence of lines and interlacing of arms. Internality is so marked that the statue suggests the impossible, the work of art as symbol of itself.

It would be difficult to assert categorically and to justify the assertion that in the instance either of the " Colleoni Monument " or the " Visitation " the specifications and perfections of technical, symbolical, and conative processes fail to satisfy aesthetic as well as factual criteria. It is notable, however, that historians and critics of art suggest a dissatisfaction with results of analyses solely in these terms.[16] The general problem is, however, a systematic one and we do well to recall at this point the issue as Rhys Carpenter has presented it.[17] The point is that Carpenter discovers considerable differences in the sculp-

[16] See, by way of illustration, the statement that Verrocchio's sculpture " reveals the realization on the part of the late 15th century artist of the limited expressive resources of unmodulated naturalism which had been in large measure the major interest of his predecessors, and shows him trying to use creatively, as it were, the vocabulary of form upon which the earlier men had exhausted their inspiration in doing no more than bringing it together." (Robb and Garrison, *Art in the Western World,* p. 520) Maud Cruttwell remarks of della Robbia (*Luca and Andrea della Robbia,* p. 43), that " the main characteristic of Luca's sculptures is vigour. Spontaneity and vital force are absent from none of them."

[17] See *supra,* Ch. I, pp. 20 ff.

tures of the Nike Temple parapet,[18] but there is no suggestion that he would so attribute superiority to one sculptor over others on grounds which would lead him to contradict the statement that the "artist's greatest and most necessary illusion is the illusion that he is creating." In fact, he denies that the artist is wholly free to create and does so, it will be recalled, on the ground that these creations take their place in an ordering of style. We have also observed, however, that, while the iconologist includes among possible analyses those of expressionalism or empathy, the history of art in modern times has largely excluded such analysis and concentrated upon the process by which a specific work of art is subsumed under its generic sign. Again, the emphasis is upon intelligibility and meaning, at the expense of aesthetic criteria. It is of value to recall the reasons for this concentration of interest and for the exclusion of the criteria of originality or uniqueness. As we have seen, the iconologist regards his art as a science, a direct descendant of the science of logic from which it sprang, and one which, by inductive and deductive processes, has as its goal certainty of judgment. And yet, as we have observed, the precision offered turns out to be impossible, precisely because we know that the individual imagination in art is not coerced but merely guided by precedent.

Aristotle is certainly correct in assuming that the field of art is that in which what happens happens for the "most part." It is probable that Carpenter's sculptor B of the metopes, were his superiority [19] wholly explicable in terms of specification of

[18] *The Sculpture of the Nike Temple Parapet.* See, for example, his remark concerning the Victory illustrated in Plate VII, p. 23: "Improbable as it may seem, the Victory at the right of this same slab is worked with a wholly different technique and in every detail betrays a different sculptor's hand . . . ."

[19] Carpenter, *op. cit.*, p. 23: ". . . Where Master 'A' relies on the minute effects of close chisel-work and almost ruins every drapery line . . . this new master (whom we shall have to dub 'B') carries his lines through in long ogival flourishes, with clear steady ridges and strongly emphasized valleys . . . . In general, his manner is flamboyant and dramatic . . . and his sense for linear design is much stronger than his feeling for plastic form. The style, with all

styles and stylizations, would turn out to be as rare a phenomenon as is the Giotto who broke with the Byzantine mosaic tradition of painting. It might similarly be asserted that it is improbable that the iconologists have in fact exhausted the possibilities for meaning by concentrating their attention upon the relation of genus and species. The direction of fine scholarship upon the history of ideas, the purport of signs with intrinsic meanings, or even the history of styles or expressions bears considerable resemblance to that ancient scholasticism which discovered in Aristotle's discussions of poetics and rhetoric only the intelligible explanation of Achilles as the ideal type of Achilles. Against that tyranny, as we have observed, the theory of genius was turned, formulated within the tradition of inspiration and rationalized in terms of imagination. The climactic point of that tradition is, as we have seen, Croce's nominalism and such estimates of rational approaches to art as Aldous Huxley's remark that there is "a beauty, a goodness, a unity that no intellectual research can discover, that analysis dispels, but of whose reality the spirit is from time to time suddenly and overwhelmingly convinced."

The latter alternative is philosophically meaningless. The issue is, rather, whether all judgments of fine art are in fact judgments of concrete significant forms, as specifications of genera, i. e., of the nonaesthetic specifying processes, considered separately or in conjunction as symbolizing, expressing, and making.

That not all symbols are in fact repetitions of anterior symbols, that not all techniques are derivative from prototypes, and that not all feelings are specifications in the sense which the theory of the freedom of choice implies, is suggested by one phenomenon in art itself. There is not only the divergence among artists which marks one as a fine artist in contrast to

its beauty, is very mannered . . . . It must however be conceded that this figure ranks with the Sandalbinder as the most memorable of all the Parapet. If it is importunate, it is at least splendidly so."

the technician nor the spontaneity with which the member of a school is often characterized by historians and critics. There is also evidence for the artist's demand for freedom of creativity in works of art. This manifests itself in a search for novelty and often ends aridly in the bizarre and fantastic,[20] in duplication and cliché. Such efforts to break the bonds of tradition are well-known in pre-Raphaelite renaissances, Gothic revivals, and efforts to revitalize the architecture and sculpture of ancient Greece. More significant, perhaps, are the attempts to individualize the work of art by duplication of design,[21] by portraits or paintings within paintings,[22] or by the use of eclectic symbols, techniques or feeling.[23]

A precise statement of the problem is possible. We inquire whether there is not some structure which will serve as a basis for a description of the work of art other than that which Hopkins suggests as "affecting the general result or type." The central issue is still the possible extension of the range of judgment beyond the area of freedom of choice in which the imagination discovers potentialities. May not such meaning as is possible of confirmation or refutation from an indefinite series of points of view be got from the area of free creativity or originality in the field of aesthetic, without recourse to the supranatural realm of the traditional theory of the artist as creator? Croce's individual and unconditioned image expressed by a freely inspired artist is meaningless for judgment, but we have also observed that his theory of artistic originality requires for completeness the hypotheses of making and symbolizing as complementary. The requirement of his theory that the unique and individual work of art be included is not satisfied,

[20] See, for example, the Ivory Coast mask illustrated in P. Guillaume and T. Munro's *Primitive Negro Sculpture,* p. 101. Euphuism, the conceit, and archaic language also illustrate the point.

[21] *Ibid.,* p. 103.

[22] See, by way of illustration, Vermeer's inclusion of maps and paintings in his studio.

[23] For example, Dali's "Soft Construction with Boiled Beans" and "Premonition of Civil War."

however, by the theory of the limited structure of art which we have here called that of concrete significant form.

Is it possible to judge the work of fine art as a unique individual as well as a specification of a genus? An affirmative answer to this question turns upon the possibility of indicating the relation between concrete significant form and the work of fine art by a reference to the mechanism of the work of art. Provided that an affirmative answer can be offered, we may extend the grounds for meaningful judgments on the basis of comparison and contrast of the work of art and the work of fine art. We may also extend the two grounds for value. To ask what the work of art ought to be in terms of perfection is to inquire concerning the value of intelligibility. To ask what the work of fine art ought to be is to inquire concerning the value of individuality in terms of uniqueness. Finally, another extension of the inquiry is possible. Additional information concerning value is available once we relate individuality and intelligibility.

More specifically, we shall inquire concerning the possibility of specifying a means-end relation holding between the work of art, the concrete significant form, now serving as mechanism, and the work of fine art. The criterion of success is the establishment of the work of fine art both as unique and meaningful and, by inference, the fine artist as both creator and maker.

To state the problem in this way is not merely to reiterate Kant's suggestion that genius is the product of both mechanism and spirit, of something compulsory and original. Rather, it is to take Kant's suggestion as an hypothesis specified in aesthetic of the general problem of freedom as more than deliverance from restraint and from the guidance of all rules. By implication, Kant holds that there is a law for mechanism and a law for freedom. More explicitly, mechanism and freedom do not differ as law from lawlessness but as laws holding for differing orders. The argument of the present essay is that there is a relation of means-end in fine art and that the work of art is the structural precondition for reconciliation in aesthetic of the traditionally bifurcated theories of demiurgic and creative making.

It will be argued, therefore, that the fine artist, as creator and maker, is an artist describable in terms of two laws, that of freedom of choice in the field of concrete significant form, and that of free originality, under which law the concrete significant form as a single organism or instrument becomes in turn the mechanism for the work of fine art, in relation to a limiting conception of individuality. The argument is that the work of fine art is both unique and meaningful.

If, as we have maintained, technique and judgment are correlative terms, then the problem of the artist as creator may be presented either in terms of the question, whether or not the artist as technician produces an individual work of fine art or whether or not the work of fine art is susceptible to meaningful judgment. We shall begin by examining the issue in the latter terms, asking ourselves whether each artist's creation does or does not take "its ordered place within a phase or style pointing back to its predecessors and forward to its successors." If the argument of the present essay of the artist as creator is sound, it is possible to classify the arts in terms of predominant aspects such as symbolism, technique, or expression and to classify within the arts any given work of art in the same terms. The issue is not now whether the work of art as concrete significant form may be classified correctly, but, rather, under what limitations it is possible to judge and so to classify a free work of fine art?

Croce, maintaining as he does that the work of art as image or expression is individual and free, infers that the notion of such judgment in aesthetic is absurd: "The so-called *arts*," he writes, "have no aesthetic limits, because, in order to have them, they would need to have also aesthetic existence in their particularity; and we have demonstrated the altogether empirical genesis of those partitions. Consequently, any attempt at an aesthetic classification of the arts is absurd . . . . All the books dealing with classifications and systems of the arts could be burned without any loss whatever." [24]

Whether, indeed, the sole choice is between such categorical affirmations as Carpenter's, which denies uniqueness, and no less categorical denials such as Croce's which denies the type, between the assertion that the freedom of the artist is illusory and the assertion that it is unconditioned, between the statemen that every work of art " takes its ordered place within a phase or style " and the statement that " any attempt at an aesthetic classification of the arts is absurd," are questions which introduce the crucial problem of the artist as creator. Let us therefore turn to an examination of the aesthetic classification of the arts.

[24] *Aesthetic,* p. 114.

9 The Aesthetic Relation of the Arts: The Structure of Value and Judgment

> The sublime (or comic, tragic, humourous, etc.) is *everything* that is or shall be *called* by those who have employed or shall employ these *words*.
>
> CROCE

Croce's assertion that an aesthetic classification of the arts is absurd is not a denial of the feasibility of such classifications as are implicit in the *Poetics* or are explicitly presented in Hegel's *The Philosophy of Fine Art.* Aristotle's analysis proceeds from the genus, imitation, to the species and differentiae. Hegel's classification presents the various arts, music, poetry, painting, sculpture, and architecture within the stages of the romantic, classical, and symbolic. But Croce contends that such classifications are science rather than aesthetic. If we take into account his denial to the artist of aim, end, or intention, it may with equal accuracy be inferred that for him the proposition, the work of art as a concrete significant form, would likewise be a scientific or technical judgment and, therefore, irrelevant to the aesthetic problem.

It is notable that this denial limits the aesthetic problem to the work of art *sui generis,* not as a limit, as is the ugly for Croce,[1] but as the product of unconditioned free creativity. It is perhaps more significant that the absurdity of classifying or relating the aesthetic arts is presumed to arise in consequence of the assumption that in the " lyric or the music of spirit . . . there is nothing philosophically contradictory because the philosophical problem has not yet arisen." [2] This statement means precisely what it says, with all of its implications, as is evident

[1] See *supra,* Ch. III.

[2] See *supra,* Ch. V, pp. 165 ff.

from the inference that " the sublime (or comic, tragic, humorous, etc.) is *everything* that is or shall be *called* by those who have employed or shall employ these *words.*" [3] Because it is held that aesthetic experience is not susceptible to philosophical analysis, this nominalism and freedom of judgment means that a man might call the same aesthetic object ugly and beautiful, comic and tragic without contradiction, i. e., that he may assert that a thing or event can have opposite attributes at the same time. Not only is it assumed that the principle of contradiction does not hold in aesthetic; it is asserted that there can be neither error nor correctness in judgment, which implies that subsumption of the work of fine art under either genus or class is neither accurate nor inaccurate.

One of our interests in the present essay has been to examine some of the arguments which have been employed to exile the fine artist from the republic in which activities are assumed to be intelligible and in which the products of those activities may be understood. It is less significant for the history of the tradition of the artist as creator that the first of these writers on the exile charges that the poet is one who writes by inspiration and not by wisdom than that he urges that one so inspired need have no " knowledge of a whole art " and that he cannot " make right judgments of the sayings and doings of that art." It was the latter aspect of the criticism, which led the author of *de Sublimitate* to conclude that the great genius evidently thought—and, indeed, need think—little of " minute correctness." As we have observed, it was this influential writing which affected the eighteenth century and influenced Kant to urge that the products of genius are ineffable. But, as we have likewise noticed, Kant stipulates that the originality of genius which produces the ineffable is nonsense unless it is associated with the " something compulsory of mechanism."

An historian of aesthetic may well grant that the interpretation of the genius in the arts as one who is both original creator and master of technique presents a laudable ideal which

[3] *Aesthetic,* p. 90.

Kant's own argument merely sketches. Still, the effort to provide perspective and body to the sketch encounters exclusive claims from both the mechanist and the expressionist which, if stated in terms of strict antitheses, appear irreconcilable. In support of the mechanist, it is difficult to deny the force of the argument that the hypothesis of artistic originality is destructive of the intelligibility of the work of art; that the unity, form, or wholeness of concrete significant form—different from the objects of distributive analyses of the embodied *and* significant *and* expressive—is an aspect of the made structure of the work of art; that there are works of art which appear to occupy their preeminent place simply and solely in consequence of artistic powers expressive of freedom of choice in craftsmanship, expression, or significance or in the conjoining of these aspects of concrete significant form. It is not without importance that the continuing judgment of Giotto's contribution to painting relates primarily to a technical innovation and that of Michelangelo is principally of one who combined technical mastery with profound thought.

Yet, strong as the claims of the mechanist are that his theory provides an adequate explanation of the artist and the work of art, originality, which escapes classification in terms of signs, techniques, feelings, and styles, presents a problem which cannot be dismissed simply by recourse to the phrase, *tour de force*. There are works of fine, in contrast to technical, art and whatever the difficulties which common sense encounters in accepting expression without technique, Croce is certainly correct in his insistence that the unique individual is integral to aesthetic theory. The soundness of Croce's intuition is unaffected by the fact that aesthetic freedom is not primitive, that intuition is an integral portion of the life of feeling, and that feeling is, no less than technique and significance, part of the structure of concrete significant form.

It is the thesis of the present essay that the rival claims of freedom of choice and freedom of originality, of mechanism and freedom, of intelligibility and uniqueness do present theory with a difficult problem but that the claims may be reconciled. Various possibilities for such reconciliation have been suggested in the preceding pages, provided that errors may be rectified. These may provide the grounds for solution to the central question, what is the artist as creator? We may, by way of illustration, attempt to rectify Croce's error [4] by reinterpreting the individual as a member of a class. We have argued, moreover, that the identification of genius and taste suggests that the artist expresses the unique and individual image, whereas he expresses the potential aesthetic experience. This, in turn, signifies in terms of taste, both that the work of fine art is in part explicable in terms of an immanent teleology and that judgment is implicit in the creative artistic processes. Finally, we have observed the imbalance of a theory which interprets ugliness as a limit and insists that its contrary the beautiful is a wholly concrete image.

Each suggestion is an error and the possibility that in the correction of each such error we open an avenue for a sound reconciliation of the demiurgic and creative theories of the artist is present. There is, however, a more central problem which suggests a direct approach. The assumptions that the artist is free without condition and that both artistic originality and aesthetic creativity are completely possible are specifications in aesthetic of Whitehead's definition of creativity as " the universal of universals." Whatever may be said of the validity of asserting, except in terms of limiting conceptions, that there is a genus which is not subsumed under the next higher genus, the history of the tradition of the artist as creator does not suggest to an historian that creativity has been preferred to perfection as the supreme value. On the contrary, the theory of value should be argued on a naturalist level in terms of what in the universe most opposes man and at the same time permits him to exert and extend his control over himself and his environment. It would appear, then, that the values man has set store by in recorded history are precisely those which are got by the

[4] See *supra*, Ch. VII, p. 238.

exertion of technique to perfect by means of instruments and by the exertion of knowledge to produce novelty.

Philosophically, in terms of the theory of value, God is the ideal of perfect attributes, and of these, along with life, omnipotence has been no less significantly predicated of Him than has omniscience. As we have argued at length, the " great analogy " is an assertion in which the conception of God is humanized in the genius, whose attributes are omniscience and omnipotence. Moreover, in the context of aesthetic, an insistence upon the uniqueness of value of originality is meaningless: without comparison to and contrast with the perfected, the unique is meaningless, precisely as the argument concerning the unique and individual image is meaningful only in terms of the specific product of technique.

It follows that precisely as it is meaningful in the aesthetic universe of discourse to argue that a work of art is a becoming or an event specified as a concrete significant form in comparison and contrast to the mechanisms of signs, feelings, and crafts, so it is meaningful to postulate the work of fine art as original in comparison with and contrast to the work of art. More concretely, intelligible originality in its aesthetic signification implies such classification (as a generalized form of judgment) of the fine arts as will relate free originality and free choice, creativity and technique. This, in its turn, implies that fine art is a possible means-end relation and a technique, relative to which meaningful judgments may be made. It is not by Young's " structure of means invisible " but, ultimately, by " skillful use of common [i. e., intelligible] tools " that originality is made comprehensible in art, and to use these tools for purposes of analysis we may avail ourselves equally of the artist's technique or the criticism, classifications, and judgments of the man of educated taste.

It suffices to point out that, with reference to the value of historical classifications of the arts and of fine arts, the analysis of the work of art as a becoming or as an event deprives history's most notable account of its immediate use. Lessing's *Laocoon* argues that the arts may be classified as spatial and temporal. But the assumption that sculpture is a spatial and poetry a temporal art is untenable if the experience and judgment of a structure as concrete significant form is a conjoining in time of technique, symbols, forms, and expressions by means of reproductive imagination.

If, however, what Croce calls the " aesthetic limits " disappear in the most influential theory of the classification of arts because all works of art are events, and temporally conditioned judgments are processes concerning processes, it does not follow from the fact that judgment is process that other possibilities for classification are precluded. It will be recalled that our argument concerning judgments of the work of art was centered upon the fact that the three processes, making, expressing, and symbolizing, lead into the work of art, contributing to it as a concrete significant form. As directed by the artist, in making, and by the aesthetic perceiver, in experiencing and judging, these processes provide grounds for the comparison and contrast of what the work of art has been in terms of mechanism, i. e., what it is no longer as mechanism, compared to what it becomes as an event, i. e., what, in the process of judging, the event is as a structure upon which making has been directed.

The processes, taken in conjunction as concrete significant form, produce a limited structure, a work of art. From this limited structure, in its turn treated as a mechanism, this conjunction of the three processes provides the ground from which comparison and contrast are directed to what the work of art becomes as it ought to be, as a value, but what it is only as mechanism. The first direction, i. e., toward the concrete significant form and within the latter event, provides us with grounds for judgments of fact and with judgments of value in the realm of free choice. The second direction, i. e., from the concrete significant form toward what ought to be, provides us with grounds for judgment of aesthetic value, provided that free choice is the condition for free originality. This means precisely that the structure of art is the condition in any case for the structure of fine art.

More specifically, for the philosopher of art, the work of art is a complex unity produced by making. The artist employs techniques on mechanisms, i. e., upon signs, materials, and feelings, in order to embody expressed and intelligible symbols of feeling. The achieved form or unity of the made work of art produces a single event. It also produces a single instrument. The unity made, in so far as the artist's powers reach, is a function of the limiting conception of absolute power to form the technically perfected work of art. Upon the completion of the technical processes in a concrete significant form, an end-point is reached in the direction of making. Making, as we have observed, is artistically the carrier of feeling and significance. In so far as the work of art is completed as an event, the immanent teleology of the regulative conception of perfection has operated through the techniques of making and judgment. A value as a work of art has been produced. Freedom of choice, as we have seen, is the discovery of potentialities. The work of art remains a specification of generic techniques, lacking uniqueness.

For the aesthetician, in contrast to the philosopher of art, the work of fine art is not only a work of art, i. e., a limited structure as a concrete significant form, evaluated in terms of the regulative principle of perfection of technique. Immanent in some complex unities called concrete significant forms is a second teleological principle which, by the redirection of the limiting conception of technical perfection toward the limiting conception of originality, individualizes by means of fine art the value of the concrete significant form into an aesthetic value.

On this hypothesis, which we shall examine, the judgment of that work of fine art as a valuable instrument is not, as Nietzsche,[5] Croce,[6] and a host of others have maintained, a prodigy, a mystery, or a miracle. It is, rather, explicable as a specification in aesthetic terms of judgments of value. It involves sub-

[5] *Thus Spake Zarathustra,* I, XV.

[6] *Aesthetic,* p. 51.

sumption as does judgment of art and judgment of fact. What is subsumed is the event called concrete significant form. That event is subsumed under aesthetic classes, specifications of the limiting conception of originality. In the course of that subsumption, the event is judged not only in terms of what it becomes, i. e., the degree to which it has approached technical perfection, but it is also judged in terms of what ought to be, i. e., in terms of the degree of its free originality.

We have sufficiently indicated the obstacles which the great analogy of the fine artist to God has placed in the way of sound evaluation of the work of fine art. It is perhaps advisable to mention briefly the principal barriers in aesthetic to attempts to differentiate judgments of fact and of aesthetic value. The main obstacle has been to determine the class or classes with reference to which such subsumption is made or, having determined the classes, to relate objects of fine art to them. Criticism in the eighteenth century provides a classic example of a period in which critics, through lack of sound iconological, historical, and archaeological techniques, failed to relate the object of art to the classes they had inherited and examined.

There are, however, subsidiary difficulties which should be mentioned here, to clear the way for the more general problem. The first arises if the two species of judgment are confused or if it is assumed that one may perform the task of the other.[7] The second arises if we suppose, as does Croce, that judgments of aesthetic value are logically prior to judgments of fact. Judgments of fact, judgments concerning concrete significant form,

[7] Kant saw this problem clearly, as is evident from his remark in the *Kritik of Judgment*, sec. 33 (trans. Bernard, p. 158): "If a man reads a poem of his or brings me to a play, which does not on the whole suit my taste, he may bring forward in proof of the beauty of his poem *Batteux* or *Lessing* or still more ancient and famous critics of taste, and all the rules laid down by them; certain passages which displease me may agree very well with rules of beauty . . . but I stop my ears, I will listen to no arguments and no reasoning; and I will rather assume that these rules of the critics are false, or at least they do not apply to the case in question, than admit that my judgment should be determined by grounds of proof *a priori*. For it is to be a judgment of Taste and not of Understanding or Reason."

are logically prior to judgments of aesthetic value and are their presuppositions. The third difficulty arises if it be assumed that, because men disagree concerning the merits of an instance of concrete significant form, such disagreement proves the soundness of the cliché, *de gustibus non est disputandum.* One judge may maintain that a work of art is beautiful, meaning only that it is technically excellent. Another may emphasize its expressive, a third its symbolic powers or the artist's skill in unifying heterogeneous parts. In such circumstances, it may be argued that a) the judges agree, in so far as they refer to the identical event or work of art; b) they disagree in so far as they refer to divergent aspects of the same event or work of art; and c) that they both agree and disagree concerning the same object or event, provided we remember first that they agree that what they denote is the object they are in fact talking about and second that they do not confuse a technical aspect of the same work of art with an aesthetic aspect in the same universe of discourse of agreement or disagreement. The significant point, clearly, is that the possibility of error is a basic assumption in each instance and that comparison and contrast are essential to sound judgment.

Our central problem is not, however, specific judgments. Once having suggested that aesthetic judgments are not invalidated in general because they may be erroneous in specific instances, the problem centers upon the relation of concrete significant form to the two limiting conceptions of perfection and originality. These limiting conceptions of human freedom, which the tradition of genius humanized through the fallacy of misplaced concreteness in the figure of the great man, provide the regulative principles for the work of fine art. The latter principles are the unique individual and the wholly specified event. Both regulative principles are required. In setting a desired but unachievable goal for productivity, limits are set toward which art and criticism move. The artist and the critic are freed by them from the immediate, empirical problems which are presented by the specific work of art. They provide the ground for the conviction of progress toward the ends of perfection and originality which are approachable without limit and serve as directions or destinations for effort. The limiting conceptions of perfection and originality become values upon being considered by the artist, the aesthetic percipient, or the critic, to be objects of desire.

It is thus necessary, in order to describe the technique of fine art and the work of fine art, as well as the artist as creator and criticism by the man of educated taste, to extrapolate from the complex unity of the work of art, the concrete significant form, to the postulated levels of value and, in explanation of aesthetic value, to the dual levels of perfection and originality. The extrapolation is made from the synthesis of the various processes, principally the three of making, symbolizing, and expressing, to a new class of value which the synthesis of processes conditions but does not wholly determine. In this interpretation of the immanent teleology of the work of art, the new class of value is a novel event under which the event called the individual work of fine art is subsumed and which serves it as the ground for judgment. In this judgment of a single instrument, understood in terms of the end, the desirable value, we are concerned at the outset not with the components of the specific event, the concrete significant form. What transformations the specifications of genera undergo in the process is our later interest.[8] We are immediately concerned with what that specific instance " ought to be " as a whole. Once the work of art as a unified mechanism or instrument is subsumed under the class, free originality, evaluational judgments of a specifically aesthetic kind may be made upon the parts of the whole which have been invested in the process of such judgment with that value.[9]

That there are two levels of judgment for the event, the

[8] See *infra*, next chapter.

[9] In this judgment of a single instrument understood in terms of an end, we rediscover the significance of the Platonic question, " Are we on the way from or to the first principles? " See Aristotle, *E.N.*, 1095 a 31 ff.

work of art which is also the work of fine art, extends the bases for meaningful judgments and so permits their " confirmation or refutation " from a second of " an indefinite series of points of view," the valuable as well as the factual. The grounds for the comparison and contrast lacking in the theory of expression are thus provided at two levels. Generically, there is possible a comparison and contrast between the work of art and the work of fine art, between judgments of fact and judgments of taste, or judgments of technique in its broadest sense, and judgments of aesthetic value. Generically also, there is possible a comparison and contrast of the work of art and the work of fine art. Specifically, there is possible a comparison and contrast of the differentiae of judgments of fact, including making, expressing, and symbolizing, and their specifications and interrelations within the work of art as concrete significant form, and the work of fine art, in which these aspects of making are reformed within the individual event by fine art and criticism.

Let us examine the relation of concrete significant form and the work of fine art, as a pattern of human freedom within the total structure of art. We shall be particularly interested in the specification of aesthetic classes within which the event produced by fine art is made unique while retaining the intelligibility of the made, symbolized, and felt work of art. The thesis is that the work of fine art is explicable in terms of a rational means-end relation and that, granted the technique called fine art, the correlative judgment of taste may be rationally grounded. If a classification of the aesthetic arts is possible, there is philosophical meaning to the phrase, artist as creator.

In the next chapter, we shall indicate how the general structure of value and judgment helps to resolve the more specific problem of the judgment of fine art within the aesthetic structure as a specification of a general theory of value.

10 The Aesthetic Relation of the Arts: Aesthetic Structure and the Judgment of Fine Art

. . . the feeling is submitted to the laws of the object.
BOSANQUET

If, as we have argued, the artist expresses by means of works of art which are also works of fine art, not the isolated datum, the individual image, but the potential aesthetic experience, it follows that aesthetic activity, whether of the artist or perceiver, provides the ground for making explicit the values of originality and intelligibility. In this connection, few more enlightening inferences have been drawn from the controversy between the supporters of the theory of art as imitation and the proponents of the theory of art as imagination than that made by Kant [1] to the effect that the ideas of the artist-genius "excite like Ideas in his pupils if nature has endowed them with a like proportion of their mental powers." Disregarding the words, "like Ideas," heritage of the imitative theory which does not explain fine art, Kant goes to the core of the problem: the product of genius, he writes, "awakens to a feeling of his own originality" another genius, "whom it stirs to exercise his art in freedom." [2]

To this inference, we need but bring a clear understanding of the significant contribution of the tradition of the genius to aesthetic theory, the identity of genius and taste, in order to arrive at the basis for the ensuing argument concerning fine art, its originality and intelligibility. On the hypothesis of the identity of genius and taste, not only the artist but the aesthetic

[1] *K.d.U.*, sec. 47, p. 192.
[2] *Ibid.*, sec. 49, p. 203.

observer or critic is awakened "to a feeling of his own originality." This event is occasioned by the work of fine art. The artist's expression of the potential aesthetic experience is the instrument for the creation of the creator, i. e., of one who also originates in freedom. Aesthetic theory in this way interprets the eighteenth-century conviction that the beautiful arts produce a novel state of mind.[3]

Let us mention some of the varieties of freedom which enter upon the making of the creative mind by the artist in his originating activities. In a vivid phrase, Bosanquet expresses the negative estimate of the freedom the artist exercises in fine art. In *Three Lectures on Aesthetic* he remarks that aesthetic experience begins when "the feeling is submitted to the laws of an object."[4] It should be added that it begins, also, when not only feeling but signs and techniques are likewise submitted to the laws of the object in order to produce a concrete significant form.

The implications of this largely negative freeing, principally a function of artistic freedom of choice, may be presented succinctly.[5] In reflecting upon our own state as we experience profoundly moving art in relation to the work of art itself, we are aware of being *freed from* various compulsions which mark our nonaesthetic life. We are freed from compulsions inherent in the relations of feelings to the natural and nonartistic objects and events by which they are aroused and to which they attach. We are liberated from the framework of reference in which signs indicate merely natural meanings. We are introduced to a world in which techniques are no longer directed to the natural ends of practice, prudence, and pragmatism. Once choice is effective, the framework of reference for signs, feelings, and techniques is the concrete significant form, product of artistic freedom of choice and a symbol of the artist's

[3] Cf. *supra*, Ch. VI, pp. 199 ff.

[4] *Op. cit.*, p. 8.

[5] It is the general basis of the argument in M. C. Nahm, *Aesthetic Experience and Its Presuppositions*, pp. 483 ff.

feelings concerning nonaesthetic signs. The laws of the object, to repeat Bosanquet's words, are the laws reciprocally imposed by technique upon a material and the conditions which are imposed by the material upon the artist. They manifest themselves in temporal spread, diversity in unity, order of specific intervals, and other of the functions of the made work of art. Their employment in the specification of general signs, techniques, and feelings differentiates the work of art from the event as it occurs in nature.

The condition for the negative freedom made explicit in the differentiation between the experience of art as product of freedom of choice and the experience of nonartistic events is the life of feeling. A brief résumé of its initial function in aesthetic experience is of value as preparation for a statement concerning the affirmative conception of freedom as originality. Of the negative freedom, it is enough to point out that by means of art and the event called the work of art, the artist frees us from compulsions which, as functions of feeling, once enslaved men to extrinsic forces and made them, as creatures of instinct and tropism, mechanisms in large degree inflexible in their reactions. Feeling, as instrumental, operates at this level in specific modes, as panic-fear or rage. It is, as overt, largely mechanical reaction, describable in mechanical terms as trigger-like reactions to stimuli.[6] In epistemological terms, however, feeling at this level is reproductive imagination, which ensures familiarity for the racial and cultural symbols which provide the common framework of reference for profoundly moving art and for the religion, the art, science and morality from which the symbols of art are derived.

Fine art, i. e., profoundly moving or freeing art, does not as such, however, teach, preach, or construct scientific, religious, moral, or practical systems. Racial and cultural symbols are material for such art. It is true, as Bosanquet remarks, that " the feeling is submitted to the laws of the object," but this is possible not only because feeling is attached to signs, objects

[6] See *supra*, Ch. VIII.

and events but also and primarily because feeling is not solely reflex reaction or reproductive imagination. In the course of man's evolution, emotion and mood have emerged as dimensions of the continuum of feeling; and within the ranges of emotion and of the mood, behavior varies directly in intensity from overt action in the instinctive range to peripheral reaction in the range of mood.[7] This means that as the behavior varies from overt to peripheral action, the alternative stimuli or modes of possible action which the organism presents to itself increase. It is this increase in the stimuli made effective by and for the organism—in contrast to the stimuli presented externally and productive of trigger-like reaction—which ensures the possibility of freedom of choice.

The behavior of the individual who feels evidences a capacity, therefore, for the presentation of alternative stimuli or images. An image is simply a stimulus effective for the production of behavior. This capacity, minimal in operation in the ranges of instinct and tropism but radically increased in emotion and mood, is productive imagination. The work of art is constructed, as we have observed, as an integration in the most complex degree of the specifications of concrete significant form. The artist, expressing his freedom of choice, presents the perceiver with stimuli for the reaction which is experience and ground for judgment. In re-making the bare work of art, which is potentially the concrete significant form, an actually experienced complex, the perceiver is freed in the education of taste.

Fine art, i. e., profoundly moving art is, however, freeing art in other than what the negative interpretation takes it to be. It is more than liberation from compulsion to action, explicable mainly as reproductive imagination in relation to the generic signs and symbols which man's animal heritage and his cultural constructions in science, morality, and religion, provide. Productive imagination is basically the presupposition of Kant's

[7] See M. C. Nahm, *Aesthetic Experience and Its Presuppositions*, Ch. x, pp. 325 ff.

"reproduction of representations," i. e., that connection of the imagination "with some one representation in preference to another."[8] In its elaboration in mood, however, productive imagination is so influenced by the specific factor of temporal spread in the stimulus presented by the artist that its activity continues in time and is maintained in productivity once the subject's contemplation of the artistic event is concluded.

The negative liberation of imagination from its scientific, moral, economic, or religious functions, for employment in its specific function of making actual the stimuli or images implicit in the concrete significant form, leads in experiences of works of art that are also works of fine art to the transcendence of the art-object and the employment of the imagination upon new total situations. The limiting conception of perfected technique is now directed toward the limiting conception of free originality. For reasons which need not here be again presented,[9] aesthetic experience provides—because it is a mood of courage—a source of energy enabling the perceiver to attack new problems which present themselves in the new event to which imagination moves in its productivity.

The individual moved by fine art to present to himself effective stimuli in ideas, objects, events, and situations, may be made creative in total situations other than art or fine art. The equilibrium achieved at the new level, i. e., the level of evaluation, may not be specified by the work of art simply because the derivation of the symbols of a work of fine art may be scientific, technical, moral, or economic. We come here to the implications of Kant's inference concerning genius that the work of fine art "awakens to a feeling of his own originality" that other genius "whom it stirs to exercise his art in freedom." The new situation of value is not limited to the experience and judgment of fine art. It is none the less true that among the new total situations which present themselves are works of fine art. We are specifically interested, for an understanding

[8] See *K.d.R.V.*, A 121.

[9] M. C. Nahm, *Aesthetic Experience and Its Presuppositions*, Ch. xv ff.

of the artist as creator, to learn more precisely what we can concerning the specific aesthetic perceiver who, *ex hypothesi,* is also a genius, whether as technical fine artist or man of taste, for whose imagination the new total situation is principally concerned with technique, symbols, feelings, forms, materials and the something more which, going beyond concrete significant form, is the work of fine art.

A man is freed to evaluate or make the work of fine art and to express the functions of its individuality. Hegel once wrote that "any content whatever may attain to being represented quite adequately, judged by the standard of its own nature." [10] For the present essay, Hegel's dictum holds for both senses of the word "nature," i. e., as applied to the work of art and to the work of fine art. Precisely as the artist is free to choose among signs, techniques, forms, feelings, and modes of unification in making the concrete significant form, so by means of technique, he is free to make of that form the new and original but nonetheless natural value, the work of fine art. This he does by bringing it within the scope of aesthetic classes. The man of taste is endowed with freedom of choice to experience fully the work of art. He is also free to subsume the concrete significant form under the novel (in the sense of different from concrete significant form) aesthetic categories which his productive imagination presents to him as the conditions and requirements of the new total situation which follows upon imagination's transcendence of the work of fine art. There are, as we have maintained, limiting conceptions which as objects of desire become values. They are, as we have argued, perfec-

[10] See *The Introduction to Hegel's Philosophy of Fine Art,* trans. B. Bosanquet, p. 178. Cf., more specifically, *ibid.*, 204–205: "Whatever can find room in the human heart, as feeling, idea, and purpose; whatever is capable of shaping into act—all this diversity of material is capable of entering into the varied content of painting. The whole realm of particular existence, from the highest embodiment of mind down to the most isolated object of nature, finds a place here. For it is possible even for finite nature, in its particular scenes and phenomena, to make its appearance in the realm of art, if only some allusion to an element of mind endows it with affinity to thought and feeling."

tion and originality. There are likewise, however, carriers of value, i. e., the fine artist and the aesthetic perceiver. Each makes the value actual, the artist by technique in converting the concrete significant form into work of fine art, the perceiver by means of taste, judgment and criticism.

The meaning of the assertion—that a new total situation related to and conditioned but not determined by freedom of choice does emerge as the product of fine art—may be made clear if we attack the problem of the possibility of classifying the aesthetic arts. If successful, the inference is that the original is also the intelligible. Let us begin with the specific works of art, the concrete significant forms, which have as their presupposition the nonaesthetic materials of craft, signs, feelings, and forms as unities and which do not determine but, rather, condition works of fine art. The classificatory names for such groups of mechanisms are readily available. Architecture, painting, music, poetry, sculpture, and the dance are generic names for the specific mechanisms of art, i. e., for the concrete significant forms specified as buildings, paintings, symphonies, and the like. As mechanisms, such specific works of art are not interchangeable.[11] Not only is it true that if a man need a habitation, neither painting nor poem will adequately protect him from the elements. It is also true that, except in a figurative sense, no man can " poem a picture." Only in figures of speech is architecture " frozen music." [12] It is equally the fact that no building, whatever its aesthetic merit, is an aesthetic object or event unless the nonaesthetic and mechanical architecture to construct it, the symbols it incorporates, the feelings its builder expresses by means of technique, symbols, and forms, are likewise present.[13]

[11] See E. A. Singer, Jr., " Esthetic and the Rational Ideal," *On the Contented Life*, p. 18.

[12] See Lessing's argument in *Laocoon* and his attempt, in terms of the differentiation between spatial and temporal arts, to indicate the power of the poet to represent the function of the painter by means of movement. Compare also such complicated classifications of the arts as Baldwin Brown's *The Fine Arts*.

[13] See Henry Adams' *Mont-Saint Michel and Chartres*, particularly p. 93.

Despite the fact that they are not interchangeable *qua* mechanisms, some concrete significant forms are interchangeable in their aesthetic meanings. Works of art which are also works of fine art are interchangeable in precisely that relation which Kant calls spirit, as he refers to originality. In this relation, the aesthetic arts as classes, within which the individual work of fine art is subject to the law of the aesthetic class, are names for instruments interchangeable with reference to the unique proximate end of stimulating the productive imagination. The latter, in its turn, fulfills the end of fine art, the creation of the creator.[14]

So much for the general pattern of the problem. Is it possible to specify the aesthetic classes of the limiting conception, originality, and so to judge the work of fine art in terms of uniqueness and intelligibility? Within the complex interrelations of artist, work of art, work of fine art, aesthetic experience and end of art called the total structure of art, the fine artist and the aesthetic relation of the arts present a conjoined problem in human freedom. The diversity of natural values in the work of art as concrete significant form, the products of expression of feeling, of capacity to symbolize and signify, and of technical skill to make, provide means for the expression of the most diverse technical potentialities. Some artists are fine artists and some tastes are educated aesthetically. In some instances, the diversities of the work of art, conditioned by the value of intelligibility, are converted into the unity of the work of fine art. This unity, in relation to the limiting conception of originality, converts the natural values of free choice in art into the aesthetic values of fine art. In these instances, if taste is educated, the aesthetic perceiver is put into a creative mood if he is trained to live, think and feel under the discipline of the artist the knowledge, information, and technical skill which have been objectified in the work of art. On such occasions, the diverse parts of the work of art, in which " any

[14] M. C. Nahm, *Aesthetic Experience and Its Presuppositions*, Ch. XVIII.

content whatever may attain to being represented quite adequately, judged by the standard of its own nature," acquire aesthetic value. They become meaningful in terms of such value when they are made part of the single instrument called the work of fine art.

The work of fine art is a new unity, a new individual. In the work of art, the artist operates technically to use signs, feelings, and media for their own sake and for the perfection of the technically definable unity. The fine artist, on the other hand, uses these same technical factors for the proximate end of stimulating the imagination to its creative task. The individual work of fine art is not the sum of its diverse parts. Its diversities do provide the variations of means, interpreted aesthetically, which are essential to the value of the work of fine art. They are required for making productive the imagination of the individual affected by value.

For what are the potential works of fine art single instruments? In providing the grounds for valid aesthetic judgment of relations to aesthetic values, the single instruments as means are related to specific aesthetic ends which are also aesthetic values. If we ask what, specifically, these value terms are, the answer is provided by the history of speculation, despite the errors which philosophers have committed and the exaggerations which critics have set store by. The great analogy of the fine artist to God centered the attention of theologians and philosophers of art upon the terms " ugly," " beautiful," and " sublime." [15] Speculation less theologically inclined applied the terms to types or classes of aesthetic, i. e., to classifications of the arts. They drew, also, upon an ancient terminology, the " comic " and " tragic," to extend the scope of classification.

There is, in this terminology, an evident conflict between the general classification and a more specific one, owing principally to an interest in specific comedies and tragedies. With reference to the ugly and the sublime, as we have noted, there has been

[15] See *supra*, Ch. III, VI.

evident a reluctance either to relate the terms to specific works of art or to relate the structures made to the classifications. It is evident that in the tradition of the " great analogy " it becomes increasingly paradoxical to attempt to associate a structure with the nonexistent ugly,[16] as it becomes increasingly obvious that difficulty arises in answering the question, whether there are in fact sublime objects or events.[17] It is notable, as well, that speculation upon technique, in contrast to that by theorists of genius who sought to resolve the problem of originality in terms of the sublime, tended to assert its claims to aesthetic autonomy by describing the beautiful in specific and structural terms.[18]

We have observed that in speculation upon both the sublime and beautiful the fallacy of misplaced concreteness was committed and, consequently, that the incompatibility of beautiful and sublime events was inferred. This is true even of Kant, who had at hand a systematic answer to the problem. To this point we shall return. At the moment, it is sufficient to maintain, as history suggests, that the beautiful is the limiting conception of perfection of technique, intended to satisfy requirements for the value of intelligibility; that the sublime is the limiting conception of originality in aesthetic intended to satisfy the requirement for the value of novelty; and that these terms, " sublime " and " beautiful," as well as " ugly," " tragic," and " comic," are not merely classificatory of fact in art but are terms denoting aesthetic value.

Our argument is that these types and values are properly to be understood in their relation to concrete significant forms, i. e., in their relation to works of art which, as events, are specifications of generic signs, feelings, materials, forms, and techniques. In their relations to the aesthetic values, the concrete significant forms are individual events related to what ought to be.

[16] See *supra,* Ch. III.
[17] See *supra,* Ch. VI.
[18] See *supra, ibid.*

The historical aesthetic types are not merely classificatory names. They do indicate, it is true, the grounds for correct classifications of works of fine art. If the fine artist succeed, however, and we, in consequence of the education of taste, succeed in sound judgment or subsumption, the painting painted and the poem expressed may be classified correctly and evaluated aesthetically. This means that the event is evaluated as an intelligible individual. The classes, tragic, comic, sublime, ugly, and beautiful, are end-events of movements of imagination. They are occasioned by some works of art which belong to the total structure of art and which are to be judged in terms of originality.

11 The Structure of Fine Art: The Specification of Aesthetic Values and Movements of the Imagination

. . . the satisfaction here concerns only the *destination* of our faculty.

KANT, *Kritik of Judgment*

A glance at the writings of the two most influential authors who have touched upon the subject leaves little doubt that sublimity is, historically, the class-name philosophers of art have preferred in describing and defining originality. Longinus maintained that sublime poetry elevated man near to God and endowed him with powers transcending those of the humble herd of brutes.[1] Kant's interpretation of the conception treats of the mind's power to achieve a totality to which no empirical concept corresponds, as well as man's superiority over the might and power of nature herself.[2]

The use of the term, sublimity, has been extended beyond the field of speculation upon great art. Kant is notably eloquent, for example, in his peroration of duty,[3] and equally notably, acute. In aesthetic, whatever connotations have been attached to the term in other branches of knowledge, sublimity has signified the type and value of the original and the creative. As we have observed, it is the aesthetic conception which has been used most widely to intimate that the artist's powers are divine and, as we have also pointed out,[4] its most radical usage

[1] *De Sublimitate.* [2] See *supra,* Ch. v.

[3] Kant calls duty that "Sublime and mighty name." It is evident, however, that duty "can be nothing less than a power which elevates man above himself . . . a power which connects him with an order of things that only the understanding can conceive . . . ."

[4] See *supra,* Ch. vi, pp. 203 ff.

implies that the artist and the aesthetic percipient are by analogy capable of creation *ex nihilo.* Some among the most acute minds of the eighteenth century were convinced that neither the rules of art nor the making of an object permitted the emergence of novelty. They tended to account for the alternative creating of a new state of mind in terms of sublimity. The subject has ancient alliances. Not only in Longinus' thought, but for the mystic, by way of illustration, it is precisely that state of mind which is personal and individual and, as Plotinus believed, beyond the dualism of thinking and object thought.

It is no less evident that, in part as a result of controversy, the beautiful is the class-name adopted by many in the eighteenth century to characterize the contrary to the sublime and to signify what they judged to be endowed with the value of perfection. To the claims for originality in the experience of the former were opposed those for the complete intelligibility of the beautiful. By exercise of freedom of choice in making, it was implied, artists produce beautiful forms, objects of generally agreed upon or universally valid judgments. The opinion of the eighteenth century that the beautiful and the sublime do present a bifurcation in philosophy of art is reflected in Francis Hutcheson's remark, " *Grandeur* and *Novelty* are two Ideas different from *Beauty* . . . ." Philosophers and critics sought to specify concrete embodiments in works of art and in nature of what in fact are norms, ideals, and limiting conceptions of unconditioned originality and of perfection wholly conditioned by technique.

Kant, to whose writings upon the sublime we again return, did not escape this error of the eighteenth century, although he does indicate the systematic method by which a correct specification of aesthetic values may be got. As we have observed,[5] Kant's is a theory of aesthetic originality expressed in terms of the sublime. Kant is well aware that the relation of imagination to reason which is the condition for his notion of creativity,

[5] See *supra,* Ch. VI.

is self-contradictory. Moreover, it should be recalled that he realizes that the analysis renders the sublime aesthetically incompatible with the beautiful.[6] And, finally, he holds that the state or condition of mind called sublime is attainable.

However interesting these aspects of Kant's theory are from the viewpoint of the historian of compulsions implicit in the notion of genius,[7] it is significant also that Kant does formulate a meaningful statement concerning the relation of intelligibility and originality, of mechanism and spirit, of technical perfection and originality. It will be recalled [8] that in writing of the faculties of mind which constitute genius, Kant maintains that imagination as the productive faculty of cognition is powerful in creating another nature out of material that actual nature gives it. More specifically, by means of productive imagination, we remold experience in accord with principles "which occupy a higher place in Reason." The consequent representation of imagination he calls ideas [9] and uses the term to indicate the striving after "something which lies beyond the bounds of experience and especially because no concept can be fully adequate to them as internal intuitions." His illustrations are illuminating: [10]

> The poet ventures to realise to sense, rational Ideas of invisible beings, the kingdom of the blessed, hell, eternity, creation, etc.; or even if he deals with things of which there are examples in experience, *e. g.*, death, envy, and all vices, also love, fame, and the like,—he tries by means of Imagination, which emulates the play of Reason in its quest after a maximum, to go beyond the limits of experience and to

[6] It should be noted, however, that he does concede the following: "Even the presentation of the sublime, so far as it belongs to fine art, may be brought into union with beauty in a *tragedy in verse*, a *didactic poem* or an *oratorio*, and in this combination fine art is even more artistic." Kant adds, however, that whether it is "also more beautiful . . . may in some of these instances be doubted."

[7] See *supra*, Ch. v.

[8] See *supra*, Ch. i and Ch. v.

[9] *K.d.U.*, sec. 49, p. 198.

[10] *Ibid.*, sec. 49, pp. 198–99.

present them to Sense with a completeness of which there is no example in nature.

Imagination may in theory create another nature out of what material nature affords it but it does not achieve in its operations the maximum limit attainable for any sensible concept, a maximum achievable, indeed, only in ideas of reason.[11] It is notable that this relation of reason and imagination produces that for which " there is no example in nature." [12] The fruitful portion of Kant's argument is that, in spite of terminological difficulties, what is in fact produced is not unnatural, in the sense of contradictory, although it is nonnatural, in the sense that it is different from what nature provides through the instrumentality of sense. Implicit in the argument is the inference that to identify creativity with unconditioned originality is meaningless. We are freed, it is true, from such conditions as the association of ideas, but we also enter the province of aesthetic ideas and so are freed in that imagination works under a new, i. e., a different principle or law.

It is to be observed that the conception of unconditioned originality, i. e., the notion with which Kant labored in analyzing the aesthetic judgment of the sublime, is here treated as a limiting conception toward which imagination strives. It is a destination for the faculty and its attainment is beyond possibility. It may be asked, therefore, what this " other nature " is and what its laws of operation? That other nature can only be the realm of free originality, as contrasted to that of freedom of choice. As for the law of this realm, it is notable that the limiting conception of free creativity may be interpreted as the genus for all the species of imaginative freedom of choice. There are no sublime objects. There are occasions which set the imagination in operation. It is the movements of the imagination in relation to the limiting conception which are important, the more so once we realize the nature of that limiting

[11] Kant in fact asserts that to these ideas " no concept can be fully adequate." He is probably recalling Addison's similar suggestion.

[12] *K.d.U.*, sec. 49, pp. 198–99.

conception: what it is is clear from Kant's insistence that aesthetic must face up to the problem that it is not merely "how we judge" but "how we ought to judge."[13]

The insistence is upon a value in contrast to a factual judgment. Such judgment is as natural as the factual one. But it is specifically different. And with this as the limit to which Kant's theory may be extended in relating freedom of choice and freedom of value we must be content, if our goal be the formal compatibility in his system of the beautiful and the sublime. Yet, while formally we encounter the incompatibility, an alternative is presented. Kant does suggest that there must be a relation in the work of genius between mechanism and originality. The force of the argument is weakened, as we have seen, by the use of the terms "ineffability" and "inspiration" in the analysis of genius. But it is also weakened by the fact that Kant tries to relate aspects of the problem which are at different levels of analysis.

If we substitute for mechanism the product of free choice operating as technique, i. e., the work of art as a concrete significant form, it is clear that, at the corresponding level, what the fine artist produces is a work of fine art. If originality is, in fact, the limiting conception of unconditioned freedom, then historically its correlative term, the aesthetic correlative of the sublime in the realm of free choice, is the limiting conception of wholly conditioned freedom of choice. This correlative is the beautiful. It is clear that Kant twice commits the identical error. Not only is the sublime judged by him to be attainable, whereas it should have been considered as a limiting conception, but the beautiful—ateleological, nonmathematical, and object of a universally valid judgment of taste—is to be judged properly at the same level of analysis as a limiting conception and not as a concrete product of technical perfection and, therefore, wholly intelligible.

The mechanism produced by making as freedom of choice

[13] *K.d.U.*, sec. 29, p. 149. He judges the "how we judge" to be empirical, rather than *a priori*. Cf. *ibid.*, sec. 8, pp. 194.

is not the beautiful but the concrete significant form, related to the beautiful which, in turn, is the extrapolated limit of technical perfection. Consequently, we can directly relate the mechanism to the work of fine art, provided that we also take into account the complex relation of the former to the limiting conception of free choice, and of the latter to free originality. We thus avoid the fallacy of misplaced concreteness which weakened eighteenth-century speculation concerning both the beautiful and the sublime. In our own terminology, the artist practises freedom of choice to produce an object subject to factual judgment and one progressively free—as progressively intelligible—from natural frameworks of reference. The concrete significant form thus produced conditions but does not determine the work of fine art. The fine artist makes an event within a framework of reference of means-end relations. What he makes is in a degree original and is subject to judgment in terms of aesthetic value.

What is the work of fine art as a structure made by the fine artist? We have implied that the artist makes an event for our imagination. We shall now try to make more explicit the nature of that event. The course of the argument is sufficiently indicated at the outset by two inferences: the first drawn from the history of aesthetic and, more particularly, resting upon the culmination of speculation upon the sublime in the eighteenth century which held that there are no sublime objects or events but only occasions for inducing movements of imagination; the second, the empirical fact which suggests the limitations of Carpenter's question, " If the artist were wholly free to create, why should not each of his creations be completely unique, instead of showing a manner appropriate to a school or group, which in turn takes its ordered place within a phase or style pointing back to its predecessors and forward toward its successors? " [14]

To this question, there is one answer which opens an inquiry

[14] " The Basis of Artistic Creation in the Fine Arts," *The Bases of Artistic Creation,* p. 31.

of another order than that which substantiates Mr. Carpenter's contention at the level of the work of art in terms of genus and species. The artist is creative and there is possible another ordered placing of the work of fine art in the phase or style dictated by predecessors and successors, provided that the predecessor and successor are the self-same fine artist. Creative artists not only specify the kind of work of art they produce; they also individualize the work of fine art they make unique. What is created is an individual, unique not in the sense that the original mind does not produce a work of art which falls into an order of phase or style or symbol or technique but that it does produce different individuals which bear traces of the same original mind.

In fine art we are not moved solely by the generic symbol, technique or feeling. The crude representation of the peasant is transformed by de Falla in *El Amor Brujo,* by Shakespeare in the characters of Caliban and Puck, and by Milton in his delineation of Satan. The fancies of the seafarer are transfigured in Wagner's *The Flying Dutchman,* in Coleridge's *The Ancient Mariner* and in Debussy's *La Mer.* The universal and common knowledge of grief is altered in the line, " She lay as though she had smiled," by the great prose of *Hydriotaphia,* and by the structure of the Taj Mahal. Illicit love loses its sordidness in Dante's line, " That day we read no more." Not only are we aware of these alterations. It is clear that one artist and one alone could have written,

> As one great Furnace flam'd, yet from those flames
> No light, but rather darkness visible . . . .

There is ultimately an identity of generic symbols in the lines,

> —here where the bone-edge frayed
> Grins white . . . .

and,

> And in this harsh world draw thy breath in pain
> To tell my story.

The lines bear, however, the imprint of two unique artistic imaginations.

If, however, fine art produces unique but intelligible symbols it does so because for the individual [15] there is a class. It is necessary, therefore, to turn to an examination of the aesthetic specifications of the class of aesthetic originality, keeping in mind the central issues of the movements of imagination and the denial that there are sublime objects and events.

It is significant that the history of the sublime tends toward the conception of a limit rather than an embodiment. We must search, in consequence, for what the artist makes as a work of art which induces the imagination to operate creatively, i. e., for what moves it in the direction of its destination, unconditioned originality. As we have remarked, making is the instrument by means of which values are imposed upon material. It is, also, the implicit recognition of the conditions laid down by the limiting conception of perfection of technique, whether the artist attempt to ignore the strictures and so to produce the wholly original or whether he accept the conditions and try to perfect the media by free choice.[16] If the goal is an originality by definition unattainable and if, as is the fact, he makes an event related to this limit, it is evident that in choosing the artist makes a choice among values, destroys some potentialities for value, and establishes others in the interest of originality. But what does he make which in the aesthetic field most nearly approximates to the limiting conception of originality, while reordering the structure, concrete significant form, the limiting conception of which is intelligibility and the approximating embodiment of which is the structure called beautiful?

In answer to this question, it is methodologically little less significant that the history of speculation has not only tended to formulate the conception of the limit of originality than that theorists have rarely failed to specify objects and events which

[15] See Carpenter's contention, quoted *supra*, Ch. I, that "The individual artist attains his own status by submission to the contemporary trend."

[16] Cf. P. Hindemith, *A Composer's World*, p. 49.

various writers have regarded as sublime.[17] The theory of originality benefits from both historical phenomena and we may well begin our answer to the question, What does the fine artist make? with some of the suggestions concerning products of technique which have been adjudged sublime.

Among the images held to induce the feeling of sublimity, there are the names for specific feelings or emotions ordinarily associated with signs presented either by nature or by means of artistic technique and associated with imaginative experiences. Among these are fear, astonishment, terror, respect, reverence, self-abasement, and humiliation. One notes that although there is, for example, reference to fear, it is not genuine fear to which the writers refer. Again, the feeling most frequently associated by writers with the sublime is exaltation. Finally, more sophisticated writers, for example Kant and Bradley, suggest that the experience of the sublime is one bifurcated in character and consists of shock or check and recovery.

If we keep these aspects of speculation in mind, is there not —leaving from consideration an aesthetic of nature—a class of structural works of art which are ordinarily related to these experiences? The answer is implicit in A. C. Bradley's illuminating essays, "The Sublime" and "Hegel's Theory of Tragedy." [18] Bradley's argument verges upon an identification of tragedy and sublimity. It is noticeable, by way of illustration, that the quotation from Tourgenieff describing the bird defending its nest [19] could equally well illustrate the tragic. Similarly, "the ocean, in those stanzas of *Childe Harold* which no amount of familiarity or of defect can deprive of their sublimity, is the untameable monster which engulfs man as lightly

[17] Longinus selects as illustrations passages from Greek poetry and oratory; Burke suggests objects of terror, and Hegel remarks on the pyramids and the conception of light. Bradley's use of Tourgenieff's brief account of the bird's effort to defend its young runs counter to the almost constant identification of the sublime with objects or events either exaggerated in size or manifesting great power.

[18] *Oxford Lectures on Poetry*. The first essay is dated 1903, the second 1901.

[19] *Ibid.*, p. 44.

as rain-drops and shatters fleets like tops. The sublimity of Behemoth and Leviathan in the *Book of Job* lies in the contrast of their enormous might with the puny power of man." [20]

The " greatness of some kind of power " which according to Bradley is requisite for sublimity is, on his own showing, no less a factor in tragedy. The catastrophe of tragedy presents two aspects, the first a " power which is irresistible and inescapable." [21] The check and recovery of the sublime is duplicated in the second, in the negation and affirmation of the tragic experience.[22] Reconciliation is common to both.[23] Even the conception of conflict, essential on Bradley's view to tragedy [24] is essential to the notion of sublimity: ". . . the greatness of soul in the sparrow is enhanced by comparison with the smallness and feebleness of its body, and pours contempt on the visible magnitude of the hound; and the stillness of night or death is sublime from its active negation of sound and motion." [25]

Additional instances of such correspondence between the two aesthetic types could be adduced. It is sufficient, however, to concentrate upon two factors in Bradley's analyses. The first is the statement, ostensibly in contradistinction to that of Burke, that " the sublime is always founded on fear . . . it can *never* be fear in the common meaning of that word, or what may be called practical or real fear." [26] The second is that for many writers upon the sublime there is need to emphasize a " checking and a recovery." [27]

[20] *Ibid.*, p. 46.

[21] *Ibid.*, p. 90.

[22] *Ibid.*, p. 86.

[23] *Ibid.*, pp. 52 and 90.

[24] *Ibid.*, p. 86.

[25] *Ibid.*, p. 56.

[26] *Ibid.*, pp. 53–54. Compare, however, Burke, *A Philosophical Enquiry into the Origin of our Ideas on the Sublime and Beautiful*, Part v, sec. 7, p. 149: ". . . if the pain and terror are so modified as not to be actually noxious . . . they are capable of producing delight; not pleasure, but a sort of delightful horror, a sort of tranquillity tinged with terror." Compare also Kant, who argues that the experience of the sublime occasioned by the might of nature depends upon our ability to contemplate nature's might from a position of security. (*K.d.U.*, sec. 28, p. 125)

[27] For example, Kant. Cf. Kames, Addison and Burke. Compare also, Bosanquet on Winckelmann, *A History of Aesthetic*, pp. 242.

The implication of the first point, that the experience of the sublime is not one of "practical or real fear," is evident. We here tread the ancient speculative path which leads from Aristotle's theory of the *katharsis* of pity and fear induced by tragedy and some kinds of music to the modern hypothesis of aesthetic emotions.[28] It need only be added that theory on the sublime has verged upon that aspect of feeling called the mood. In it, overt behavior is minimal, while productive imagination is enhanced and the aesthetic percipient brings himself to the attitude best described as empathy.[29]

The need to act overtly does not arise. The simplest answer to the obvious question, Why does it not arise? is that the event which induces the mood is so made by technique that it expresses the aesthetic experience in which productive imagination is dominant. The simple answer is, however, in fact a simple description of a complex problem. The capacity to produce and the capacity to experience aesthetically an object or event such as is properly called aesthetic imply that man has progressed from the stage of the brute and from that of the absolutism of cultural demands and has moved toward the rationalization of feeling. Consequently, the signs incorporated by technique in works of art which are selected for their generic significance no longer induce tropic action. Feeling is, as we have observed not only productive but reproductive, as well. In their operations as reproductive imagination, the reactions rooted in the bodily structure enable men to act generically and mechanically in ways predisposed for survival in the context of our lives and actions.

The recovery which theorists of the sublime have emphasized is, I believe, induced by the operation of productive imagination after the check which is the consequence of the operation of reproductive imagination. Productive imagination presents stimuli permitting possible action or making characterized by

[28] See M. C. Nahm, *Aesthetic Experience and Its Presuppositions*, Ch. IX and XVII.

[29] *Ibid.*, Ch. XVI.

freedom of choice.[30] It is the redirection of imagination in recovery which characterizes aesthetic experience as revaluation. What in the analysis of the sublime has been referred to as shock and recovery is the break-down of equilibrium and its re-establishment at another level. Classical writers upon the sublime have thus brought the experience within the scope of the teleology of feeling. May we proceed farther? What has been described thus far is mere potentiality for the aesthetic mood. The conditions for its actualization have been obscured by the vagueness of the terms "boundless," "formless," and "infinite," employed in describing the sublime. Bradley's essays, with their suggestions of relationship between the sublime and the tragic, suggest that such vagueness is unnecessary. It disappears once the conditions theoretically laid down for the sublime as the original are in practice observed to be fulfilled by the structures of fine art, the tragic and the comic. We shall take Bradley's and Kant's writings as illustrative of the relation of the structure of fine art, the relation of "what becomes," to what "ought to be."

Let us first consider tragedy in Bradley's terms. What, he asks, is more sublime than the "noble endurance" of the tragic hero? What is more likely to produce shock than the tragic conflict? What more nearly describes the recovery from shock than the fact that "the hero never shows himself so grand or noble as in the death which seals his failure?" What, in concrete instance, more nearly satisfies the abstract problem of shock and recovery than the following: ". . . the catastrophe . . . has two aspects, a negative and an affirmative . . . . On the one hand it is the act of a power immeasurably superior to that of the conflicting agents, a power which is irresistible and inescapable, and which overbears and negates what is incom-

[30] *Ibid.*, p. 446: "The individual impelled to instinctive and overt behavior is blind to alternative stimuli. The 'monitory function' of emotion is the 'compelling announcement of needed adjustments.' It is a report of 'unstable equilibrium' and it may, as Bergson suggests, 'express the fact that the disturbance is a systematic readjustment with a view to equilibrium on a higher level.'"

patible with it." [31] Bradley remarks that if this were all, it would "horrify, depress, or at best provoke indignation and rebellion." But the catastrophe ". . . must have a second and affirmative aspect, which is the source of our feelings of reconciliation . . . . He dies, and our hearts die with him; and yet his death matters nothing to us, or we even exult." [32]

This verging of the tragic and the sublime in Bradley's analyses of spiritual conflicts, wastage and recovery of value, suggests the relationship of the tragic as the most nearly perfected structure produced by making to sublimity, the aesthetic limiting conception of originality. It also suggests the relation holding between free choice and free originality for the production of an event fittingly called fine or freeing art. As we shall see, the tragic artist makes a whole event which is not determined by its parts. Before we infer, however, that the description warrants consideration of an identification of the tragic and fine art, it is well to examine the comic artist as a creator, into the product of whose making perfection and originality likewise enter.

From the beginnings of systematic criticism, in Plato's *Philebus* and in Aristotle's *Poetics*, comedy, no less than tragedy, has been subject to analysis in terms of techniques, symbols, and feelings. It is noteworthy, in the context of our present argument, that speculation upon the comic and the comic spirit has shown extraordinary agreement upon the significance, for the comic artist, of the mechanism which is so obvious a condition of the human situation. In this connection, Bergson elaborates the formula, "something mechanical encrusted upon the living"; Freud, the escape by wit from the censor; and Palmer, the fact that man is "an angel in the body of a beast." The most

[31] *Oxford Lectures on Poetry*, p. 90.

[32] *Ibid.*, p. 91. Compare Kant's observation concerning "the might of nature, on which we are utterly dependent." It is "nevertheless, a power beneath which we need not bend if the maintenance of our highest principles were at stake." Kant knew Kames' *Elements of Criticism*, translated into German in 1763. Kames held that the sublime is humiliating as well as exhilarating. I am far from arguing, however, that Kant's is a mere reflection of Kames' theory.

general speculative ground for these elaborations in terms of movements of imagination, would appear to be Kant's famous remark, in describing a comic incident that "our expectation was strained [for a time] and then was suddenly dissipated into nothing . . . expectation is transformed into nothing."[33]

Acute as Kant's remark is, it nevertheless overstates the case in a significant fashion. That deception and illusion pervade many forms of the comic may be admitted. The significant aspect of Kant's statement is, however, his use of the word "nothing." It is of little consequence that, in the tragic, shock would appear to precede recovery and that, if we believe Kant, in the comic affirmation precedes shock. The important point is that Kant's suggestion, if generalized, would identify the movement of the imagination in the comic with what tradition in the "great analogy" judged to be the ugly, namely, the nonexistent. This identification would imply destruction of values by the comic artist. It may be stated categorically, however, that whatever strictures the comic artist places upon the values of ideas, situations, objects, events or characters, the comic as a form of art does not permit their annihilation. The essence of comic is the offer by the artist of a possible return to the same level of evaluation as that from which the artist began.

In contrast, the tragic artist, by the nature of his task, permits no return to the values with which his work began. The divergence of tragic and comic is, in this respect, important but it is more notable for our discussion that, as concerns values, the tragic and the comic conform to the same generic pattern of shock and recovery, a movement toward the destruction or negation of values and a reaffirmation—that "second and affirmative aspect" of Bradley's analysis—of what "ought to be." The second point of significance is that the experience of both the tragic and of the comic is one of freedom from values accepted at the outset, temporary in the case of the comic, permanent in that of the tragic.

The immediate inference to be drawn is that tragic and comic

[33] *K.d.U.*, sec. 54, p. 224.

are related in the initial movements of the imagination. Each is a function of concrete significant form, which, as we have seen, is the event in which freedom of choice is exercised, principally in achieving negative freedom from natural values. The second inference is related to the implication drawn in the demiurgic theory, that ugliness is a contrast essential to establish the beautiful whole. In terms of the movements of imagination, it is evident that the initial direction of our imagination is toward the destruction of value, that the artist is, as Nietzsche observed, a destroyer. Indeed, the core of Nietzsche's argument concerning the revaluation of values is in the assumption that the originality of the creator is presupposed by the destruction of values. It may be argued, indeed, that the construction or making of an art object means the sacrifice of natural values. In producing a concrete significant form, value is not only made explicit by the artist's freedom of choice, but some natural values are negated or subordinated. The value of wood as fuel is subordinated to its value in a sculptured figure and another sacrifice of the intrinsic values produced by art is necessary in order to make explicit the values of the artistic whole. The arches in the Council Hall in the Bargello are bent to secure the overall effect of the room itself. Of the natural values of justice and love of brother, one must be sacrificed in *Antigone.* The dead body mentioned by Aristotle loses its natural value as it is imitated or represented.

Considering shock as an aspect of the life of feeling, the inference is obvious that the ugly is a destination of imagination from the standpoint of theory of value. The ugly is the extrapolated limiting conception, in the context of aesthetic, of nonvalue. It is not the contrary to originality, inasmuch as the artist may produce novel works of art which are ugly. The ugly is the contrary to that total structure of fine art, which is concrete significant form, originality and intelligibility, and the end of art, the creation of the creator. We do well to consider more fully some of the implications of ugliness, which is not negation but affirmation of certain aspects of art [34] which lead the imagination toward the ugly. Such consideration will aid in an understanding of our general problem.

It is trite, but true, to suggest that sacrifice of value must be justified in the result, i. e., in the production of a more desirable or suitable value. The sacrifice implicit in free choice as a process of making may not be avoided and moreover, ugliness is not nonexistent. The artist makes a work of art and what is naturally ugly may become, in fine art, beautiful, tragic, sublime, or comic. In terms of the limited structure of art, even if it were granted that a specific work of art is deficient in one of its four principal aspects, i. e., of making, symbolizing, expressing or forming, we need only to recall such intentional omissions of structure as are evident in Cezanne's "The Bathers," omissions necessary to enable the painter to concentrate upon feeling, to deny the applicability of the negative notion to the limited structure of art. Even the plausible notion that the ugliness of a work of art may derive from a lack of wholeness is so ambiguous as to become meaningless upon application, as is clear once we consider such exaggeration of individual figures as in El Greco's paintings or the exaggerations implicit in satire, burlesque, and caricature.

It is no less plausible—and no less erroneous—to suppose that the ground for ugliness is to be sought in the artist's failure to achieve originality. The Minotaur and Medusa, Dali's furlined teacup, Dunsany's and Massinger's dead men standing erect at the end of the drama, and even Venus with an alarm clock in her navel, sufficiently indicate the failure of the hypothesis that lack of novelty by itself accounts for ugliness. In specific works of art, novelty may be unconvincing and may suggest lack of artistic integrity. The "slick," shocking, or perverted may be due to the fact that the originality of the artist has no organic, technical, or rooted relation to the technique which produces the whole work of art. Yet, in abstraction, aspects of art no less than aspects of experience, may be

[34] See *supra*, Ch. III.

significant form; the second, the end of fine art in the creation of a creative and original mind; and the third is the aesthetic classes, the beautiful, the sublime, the tragic, and the comic.

The artist makes an event, the concrete significant form, the judgment of which relates to what it was, and what it becomes as fact. The fine artist likewise makes an event. He, however, relates the what it was and what it becomes as fact to what it ought to be as an aesthetic value. What he makes by means of art is a concrete significant form; what he makes by means of fine art is a tragic or comic whole which is also a building, a painting, a sculptured figure, a sonata, or a poem. What the work of art ought to be is intelligible in relation to the classes which derive their meaning as values from the sublime, the limiting conception of originality in aesthetic. What the fine artist produces is an aesthetic potentiality, actualized in terms of sublimity, once the percipient is, in ancient phrase, "carried out of himself," i. e., once the perceiver relinquishes nonaesthetic values and establishes aesthetic ones.

What the event becomes in relation to this extrapolated limit, i. e., what fine art makes of the concrete significant form, is a structure. Intelligibility is provided by the classes tragic and comic. The beautiful is the structural limit of perfection, the sublime of uniqueness. Originality is expressed in the individuality of the work of fine art. Intelligibility is again owing to the reference to the limit of technical perfection in the production of the tragic or comic painting, poem, symphony, or dance.

On the side of aesthetic experience, the correlative to the making of the tragedy, comedy, symphony, or painting is the judgment, formulated in terms of aesthetic criticism. The tragic and the comic, classes which principally govern the structures called fine art, are not merely specifications of significance, expression, and technique. Their meaning is not exhausted by description in terms of the values of discovery in free choice, whether the description relates to the collective event or to the event taken distributively.

The tragic, comic, sublime and beautiful, provide the intelligible classes [35] under which the specific work of art is subsumed. In the processes, the specific instance of concrete significant form becomes an individual work of fine art. The process by means of which the artist effects this transformation from one level for judgment of fact to the other level for judgment of value will shortly be examined, but certain general aspects of the process should be made clear before we present details. The first is that the fine artist makes the concrete significant form into a single instrument related to the proximate ends of tragic or comic and to the end of creating the creator. The concrete significant form and the limited structure of the work of fine art, the latter the means to the end of fine art, are the same event in isolation. The first is, however, described in distributive, the second, in collective terms.[36] The first meaning is that not infrequently associated with form as the unity of such an object as a work of art described in terms of ratio, boundary, or delineation.[37] The second meaning is of a whole unified in terms of end or ends subserved.

The second point to be noted is that the intelligible aesthetic classes or types which are likewise values, are not discoveries or functions of freedom of choice. Nor are they to be interpreted merely in negative terms, as freeing the artist or the aesthetic percipient from the compulsions of signs, expressions, or techniques. More specifically, they are not discoveries [38]

[35] The range is beautiful, comic, tragic, sublime in terms of specification of structure.

[36] See E. A. Singer, Jr., *Mind as Behavior,* Ch. IV, p. 68. The entire chapter of the book cited is called "The Pulse of Life" and is basic to the argument here presented.

[37] See M. C. Nahm, *Aesthetic Experience and Its Presuppositions,* Ch. IV, particularly p. 170.

[38] Carpenter, "The Basis of Artistic Creation in the Fine Arts," *The Bases of Artistic Creation,* p. 36, touches upon the problem in a way significant for his own technical interpretation of the fine arts: "Yet teach a modern student to model like Signorelli, foreshorten like Mantegna, envelop like Rembrandt, and nothing of importance will result. Why? For a very simple reason. Signorelli, Mantegna, Rembrandt were excitedly discovering the technical resources on

because they have no natural cognates or correlatives in natural signs, expressions, or techniques. The song of the bird, the sighing of the wind, the harmony of the spheres, the animal's den, the eagle's eyrie, the dance of mating birds—all have seemed at one time or another to be of the same order as man's music, the intricacies of choreography, and the products of the architect's techniques.

Nature, however, does not produce either the tragic or the comic. Man is a "thinking reed," the "most feeble thing in nature . . . . But, if the universe were to crush him, man would still be more noble than that which killed him, because he knows that he dies and the advantage which the universe has over him; the universe knows nothing of this . . . ." A metaphysic of aesthetic might well be grounded on man's knowledge of his mortal lot and of the human situation. He builds monuments in bronze. Plato remarks that the inventors, the poets and artists are more creative in their souls than in their bodies and produce immortal children.[39] And if men alone know that they die, men alone, also, not only erect monuments in bronze but present in great art the creativity which, against the background of loss of value and in the effort to produce value, objectify their own powers to experience aesthetically the fact of their own mortality. The tragic and the comic not only transcend nature but go beyond the literal rule of art and technique as well.[40] The fundamental criterion of technique is correctness

which they laid such emphasis; and for an artist thus absorbed and involved, there will be no distinction (such as the schoolmen draw) between discovery, invention, and creation. Signorelli must have felt that he was himself creating the device of sculptural modelling in paint; Mantegna may well have thought that he had invented certain extreme devices of foreshortening; Rembrandt must have been convinced that he himself had discovered a new painter's world of light amid darkness. And thus it was possible for these coldly academic matters of technique to convert themselves into flaming emotional resources by which craftsmen were transmuted into master artists." But what, it may be asked, of the originality of a Giotto or a Mozart?

[39] *Symposium*, 209.

[40] Hindemith, *A Composer's World*, pp. 89–90, gives an interesting instance of the limitations of technical experimentation in his answer to the question,

in specifying a kind, but not even the definition of a tragedy as that which ends unhappily holds for all tragedies. The classes of the tragic and the comic are structures in aesthetic of the category, originality.

The third point we should notice is that the new series, the ground for originality and, in conjunction with choice, for creative freedom, makes possible the individualization of specifications of genera by the individual fine artist.[41] Our judgments concerning free or fine art are thus susceptible to confirmation or refutation by reference to the series from fact to form, in the operation of free choice; from form to value, in the operation of originality. The series will shortly be extended from value to the portions of the work of fine art as an instrument, portions of which pertain originally to the specifications of the genus, but which in this later process are properly considered to be modes of individualization. In general, each work of fine art is unique in the sense that as an individual it is different from all other works of fine art. Despite the individuality of all works of fine art, in any circumstance in which an original artist produces more than one individual work of art, the unique individuals bear the mark of the same mind. Originality can produce individuals but the individuals are identical, in terms of factual judgment and in terms of the mind which produces them.[42] El Greco's varying paintings of " El Despolio " are unique, as are the varying versions of the *Leonore Overture*, and the " Mona Lisa." But each bears the

" Could not the stimuli afforded by this carefree calculation be heightened if we replaced our twelve-tone division of the octave by a different number of tones? " His conclusion is that " apart from a greater number of tones, the multiples of twelve would yield nothing new, because the deviations from the main intervals would remain the same as in the twelve-tone temperament . . . ."

[41] It is well to remind ourselves of Singer's injunction concerning judgments: " Insofar as a judgment lays claim to truth, insofar does it pretend to have grasped an objective reality, and insofar must it be capable of confirmation or refutation from an indefinite series of other points of view." *Mind as Behavior*, p. 197.

[42] See *supra*, Ch. IV, p. 146 ff.

mark of the artist's technique and all have in common the end of creating an original state of mind.

The more specific problem is the one which has been implicit in this essay of the artist as creator from its beginnings: Is there a technique for the production of a work of fine art? In general, our answer is that the fine artist produces not only the concrete significant form which is meaningful in relation to the limiting conception of perfection of technique but that he simultaneously produces a whole which functions, in terms of such values or ends of originality as the tragic, the comic, and the sublime, as a single instrument. He produces a work of fine art which is an individual event and potential aesthetic value. John Addington Symonds put the problem clearly in discussing Signorelli's paintings at Orvieto: " His composition sways our souls with all the passion of the terrible scenes he depicts. Yet what does it contain? Two stern angels on the clouds, a blank gray plain, and a multitude of naked men and women." [43]

The order in which Symonds frames the parts of the problem offers a clue to its immediate difficulty. What the critic as judge and aesthetic perceiver is able to describe only in a sequence of propositions and questions, the artist makes simultaneously. We have observed that the artist's technical making is imagination in process of producing the work of art. It is also the productive imagination in process of making the work of fine art. Artistic creativity involves a technical process simultaneous for the production of the concrete significant form and of the individual event called sublime, beautiful, tragic, comic, or ugly. The fine artist makes, in the latter instance, an event meaningful aesthetically in terms of immanent teleology—what Kant implies in the phrase, " purposiveness without purpose." That teleology refers the work of fine art to the ends of perfection and originality. Committed as he is to the first by the fact of making, the artist may likewise commit himself to the second,

[43] *Sketches in Italy*, p. 105.

provided that he proposes to individualize as well as to specify the components of concrete significant form. This means subordinating freedom of choice to freedom of originality. It does not consist in choosing freely among media, signs, and techniques solely in terms of discovery or caprice.

But, as Plato saw clearly that there is a difference between going toward and coming away from the good, so there is a difference between going toward and coming away from the limit of originality. What the artist makes is a work of fine art; what he expresses is a potential aesthetic experience. What for the artist is a simultaneous process, a use of technique for a dual purpose, must for the perceiver be no less actualized than is the bare work of art.[44] In aesthetic judgment, the evaluation of the single instrument directed to the end of creativity, a judgment of the whole, is made which necessarily[45] includes the procession from categories of value—the class of originality as specified in the sublime, the beautiful, the tragic, and the comic—back to the instrument. That procession of judgment and evaluation transforms the parts of the instrument into modes of symbols, forms, expressions, and techniques specified at the nonaesthetic level but also individualized at the aesthetic level. In this way, the duality of the artist's technique is made evident in a different time sequence. The ground for the difference between the individualization and the specification of the parts of the work of fine art and the work of art is, morphologically, the difference between a limited structure of a work of art and a total structure of the work of fine art. The principal difference becomes explicit in the actualization of the immanent teleology in the aesthetic experience. The differentiation between the two structures provides the new series for comparison and contrast by which judgments may be confirmed or refuted. Genius and taste are both essential to creativity in the artist.

[44] Cf. *supra*, Ch. VIII, pp. 248 ff.

[45] If, as is suggested, the identical technique serves to produce specification and individualization, the immanent teleology of the work of art is a methodological necessity for judgment.

The artist achieves his freedom by producing an individual work of fine art which is correctly subsumed in judgment under the class of value. In the new relation of the work of art, what used to be and what becomes is now what ought to be as a whole. Our principal interest concerns the comparisons and contrasts which are implied. Inasmuch as the teleology of the work of fine art is immanent, our obvious course for indicating the grounds for such judgment is the examination of the technical means employed by the artist after the procession of events constituting the parts of the whole has been affected by the class of value. We shall proceed by such reference as is necessary to instances of fine art which were mentioned in the first chapter of this essay. We shall concentrate attention, however, upon one illustration in order to indicate by comparison and contrast the duality of technique employed by the fine artist in the means-end relations which produce both the concrete significant form and the work of fine art, once the latter has been affected by originality. We may do this because the parts of the whole, of the work of fine art as an instrument, are invested with that value once the imagination has been induced by great works of art to move toward its destination.

Some facts relevant to Verrocchio's "Colleoni Monument" and della Robbia's "The Visitation" have already been mentioned [46] and the references to these works of fine art will in the main sufficiently serve our purpose at the moment in emphasizing the variety of objects and events a work of fine art may be, as well as to suggest again the fact that in their nonaesthetic aspects works of fine art are not interchangeable. The latter point is illustrated by the contrast of George Kolbe's "Dancer" in bronze and Verrocchio's commemorative statue of the great condottiere. A similar contrast is afforded within the classification, work of art, by the Greek temple at Segesta and the cathedral at Pisa. The former dates from the early fifth century B. C., and is a hexastyle peripteros, with thirty-six columns,

[46] Ch. VIII, pp. 262 ff.

unfluted, and without cella, standing alone on a hill below the theater. The cathedral has as its basic plan the Latin cross, nave with double vaulted aisles and the transepts single. The pillars of the side aisles were brought by Pisan galleys from Greek and Roman buildings. The cathedral stands between the baptistery and the campanile. A similar variety holds among the paintings. Van Dyck, a native of Flanders, a student of Rubens, and painter at the court of Charles I, painted " The Head of a Man "; Vermeer, a Hollander of the mid-seventeenth century, " A Woman Weighing Gold "; a Greek, Domenico Theotocopuli (El Greco) painted " Toledo " and " Ecstasy in a Garden "; while Turner's " Steam, Speed, and Rain " is an English anticipation and Monet's " Rouen Cathedral " a French fulfilment of impressionism. The extrinsic facts relating to *King Lear, Concerto No. 21 in C,* the Medici Chapel and the Sistine Chapel are too well known to require presentation here. " A shelfy coast . . ." is from John Dryden's translation [47] of Virgil's lines [48] concerning the Sirens.

In the more general ranges of description, these works of art which are also works of fine art are susceptible to an almost unlimited number of approaches. The extraordinary " Head of a Man " by Van Dyck is a technical masterpiece, as well as an illustration of that ancient compulsion described by Berenson as " the longing for the perpetuation of one's fame " which ". . . brought with it the more universal desire to hand down the memory of one's face and figure." [49] El Greco's " Toledo " or his " Ecstasy in a Garden " could easily illustrate either the movement of Tintoretto's technical mastery to the Iberian peninsula, the influence of Alexandrian grave-painting, or the use of cultural symbols. Mozart's *Concerto,* with its extraordinary descending cadences, is a superb illustration of the way in which this master of music attained to a perfection

[47] *The Works of John Dryden,* eds. Sir Walter Scott and George Saintsbury, Vol. XIV, *Aeneïs,* V.1125-27.

[48] *Aeneid,* v, 864–71.

[49] *The Italian Painters of the Renaissance,* p. 16.

unexcelled before Beethoven in a form of great complexity which grew from the Aria, as the *da capo* form was taken into the polyphonic concerto.

As we have observed,[50] however, the criteria for evaluation of the work of art may be reduced in number and related more closely to the work of art by what we have referred to as the specifications of the genera: complexity, temporal spread, unity, internality, the law of organic wholes, diversity in unity, the order of specific intervals, style, mode, balance, rhythm, harmony, and repetition. We have suggested,[51] as well, that these criteria operate at two levels, of specification and of individualization. Let us now concentrate upon one of the events which we called work of fine art, and by reference to John Dryden's lines, " A shelfy coast . . ." indicate the movements of the series for judgment from fact to value by way of specification of kind and by individualization of concrete significant form into a work of fine art. We shall proceed by indicating the methods by which the artist specifies and makes explicit the genus or kind of technique, feeling, or symbol; the method by which the fine artist makes of the concrete significant form a single instrument; the influence of the classes of aesthetic originality; and, finally, the series of individuality into which the work of fine art falls.

John Dryden's lines,

> . . . a shelfy coast,
> Long infamous for ships, and sailors lost,
> And white with bones,

are a portion of the translation of the following lines from Virgil's *Aeneid*:

> currit iter tutum non setius aequore classis
> promissisque partis Neptuni interrita fertur.
> iamque adeo scopulos Sirenum advecta subibat,
> difficilis quondam multorumque ossibus albos.

---

[50] Ch. VIII, pp. 259 ff.

[51] *Ibid.*

> tum rauca adsiduo longe sale saxa sonabant,
> cum pater amisso fluitantem errare magistro
> sensit et ipse ratem nocturnis rexit in undis,
> multa gemens casuque animum consussus amici:
> 'o nimium caelo et pelago confise sereno,
> nudus in ignota, Palinure, iacebis harena.'

Their immediate context in *Aeneid* is the sailing of the ships which Juno has failed to burn. The seas are calm and the breezes favorable. The passage appears at the end of Book V, with the loss of Palinurus. Dryden translates the final lines, after the loss of the pilot,

> For faith repos'd on seas, and on the flattering sky,
> Thy naked corpse is doom'd on shores unknown to lie.

What Dryden renders *idem in alio* is the generic symbol of death, in verse of rhymed couplets. To the great natural generic sign, are added the cultural symbols of the wanderer, belief in supernatural beings, the seas, and escape from shipwreck. The dominant cultural generic symbol is that of the Sirens. Its literary context is the *Odyssey* and the incident that of the great wanderer who sailed past " the curst shore " on which " wide around/ Lie human bones, that whiten all the ground." [52] So striking is the tale of the Sirens that the word has assumed a meaning allied with carnage and destruction. Classically the image is well-known through Homer's verse. For the scholar, the referrent for the symbol is obscure. As is notable with most generic symbols, its precise meaning is likewise obscure. Some of the more plausible hypotheses [53] interpret the Sirens as " the stranglers," akin to the Keres, Erinyes, and Harpies. They promised Odysseus knowledge and were associated originally with birds. Shorey suggests that Sirens are not only lurers and temptresses but are widely associated with

[52] *The Odyssey*, trans. Alexander Pope, Book XII, *The Works of the English Poets*, ed. Alexander Chambers, Vol. XIX, p. 221.

[53] Paul Shorey, article on " Sirens," *Encyclopaedia of Religion and Ethics*, ed. James Hastings, Vol. XI, pp. 577–79. Shorey mentions many modern poetic uses of the image.

the " wings of a bird or the magic of the bird's song," signifying not only the bird's song and its spell but the " treacherous lure or the magic spell of the smiling sea," as well as the association of the " fleeting soul with the wings of a bird or the magic of the bird's song."

Shorey believes that the Sirens already embody a conscious allegory in their first appearance in the *Odyssey*. None of the fancied interpretations, he maintains, admits of proof, " but their suggestions for the poetic and the moral imagination can never pass away." To it, the culture of the Western man, through literature, language, and folklore is predisposed to react in monolithic ways.

The problem is, how has Dryden specified and made explicit the generic symbol? First, as a translator, he disavows the task of copying.[54] The way he has chosen is " not so strait as metaphrase, nor so loose as paraphrase: some things too I have omitted, and sometimes added of my own." The " regularity " of French and Italian translators, he believes, have "unsinewed " their heroic verse by affected purity. He himself seeks "strength" and " elevation."

The limits of translation allow freedom but do not permit license. Dryden follows Virgil in the specific scene, relating the symbol of death specifically to that of Palinurus, the pilot. Tempted to sleep by the god who offers to take the rudder, Palinurus succumbs finally to " A branch in Lethe dipp'd, and drunk with Stygian dew." Rudder and pilot are borne into the deep. Then, the fleet,

> Glides by the Syrens' cliffs, a shelfy coast,
> Long infamous for ships and sailors lost,
> And white wth bones . . . .

Considered as a structure produced by the poetic art in terms of intelligibility, the passage in the Virgilian-Dryden version is complex to a degree. Its symbols are those of death, danger,

[54] " Dedication of the Aeneïs," *The Works of John Dryden*, Vol. 14.

the seafarer, sleep, and the movements of a dream. The feelings it expresses are fascination, surprise, and wonder. Its technique is, in barest terms, provided by the dexterity of a master of the rhymed couplet. In brief scope, we are presented with a spread of images more than adequate to show the sleep and death of Palinurus, the vision of the coast, the gliding of the fleet, and, finally, the pilot, who cried out " for helping hands, but cry'd in vain." Sleep, danger, the sea, the ships specify the symbol of death. The external referrent of the Sirens is specified in the poem by the dominant themes, although the diversity of the varied images does not blur the unified image.

The order of specific intervals is, as regards symbols, natural —the introduction of the pilot, of the infuriated God, of the Sirens, the dangers, the debacle and the recovery. The intervals are, however, emphasized by the meter and by the rhyme of the couplet and given a specific context and interpretation. Of his powers in verse, Dryden is well aware: ". . . I have endeavoured to follow the example of my master, and am the first Englishman, perhaps, who made it his design to copy him in numbers, his choice of words, and his placing them for the sweetness of sound." [55] But, within the realm of his own freedom he shuns the cæsura: " for, wherever that is used, it gives a roughness to the verse; of which we can have little need in a language which is overstocked with consonants."

Freedom of choice is thus displayed in the use of rhymed verse and language. With specification, we have come to the style, exemplified in techniques which employ rhythm, harmony and repetition. The structure is pictorial and concrete, a specification of a generic sign, and a poetic expression, completely unified and clearly intelligible.

[55] *Op. cit.*, pp. 204–05. See *ibid.*, p. 206: " You may please also to observe, that there is not, to the best of my remembrance, one vowel gaping on another for want of a *cæsura,* in this whole poem: but, where a vowel ends a word, the next begins either with a consonant, or what is its equivalent; for our *W* and *H* aspirate, and our diphthongs, are plainly such. The greatest latitude I take is in the letter *Y*, when it concludes a word, and the first syllable of the next begins with a vowel."

Originality, as well as freedom of choice, must be considered and it presents a peculiarly difficult problem in the evaluation of a passage translated from the work of a greater poet than Dryden himself. Obvious dangers present themselves to the seeker after originality for its own sake and Dryden is well aware of at least some of them.[56] He shuns the grotesque and weighs what, available for the heroic or epic poet, would appear absurd on the stage. Yet, " for a poet is a maker . . . and he who cannot make, that is, invent, has a name for nothing." [57] The measure of Dryden's powers is evident as we glance at Pitt's translation of the same Virgilean lines: [58]

> Now they approach the siren's dangerous coast,
> Huge heaps of bones still whiten all the shore;
> And, dashed from rock to rock, the hollows roar.

It is notable that Virgil, Dryden, and Pitt all use the letter " s " as a structural factor in the unification of the diverse letters. All, similarly, use the symbols and specify them. Dryden's mastery over Pitt begins at the foundations of the lines, in the succinctness of his expression, in the avoidance of prose—compare " shelfy coast " to Pitt's uninspired rendition—and in the clarity with which the scene is envisaged.

The mastery is displayed, however, not merely at the level of structural specification. The succinctness, the diversity in unity, and the complexity of the image of the shelving coast, the sinister fame, and the " white with bones," are at first a unity, are then organized into an organic whole by the verse, the repetition of the letter " s," and the rhythm of the lines. They are then converted into an image comparable only to that which emerges in pictorial art,[59] and one of great power it

[56] *Ibid.*, p. 139.

[57] *Ibid.*, p. 184.

[58] *The Works of the English Poets,* Vol. XIX, p. 570. Dr. Johnson compared Dryden's and Christopher Pitt's translations and wrote of the former that it is read with a " hurry of delight."

[59] John Marin's remark in not inapropos: " The glorious thing is that we cannot do, elementally do, other than our ancestors did. That is, that a round

is. The " infamous for ships and sailors lost " is an individual interpretation, the " white with bones " a rendition of the original. Dryden has seen as a painter what Pitt has rendered as a prose writer.

The thoroughly specified unity, intelligible in terms of technique, significance, and expression of feeling, has been converted from an organic whole into a single individual with aesthetic value. What that individual is is to be understood in terms of the tragic class of value, the structure of the work of art once it has been related to that value, and as it displays the poet's own individuality. The fury of the god, the struggle and death of Palinurus, the saving of the fleet—here are all the ingredients of high tragedy, conflict, shock, recovery. In terms of the tragic and original aspects of the process, the descriptive and explanatory adjectives, " shelfy," " infamous," and " white," assume their tragic connotations in terms of danger and death. The winds of rumour play around the invention, " long infamous for ships, and sailors lost." The unity got by the letter " s," the verse, the associated symbols, and the rhythm, is now a single individual, the counter-part for which is the mood in which the play of productive imagination is dominant.

The lines evidence artistic originality in being converted into the tragic. But they display it no less in being unique and individual. The interpretation of the symbol of the Sirens differs from that of Homer, as it differs from that of Tennyson and Ruskin. It is unique in this sense but it is individual in the sense that it also belongs to the series of what Dryden himself believed to be the core of the poetic problem of the poet's own inventions.

> . . . a shelfy coast,
> Long infamous for ships, and sailors lost,
> And white with bones,

---

conveys to all who see it a similar definite, a triangle a similar definite, solids of certain forms, similar definites . . . the true artist must perforce go from time to time to the elemental big forms—Sky, Sea, Mountain, Plain—." (Carl Zigrosser, *The Artist in America*, pp. 9–10)

belongs to the series of images created by Dryden. It is original in being unique to him. It is intelligible in that it fits into the familial line of what Pope called the " majestic march " of his poetry. Dryden himself lays down the general conditions for what is original.[60] The Elizabethans having, in his opinion, " ruin'd their Estates themselves before they came to their children's hands " because " There is scarce an Humour, a Character, or any kind of Plot, which they have not us'd," the modern must " either not write at all or [to] attempt some other way . . . . the Genius of every Age is different."

The laconic character of the lines of poetry we have quoted, their conciseness, their march are evident. The variability of rhythm is evident in the following lines, which are nonetheless akin to those which lend power to the Sirens' song and the story of the death of Palinurus. They are of an age which, Dryden believed, must invent anew. But they are none the less his own and belong to their own family:

Then down the precipice of time it goes,
And sinks in Minutes, which in Ages rose.

(*The Conquest of Granada*)

Yet had she oft been chas'd with horns and hounds,
And Scythian shafts; and many winged wounds
Aim'd at Her heart; was often forc'd to fly,
And doom'd to death, though fated not to dy.

(*The Hind and the Panther*)

Just in the gate, and in the jaws of hell,
Revengeful Cares and sullen Sorrows dwell,
And pale Diseases and repining Age,
Want, Fear, and Famine's unresisted rage;
Here Toils, and Death, and Death's half-brother Sleep,
(Forms terrible to view) their sentry keep.

(*Aeneid*)

I have a soul that like an ample shield
Can take in all, and verge enough for more.

(*Don Sebastian*)

[60] *Essay Of Dramatick Poesie.*

The first in loftiness of thought surpassed
The next in majesty; in both the last.
(*Under Mr. Milton's Picture*)

Dryden's genius, according to Coleridge, " was of that sort which catches fire by its own motion; his chariot wheels get hot by driving fast." [61] He caught fire often and in the same way.

What we have inferred from this brief relating of John Dryden's poetic method to the lines translated from Virgil's *Aeneid* could be applied to all artists as creators. The culmination of the ancient theory of the inspired artist in the eighteenth century's search for novelty led in the writings of Kant to the inference that there are no unique works of art. There are, rather, unique and original minds which, in the sameness with which they produce works of fine art, however varied the latter may be, express their creative freedom while yet retaining for the products of their relating of means and end the intelligibility which the classical theory of genius had sacrificed. Mozart's *Concerto* belongs to the class of the tragic but it is also of the family of Mozart. El Greco's " Toledo " is no less tragic and it belongs no less to the art of the man who produced " The Burial of the Count of Orgaz " than do the anatomical drawings by Leonardo da Vinci belong to the family of pendulum clocks, tanks, studies in fossils and of heliotropism, battlements, and paintings produced by that great Italian.

The point is reinforced in all great criticism which is likewise a creative act and proof of the validity of the proposition that genius and taste are identical. The profound and perceptive critic knows that some portion of his task is to discover precisely what it is that distinguishes an individual from his fellow artists. One may cite in support of this assertion excerpts from Berenson's *The Italian Painters of the Renaissance* and from Malraux's analysis of El Greco in *The Psychology of Art*. We shall then have before us the material from which

[61] *Table Talk,* Nov. 1, 1833.

we may draw a final inference concerning the artist as creator in his combination of freedom of choice and freedom of originality.

What, for Berenson, distinguishes Titian, Tintoretto, Verrocchio, Botticelli, Michelangelo, and Raphael from each other? Of Titian, he writes that his real greatness " consists in the fact that he was as able to produce an impression of greater reality as he was ready to appreciate the need of a firmer hold on life "; [62] of Tintoretto, that " it was a great mastery of light and shadow which enabled " him " to put into his pictures all the poetry there was in his soul without once tempting us to think that he might have found better expression in words "; [63] of Verrocchio, that he was, " among Florentines at least, the first to feel that a faithful reproduction of the contours is not landscape, that the painting of nature is an art distinct from the painting of the figure "; [64] of Botticelli, " that in European painting there has never again been an artist so indifferent to representation and so intent upon presentation "; [65] of Michelangelo, that " nowhere outside of the best Greek art shall we find . . . forms whose tactile values so increase our sense of capacity, whose movements are so directly communicated and inspiring "; [66] and, finally, of Raphael, that we go to him " for the beautiful vesture he has given to the Antiquity of our yearnings . . . a world where the bird of morning never ceased to sing." [67]

Malraux's study of El Greco is illuminating. It tells us what the painter took from Venice—" that supple, yet bold manner of drawing, in which all lines seem interwoven, like seaweed on rocks, and which, in the central group, he achieved decisively." [68] It tells us from what he freed himself—" from . . . all the accessories dear to pleasure-loving Venice." [69] It suggests a " conversion " [70] but argues that it was no conversion to

[62] *Op. cit.*, p. 22.
[63] *Ibid.*, p. 25.
[64] *Ibid.*, p. 63.
[65] *Ibid.*, p. 67.
[66] *Ibid.*, p. 74.
[67] *Ibid.*, p. 128.
[68] *The Psychology of Art*, p. 180.
[69] *Ibid.*, p. 183.
[70] *Ibid.*, p. 186.

Spanish art and not alone from Tintoretto, for " what is being built up by this welter of bodies is not depth, but a surface . . . colour is being treated not as the handmaid of portrayal, but as means of expression of a special kind." [71] Toledo, we are told, " freed him from Italy," [72] as it freed him from his experience of icons. It was " the supreme gift . . . of *silence* in painting " that Spain offered him [73] but El Greco attained " complete mastery of his art " when " he created the sky . . . not like infinite space, nor yet recession, but treated as a *plane*." [74]

Just and perceptive criticism attempts to find the ground for the products of art which we call works of fine art in the history, continuity, and identity of the self-same original mind which has its own unique and individual history. The work of fine art is many things, but to be many things it must not only be specified as a work of art but individualized also as the product of an original mind which imposes its unique imprint upon it, as it does on all of its products.

The original mind, of the artist as creator, accepts the conditions of making and specifying in a given art. It practises freedom of choice as the skilled maker selects by technique among forms, symbols, media, and feelings. But it is genuinely creative and free, granted the presupposition of freedom of choice, in the sense that the same mind persists and is purposive in the same way under the differing conditions of making which are presented to it and which it presents to itself. The measure of its freedom is the measure of its capacity, like that of Spinoza's *conatus,* " to persevere in its own being " in a world external to it. In this sense, the freedom of the artist as creator is measurable in terms of its self-determination and such self-determination is manifested in the external events called the work of fine art.

[71] *Ibid.,* p. 191.
[72] *Ibid.,* p. 184.
[73] *Ibid.,* p. 184.
[74] *Ibid.,* p. 191.

12 Conclusion: The Freedom of the Fine Artist

. . . to give this material a new shape, the form of his own mind or imagination.

ERICH FRANK

If the argument of this essay of human freedom is sound, the creativity of the artist is explicable on natural grounds. As we have observed, the aesthetic problem of the artist as creator has been obscured by a confusion between two quite diverse levels of speculation. At the first level, the long tradition of the analogy of the artist to God, the creator, and to God, the demiurgic maker, has made of the original mind and the adept craftsman an agent endowed with attributes of omniscience and omnipotence. The attraction for imagination of the figure of the genius lent this an obscurity which persisted even as the notion of genius impinged upon the aesthetic field. The benefits for aesthetic speculation of this tradition in the history of ideas are not, however, to be underestimated. More particularly, it served as a carrier of values which might well have disappeared.

At the second level of speculation, the aesthetic problem of freedom has been only somewhat less obscured by the antinomic aspects of an argument which made man's imagination the ground for unconditioned originality and, later, tended in reaction against one extreme form of speculation to reduce art to science. We have argued that to consider the work of fine art merely as a sign, a product of craft, or an expression of feeling is no less an error than to consider it as a product of one who believed that he could " make a braver show on the back of a wild horse than on the back of a trained animal." The value of the second level of speculation has been twofold: speculation which expended the energies of able men in a confusion of aesthetic and theology is now directed to the work of art, within confines of knowledge garnered from science and the arts. The failure is, however, little less evident, principally consisting as it does in the reduction of all judgments of aesthetic value to judgments of fact.

We have argued that there is an art of fine art, properly designated, in so far as it is both free and art. It has been maintained that fine art produces works of fine art which are both intelligible and original. We have interpreted the terms within the aesthetic universe of discourse to mean classifiable and individual. It has not been argued that a metaphysician like Erich Frank, to whose writing we referred in the initial chapter of this essay, is incorrect in asserting that " even the finest accomplishment of the human spirit is not real creation, for all human creation presupposes as its matter the world which man has not created himself." We have in fact agreed with Frank's continuing observation that " All he can do is to give this material a new shape, the form of his own mind or imagination." We have asserted, however, that to produce the new in this way, within the limitations imposed by material, signs, feelings and under the conditions of limiting conceptions and values, is to specify the meaning of human freedom in art.

We have meant by creativity neither perfection alone nor originality alone but such combination of the two as defines the value of the work of fine art. In terms of these values, we have argued that it is precisely the function of fine art to create the creator, in Kant's words, to awaken the man of taste " to a feeling of his own originality " and to stir him " to examine his art in freedom." The principal points concerning freedom are, first, that the word is meaningless unless its usage refers to the conditions under which it is effective and, second, that the artist who is creative makes under laws operative at two levels.

If we are correct, taste and criticism are correlative to artistic making and free art. The terms all relate to the sublime, the beautiful, the tragic and the comic. The test of the freedom of the fine artist is his success or failure in leading the man of taste to create new values by specifying generic facts and by individualizing the content of aesthetic classes. In this sense, the task of the creative critic is no less one of human freedom and one scarcely less difficult than is that of the creative artist. In art that is predominately expressed in language, a medium more complex than are the media presented for the artist in others of the fine arts, the great critic must specify by application the taste that is correlative to the powers of the creative genius. The critic it is who is closest to the fine artist in terms of freedom. He must be original but he must also " exercise his art in freedom." His evaluations must be at once original and intelligible, their accuracy measurable in terms of the concrete significant form, their originality in terms of the work of fine art. Critical reflection upon fine art is no less significant for our understanding of human freedom than is aesthetic experience or the creativity of the fine artist.

The specification of rules for such judgment as is genuinely critical is a task beyond the scope of the present essay. Our aim has been to illuminate one obscure aspect of that human freedom which comes within the bounds of the poet's vision:

> How exquisitely the individual Mind
> (And the progressive powers perhaps no less
> Of the whole species) to the external World
> Is fitted:—and how exquisitely, too—
> Theme this but little heard among men—
> The external World is fitted to the Mind;
> And the creation (by no lower name
> Can it be called) which they with blended might
> Accomplish:—this is our high argument.

Bibliography

Abbott, T. K., *Kant's Critique of Practical Reason and Other Works on The Theory of Ethics.* London, Longmans, Green and Co., 1927.

Abercrombie, Lascelles, *The Theory of Poetry.* London, Martin Secker, 1924.

Adams, Henry, *Mont St. Michel and Chartres.* New York, Houghton, Mifflin Co., 1927.

Addison, Joseph, *The Spectator,* with notes by Richard Hurd. London, George Bell and Sons, 1893.

Addison, Joseph, *The Spectator,* edited by Henry Morley. London, Routledge's Popular Library, 1891.

Addison, Joseph, *The Spectator.* London, William Tegg, 1867.

Akenside, Mark, *The Pleasures of Imagination.* London, T. Cadell and W. Davies, 1818.

Alexander, Samuel, *Art and Instinct.* Oxford, The Clarendon Press, 1927.

Alexander, Samuel, *Beauty and Other Forms of Value.* London, Macmillan and Co., 1933.

Alison, Archibald, *Essays on the Nature and Principles of Taste.* London, Ingram, Cooke, and Co., 1853.

Anselm, St., *Proslogium,* translated by S. N. Deane. Chicago, The Open Court Publishing Co., 1903.

Aristotle, *Aristotelis Opera,* edited by I. Bekker. Berlin, Academia Regia Borussica, 1831–1870.

Aristotle, *Nicomachean Ethics,* translated by W. D. Ross. London, Oxford University Press, 1931.

Aristotle, *The Works of Aristotle Translated into English,* edited by J. A. Smith and W. D. Ross. Oxford, The Clarendon Press, 1908–1931.

Athanasius, *A Select Library of the Nicene and Post-Nicene Fathers of the Christian Church,* edited by P. Schaff. New York, The Christian Literature Co., 1886–1890.

Augustine, Saint, *A Select Library of the Nicene and Post-Nicene Fathers of the Christian Church,* edited by P. Schaff. New York, The Christian Literature Co., 1886–1890.

Augustine, Saint, *Confessions,* translated by William Watts. New York, W. Heinemann, 1912.

Augustine, Saint, *Opera Omnia,* edited by J. P. Migne. Paris, Garnier Fratres, 1841–1877.

Bacon, Sir Francis, " On the Dignity and Advancement of Learning," *The Physical and Metaphysical Works of Lord Bacon,* edited by John Devey. New York, P. F. Collier and Son, 1901.

Baeumker, Clemens, *Das Problem der Materie in der Griechischen Philosophie.* Münster, Druck und Verlag der Aschendorffschen Buchhandlung, 1890.

Bailey, Cyril, *The Greek Atomists and Epicurus.* Oxford, The Clarendon Press, 1928.

Baker, Courtland D., " Certain Religious Elements in the English Doctrine of the Inspired Poet during the Renaissance," *E.L.H.*, Vol. 6. Baltimore, The Johns Hopkins University Press, 1939.

Bedel, Maurice, " The Rights of the Creative Artist," *Freedom and Culture.* New York, Columbia University Press, 1951.

Berenson, Bernard, *The Italian Painters of the Renaissance.* New York, Phaidon Publishers, Inc., 1952.

Bergson, Henri, *Matière et Mémoire.* Paris, F. Alcan, 1908.

Bergson, Henri, *Matter and Memory,* translated by N. M. Paul and W. S. Palmer. New York, The Macmillan Company, 1912.

Bergson, Henri, *Le Rire, Essai sur la Signification du Comique.* Paris, F. Alcan, 1932.

Bergson, Henri, *Les Deux Sources de la Morale et de la Religion.* Paris, F. Alcan, 1932.

Bergson, Henri, *The Two Sources of Morality and Religion,* translated by R. A. Audra, C. Brereton, and W. H. Carter. New York, Henry Holt & Company, Inc., 1935.

Bigg, Charles, *The Christian Platonists of Alexandria.* Oxford, The Clarendon Press, 1886.

Blunt, A. W. F., *The Prophets of Israel.* Oxford, The Clarendon Press, 1929.

Blunt, Anthony, *Artistic Theory in Italy, 1450–1600.* Oxford, The Clarendon Press, 1940.

Bosanquet, Bernard, *A Companion to Plato's Republic.* London, Rivingtons, 1906.

Bosanquet, Bernard, " Croce's Aesthetic," *Proceedings of the British*

Academy, Vol. 9. London, H. Milford, Oxford University Press, 1914.

Bosanquet, Bernard, *Three Lectures on Aesthetic*. London, G. Allen and Unwin, 1934.

Bosanquet, Bernard, *The Value and Destiny of the Individual*. London, Macmillan and Co., Ltd., 1923.

Bosanquet, Bernard, *A History of Aesthetic*. London, G. Allen and Unwin, 1934.

Boswell, James, *London Journal*, 1762–63. New York, McGraw-Hill, 1950.

Bradley, A. C., *Oxford Lectures on Poetry*. London, Macmillan and Co., 1923.

Brehaut, Ernest, "An Encyclopedist of the Dark Ages, Isidore of Seville," *Studies in History, Economics and Public Law*. New York, Columbia University Press, 1912.

Brehier, E., *La Philosophie de Platon*. Paris, Boivin et Cie., 1928.

Brehier, E., *La Philosophie de Plotinus*. Paris, Boivin et Cie., 1928.

Bridges, Robert S., *The Testament of Beauty*. New York, Oxford University Press, 1930.

Burch, George Bosworth, *Early Mediaeval Philosophy*. New York, King's Crown Press, 1951.

Burckhardt, Jacob, *The Civilization of the Renaissance*, translated by S. G. C. Middlemore. London, The Phaidon Press, 1944.

Browne, Isaac Hawkins, *On Design and Beauty. An Epistle*. London, J. Roberts, 1734.

Browning, Robert, *The Poetical Works of Robert Browning*. London, Smith, Elder and Co., 1900.

Browning, Robert, *Poems of Robert Browning*. London, Oxford University Press, 1925.

Burke, Edmund, *A Philosophical Enquiry into the Origin of Our Ideas on the Sublime and Beautiful*. London, J. Dodsley, 1770.

Burke, Edmund, *A Philosophical Enquiry into the Origin of Our Ideas on the Sublime and Beautiful*. London, Oxford University Press, 1925.

Burke, Edmund, *The Works of the Right Honorable Edmund Burke*. London, G. Bell and Sons, 1913.

Butcher, S. H., *Aristotle's Theory of Poetry and Fine Art*. London, Macmillan and Company, 1932.

Bywater, I., *Aristotle on the Art of Poetry.* Oxford, The Clarendon Press, 1909.

Carpenter, R., *The Sculpture of the Nike Temple Parapet.* Cambridge, Harvard University Press, 1929.

Carpenter, R., " The Basis of Artistic Creation in the Fine Arts," *The Bases of Artistic Creation.* New Brunswick, Rutgers University Press, 1942.

Cassirer, Ernst, *Individuum und Kosmos in der Philosophie der Renaissance.* Leipzig, B. G. Teubner, 1927.

Cassirer, Ernst, *The Renaissance Philosophy of Man,* edited by P. O. Kristeller and J. H. Randall, Jr. Chicago, University of Chicago Press, 1948.

Castelvetro, Lodovico, *Poetica d'Aristotele Vulgarizzata et Sposta.* Basel, 1576.

Casson, S., *The Technique of Early Greek Sculpture.* Oxford, The Clarendon Press, 1933.

Chadwick, N. Kershaw, *Poetry and Prophecy.* Cambridge, Cambridge University Press, 1942.

Chapman, E., *St. Augustine's Philosophy of Beauty.* New York, Sheed and Ward, Inc., 1939.

Childe, V. Gordon, *Man Makes Himself.* London, Watts and Co., 1936.

Cochez, M., " L'Esthétique de Plotin," *Revue Néo-Scolastique,* Vol. 20, 21, 1913–1914.

Collingwood, R. G., *The Principles of Art.* Oxford, The Clarendon Press, 1938.

Colman, George, *Prose on Several Occasions, accompanied with some Pieces of Verse.* London, T. Cadel, 1787.

Cornford, F. M., *Plato's Cosmology.* New York, Harcourt, Brace and Co., 1937.

Croce, B., *Estetica come Scienza dell'Espressione Linguistica Generale.* Bari, G. Laterza e Figli, 1908.

Croce, B., *Breviario di Estetica.* Bari, Laterza e Figli, 1913.

Croce, B., *What is Living and What is Dead of the Philosophy of Hegel,* translated by Douglas Ainslie. London, Macmillan and Co., 1915.

Croce, B., *Philosophy of the Practical: Economic and Ethic,* translated by Douglas Ainslie. London, Macmillan and Co., 1913.

Croce, B., *The Essence of Aesthetic*, translated by Douglas Ainslie. London, Macmillan and Co., 1921.

Croce, B., *Aesthetic*, translated by Douglas Ainslie. London, Macmillan and Co., 1929.

Cruttwell, Maud, *Luca and Andrea della Robbia*. London, J. M. Dent and Co., 1902.

D'Arcy, N. C., *A Monument to St. Augustine*. London, Sheed and Ward, 1934.

Dessoir, Max, *Ästhetik und Allgemeine Kunstwissenschaft*. Stuttgart, 1923.

De Wulf, Maurice, *History of Mediaeval Philosophy*. London, Longmans, Green and Co., 1926.

Dionysius Areopagita, *Opera Omnia*, edited by B. Corderius [in *Patrologiae Cursus Completus . . . Graeca*, edited by J. P. Migne]. Paris, 1857–1884.

Dionysius Areopagita, *The Works of Dionysius the Areopagite*, translated by The Reverend John Parker. London, J. Parker and Co., 1897.

Dryden, John, *The Works of John Dryden*, edited by Sir Walter Scott and George Saintsbury. Edinburgh, William Paterson, 1889.

Duff, William, *An Essay on Original Genius*. London, Edward and Charles Dilly, 1767.

Ebreo, Leone, *Dialoghi D'Amore Hebraeische Gedichte*, edited by Carl Gebhardt. Heidelberg, Curis Societatis Spinozanae, 1929.

Ebreo, Leone, *The Philosophy of Love*, translated by F. Friedeberg-Seeley and Jean H. Barnes. London, Soncino Press, 1937.

Ferguson, A. S., "Plato and the Poet's ΕΙΔΩΛΑ," *Philosophical Essays Presented to John Watson*. Kingston, Queen's University, 1922.

Foster, M. B., "The Christian Doctrine of Creation and the Rise of Modern Science," *Mind* (N.S.), No. 43 (1934).

Forster, E. M., *Two Cheers for Democracy*. London, Edward Arnold and Co., 1952.

Fracastoro, Girolamo, *Naugerius, Sive de Poetica Dialogus*, translated by Ruth Kelso, *University of Illinois Studies in Language and Literature*, Vol. IX. Urbana, 1924.

Frank, Erich, "The Fundamental Opposition of Plato and Aristotle," *American Journal of Philology,* Vol. 61.

Frank Erich, *St. Augustine and Greek Thought,* Cambridge, The Augustinean Society, 1942.

Frank, Erich, *Philosophical Understanding and Religious Truth.* New York, Oxford University Press, 1945.

Freud, S., *Wit and Its Relation to the Unconscious.* New York, Moffat, Yard, and Co., 1916.

Freud, S., *Introductory Lectures on Psychoanalysis,* translated by Joan Riviere. London, G. Allen and Unwin, Ltd., 1922.

Fuller, B. A. G., *The Problem of Evil in Plotinus.* Cambridge, Cambridge University Press, 1912.

Galsworthy, John, *The Creation of Character in Literature.* Oxford, The Clarendon Press, 1931.

Gerard, Alexander, *An Essay on Genius.* London, W. Strahan, 1774.

Gerard, Alexander, *An Essay on Taste* (2nd edition). London, W. Strahan, 1764.

Gilbert, Allan H., *Literary Criticism–Plato to Dryden.* New York, American Book Co., 1940.

Gilbert, K., and H. Kuhn, *A History of Esthetics.* New York, The Macmillan Co., 1939.

Gilson, Etienne, *Introduction a l'Étude de Saint Augustine.* Paris, J. Vrin, 1931.

Hanslick, Eduard, *The Beautiful in Music,* translated by Gustav Cohen. London, Novello and Co., 1891.

Harnack, Adolph, *History of Dogma,* translated by Neil Buchanan. Boston, Roberts Brothers, 1897.

Hegel, G. W. F., *The Introduction to Hegel's Philosophy of Fine Art,* translated by B. Bosanquet. London, Kegan Paul, Trench, Trübner & Co., 1905.

Hegel, G. W. F., *The Philosophy of Fine Art,* translated by F. P. B. Osmaston. London, G. Bell and Sons, 1920.

Hindemith, Paul, *A Composer's World.* Cambridge, Harvard University Press, 1952.

Holt, Elizabeth Gilmore, *Literary Sources of Art History.* Princeton, Princeton University Press, 1947.

Home, Henry (Lord Kames), *Elements of Criticism* (5th edition). Edinburgh, A. Kinkaid, W. Creech, and J. Bell, 1774.

Hopkins, Gerard Manley, *The Note-Books and Papers of Gerard Manley Hopkins.* London, Oxford University Press, 1937.

Huarte, Juan, *Examen de Ingenios or, The Tryal of Wits,* translated by M. Bellamy. London, Richard Gare, 1648.

Huarte de San Juan, *Examen de Ingenios para las Ciencias.* Madrid, La Rafe, 1930.

Husik, Isaac, *A History of Mediaeval Jewish Philosophy.* New York, Macmillan Co., 1930.

Hutcheson, Francis, *An Inquiry into the Original of our Ideas of Beauty and Virtue* (5th edition). London, R. Ware etc., 1753.

Huxley, Aldous, *Point Counter Point.* New York, Modern Library, 1928.

Irenaeus, Saint, *Five Books of S. Irenaeus Against Heresies,* translated by John Keble. Oxford, J. Parker and Co., 1872.

Jackson, William, *Whether Genius be born, or acquired?* London, 1748.

Jaeger, Warner, *The Theology of the Early Greek Philosophers.* Oxford, The Clarendon Press, 1947.

Joachim, H. H., *Aristotle: The Nicomachean Ethics.* Oxford, The Clarendon Press, 1951.

Johnson, Samuel, *The Rambler.* London, T. Tegg, 1826.

Jowett, Benjamin, *The Dialogues of Plato.* Oxford, The Clarendon Press, 1921.

Joyce, G. C., *The Inspiration of Prophecy.* New York, Oxford University Press, 1910.

Jung, C. G., *Modern Man in Search of a Soul.* New York, Harcourt, Brace and Co., 1933.

Kant, I., *Kant's Kritik of Judgment,* translated by J. H. Bernard. London, Macmillan and Co., 1892.

Kant, I., *Kant's Critique of Aesthetic Judgement,* translated by J. C. Meredith. Oxford, The Clarendon Press, 1911.

Kant, I., *Immanuel Kants Werke,* edited by Ernst Cassirer. Berlin, B. Cassirer, 1922.

Kant, I., *Kant's Critique of Pure Reason,* translated by N. K. Smith. London, Macmillan and Co., 1929.

Kaufman, Walter, " Heralds of Original Genius," *Essays in Memory of Barrett Wendell.* Cambridge, Harvard University Press, 1926.

Keats, John, *The Poetical Works of John Keats,* edited by H. Buxton. London, Oxford University Press, 1926.

Kretschmer, Ernst, *The Psychology of Men of Genius.* New York, Harcourt, Brace and Co., 1931.

Lange-Eichbaum, Wilhelm, *The Problem of Genius,* translated by Eden and Cedar Paul. New York, The Macmillan Co., 1932.

Leone Ebreo (see Ebreo).

Leonardo da Vinci, *The Notebooks of Leonardo da Vinci,* edited by Edward McCurdy. New York, Reynal & Hitchcock, 1938.

Leonardo da Vinci, *The Literary Works of Leonardo da Vinci,* edited by Jean Paul Richter. London, Oxford University Press, 1939.

Leonardo da Vinci, *Paragone A Comparison of the Arts,* edited by Irma A. Richter. London, Oxford University Press, 1949.

Lessing, G. E., *The Laocoon and Other Prose Writings of Lessing,* translated by Ellen Frothingham. Boston, Roberts Brothers, 1877.

Listowel, Earl of, *A Critical History of Modern Aesthetics.* London, G. Allen and Unwin, 1933.

Longinus, C., *De Sublimitate,* ed., Otto Iahne. Bonn, Marcus, 1867.

Longinus, C., *On the Sublime,* translated by William Smith. London, F. C. and J. Rivington, 1819.

Longinus, C., *On the Sublime,* translated by W. R. Roberts. Cambridge, Cambridge University Press, 1899.

Longinus, C., *On the Sublime,* translated by W. H. Fyfe. London, W. Heinemann, 1927.

Lovejoy, A. O., " The Parallel of Deism and Classicism," *Modern Philology,* XXIX (1932), No. 3. Chicago, University of Chicago Press.

Lovejoy, A. O., *The Great Chain of Being.* Cambridge, Harvard University Press, 1936.

Lucretius, T., *De Rerum Natura,* edited by Cyril Bailey. Oxford, The Clarendon Press, 1947.

Lucretius, T., *On the Nature of Things,* translated by H. A. J. Munro. London, G. Bell and Sons, 1914.

Mackenna, Stephen, *Plotinus.* London, The Medici Society, Ltd., 1917–1926.

Malraux, André, *The Psychology of Art,* translated by Stuart Gilbert. New York, (The Bollingen Series XXIV), Pantheon Books, 1949.

Mann, Thomas, *Dr. Faustus,* translated by H. T. Lowe-Porter. New York, Alfred A. Knopf, 1948.

Maritain, J., *Art and Scholasticism,* translated by J. F. Scanlan. New York, Charles Scribner's Sons, 1930.

More, Paul Elmer, *The Religion of Plato.* Princeton, Princeton University Press, 1921.

Morgann, Maurice, *Essays on the Dramatic Character of Sir John Falstaff,* edited by William Arthur Gill. London, Henry Frowde, 1912.

Munro, T. and Guillaume, P., *Primitive Negro Sculpture.* London, J. Cape, 1926.

Nahm, Milton C. (ed.), *Selections from Early Greek Philosophy,* New York, Appleton-Century-Crofts, 1944.

Nahm, Milton C., *Aesthetic Experience and Its Presuppositions.* New York, Harper and Brothers, 1946.

Nahm, Milton C., "The Theological Background of the Theory of the Artist as Creator," *Journal of the History of Ideas,* Vol. VIII, No. 3, June, 1947.

Nahm, Milton C., *Aristotle on Poetry and Music.* New York, The Little Library of Liberal Arts, 1948.

Nietzsche, F., *The Complete Works of Friedrich Nietzsche,* edited by Oscar Levy. Edinburgh, T. N. Foulis, 1910–.

Oehler, Gustav Friedrich, *Theology of The Old Testament.* New York, Funk and Wagnalls, 1883.

Okakura-Kakuzo, *The Book of Tea.* New York, Duffield and Co., 1912.

Orr, James, *Revelation and Inspiration.* New York, Charles Scribner's Sons, 1910.

Palmer, John L., *Comedy.* London, Martin Secker, 1914.

Panofsky, E., *Idea.* Leipzig, B. G. Teubner, 1924.

Panofsky, E., *Studies in Iconology.* New York, Oxford University Press, 1939.

Panofsky, E., *Albrecht Dürer.* Princeton, Princeton University Press, 1943.

Picolli, Raffaello, *Benedetto Croce*. New York, Harcourt, Brace and Co., 1922.

Pico della Mirandola, "On the Dignity of Man," translated by E. L. Forbes, *The Renaissance Philosophy of Man*. Chicago, University of Chicago Press, 1948.

Pinkerton, John, *Letters of Literature*. London, G. J. and J. Robinson, 1785.

Plato, *Opera Omnia*, edited by G. Stallbaum. Gothae, Hennings, 1857–1885.

Plato, *The Republic of Plato*, translated by J. L. Davies and D. J. Vaughan. London, Macmillan and Co., 1907.

Plato, *The Dialogues of Plato*, translated by Benjamin Jowett. Oxford, The Clarendon Press, 1921.

Plato, *Timaeus and Critias*, translated by A. E. Taylor. London, Methuen and Co., 1929.

Plotinus, *Ennéades*, edited by E. Bréhier. Paris, University of France, 1924–1938.

Plotinus, *Plotinus*, translated by Stephen Mackenna. London, The Medici Society, Ltd., 1917–1926.

Portnoy, Julius, *A Psychology of Art Creation*. Philadelphia, University of Pennsylvania, 1942.

Prickard, A. O., *Longinus on the Sublime*. Oxford, The Clarendon Press, 1906.

Puttenham, George, *The Arte of English Poesie*. Cambridge, Cambridge University Press, 1936.

Raleigh, Sir Walter, *Style*. London, E. Arnold, 1901.

Ritter, Constantin, *The Essence of Plato's Philosophy*. London, George Allen and Unwin, Ltd., 1933.

Robb, D. M., and Garrison, J. J., *Art in the Western World*. New York, Harper and Brothers, 1942.

Robb, Nesca A., *Neoplatonism of the Italian Renaissance*. London, George Allen and Unwin, 1935.

Robertson, J. G., *Studies in the Genesis of Romantic Theory in the Eighteenth Century*, Cambridge, Cambridge University Press, 1923.

Rodin, A., *L'Art*. Paris, Bernard Grasset, 1911.

Rodin, A., *Art*, translated by R. Fedden. London, Hodder and Stoughton, 1912.

Rosenkranz, Karl, *Aesthetik des Hässlichen.* Königsberg, Borntrager, 1853.

Schaff, P. (editor), *Nicene and Post-Nicene Fathers of the Christian Church.* Buffalo, Christian Literature Co., 1887–.

Schevill, F., *History of Florence.* New York, Harcourt, Brace and Co., 1946.

Schlapp, Otto, *Kants Lehre vom Genie und die Entstehung der 'Kritik der Urtheilskraft.'* Göttingen, Vandenhoeck & Ruprecht, 1901.

Schlapp, Otto, *Die Anfänge von Kants Kritik des Geschmacks und des Genies, 1764 bis 1775.* Göttingen, E. A. Huth, 1899.

Schopenhauer, Arthur, *The World as Will and Idea,* translated by R. B. Haldane and J. Kemp. London, Kegan Paul, Trench, Trübner & Co., 1883–1896.

Shaftesbury, Anthony, Earl of, *Characteristics of Men, Manners, Opinions, Times,* etc., edited by John M. Robertson. London, Grant Richards, 1900.

Sharpe, William, *A Dissertation upon Genius.* London, C. Bathurst, 1755.

Shelley, Percy Bysshe, *A Defense of Poetry.* Oxford, B. Blackwell, 1923.

Shelley, Percy Bysshe, *Selected Poems, Essays, and Letters.* New York, The Odyssey Press, 1944.

Shorey, Paul, *What Plato Said.* Chicago, University of Chicago Press, 1933.

Sidney, Sir Philip, *The Defense of Poesy,* edited by A. S. Cook. Boston, Ginn and Co., 1891.

Singer, E. A., Jr., *On the Contented Life.* New York, Henry Holt and Co., 1936.

Singer, E. A., Jr., *Mind as Behavior.* Columbus, R. G. Adams and Co., 1924.

Solmsen, F., *Plato's Theology.* Ithaca, Cornell University Press, 1942.

Spingarn, Joel Elias, *A History of Literary Criticism in the Renaissance.* New York, The Macmillan Co., 1899.

Spingarn, Joel Elias, *Critical Essays of the Seventeenth Century.* Oxford, The Clarendon Press, 1908-09.

Spingarn, Joel Elias, *Creative Criticism.* New York, Henry Holt and Co., 1917.

Svoboda, K., *L'Éstetique de Saint Augustin et ses Sources.* Brno, Masarykova Universita, 1933.

Symonds, John Addington, *Sketches in Italy.* Leipzig, B. Tauchnitz, 1883.

Taylor, A. E., *Varia Socratica.* Oxford, J. Parker and Co., 1911.

Taylor, A. E., *Plato: The Man and His Work.* New York, The Dial Press, 1927.

Taylor, A. E., *A Commentary on Plato's Timaeus.* Oxford, The Clarendon Press, 1928.

Taylor, A. E., *Timaeus and Critias.* London, Methuen and Co., 1929.

Tertullian, *Tertullianos Against Marcion, Ante-Nicene Christian Library Translations of the Writings of the Fathers.* Edinburgh, T. and T. Clark, 1865.

Tillyard, E. M. W., *The Elizabethan World Picture.* London, Chatto & Windus, 1943.

Tolley, W. P., *The Idea of God in the Philosophy of St. Augustine.* New York, Richard R. Smith, 1930.

Trapp, Joseph, *Lectures on Poetry, Read in the Schools of Natural Philosophy at Oxford.* London, C. Hitch and C. C. Davis, 1742.

Vacant, A., and Mangenot, E., *Dictionnaire de Théologie Catholique.* Paris, Letouzey et Ané, 1900–1905.

Volkelt, J. I., *System der Ästhetik.* Munich, Beck, 1905–1914.

Westcott, B. F., *Introduction to the Study of the Gospels.* New York, Macmillan and Co., 1882.

Whittaker, Thomas, *The Neo-Platonists.* Cambridge, Cambridge University Press, 1918.

Whitehead, A. N., *Process and Reality.* New York, The Macmillan Co., 1929.

Windelband, W., *A History of Philosophy,* translated by J. H. Tufts. London, The Macmillan Co., 1901.

Wolf, Herman, "Versuch einer Geschichte des Geniesbegriffs in der Deutschen Ästhetik des 18. Jahrhunderts . . . von Gottsched bis auf Lessing," Beitrage zur Philosophie. Heidelberg, Carl Winter's Universitätsbuchhandlung, 1923.

Wolfson, Harry Austryn, "Philo on Free Will," *Harvard Theological Review*, Vol. xxxv, No. 2, 1942.

Wolfson, Harry Austryn, *Philo*. Cambridge, Harvard University Press, 1947.

Wordsworth, William, *The Poems of Wordsworth*, edited by Thomas Hutchinson. London, Oxford University Press, 1926.

Young, Edward, *Conjectures on Original Composition*, edited by M. W. Steinke. New York, F. C. Stechert Co., 1917.

Zeller, E., *Plato and the Older Academy*. London, Longmans, Green, and Co., 1876.

Zigrosser, Carl, *The Artist in America*. New York, Alfred A. Knopf, 1942.

Zilsel, Edgar, *Die Entstehung des Geniesbegriffes, ein Beitrag zur Ideengeschichte der Antike und des Frühkapitalismus*. Tübingen, J. C. B. Mohr (Paul Siebeck), 1926.

Index